CONTEMPT
OF COURT

ALSO BY MARK CURRIDEN

Cause of Death (with Dr. Cyril Wecht)
Grave Secrets (with Dr. Cyril Wecht)

CONTEMPT OF COURT

THE TURN-OF-THE-CENTURY LYNCHING
THAT LAUNCHED 100 YEARS
OF FEDERALISM

MARK CURRIDEN AND
LEROY PHILLIPS, JR.

ff

FABER AND FABER, INC.

An affiliate of Farrar, Straus and Giroux

NEW YORK

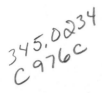

FABER AND FABER, INC.
An affiliate of Farrar, Straus and Giroux
19 Union Square West, New York 10003

Designed by Gretchen Achilles

FIRST EDITION, 1999

Library of Congress Cataloging-in-Publication Data

Curriden, Mark.
    Contempt of court : the turn-of-the-century lynching that launched 100 years
of federalism / Mark Curriden and Leroy Phillips. — 1st ed
      p.   cm.
    Includes bibliographical references and index.
    ISBN 0-571-19952-6 (alk. paper)
    1. Contempt of court—United States—History. 2. Lynching—Tennessee—
Chattanooga—History. I. Phillips, Leroy, 1935- .
II. Title.
KF224.J63C87   1999
345.73'0234—dc21   99-19327
                                             CIP

To my daughter, Nancy Michelle Phillips,
who wants to be a lawyer.

LEROY PHILLIPS, JR.

To my grandparents, Joe and Edna Curriden and Donald
and June Dawson, whose never-wavering support
helped me through this project.

MARK CURRIDEN

CONTENTS

ACKNOWLEDGMENTS

Many friends and colleagues made it possible for us to do the decade's worth of research this project involved. We especially thank Lauren Osborne and Catherine Newman, our editors at Farrar, Straus and Giroux. Their patience was merciful and their guidance was sorely needed and welcomed.

We also would like to thank Joel Fishman, our agent. He spent many hours on the proposal and guided us in writing the book. His insight was extremely valuable.

Several of our colleagues also deserve our gratitude. My editors at the *Dallas Morning News*, especially business editor Chuck Camp, gave me both encouragement and precious time off. The support Leroy received from his colleagues at Phillips & Caputo was also immeasurable. We especially praise Vickie Finnell for typing thousands of pages of notes and research materials for us over the past few years.

A special thanks goes to Rebecca Adams, a reporter at the *Congressional Quarterly* and formerly with the *Chattanooga Times*. Without her research assistance, this book would be missing many of its incredible details.

The same goes for Ron Smith, a great friend and former managing editor of the *Chattanooga Times*. Ron was our personal editor and adviser. His tremendous insight kept us focused on our mission. He also challenged us to provide better writing and reporting every step of the way.

There are three friends and colleagues who acted as informal consultants. To those individuals—Keith Summa of ABC News, Dan Lothian of NBC News, and Bill Oliphant, a longtime journalism professor from Tennessee—we offer a sincere thank you. Their fingerprints can be detected throughout the book. My brother and good friend, Jason Curriden, saved me from many slips of grammar and spelling.

In developing the legal and historical importance of this case, we spent many, many hours with some of the most prominent and respected scholars in our country. We owe a great debt to University of Georgia law professor Eugene Wilkes, who has studied this case and its importance and gave us unlimited access to his knowledge and understanding of the story.

There is no way for me to express my appreciation for Drake University law professor Thomas Baker. Professor Baker, an expert on the U.S. Supreme Court, helped us interpret the *role* of each member of the Court. Texas Tech Law School Dean Frank Newton also deserves a considerable amount of credit for helping us put the issues in this case in perspective. He was a constant sounding board.

Professor James Gordon at Western New England College School of Law helped us develop Justice Harlan as the key character he was in this project. Professor Gordon's insight into Harlan allowed us to write about him with more authority.

The learning curve for me continued at Howard University School of Law in Washington, D.C. Not only did Howard provide us with tremendous resource materials directly associated with this case, but a law professor at the school, J. Clay Smith, really helped us understand the role and dilemma of African-American lawyers in 1906.

Special thanks go to the library officials at Tennessee State University, Vanderbilt University, the University of Tennessee at Chattanooga, the University of Tennessee at Knoxville, Atlanta University, the University of Georgia, the University of South Carolina, and Howard University in Washington, D.C.

This project could never have been done without the incredible resources and assistance of the public-library system. The public libraries in Atlanta, Knoxville, Nashville, Cincinnati, Indianapolis, and Findley, Ohio, offered us their records and expertise. Clara W. Swann, director of the Local History and Genealogy Section of the Chattanooga–Hamilton County Bicentennial Library, was especially gracious. Another wonderful resource was the state archives in Tennessee, Georgia, and Oklahoma. The National Archives, the Library of Congress, and the U.S. Supreme Court also cooperated with us.

Officials at the Tennessee Supreme Court, including media

spokeswoman Sue Allison and former state Chief Justice Lyle Reid, also helped us gain access to some important documents.

The McCallie School in Chattanooga was a gold mine. McCallie's public-relations director, Bill Steverson, gave us access to dozens of boxes of old letters, memos, and other records from 1900 to 1920. The records included wonderful details and taught us about Dr. T. H. McCallie and his role in this case.

Many of the details included in this book were obtained through several days of research at Tuskegee University in Alabama. We cannot say enough about the tremendous aid provided us by the officials at Tuskegee, especially Daniel Williams, the school's archivist. I was so overwhelmed by the materials they had gathered on this case and other lynchings that I ended up staying in the school's library and archives longer than expected. The college has dozens of file drawers filled with reports on every reported lynching that ever occurred in the country. These files, with their many documents gathered by Tuskegee for more than a century, are an invaluable piece of history. However, the original documents are in poor condition and the school simply does not have the money to have them restored and preserved. From the proceeds we earn from this book, we plan to make a contribution to Tuskegee University library officials for the purpose of restoring these documents. They are evidence of horrible things that have occurred in our country's history, and they must not be forgotten. We would plead for some major contributor to step forward and provide the necessary resources to preserve these priceless documents.

No book about Chattanooga or Tennessee can be thoroughly written without a consultation with Dr. James Livingood. The author of several books himself, Dr. Livingood is the region's definitive historian. We learned from him not only what occurred, but why things happened.

There are countless other people and institutions who helped us along the way, and we hope they will forgive us for omitting their names from this brief gesture of thanks.

MARK CURRIDEN

PREFACE

On the side of Chattanooga's Missionary Ridge, a crucial battle site in the Civil War, sits a small cemetery. A rusty old sign announces it as the Pleasant Garden, a final "resting place for Negroes." The lot is blanketed with thorns and thick brush. Every person buried here was a man or woman or child of color. Most were poor. The broken-down iron fence and sunken tombs are evidence that the cemetery closed decades ago.

Deep within the graveyard, on a small slope, lies an undistinguished granite stone. A barely readable inscription is chiseled on its aging and molded surface:

> GOD BLESS YOU ALL. I AM A
>
> INNOCENT MAN
>
> ED JOHNSON
>
> BORN 1882
>
> DIED MARCH 19, 1906
>
> FAREWELL UNTIL WE MEET AGAIN IN THE
>
> SWEET BY AND BY

Ed Johnson was not a significant man, except in the sense that all people have significance. He was a young, uneducated black man living in the South. He had no regular occupation, no home, no wife or kids. Unfortunately, the means by which Johnson's life abruptly ended was not unusual for his time. American history is replete with tales of black men lynched for nothing more than watching a white woman walk across the street or trying to talk to a white woman when no white man was present.

But the story of Ed Johnson remains of supreme importance to this day. Buried deep in the court files in Chattanooga, Tennessee, is the tale of this African-American wrongly accused of a crime, railroaded through the criminal-justice system, and rescued by the U.S. Supreme Court. His reprieve, however, was temporary. He became the symbolic target of white vigilantes who felt the federal government had become too big and too intrusive into states' rights. The written law, they concluded, was not good enough, and they decided to enforce their own code of morals.

The story of Ed Johnson brings to life a Supreme Court case that moves both the heart and the mind—to demonstrate that the liberties and prerogatives we so frequently take for granted were written in blood. Legal scholars say it signaled a change in the nation's entire criminal-justice system.

The events considered in this book culminate in a unique and historical trial before the nation's highest tribunal. They represent a step in the long march of African-Americans seeking freedom, equality, and justice. The story provides unique insight into our dual criminal-justice system, that of state and federal courts.

From the time of the Magna Carta in 1215, English Common Law and American jurisprudence have rested on a bedrock of accumulated legal precedents. Behind each case lies a story involving real people. Sometimes these are merely the stories of expectations interrupted. At other times they tell of anguish and suffering the likes of which most of us will never witness.

The case of Ed Johnson is a fascinating and heartbreaking tale of an innocent man, a politically motivated Southern sheriff, two heroic African-American lawyers, and a state-court system that refused to provide equal justice for all. The story touches on a number of important issues, including race relations, protection of the innocent, the threat of mob rule, the potential influence of politics on jurisprudence, and the history and development of the U.S. Supreme Court. The Court championed an innocent black man, shouting loud and clear to the nation's law-enforcement officials that it would not tolerate those who violated its orders. Yet, even though it established a precedent that stands to this day, the story of Ed Johnson has never been fully told or had its importance thoroughly examined.

The case first came to Leroy Phillips's attention in the late 1960s. Phillips, a young lawyer in Chattanooga and a lifelong resident of Tennessee, loved history, especially legal history. In 1968, he bought a set of the 100-volume *United States Supreme Court Reports*, which detailed every case and order of the high court since its inception. In its pages Phillips came across *United States* v. *Shipp*, a case in which the Court itself had initiated contempt charges against Sheriff Joseph F. Shipp of Chattanooga, his deputies, and numerous members of a lynch mob because of their actions in a previous case, *State of Tennessee* v. *Ed Johnson*.

Over the next two decades, Phillips read countless newspaper articles about the cases. He researched the law for every citation, and he traveled to Washington to scour the Supreme Court files on the case.

In 1988, I covered a high-profile murder trial in which Phillips defended a suspected killer. During the jury deliberations, Phillips told me about his research into the Ed Johnson case. Fascinated, I spent the next several months reading the materials he had collected. I was astonished to discover that no one had written about the case. Together, we decided to change that.

Over the next ten years, Phillips tracked down relatives of and background materials on the woman Johnson was accused of raping, while I dug through Tuskegee University's incredible archive on lynchings.

We discovered previously secret memos and reports from the U.S. Secret Service agents who investigated the lynching. We searched through the private papers of each member of the U.S. Supreme Court in 1906. We studied thousands of newspaper articles, from the *Washington Post* and the *New York Times* to the *Voice* and the *Independent*, and we read dozens of black-owned newspapers. We mined state archives, the historical records of several schools, colleges, and law schools, U.S. Census Bureau data, and various state public records, and we interviewed historians and legal experts.

This is not to imply that we found everything we sought. There were key details that, despite our efforts, we were unable to locate.

For example, we never found any photographs of the central character, Ed Johnson. Nor could we locate any of his relatives. Unfortunately, the Hamilton County Courthouse burned to the ground a few years after this case, and most of the local court and law-enforcement records were destroyed. Some had been copied when the case was moved into the federal courts, but many important specifics were forever lost.

Fortunately for us, Noah Parden, one of the lawyers leading Johnson's appeal, was a prolific writer. His articles appeared mainly in the *Blade*, a black-owned newspaper in Chattanooga, and the *Independent*, a black newspaper in Atlanta. However, we discovered his handiwork reprinted in newspapers and magazines across the country. Parden's meticulous work provided us with a tremendous amount of invaluable detail.

While we are confident that every statement and fact in our book is true and based on the historical record, we have reconstructed several scenes. Those reconstructions are the result of combining multiple sources—people's letters, federal court testimony, interviews with federal law-enforcement officers, and newspaper accounts. A good example of this frequently used journalistic technique unfolds in Chapter 6, where lawyers for Ed Johnson meet with their client to discuss his case. This scene is reconstructed from six separate but very authoritative sources—a detailed summary of the meeting by one of his lawyers, a newpaper account of the event, sworn federal court testimony of three of the individuals present, and a federal investigative report based on interviews with the people who attended the meeting. Instead of recounting what each of those sources claimed happened or was said, we have used the sources to reconstruct the event itself. Specific sources for each section of the reconstruction are listed in the Note on Sources.

Possibly the most invigorating day of my research came in 1991, when I interviewed Supreme Court Justice Thurgood Marshall. I asked the nation's first black justice if he remembered or had any thoughts on the 1906 case. In his distinctively scratchy voice, Justice Marshall said he was keenly aware of the Shipp case.

"Very few people understand the import of the Shipp trial," he told me,

> Its significance has never been fully explained. Shipp was perhaps the first instance in which the Court demonstrated that the Fourteenth Amendment and the equal-protection clause have any substantive meaning to people of the African-American race. The Shipp case served as a foundation for many cases to come. At a time when racism and white supremacy ruled the day, the Shipp case demonstrated a real moment of courage by the Court, especially for Justice Harlan, who has always been one of the legal champions I have admired and studied. Unfortunately, the Sheriff Shipp case has never received the attention or the scrutiny it deserves. The import of the Sheriff Shipp case on the federal court's authority over state criminal cases should not be underestimated.

The legacy left by the Johnson and Shipp cases is multifaceted. While the set of events grew out of one incident, two separate cases were litigated. Each case has its own important historic developments. They each have individual lessons, which will become obvious as our story unfolds. But for all its legal importance, this story also has another attribute: it is simply a fascinating tale. It is an incredible glimpse into history.

MARK CURRIDEN

CONTEMPT
OF COURT

CHAPTER ONE

A PLEA FOR JUSTICE

ON MARCH 17, 1906, Noah Walter Parden stood at the steps of the U.S. Capitol in Washington, D.C. It was early Saturday morning, barely dawn. The temperature was cold, just above freezing. The fog was thick and the rain intermittent. He could barely see the top of the dome.

With a colleague at his side, Parden marched up ninety-five marble steps. He was about to do something no black man had ever done in the United States: argue a case before a justice on the United States Supreme Court.

The heavy metal door was already open. Inside, armed security guards searched the two men and their briefcases for weapons; sidearms were specifically prohibited. The security officers recognized Parden's companion and did not stand in their way any longer. The men made their way through a maze of hallways and spiraling stairways.

Finally, room 38. Offices of the U.S. Supreme Court.

They were directed to a waiting room for people desiring to see the justices on the days when the Court was not in session. The room doubled as a robing area for the justices when the Court heard arguments. Adjacent to the courtroom, the waiting room was basically a long, elaborate hallway. The walls were marble. Three large windows about eight feet apart extended from the floor to the ceiling twenty feet above. Against the left wall in the middle of the room was a fireplace. Two padded couches and six leather chairs lined the walls. Paintings of past justices hung between windows. The Supreme Court had moved into this area of the Capitol, commonly referred to as the Old Senate Chamber, in 1860, when the Senate moved to its more plush, expanded chambers down the hall.

At one side of this hall were two desks, from which three women answered the telephone, took messages, made appointments, processed paperwork, and accepted court briefs. They also served as gatekeepers to whoever sat in the next room.

Parden introduced himself and his co-counsel, prominent black Washington, D.C., lawyer Emanuel D. Molyneaux Hewlett, to the receptionist. The lawyer explained they had called ahead about an important case from Tennessee that required immediate consideration. A man's life was at stake, he said. They had filed the necessary paperwork the day before and were told to return this day to answer any questions the Court might have in determining the request. The secretary nodded, jotted down their names, and pointed the two men toward a couch in the middle of the hallway.

The wait was long. Parden's hands trembled as beads of sweat outlined his receding hairline. His dark-gray suit and white shirt had been perfectly pressed, but his shoes were damp from walking nine blocks in the rain. He had come 700 miles by rail in hopes of finding mercy and justice, in hopes of saving his client from a horrible death. Back home, Ed Johnson sat in a jail cell, hours away from an appointment with a hangman's gallows. The folks back in Tennessee were thirsty for blood. They demanded that punishment be delivered.

But Parden knew the truth: Ed Johnson was innocent. His client had not raped the young lady. He was at least a mile away at the time of the vicious crime. A dozen witnesses were his alibi. Despite this, Johnson had been arrested, convicted, and condemned to die.

Three different state and federal courts had rejected Parden's efforts to appeal. He claimed he had overwhelming evidence to show that his client had not gotten a fair trial. The defendant was merely an uneducated Negro laborer who had been railroaded by a judge and a sheriff who were more interested in getting re-elected than in administering justice.

With the clock ticking on Johnson's life, the race was on. Authorities back in Chattanooga were rushing to get the noose around Johnson's neck; Parden was hustling to intercept the executioners. This truly was Parden's court of last resort. There were no more appeals, no more emancipators with whom to plead. If this attempt failed, God would have turned his back on Johnson.

All morning, people came and went from the office. I spent a great portion of that day praying, studying my legal application, and praying some more.

Mr. Hewlett and I were the only Negroes present, except for the man handing out towels in the bathroom. He sure seemed surprised when I walked in. He looked at my new suit and new shoes and just smiled. Never had I felt so far away from home.

I was afraid to leave the couch even to get a drink of water or lunch. I didn't want them to call for me and I not [to] be there.

As the day expired, I prepared my soul for failure. Then I convinced myself this effort required nothing short of a miracle. It was late in the evening and I had all but given up. I folded my hands and asked God for guidance on how to tell Ed Johnson's family that I had failed.

Parden read and reread his court briefs. He practiced what he would say and how he would say it. But would he even get the chance? It had been years since the nation's highest court had stayed an execution or reversed a murder conviction. And no one could remember a single black man the justices had ever saved from the gallows. If getting on the docket was a long shot, obtaining a favorable ruling was unthinkable.

The intermittent rain only dampened his spirits further. As if preparing to accept his failure, the black lawyer folded his hands and bowed his head as he had been taught at the orphanage where he grew up. He begged God for mercy and for strength.

Many back home in Chattanooga believed Parden had missed his true calling. He often sounded more like a preacher than a lawyer. And sometimes he seemed like both. But no one doubted his ability to practice law. Having graduated at the top of his class, Parden knew the words in the law books by memory, and he felt the spirit of the law in his soul. He fought vigorously for his clients. Parden was so zealous that he made very few friends at the courthouse. Prosecutors often referred to him as a "troublemaker."

White lawyers believed that Parden was too emotional, that he took defeat in the courtroom too personally. The black lawyer was frequently seen kneeling in the back of the courtroom praying with his clients before a court hearing or crying with the family of a client who had been sentenced to prison. Many attorneys considered such conduct unbecoming an officer of the court. And the judges felt he was too young, too inexperienced to challenge their decision-making in open court and in subsequent appeals.

Their concerns and objections, of course, were less about who he was or what he did than about the color of his skin.

"What can a Negro lawyer know that a white lawyer does not?" the trial judge in the Johnson case had asked him. "Do you think a Negro lawyer could possibly be smarter or know the law better than a white lawyer?"

Yet Parden enjoyed true success in the courtroom. He won scores of jury verdicts for his clients that were deemed unachievable by other attorneys. "Even though he's black and they're white, Noah Parden develops a bond with a jury faster than any lawyer I have ever seen," a white lawyer told a newspaper. "He makes jurors like him and trust him, and in return, they like and trust his client."

Indeed, Parden was such an extraordinary speaker that even his wife believed God had called him to be a preacher. His voice could be powerful. His words were filled with meaning. To illustrate a point, he always had a story to tell. Most of the time, it involved the missteps of a client or some experience he had growing up in an orphanage. Preachers around town were constantly asking Parden to speak at their services. He knew the Bible, too. He would frequently cite complete chapters from the book of Psalms or Proverbs or use parables from the New Testament in arguments to juries.

Like innumerable lawyers before and after him, Parden loved to write. Many of his articles were printed by black newspapers and magazines around the country. For a short time in 1904, he published his own weekly newspaper. Though he loved writing, he quickly learned that printing a newspaper was expensive and time-consuming. It also took too much time away from his law practice.

But to people in Chattanooga's black community, he was simply one of them, a local who had grown up poor. In thirteen years of practicing law in Chattanooga, Parden had developed a reputation among the black community as a person who would stand up for their rights. He was the lawyer black people called when they had no money to pay a white lawyer. Many times, a home-cooked dinner at the residence of a defendant's mother, grandmother, or spouse was about all he could expect as payment.

At age forty-one, Parden was in the best physical shape of his life. Gray was lightly sprinkled through his curly hair and full mustache. Cheap wire-rimmed glasses fit loosely on his nose. He was married but had no children. His family had consisted of the parents and brothers and sisters at the orphanage who discovered him one afternoon abandoned on their doorstep. He had spent his teenage and early-adult years working days in the tobacco fields and nights in a factory trying to save money for law school.

After studying two years at Central Tennessee College in Nashville, Parden returned to Chattanooga to open a law firm with his mentor, former Tennessee Representative Styles L. Hutchins. Hutchins was the first black person to be elected to a state office from Chattanooga. The two men were exact opposites. As deliberate and cautious as Parden was, Hutchins was flamboyant and rebellious. Together, they represented most of the black people who found themselves in trouble with the law in southeastern Tennessee. This case that brought Parden to the nation's highest court was the biggest either man had ever handled.

All that said, this also was a case he didn't want. Twice Parden had told Ed Johnson to find another lawyer. He rejected requests by white lawyers and leaders within the black community to get involved in Johnson's defense during the trial. Even after Johnson had been condemned to die, Parden initially turned away Johnson's father, who pleaded for help in saving his son's life. But Hutchins insisted they accept the case. The older lawyer saw it as their duty and eventually browbeat his young associate into handling the appeal.

Parden's public message was usually low-key and gentle. He seldom raised his voice, except at the stupidity of his own clients. Publicly, he sought justice or mercy from the courts for his clients and never wavered as an advocate for the people he represented. Privately, he chastised his clients for their wrongdoings and tried to help them mend their ways. Though Parden never backed down from a fight, he certainly didn't go looking to pick one, either. Even when disagreeing with a prosecutor or a judge, Parden seemed reluctant or embarrassed to challenge their authority.

"Mr. Hewlett. Mr. Parden."

The voice was startling. It came from across the room, where the secretary stood in the doorway. She nodded for them to step forward.

"Yes."

"He will see you now."

Nervously, Parden picked up his briefcase, cleared his throat, and walked toward the open door. Hewlett patted him on the shoulder and followed him into the room. Above the thick wooden door was a sign:

SUPREME COURT CONFERENCE ROOM

The justices' courtroom was directly above their old chambers, which they had called home for the eighty years before their 1860 move. Their new space was elegant, but not as expansive as the Court desired. None of the justices had his own office. Instead, they shared a conference room, a robing area, a law library, and the courtroom. A new Supreme Court building was in the planning stages, but it would not be completed until 1935.

This was a moment few lawyers ever experience. Parden had no idea what to expect. He thought maybe two or three of the justices would be there. Or possibly all of them.

The conference room was huge, larger than Parden's entire house. Law books packed dark oak shelves that lined every wall from the floor to the ceiling twenty feet above. The only light in the room was a gas-fueled chandelier hovering above a long table. Shades over a large window were drawn shut. This was the room where the justices met regularly to discuss cases among themselves and decide how they would rule.

Nine wooden chairs were neatly fitted around the table. About a dozen more chairs lined the walls. The floors were of hardwood and gave under Parden's step. A cigar on the table left a trail of white smoke.

"Mr. Justice," said Hewlett, "it's an honor, sir. I'm E. D. Hewlett, a member of the bar of the Supreme Court, and this is Noah Parden, a lawyer from Chattanooga, Tennessee."

Parden was starstruck. He was here, standing before a justice of the United States Supreme Court. All of the chairs were empty except one. At the far end of the long, grandiose oak table, behind a stack of papers and law books, sat an old man with barely a red hair or two on the side of his head. He was studying a document and did not even look up as he waved them over. There was no friendly welcome to Washington, D.C. There was no handshake or apology for the day-long wait.

Even though the cantankerous codger was seated, Parden could see that he was a large specimen, about six feet two inches tall and well over 260 pounds; he had not missed many meals. His face was stern and red. The buttons on the black double-vested suit and the black bow tie that choked his white collar strained to gather in his flesh. A few feet behind him, several black robes hung on thin wooden hangers.

To Noah Parden, this man needed no introduction. He was U.S. Supreme Court Justice John Marshall Harlan, a legendary member of the Court who has frequently been overshadowed by Justice Oliver Wendell Holmes. Known as the "Great Dissenter," Harlan had a reputation for being bombastic and somewhat pompous from the bench. His words were biting, and many who appeared before the jurist considered him a grumpy old man.

Justice Harlan never hesitated to tell lawyers appearing before the Court that they were doing an awful job and that their clients should demand a refund for ineffective assistance of counsel. He would openly berate his fellow justices in the strongest of terms. He often violated the Court's judicial decorum; once he had pounded his fist on the desk and waved his finger in another justice's face while reading a dissenting opinion from the bench. His scathing written and oral attacks upon litigators and fellow judges were legendary.

The other justices joked that Harlan suffered from "dissent-ery." "He could lead, but could not follow. His was not the temper of a negotiator," said a former U.S. attorney general. In a court ruling, Justice Felix Frankfurter described Harlan as "an eccentric exception."

Yet Justice Harlan's written opinions, though colorful and haughty, delivered a clear message: he was a friend to the poor, the underprivileged, and the people of color in our society. He believed in equal rights and equal protection under the law. The most obvious evidence of his views came in 1896, in a case called *Plessy* v. *Ferguson*. The Supreme Court was reviewing an appeal by Homer Plessy, a man from Louisiana, who complained about the state's law compelling segregation of the races in railroad coaches. Plessy, who was one-eighth black, said he wanted to be able to sit in the passenger cars reserved for white people. The Louisiana courts ruled against Plessy, who appealed to the Supreme Court. In deciding the case, the Court, led by Justice Henry Brown, said that the fallacy in Plessy's argument was in his "assumption that the enforced separation of the two races stamps the colored race with the badge of inferiority." However, Justice Brown said that if the law branded black people as inferior it was "solely because the colored race chooses to put that construction upon it." Six other justices signed off on Justice Brown's opinion that segregation did not and should not stigmatize black people. In doing so, the Supreme Court gave its stamp of approval to Jim Crow laws and the public policy of "separate but equal."

Only one justice dissented in the Plessy case: John Marshall Harlan. He blasted his fellow members of the Court for being disgracefully bigoted in their decision-making. He argued that all men are created equal and insisted that no one—black or white—should be discriminated against or awarded preferential treatment because of the color of his skin.

In the view of the Constitution, in the eye of the law, there is in this country no superior dominant ruling class of citizens. There is no caste here. Our Constitution is color-blind, and neither knows nor tolerates classes among citizens. In respect of civil rights, all citizens are equal before the law. The humblest is the peer to the most powerful. The law regards man as man and takes no account of his surroundings or of his color when his civil rights as guaranteed by the supreme law of the land are involved.

Justice Harlan said that "separate but equal" operated under the "guise of giving equal accommodation for whites and blacks" but instead "compelled the latter to keep to themselves." Harlan was correct in his prediction. The high court's decision opened the door to unprecedented segregation through the acceptance of Jim Crow laws across the South.

As confrontational as Justice Harlan was on the bench, he was equally approachable in person. Most of the great mustachioed justices who sat on the Court were considered haughty and aloof, but Harlan was a man of the people. Justice Holmes called him the last "tobacco chomping justice." Harlan was known for leaving the Supreme Court chambers in the afternoon and walking around the capital. He would stop at a fruit stand to buy apples for himself and anybody else standing nearby—white or black. If lawyers thought he was a tyrant, the laypeople who met him felt the exact opposite way.

Now, a decade after the infamous Plessy decision, here was Parden, a black man from the South, standing before Justice Harlan seeking emergency relief. Parden was one generation removed from slavery, yet he was across the table from one of the most powerful men in the United States. He might not have been the first black attorney to enter the U.S. Supreme Court building, but he certainly was the first to sit before a justice with such a sober purpose. Only once before had a black lawyer from the old Confederacy taken a petition to the nation's highest court.

Back home, Parden was given little chance of winning relief for his client. Instead, he was viewed as a community agitator. Just another Negro trying to stir up trouble, misusing the court system to delay the inevitable, people said. Most white people, especially lawyers and court authorities, laughed at Parden and Hutchins when they announced they would take their case to Washington. Then again, most lawyers back in Chattanooga never thought Parden would even get an audience with a Supreme Court justice. Even many prominent black leaders had tried to persuade Parden to turn the appeal over to a white lawyer, who they believed might be more effective or at least better received.

The federal courts had never been a friend to the black man in America. Just decades earlier, this very Supreme Court had publicly stated, as a matter of law, that there were no rights belonging to a black man that white people were bound to respect.

For Parden, just being in the room was intimidating. He struggled to keep his focus. He needed to make the strongest argument he could and not forget any key points. He must remember that he was there not for himself but for his client.

"I represent Ed Johnson, the condemned man," said Parden.

"Mr. Parden, Mr. Hewlett," the old man responded without standing up and without stating his own name, "tell me why the United States Supreme Court should care about this case?"

The justice's hands continued to grasp a document. Parden was unsure if it was the request for writ of error and petition for habeas corpus that he had filed a day earlier, asking the Court to stay Johnson's execution and grant a full review of his case. He also was unsure if the justice had read his petition or how much he knew about the case.

"Your Honor, never has there been a more obvious injustice than in this case," Parden began. "Here we have a defendant who is certainly innocent, but who has never been afforded the presumption of innocence."

"Why do you think this Negro is innocent?" Justice Harlan interrupted.

"Because he told me so," Parden responded. "I have met with him, I have met with his friends, I have reviewed the evidence. I believe he is telling the truth."

"All criminals claim they're innocent." Harlan smirked, displaying the only glimpse of emotion Parden would see.

"But Ed Johnson is telling the truth," Parden answered. "The evidence unequivocally supports his plea of innocence."

The Chattanooga lawyer took this as an opportunity to make his pitch. He told Harlan that neither of the key witnesses against his client was to be believed. The victim admitted she had not gotten a good look at her attacker. In fact, the man who claimed he saw Johnson in the area of the attack carrying a leather strap like the one used against the victim came forward only after he was offered a $375 reward. And other witnesses put his credibility in doubt, Parden told Justice Harlan.

> Miss Nevada Taylor was raped by someone, but who it was she could not say. On the night the outrage was committed, several officers were called to the home of the young woman and the first question propounded to her was if she knew who her assailant was. She said she did not know. Then she was asked if he was white or black, and she said she did not know, as it was too dark for her to tell.

"I'm not here to retry this case. A jury has already done that," Justice Harlan again interrupted. "Was the trial flawed? Was the defendant denied some constitutional right?"

Parden said there were specific violations of the Fourth, Fifth, Sixth, and Fourteenth Amendments. Two of the lawyers appointed to defend Ed Johnson had never handled a criminal case before. They were denied enough time to investigate adequately and research properly the case against their client.

The black lawyer argued that his client was denied his right to be tried by a jury of his peers. Not one person in the jury pool was black, and there was evidence that the judge and other court officials had gone to great lengths to make sure that no black man could be called for jury duty in this case. Parden pointed out that the Supreme Court had ruled two decades earlier that states and counties that systemati-cally kept black people out of the jury pool were violating the Four-teenth Amendment's equal-protection clause. "That's what happened here," Parden said.

The defense attorney said that the trial should have been moved to another jurisdiction, because the Chattanooga community was con-taminated by overwhelming anger and a thirst for revenge in this case. Such feelings were evident, if not encouraged, by newspaper reports detailing the brutality of the crime and the desire for swift and severe punishment. Just days before the trial, thousands of citizens had formed a lynch mob and stormed the county jail in an unsuccessful attempt to kill Johnson.

"Three times in the two weeks prior to trial, the mob went to the jail to administer its own justice. The atmosphere in the community was so poisoned that there was no way Ed Johnson could have received a fair trial from an impartial jury." Parden's voice rose with confidence. "Everybody in that courtroom knew going in what they were going to do. They were there to give Ed Johnson a trial and then they were going to hang him."

There was so much pressure on the sheriff, the district attorney, and the judge to act quickly and punish severely that the basic rights of the defendant were ignored. The elected officials were trying to preserve the rule of law and quell the bloodthirsty appetites of the mob by proving to the public that the court system would provide the justice, or at least the result, it wanted, Parden said. Instead, the case became a race to see which would kill Ed Johnson first—the court offi-cials or the lynch mob.

Parden argued that the jury was biased and tainted, noting that in the middle of the trial two separate jurors had made either derogatory statements or threatening gestures toward the defendant. When jurors have to be restrained, how can that be a fair trial? he asked. He also noted that after the trial Johnson's own lawyers—either fearing that the lynch mob might turn on them or worrying that their reputations in the community might be irreparably harmed—had betrayed their client by encouraging him to waive his rights to appeal.

The words leaving the black lawyer's mouth focused on the case of Ed Johnson. After all, he was the client and Parden's primary concern. But Parden realized the message he was delivering was unmistakably broader and more complex. He was asking the Supreme Court to do much more than rescue his client from pending death.

In reality, Parden sought a condemnation of a state criminal-court system buried in tyranny. To achieve his goal of liberating Johnson, he needed to convince the Supreme Court to make the right to a fair trial, as guaranteed in the Sixth Amendment of the United States Constitution, binding on state courts. The message subtly asked the Supreme Court to take a much more pragmatic and active view in determining an individual's right to due process and equal protection. Due process is not whether a procedure written in a Tennessee law book has been followed, Parden said, but whether the petitioner was given a full and fair hearing and whether he was presumed innocent by the jurors who decided his fate. Equal protection is more than providing black people with a lawyer and a trial, he argued. It's about according black defendants the same privileges and respect as white suspects.

In essence, Parden was asking the Court to intervene directly in a state-court criminal trial for the first time in the nation's history. He sought a landmark decision that would forever change how criminal defendants were tried. And he wanted the Supreme Court to expand the Constitution and begin an era of federalism that would forever change how state courts treated their prisoners.

The black lawyer had done his homework on Justice Harlan. From all Parden had read and been told about Harlan, he was certain his argument went straight to the heart and soul of the justice. Indeed, if Harlan believed in any legal principle, it was that the U.S. Constitution was there to right wrongs, to protect people, and to guarantee that all the citizenry were treated equally and fairly. The law was not some procedural technicality to Harlan but, rather, a model code for morality in determining right and wrong, and separating justice from injustice. Parden knew Justice Harlan advocated the expansion of the federal

Constitution to state courts, and that the other justices had rejected those arguments in the past. But never had they seen a case where the facts so clearly invited federal intervention. Parden continued to press his case.

It was one of the most remarkable trials known in criminal history. He was a poor young man and not able to hire counsel. The court appointed three white lawyers, men of ability, to represent Johnson.

They claim that the reason they could not conduct the trial as it should have been is that they were told that if they should undertake to file a plea to the array of jurors that Johnson would be lynched.

Then they thought that, under the circumstances, they should file a motion for change of venue, and they were again informed that Johnson would be lynched. They also thought that at that time prejudice in Hamilton County was at such a pitch that the case should be continued until the next term of court, and again they were informed that any dilatory plea would again cause the mob to make another attack on the jail.

And there was more solid evidence that Johnson's right to a fair and impartial trial and due-process rights were violated, Parden said. But before he could enumerate them, the office door opened. It was the same silver-haired, bespectacled secretary. Ten minutes were up. Parden laid a copy of a detailed legal brief outlining his arguments in front of Justice Harlan.

"Sir, there's not much time," Parden quickly inserted. "They are going to hang him in seventy-two hours. I beg of Your Honor to give him this review."

With that, the two lawyers said thank you and goodbye. Harlan nodded without looking up. There were no words of encouragement from the old judge, no promise to give the case full consideration, not even a wish for a safe trip back to Chattanooga. Just a nod. Parden hoped the silence meant the judge was in deep thought and not that he was bored with the argument.

Minutes later, Parden grabbed Hewlett's hand. His hearty hand-shake said it all. Hewlett said he had another case for which he needed to start preparing. They wished each other the best and parted ways. Once again, Parden found himself alone. The rain had stopped, but the newspapers were predicting snow. His bones were chilled, and he needed to return to the guest home where he had rented a room. But he had promised to inform the editors of a black-owned newspaper in Chattanooga how the Supreme Court hearing had gone. Sitting under an electric lamp on the steps of the Capitol, Parden gazed down the Mall toward the Washington Monument. Across the walkway was the thirty-foot-high Bartholdi Fountain with its tiered basins. Feeling inspired, he jotted down a few notes that he would dictate the next morning via telephone.

We met with Justice Harlan. He seemed open to our argu-ments. We had only a few minutes to present our case. Judge Hewlett and I summarized each point in our writ carefully. Justice Harlan displayed no opinion. He did ask many ques-tions. Judge Hewlett agreed that the meeting went well and we are hopeful.

Justice Harlan is the jurist in our case and that is good for Mr. Johnson. He is a fair and honorable judge with regards for the Negro people and his opinion is that the Constitution is colorblind.

I request every man and woman, Negro and white, to pray with me that God's will be done. I beg God for forgiveness for my own arrogance and I apologize to the Almighty for thinking I could do this all by myself and I ask God to not condemn my client because of my own shortcomings.

The next morning, before breakfast or even a first cup of coffee, Parden walked to the Supreme Court clerk's office to see what, if any, action Justice Harlan had taken. He prayed aloud the entire nine-block walk to the Capitol. He walked quickly, because he had a ticket for a train back to Chattanooga that left Washington at 11:00 a.m.

Only after he arrived and found the doors to the Capitol locked did it occur to Parden that it was Sunday. The Supreme Court was not in session. Disappointed, the lawyer retrieved his luggage and prepared to leave Washington.

The train trip back to Chattanooga was a time of introspection for Parden. He sat alone, drinking coffee, in the passenger car designated for black people. He had gotten no sleep the night before his meeting at the Supreme Court, nor had he slept any this past night. Even on the trip home, he was anxious, unable to close his eyes for any extended period.

His thoughts focused on his client. If ever he had represented a man he believed was innocent, it was Ed Johnson. The two had talked several times during the trial and a few times since. Parden had connected with the young black man. He could see the plight of many black men in the eyes of Johnson. "But for the will of God," the lawyer said of his client, "that is me."

But what did he really know about his client? Not much. They didn't exactly run in the same social circles. Parden was well established in the city's black middle class and had many prominent white people as friends. Well educated, he had doctors, lawyers, and ministers as close friends. And he worked to obtain a better life for himself and all minorities. To Parden, the American Assumption was very real—that wealth and influence could be obtained through hard work and achievement in the capitalistic system.

Ed Johnson, on the other hand, hadn't finished the fourth grade. He was illiterate. His only friends were those he met at the Last Chance Saloon, where he also worked part-time. None of them were exactly pillars of the community. Johnson's dreams for the future were of having a place to sleep and food to eat, and avoiding the very predicament in which he now found himself.

At that moment, a young porter offering coffee refills interrupted. Parden took some with cream and sugar. Then the thought pattern started all over again.

That was the longest train ride of my life. I relived every word spoken in our meeting with Justice Harlan. I remembered every expression he exhibited. What I didn't know was if those memories would forever bring joy or sadness. Had my attempts saved Ed Johnson's life or had my efforts only assured my client certain condemnation?

NOAH PARDEN, in a speech to the Galbraith African Methodist Episcopal Zion Church in Atlanta in April 1906

CHAPTER TWO

SCENE OF THE CRIME

BY ALL ACCOUNTS, Chattanooga is deserving of its motto "the scenic city." The name "Chattanooga" is Indian in origin, meaning "a mountain coming to a point." The city sits in the shadows of historic Lookout Mountain and Missionary Ridge—two well-known Civil War battlegrounds. Through the heart of town cuts the mighty Tennessee River.

The birth of Chattanooga was strongly associated with racism, but it was not directed against African-Americans. At the beginning of Tennessee's statehood, in 1796, most of its land was Indian territory, dominated by the proud Cherokees. It was the Western frontier of the nation, the Appalachian Mountains having formed a substantial barrier to earlier development.

In 1815, John Ross started a ferry service down the Tennessee River. He developed a trading site in the state's southeast corner that would later be called Chattanooga. By the 1830s, Ross had become a prominent business leader among the Cherokees and white men. But as commerce in the new territory prospered, white business and political leaders in the East decided the nation needed to take possession of the area. Employing fraudulent and bogus treaties, the United States took the position that the Cherokees had ceded or sold their lands to whites in Tennessee and Georgia.

Ironically, the Cherokees had made the greatest effort of all Indian tribes to adopt the ways of the white man. They became successful farmers and established a government emulating the white man's. They had established excellent business relations with their white counterparts.

But the Cherokees were occupying land that the white man wanted, and the white man was determined to seize it and not share it. Congress gave the Cherokees two years to leave Georgia and East Tennessee for a new territory, now known as Oklahoma. When government officials realized that most of the Cherokees had not moved, President Andrew Jackson sent troops to escort the Indians forcibly to their new home west of the Mississippi River. On this expedition, known as the "Trail of Tears," thousands of Cherokees died.

By the time the Civil War rolled around, Chattanooga had actually transformed itself into a progressive city. Very few of its residents owned slaves. This wasn't because the people were morally opposed to slavery. The terrain of East Tennessee was so mountainous and hilly that there was very little farming, so that the city grew by developing manufacturing and commerce. As a result, slavery was not a major controversy for the people of Chattanooga.

Most of the people living in Chattanooga had moved to the city from North Carolina, Pennsylvania, and northeastern Virginia. Their ancestors had fought the British only a century before, and their forefathers had played significant roles in the creation and survival of the United States of America. They were not about to turn away from their nation. Thus, Chattanooga remained a Union stronghold throughout the Civil War.

Confederate loyalists considered Chattanooga "occupied territory" because there were so many Northern transplants living there. It was the only metropolitan area in Dixie that voted to stay in the Union; the rest of Tennessee decided to secede. The city had overwhelmingly favored Lincoln, strongly supported the Republican Party, and overwhelmingly ratified the Fourteenth Amendment to the U.S. Constitution, also known as the equal-rights amendment.

With near-unanimous support from black people, Republican candidates won most of Chattanooga's elections following the war. White

politicians therefore rewarded black supporters with key appointments to the school board and other political-patronage positions. A
majority of the city's police force was, for a while, made up of black
officers. In fact, the GOP even nominated and elected a handful of
black men as magistrates, aldermen, clerks, school-board members,
and the first superintendent of the Chattanooga City School System.
Between 1880 and 1890, two of the area's representatives to the Tennessee Legislature—Styles L. Hutchins and William C. Hodge—were
black.

Most Southern towns experienced rashes of lynchings, but Chattanooga was much more restrained. Between 1880 and 1930, the
period in which race-based lynchings were commonplace, there were
only three in Chattanooga. By comparison, Nashville, Birmingham,
Knoxville, and Atlanta recorded at least a dozen mob hangings.

But as some Chattanooga leaders pushed for racial harmony and
acceptance, the rest of the state sought to draw clear boundaries for the
races. "Black people may no longer be slaves," a Nashville columnist
wrote, "but whites must find means to retain control over the coloreds." By 1890, the Ku Klux Klan, which was organized and founded
in a small town west of Chattanooga, had become politically and
socially active in the state.

Chattanooga eventually followed other Southern cities in adopting
so-called "black codes." Such codes had one intention: countering
emancipation and disenfranchising black people. One code, for example, required that voters be able to read and interpret various sections
of the U.S. Constitution. Officials waived the requirement for white
people at the voting precincts but stringently enforced it when a black
person wanted to cast a ballot. Combined with strict property-owner-
ship requirements and hefty poll taxes for voters, the laws effectively
deterred black people from exercising their constitutional right to
vote.

The state also enacted criminal statutes that were exclusively
punitive toward black people. For instance, Tennessee laws provided
that any black person found guilty of assault upon a white woman,
impersonating a white man for carnal purposes, or stealing a horse, a

mule, or baled cotton would automatically be punished by death. There were no similar laws for white people.

Chattanooga's white leaders also journeyed down the path of segregation through the implementation of Jim Crow laws. Black people were separated from their white neighbors when using trains, schools, parks, theaters, restaurants, public bathrooms, water fountains, and even cemeteries. These segregationist laws were ignited by the 1896 U.S. Supreme Court decision in *Plessy*, which promoted the idea of "separate but equal." They remained in effect until 1954, when the U.S. Supreme Court reversed itself in the famed *Brown* v. *Board of Education*.

Chattanooga's attitude toward race was best expressed just weeks before Noah Parden's trip to Washington, D.C. As various civic and community groups struggled with how to deal with the race problem, a prominent Baptist church voted seventy-four to seventy-one that black people do have souls and can go to heaven. "Thank God for the Soddy Baptist Church," Parden responded sarcastically. "I just hope they notified God about their decision."

When it came to business, Chattanooga was good to both black and white people. With a major river flowing through the middle of town, the city had positioned itself as a transportation hub. That reputation only increased when the railroad companies decided to route their north-south lines through the city.

City fathers possessed an almost religious enthusiasm for iron factories and steel mills—industries aided by the ability to transport large amounts of supplies and materials by train and river barge. Cast-iron stoves, frying pans, and iron skillets were made in Chattanooga and exported throughout the rest of the country. City leaders boasted that there were enough jobs available for everybody and that no man need be out of work. By the end of the century, Coca-Cola had become a national brand, rewarding the foresight of the Chattanooga businessmen who first decided to bottle and distribute the soft drink.

However, the town's economic successes tended to overshadow the definite social ills that existed. The community suffered from an extremely poor educational system. More than 15 percent of the adults living in Chattanooga were illiterate. The city recorded a considerably higher infant-mortality rate and shorter life spans than the rest of the nation.

If commerce in general was prospering, black-owned businesses in Chattanooga were thriving. With money came opportunities for education. By 1906, two generations since the Civil War, there were an unusually high number of black lawyers, doctors, and other professionals practicing in Chattanooga, compared with other Southern cities. The city itself had a population of about 60,000—one-third of whom were black.

Chattanooga's economic prosperity actually promoted a more relaxed racial attitude, or at least indifference. More important than black and white was green and silver. And if black people were spending their newfound wealth in white-owned stores, white business leaders were more than happy to welcome them through the front door and treat them hospitably.

Chief among those to encourage people toward the idea of a progressive South was Adolph Ochs, owner and publisher of the *Chattanooga Times*. Ochs promoted fair and truthful writing, and less sensationalism. He used the profits from the Chattanooga paper to buy a struggling newspaper in the Northeast called the *New York Times*. Ochs's editorials displayed his views on race and community.

> Chattanooga knows no North, no South, no East, no West. The perfect harmony that has been apparent throughout, the energy with which the ex-Confederates and the ex-Federals took hold of the work assigned them, and worked side by side, was the pleasing feature of the occasion, and one particularly characteristic of Chattanooga.
>
> We must learn to set aside or suppress our prejudices against the Negro. If we are to succeed as a city, they must be successful as a people. They must be fully educated and respected as a people.

It was in this world that Nevada Taylor was raised and lived. In 1906, she was twenty-one, blond, and beautiful. For two years, she had worked as a bookkeeper for a downtown shop, the W. W. Brooks grocery store on Market Street. She had a boyfriend, but they were not serious. She lived at home with her father, in a cottage in the middle of the Forest Hills Cemetery, where her father was the groundskeeper. He was known throughout the area for his superior abilities as a florist; some of his work even made a display at the Smithsonian Institute in Washington, D.C., in 1901.

On the evening of January 23, 1906, Miss Taylor left work at 6:00 p.m. She rode home from work aboard one of Chattanooga's new electric trolleys, which had replaced the mule-drawn streetcars. The trolley ran three miles, from downtown to the base of Lookout Mountain. The first automobile dealership opened in 1903, selling Cadillacs, Stearns, Marmons, Franklins, and Stanley Steamers. By 1906, sixty Chattanoogans owned cars. For many people, bicycles and the horse and buggy were still the preferred methods of transportation, even in this town of steep hills.

Miss Taylor, however, was partial to the electric trolleys, which were much smoother and faster than the old horse-drawn carriages. They allowed her to read the newspaper, especially the gossip columns, and check out the sales in the advertisements. The trolley ride also provided her extra time to plan for supper—a task that had fallen to her since her mother's death a few years earlier.

Winters in southeastern Tennessee could get bitterly cold. Highs would reach the mid-thirties, but temperatures in the teens or lower were not uncommon at night. On this particular day, the afternoon had warmed up to near forty. The skies were clear. But now the sun had set behind Lookout Mountain, casting the city in deep darkness. The temperature was dropping quickly.

For Miss Taylor, the twenty-minute ride cost three pennies. The big Coca-Cola sign she passed every day on the right-hand side of Broad Street never failed to make her thirsty. Even though Coca-Cola still advertised its product's medicinal value, this billboard was simple:

**DRINK A BOTTLE OF COCA-COLA,
FIVE CENTS AT ALL STANDS,
GROCERS AND SALOONS.**

With an umbrella in one hand and her purse in the other, Miss Taylor stepped off the trolley near 35th Street at about 6:30 p.m. It was very dark. Lights from several nearby businesses offered what little illumination there was in the neighborhood. In the distance, she could see the lights of the electric incline railway making its way up the side of Lookout Mountain. The incline appeared to go 4,400 feet straight up. In reality, it was a thirty-three-degree grade, which is still quite steep by any standards.

After waving goodbye to the trolley conductor and promising to see him at the same time the next day, she started her brief walk home. On a shortcut between buildings, she could hear faraway voices. The skies offered almost no light, and she was a considerable distance from the nearest gas-operated street lamp.

As Miss Taylor neared the cemetery gate, she heard footsteps behind her. Before she could turn around, something was around her throat, choking her. She started to fight. She started to cry out for help.

"If you scream, I will kill you," the attacker promised.

The brutal attack lasted no more than ten minutes. Miss Taylor was devastated. The public outcry was immediate, as demonstrated in the next day's newspaper.

THE CHATTANOOGA NEWS

Wednesday, January 24, 1906
BRUTAL CRIME OF NEGRO FIEND

DETAILS SHOCK ENTIRE COMMUNITY

A CRIME WITHOUT PARALLEL IN CRIMINAL ANNALS
OF HAMILTON COUNTY

No Clue of Whereabouts or Identity of Dastardly Assailant
An unknown Negro man committed the most fiendish crime in the history of Chattanooga last night when he attacked Miss

Nevada Taylor, and after choking his victim into insensibility by means of a leather strap drawn tightly about her throat, accomplished the terrible purpose for which he had waited in the dark for the woman.

The crime was committed within sight of the victim's house, inside the triangular enclosure occupied as a marble yard and strewn with marble shafts and tombstones.

The lights of her home could be seen from the point where she was attacked. She heard footsteps behind her and turned only to be caught in the powerful arms of a Negro man, whom she cannot identify.

A leather strap was quickly thrown over her head and drawn tight to hush her screams. He then picked his victim up from the ground and hurled her over the fence into the marble yard near the southeastern corner of the cemetery.

There he accomplished his terrible purpose and there he left his victim unconscious, choked into insensibility.

About 6:45 p.m., Miss Taylor regained consciousness. At first, she was unsure what had happened or where she was. Slowly standing up, she noticed that her dress was ripped and soiled. Her body ached, as if she had been beaten. Her throat was terribly sore. That's when she remembered the footsteps.

The young woman slowly looked around. She expected to see him, fearing it was not over. But the attacker was nowhere in sight. Nor was her purse or umbrella. She did not wait for him to return. Her home was less than 100 yards away. There she told her father and brother what had just happened.

Both immediately ran outside to see if they could get a glimpse of the assailant. The alarm went out. The sheriff was called. The family doctor was also summoned.

By 7:00 p.m., Hamilton County Sheriff Joseph F. Shipp had received news of the attack at the jail downtown. He called several of his best men, gathered a couple of bloodhounds, and quickly took a horse-drawn carriage to the Taylor home. By 7:40 p.m., Shipp was at the scene of the crime. He directed his deputies to search the area for the perpetrator, witnesses, or possible evidence while he went alone to visit with Miss Taylor and her father.

All eyes were on Sheriff Shipp. A Confederate Army officer whom everyone called Captain, the sheriff was nearing the end of his two-year elected term. Tall and thin with a full mustache, Shipp expressed a sense of purpose in his every movement. He never hesitated to tell people his thoughts or opinions. At the same time, he played the role of a gentleman perfectly. He was, after all, a Southern politician.

Joseph Franklin Shipp was born February 3, 1845, in Jasper County, Georgia. Two months after his sixteenth birthday, he enlisted as a volunteer in the Confederate Army. But his initial stay was short-lived. Confederate officials soon learned that young Joe had run away from home and did not have the permission of his parents—Gustavus and Caroline Shipp—to join the men in gray. A year later, he joined the Confederate soldiers again, this time legitimately as a private.

Shipp's military experience began with the Fourth Georgia Regiment. He spent his entire service as a soldier in Virginia, finally retiring as a captain in April 1865. He was wounded three separate times during his three-plus years in the Confederate Army, including a serious injury at the Battle of Malvern Hill. He also was a witness to the battle between the Civil War battleships the *Monitor* and the *Merrimac*—a story he would repeat many times in vivid detail to friends and supporters.

Returning to his parents' home in northern Georgia in the spring of 1865, Shipp had only a seventh-grade education, no money, and no business experience. His first job was as a message carrier between Atlanta and Augusta. For several years, he joined his father in the cotton-gin business in Social Circle, Georgia. This is where he met and married Lily Echols. They had four sons and three daughters.

By 1874, the couple had moved to nearby Chattanooga, which was becoming a major Southern city, to build and operate a water-pump manufacturing plant. Thanks to hard work and strong demand, Joseph Shipp was estimated to be worth about $25,000, making him one of the wealthiest men in the city. Then a tremendous flood in 1876 destroyed most of the factory and its stock. He spent nearly all of his personal savings to rebuild the plant—an effort that took six months.

But the new struggle proved very profitable, and soon Shipp's bank account and influence equaled and surpassed his earlier successes. He also opened a furniture factory right next to his pump plant. Shipp took a large portion of his profits and reinvested in real estate throughout town. Records show that in 1880 he owned only one six-room house. By 1896, fourteen homes and several other pieces of property were listed in his name.

For years, he had told his friends he wanted to run for public office. In 1900, he decided to seek the Democratic nomination for tax assessor. His only competitor was a seventy-nine-year-old saloon owner who died two weeks before the election. Shipp won by default. However, he always pointed out that his recently deceased opponent had still attracted 800 votes.

In 1904, he was elected to a two-year term as Hamilton County sheriff. He was considered an astute politician and community leader. As a businessman, he was active in the Chattanooga Chamber of Commerce and numerous other clubs and organizations. When he came into office, Shipp fired the deputies who had actively campaigned against him during the election and replaced them with his faithful supporters. He demanded loyalty, but he would never ask one of his deputies to do something he would not. And he was a darling of the newspapers, who described him as a "natural born leader." They said he was a "tender and devoted husband and a loving father." Not that he didn't enjoy frequent visits to many of the city's taverns and saloons. He preferred drinking whiskey and gin, always took pleasure in smoking fine cigars, and could never turn down a good game of pool or a competitive hand of poker.

Shipp was a take-charge kind of guy who didn't suffer fools, had no use for practical jokesters, and hated losing. As a lawman, the sheriff's reputation was that of a bulldog: he relentlessly pursued criminals. Get him mad and he cursed like a sailor, but he could never hold back the tears when forced to console a grieving widow.

Though his law-enforcement techniques certainly would have failed to gain the endorsement of today's American Civil Liberties Union, they were effective in his time, and the public appreciated that. A shoplifter or low-level thief might leave the sheriff's office without criminal charges but with a black eye and a lesson learned.

In the winter of 1906, however, he was facing re-election, and the crime against Nevada Taylor could not have come at a worse time. The community was in the midst of what the newspapers referred to as a crime wave. It began on the night of December 11, 1905, when a fifteen-year-old white girl living at the Vine Street Orphanage was raped in her sleep by a black man. Eight days later, a sixteen-year-old white girl surprised a black intruder apparently burglarizing her home. In his attempt to escape, the man stabbed the girl, inflicting serious injuries. The very next day, a young white schoolgirl was attacked downtown by a black man. On Christmas Eve, a Chattanooga constable was gunned down by an infamous black gambler named Floyd Westfield. And on Christmas Day, police received eight reports of assaults or robberies by black people.

The incidents filled the newspapers. Many of the citizens were in an agitated mood. On December 26, the *Chattanooga Times* trumpeted the crime spree in a front-page editorial with huge headlines that read: "Desperadoes Run Rampant in Chattanooga; Negro Thugs Reach Climax of Boldness."

The newspaper editorial clearly put some of the blame on Shipp for not being tough enough on the "Negro Thugs." The attack on Nevada Taylor made the public even more fearful. And with an election just two months away, Sheriff Shipp knew he needed to solve the rape case and do it quickly.

As the sheriff approached the small cottage, William Taylor greeted him on the porch. Shipp had known the Taylor family for many years. For several minutes, the sheriff consoled his longtime friend and supporter. He assured Taylor that everything would be done to swiftly apprehend and severely punish the culprit.

About that time, Dr. H. B. Wilson opened the front door and walked out onto the porch. An older man with long stringy white hair and wire-rimmed glasses, Dr. Wilson was the only physician Nevada Taylor had ever known. He treated most of St. Elmo, the small community at the foot of Lookout Mountain where the Taylors lived.

Dr. Wilson put his arm around William Taylor's shoulders and gave him a tight squeeze. Nevada had been through a very traumatic experience, the doctor said. There would be many scars—physical and psychological.

The physician had fully examined the victim, finding a livid red streak around her neck and bruises on her arms and legs, which he believed were injuries from being thrown over the fence by the attacker. Then came the most devastating news: she had been raped.

The three men—Sheriff Shipp, Dr. Wilson, and Mr. Taylor—stood silently on the porch for several minutes. Tears filled Taylor's eyes, anger filled his soul. The sheriff simply nodded and patted his friend on the arm as a condolence, then opened the screen door and walked inside.

Miss Taylor was lying on top of the bed, wrapped in a quilt her grandmother had sewn together from a hodgepodge of fabric pieces. She stared out the window as Shipp approached. No words of comfort came to mind. He asked if there was anything he could get her. She shook her head no. He sat beside her for several minutes in silence. Finally, he spoke up.

"Nevada, you must tell me exactly what happened. I need to know every detail that you can remember."

The story didn't take long, because there wasn't much she could recall. She told about leaving work, about riding the trolley and then walking toward her house. She remembered noise behind her, like footsteps. She hadn't gotten a good look at the man, but she said the attacker was about her height—five feet six inches—or maybe a little taller. He wore a black outfit and a hat. His arms were thick with muscles.

"Was the man white or Negro?" Shipp inquired.

At first she didn't know. She repeated that she'd never really gotten a look at him. Then she stated she believed the man was black.

She told Shipp she'd tried to scream, hoping someone nearby would hear her cries for help. And she remembered the attacker's threat to kill her. The sheriff again asked if she remembered anything about the man physically. She repeated that she couldn't give a reliable description of her attacker. But one thing stuck out in her mind:

"He was a Negro with a soft, kind voice."

Shipp gave the young woman a hug, said a prayer with her and her father, and promised that he would track down the criminal who had committed this horrible act.

Sheriff's deputies scoured the neighborhood for the assailant, or at least for evidence. They were soon joined by an informal posse of locals who had heard of the attack upon their neighbor. Despite questioning every person in the area where the attack occurred, police could not find a single witness who had seen or heard a thing. Every person questioned pointed out just how dark it was on this particular night.

Bloodhounds were on the scene by 8:00 p.m. to track the assailant. The dogs were allowed to smell Miss Taylor's dress in order to pick up the scent of the attacker. It appeared to work: the bloodhounds dragged their handlers quickly away from the crime scene and toward the road. However, the dogs lost the trail at the tracks for the electric streetcar. Sheriff's deputies repeated the effort several times, but each ended with the same unsuccessful result.

The only piece of evidence recovered was a black leather strap. The piece of rawhide was twenty-five inches long and about three-fourths of an inch wide. There was a split in the leather at one end, and a narrower edge at the other. This allowed the narrow end to be inserted into the split end, producing a noose that would tighten when pulled.

Deputies immediately took the strap to Shipp. A few minutes later, the sheriff showed the strap to Miss Taylor to see if she could identify it as the weapon used against her. She stared at the piece of rawhide for several minutes, holding it in her hands. However, she was unable to say for sure that this was the exact strap.

The sheriff then asked if he could gently put the strap up against her neck. He promised it would not hurt and that it would take only a few seconds. Holding the straps from behind and placing them around Nevada Taylor's neck, the sheriff called out for Dr. Wilson to come into the room and view the demonstration.

The strap matched perfectly with the red streaks around her throat. There was no doubt that this was the weapon used in the crime. Now they had simply to find out who the strap belonged to.

———

BY THE NEXT morning, public anger over the incident was obvious and growing:

> The fiendish and unspeakable crime committed in St. Elmo last night by a Negro brute, the victim being a modest, pretty, industrious and popular girl, is a sample of the crimes which heat southern blood to the boiling point and prompt law abiding men to take the law into their own hands and mete out swift and horrible punishment.
>
> No crime has so shocked the community within the memory of its oldest citizens.

Chattanooga News, January 24, 1906

CHAPTER THREE

SOMEONE MUST PAY

THE CHATTANOOGA TIMES

Thursday, January 25, 1906
FEELING AT HIGH PITCH

BLACK BRUTE MANAGED TO COVER UP TRACKS WELL
AND NO TRACE OF HIM HAS YET BEEN FOUND

One Course Suggested in Case of Capture

Feeling continues to run high, not only in St. Elmo and vicinity, but all over Hamilton County because of the terrible outrage committed Tuesday night near the cemetery gate, and of which Miss Nevada Taylor was the victim.

It was acknowledged by everybody, including officers of the law, that no power could save the criminal from summary vengeance in case he should be caught. The humor of the citizens of St. Elmo was one of quiet determination to deal punishment to the Negro which would be a warning to others of his stamp to abandon the present tendency toward outlawry in this community.

Neither is there any likelihood of any dying out of public sentiment along these lines. The crime was so horrible in every particular and the victim so popular in her neighborhood that any mention of the affair, it is stated, will stir up the wrath of the citizens for weeks and months to come.

Many citizens who were never before heard to use any intemperant expressions on account of crime were open yesterday in their vile desire to aid in meting out punishment to this Negro whenever caught. It was a frequently expressed desire to help pulling the rope or wielding the weapon that would send such a brute into eternity at the earliest possible moment.

Sheriff Joseph Shipp readily admitted he had no clues to the identity of the perpetrator of such a horrible crime. The victim couldn't give a description of her attacker, and there were no eyewitnesses. All he had was a leather strap. And this was decades before the days of fingerprinting and DNA testing.

By Wednesday afternoon, the sheriff was desperate. The more time that passed, the less chance there was that credible evidence would surface. People's memories get worse, not better, with time. In an effort to encourage tips from the community, Sheriff Shipp publicly announced that he was offering a $50 reward to anyone providing information that led to the arrest and conviction of the rapist.

W. W. Brooks Grocery Store, where Nevada Taylor worked, matched the reward offer with $50 more. Governor William Cox had also heard about the attack. He put an additional $200 into the reward pot. By Thursday, the Forest Hills Cemetery Association, which employed William Taylor, had added another $50 and a group of individuals from the St. Elmo area had put in $25 more.

The total reward offered stood at $375—more than many people in Chattanooga earned in a year. If this didn't shake a witness from the trees, Shipp believed nothing would. Published reports say that Sheriff Shipp frequently made offers of money and other favors in return for information about a crime. Asked about it during the political campaign, the sheriff said that if the Pharisees and Romans could pay

Judas thirty pieces of silver to snitch on Jesus, why should he be prohibited from paying a few dollars to capture a criminal?

Even churches in the black community were expressing their outrage at the crime and offering their support to the victim. The pastor of
the St. Elmo Baptist Colored Church visited William Taylor to offer
his apologies, promising to do everything within his ability to help the
authorities bring the man who had committed the crime to justice.

Other churches, such as the AME Zion Church on E Street, also
publicly condemned the assault and offered any assistance in identifying and capturing the criminal. Meanwhile, Sheriff Shipp was beginning to feel the public pressure. With the election only two months
away, he issued a statement to the city's two newspapers:

> I know the people thirst for judgment of the Negro who did
> this. I can assure the people that all at the courthouse agree
> and will be satisfied with nothing less. I am confident we will
> find this beast and he will feel the vengeance of our commu-
> nity upon him.

For their part, the two newspapers in Chattanooga were only
inflaming the passions in the community. Both the *Times*, which was
the morning newspaper, and the *News*, which published in the afternoon, featured front-page stories on the crime. Both ran editorials
expressing community outrage.

In story after story, the newspapers printed the most gruesome
details of the St. Elmo crime. Each played on stereotypes, repeatedly
referring to the attacker as a "Negro brute" and Nevada Taylor as a
"young white princess." They kept stating that the man arrested for
this crime would undoubtedly be lynched. Never did either newspaper use its pages to seek to calm the community.

It was the *Times'* use of incendiary language that was so surprising.
After all, many of the editorials in the *Chattanooga Times* in 1906 were
written or approved by its owner and publisher, Adolph Ochs. *The
Times* fashioned itself as a newspaper of the New South, supporting
liberal political and social ideals as well as equal rights and equal treatment for black people. With that mission in mind, its coverage of this

crime demonstrates how emotional and intense the community had become.

THE FIRST MAJOR break in the case came late Wednesday. For reasons that the sheriff kept completely to himself, a young black man named James Broaden, also known as Wyatt, became the prime suspect. He was said to have been studying to be a minister. Sheriff Shipp led a group of deputies and a full posse to arrest Broaden and return him to the Hamilton County Jail.

By all accounts, Mr. Broaden fit the minimal description given by Nevada Taylor of her attacker. About twenty-five years old, short and stocky, he lived near the foot of Lookout Mountain. Broaden worked at a grocery store, delivering goods to people throughout St. Elmo. Deputies said that he was "very familiar" with the neighborhood, and might have known when and where Miss Taylor came home every day.

At the jail, Shipp began questioning Broaden intensively. However, the sheriff never revealed if Broaden was truly a suspect in the attack, or if he was believed to be a witness or thought to have information regarding the crime.

Early Thursday morning produced a second break. Responding to the offer of the reward, a white man named Will Hixson, who worked at the Chattanooga Medicine Company, near the St. Elmo cemetery, telephoned Shipp at home. He wanted to know if the money was still being offered for information about the rape. The sheriff, who was reading the morning newspaper and eating breakfast when the call came in, immediately drove to St. Elmo to meet with Hixson. The informant claimed he had been standing at the St. Elmo trolley station about 5:50 p.m. the night of the attack and had seen a black man standing nearby "twirling a leather strap around his finger." Hixson said his attention was directed to the man because of the reported purse-snatching that had occurred the night before; he wondered if this could be the same culprit.

Hixson told the sheriff that a few minutes later a streetcar had come by and cast a light upon the black man, whom he recognized as a man he had given a match to earlier that morning. When the black man realized Hixson had seen him, he immediately fled into the darkness, the informant said. About a half-hour later, Nevada Taylor's trolley arrived at the depot.

Shown the strap recovered by deputies, Hixson said it appeared to be the same strap he had seen, or one identical to it. He said he did not know the name of the man he had seen, but would be able to identify the suspect if he ever saw him again.

For an hour, the sheriff and Hixson rode around St. Elmo looking for the attacker, but no one caught the witness's eye. Later that morning, Shipp received a second telephone call from Hixson. The informant had just seen the suspect walking toward town with a tall black man. Within minutes, the sheriff and his deputies were back in St. Elmo.

The lawmen searched the houses near where Hixson had seen the two men walking. Inside one of the homes, police found the tall black man, but not the suspect. Shipp assured this second black man they were not there for him, just wanted the name and whereabouts of the man he had been walking with forty minutes earlier.

That man, he said, was Ed Johnson. But he didn't know where the suspect was going.

Orders went out to all deputies, city police officers, and county constables: arrest Ed Johnson for the rape of Nevada Taylor.

Employing typical law-enforcement techniques, the sheriff quickly learned that Johnson was a drifter who had been working as a carpenter for several local churches doing remodeling or expanding. Shipp's first step was to visit the small frame hovel of the suspect's father, but Johnson was nowhere to be found. The sheriff searched through the suspect's belongings, hoping to find Miss Taylor's purse or umbrella or some other piece of evidence that would conclusively connect him to the crime. They found nothing, but neighbors said that Johnson frequently stayed with his sister, who lived only a few blocks away.

This was long before lawmen needed search warrants signed by judges; the sheriff and his deputies immediately left for Johnson's sister's house. Although she said he was not there and she did not know where he was, Shipp thoroughly searched her home, too. Again, nothing incriminating surfaced. But the sheriff was convinced that the sister was protecting Johnson, so he pretended to leave, only to hide around the corner of a nearby house. His suspicion paid off. Within a few minutes, Johnson's sister hurried from her house toward town. The sheriff had his deputies follow a short distance away.

Less than a mile from their neighborhood, Shipp spotted the sister waving toward an ice wagon to stop. On the back of the ice wagon sat Ed Johnson. The sheriff ordered his armed deputies to move in immediately and place handcuffs on the suspect.

"Why are you doing this?" Mr. Johnson asked.

"We will tell you more at the jail," a deputy responded.

A few minutes later, at the jail, Will Hixson gave a positive identification of Ed Johnson as the man he had seen with the leather strap the night Nevada Taylor was raped, and Johnson was officially charged with the crime.

In a quiet but scared voice, Johnson repeatedly denied he was the attacker. He could not have done it, he said, because he was miles away, at the Last Chance Saloon, most of that afternoon and evening. There were dozens of witnesses who could vouch for him, most of them black. He gave the sheriff a list of a dozen men he claimed would vouch for his whereabouts the night of the attack.

In 1906, suspects in crimes had few if any rights. It would be six more decades before the U.S. Supreme Court would rule that defendants had a constitutional right to have a lawyer present when questioned by police. The newspaper said Johnson was "subjected to some severe sweating and tested in many ways."

For more than three hours, Sheriff Shipp personally questioned the suspect. Together, they went over every detail of Johnson's story and the information that Nevada Taylor and Will Hixson had provided. They relived every waking moment of the defendant's life during the past few days.

Ed Johnson was very much a mystery man to Sheriff Shipp. He had never met or seen the young black man. Johnson had no wife or kids. His mother was said to have been a Christian woman who cried when she heard her son had been arrested. His father was known only as "Skinbone," apparently for his thin features.

The suspect had dropped out of school in the fourth grade and was generally known as "not an intelligent" person, according to court records. He enjoyed working with his hands, especially doing carpentry. For the past year, he had helped put roofs on two churches and worked on additions to three houses. For a few hours most evenings, he would do odd jobs around the Last Chance Saloon, including sweeping, mopping, and tending to the pool tables in the basement.

The sheriff knew little else about his prime suspect. Local residents didn't know where his family came from or why they were in Chattanooga. Johnson was simply a black man accused of a crime against a white woman. In the South, committing such a crime was a deadly sin.

The first indication that authorities had a suspect in the crime surfaced Thursday afternoon in the courtroom of Hamilton County Criminal Court Judge Samuel D. McReynolds. The judge was in the middle of an arson trial when he was handed a note. Sheriff Shipp and District Attorney General Matt Whitaker were standing at the back of the courtroom. Judge McReynolds immediately announced to the room that he needed to call a recess.

For the next hour, the three men huddled in the judge's chambers. Sheriff Shipp briefed the two men on the arrests of Ed Johnson and James Broaden. Having personally questioned both suspects, the sheriff said he was convinced that Johnson was their man. Though the suspect insisted on his innocence, the sheriff believed that his testimony about where he had been the evening of the assault contained too many inconsistencies. And he generally fit the vague description given by Nevada Taylor. Meanwhile, the two suspects remained locked up in the county jail.

In the courtroom, the emergency conference had created quite a stir. At first, people were unsure what the excitement was about. But it didn't take long to determine that the St. Elmo rapist had been caught.

News of Ed Johnson's arrest quickly spread throughout the community. As the sun went down, hundreds of people—mostly young and middle-aged white men from the suburbs—journeyed on streetcars and by horse into town for drink and conversation. But the only topic on their mind seemed to be the "Negro brute." After a brief stop at one of the downtown saloons, most of the men walked over to the corner of 7th and Walnut Streets, home of the Hamilton County Jail, to see what was happening.

Inside the jail, Chief Deputy Fred Frawley was antsy. The inmates were finishing dinner when a deputy came in from patrol with bad news. Word was circulating throughout town that there would be a mob gathering at the jail to lynch Ed Johnson. However, two other deputies were convinced that the rumors were just talk among a few of the drunken hotheads. These are men too spineless to kill someone, they said. Besides, they could handle any situation that developed.

Frawley peeked out the window overlooking the courtyard. There were maybe a dozen or so men standing around talking, but none seemed threatening or suspicious. Even so, the top deputy told the prisoners to finish up their meals so he could lock them down for the evening. He also told his wife and two sons, who had visited him at the jail for dinner, that they should probably eat their desserts and head home.

Less than ten minutes later, Frawley was called to the front office by another deputy who pointed outside. Frawley was amazed: at least 300 or 400 men were standing around in the courtyard, many of them brandishing pistols and Winchester rifles. He ordered two deputies to remain at the front entrance to keep watch on the crowd, to let no one in and keep the gate locked. He told two other deputies to secure the inmates and prepare to defend the jail.

The moment the chief deputy walked into the dining room, his wife knew there was trouble. A large mob was already gathering outside, he told his family. As much as he wanted to get them out of the jail, he couldn't let them leave. For them to exit the building, the doors would have to be unlocked, and that could provide an opportunity for the agitators to get in. Instead, he led his wife and two sons to the basement of the jail and told a deputy to stay with them at all times. "I promise, you will be safe here," Frawley told them. "I will check back with you every few minutes." He kissed his wife, hugged his kids, and ran back upstairs.

Frawley looked at the clock. It was 7:30 p.m. Then he glanced back outside. The crowd was enormous. He guessed there were now

1,500 people standing around in the courtyard, on the sidewalks, and in the street directly in front of the jail—many with weapons, some with rope. Frawley noticed that a few of the men near the front of the mob seemed to be the most vocal, acting as leaders. The large majority were mere spectators, hoping to get a glimpse of Ed Johnson if there was to be a lynching.

Even at this point, Frawley and his deputies considered the crowd to be benign. Frawley tried asking several members of the mob who were close to the jail door what their intentions were, but those men shrugged their shoulders or refused to respond.

Then the speeches began, and Frawley knew he was in trouble. Hatred and prejudice permeated the night. Riled to a fevered pitch, anonymous members of the mob started throwing bricks and rocks at the jail door and windows. Some of the approximately 200 men carrying guns fired them into the dark sky. The situation was pure chaos. A few of the pistols and rifles fired accidentally, resulting in a handful of minor injuries.

The chief deputy, realizing the situation was out of control, picked up the telephone in the jail to try to call the nearby city police department for assistance. The line was dead, severed by the mob. The five deputies were alone to confront the terrorism that threatened outside. Frawley had each deputy load his pistols and grab an extra rifle from the sheriff's gun closet. They had to be ready to defend the jail, themselves, the inmates, and their families.

The situation only grew worse when Nevada Taylor's younger brother arrived on the scene. He was immediately ushered to the front of the mob and asked to speak. A hush came over the crowd. His voice trembling, his eyes filled with tears, the victim's teenaged brother spoke only a few words. But they functioned as a volatile incendiary device: "The time for justice and punishment has come. We want the Negro. He must be punished for what he did to my sister. We want the Negro."

The crowd cheered and pushed forward toward the door. Inside the jail, three deputies had locked and barricaded the doors. The prisoners—especially the black inmates—feared for their lives. Even though the mob wanted Ed Johnson, they might take just any black man.

Up to this point, Frawley and the other deputies had actually con-

sidered themselves fortunate. Even though the crowd gathering outside had continued to swell, they'd remained unorganized. No leader
had stepped forward to collect and direct the mob's anger. But that
changed at about 8:30 p.m., when an immense man fresh from the
mill, his face smeared with soot and dirt, got the mob in motion. Carrying a double-barreled shotgun, he announced that he and the mob
had come to get Johnson.

Captain George Brown, the second in command at the jail, pleaded
with the man and his nearby followers for the better part of an hour, to
stop their attack. He said there were innocent women and children,
families of the jailers, living in the private quarters of the building. But
this did not deter the mob. Finally, Brown told them the man they were
there to kill, Ed Johnson, was not even being housed in the jail: the sheriff had moved him out of town earlier in the day. The leader of the mob
said he did not believe Brown. And with that, the real assault on the
facility began, as witnessed by a reporter for the *Chattanooga News*.

Finally, the smut-begrimed leader shouted that he would
allow just five minutes for some person to yield up the keys
and that if they were not produced in that time there would be
made a trail of powder and bullets to determine their influence
upon the officers.

Captain Brown gave those nearest him to understand that
if any person tried to pass through the door, it would be over
his dead body.

All the while, members of the mob were launching a fusillade of
rocks against the three-story brick jail. Every glass window was broken. Deputies, jailers, and inmates walking around inside the building
were dodging stones, bricks, and pieces of iron that acted as dangerous
missiles.

The leaders of the mob found a large hollow steel post nearby, and
used it as a battering ram against the front door. Several strong blows
from the big beam shook the jail from its foundation to the roof. But
even the mighty force of the battering ram did little to dislodge the
steel door frame.

During the height of the attack, the mob gained another advantage. A small number of the group had walked to the powerhouse a few blocks away. Overwhelming the night engineer and watchman, the members of the mob shut down the electric plant that supplied light to the jail.

The sudden darkness startled the already edgy deputies. Frawley raced downstairs to check on his family; they were all right. The deputies quickly determined what had happened and remembered that the jail was still piped with gas. When the mob outside saw the gas lamps illuminating the inside of the jail, many of its members became even more infuriated.

At this point, a dozen of the younger members of the mob stepped forward with heavy sledgehammers they had stolen from Deshay's Blacksmith Shop nearby. The men started using sledgehammers to beat on the hinges that held the door to the wall.

Inside, Frawley and the other deputies were divided on what they should do when the mob broke through. Should they shoot? Should they bluff? Should they use deadly force or put their own lives in danger just to protect a black man they believed had raped an innocent white girl? If they shot and injured one or two, and threatened to shoot more, would that deter the crowd? Or should they simply stand back and allow the mob to have its way?

The vigilante mind-set underscored an old Tennessee adage: "Disputes are not settled at the courthouse until they're settled up the holler." The history of the Deep South regarding lynchings is well told. Just a few years earlier, sixteen black men and women were lynched in one day in Trenton, Tennessee. Still, it had been nearly a decade since the last known lynching in Chattanooga, and records showed only two since the end of the Civil War. But as the people stood outside the jail the night of January 25, 1906, the memories of those two hangings filled the air and frequently escaped the whiskey-wetted lips of those in the crowd.

The first lynching had taken place the night of February 14, 1893. The sheriff arrested Alfred Blount, a slightly built black man, for allegedly assaulting an older white woman in her home. When police brought the suspect before the woman for identification, she was confused and could not positively say he was the man. Even so, the sheriff kept the suspect locked up in the county jail for the night.

That afternoon, the *News* printed the details of the attack and the capture of Blount. The article could be described as nothing short of an invitation to a lynching.

The atrocious crime that was committed upon the person of Mrs. Mary Moore this morning must have caused the devils in hell to shudder.

The inhuman act will be placed in the annals of crime as one of the blackest and most revolting. A brute alone, devoid of any sensibilities excepting those of sensuous frenzy, could have been guilty of the incarnate deed, and if caught, the buzzards should be allowed to tear the flesh from his infernal body.

Hanging would be too good for this contemptible villain, who has destroyed a pure, good woman's honor and virtue, and probably her life. Since noon, the best citizens of the city have spoken in open condemnation of the affair and a lynching is expected before tomorrow morning.

Mrs. Moore was alone in the house this morning . . . when she beheld a Negro man about 32 years of age. Like a panther after its prey, the strong brute approached the weak, sick, defenseless woman.

He placed his hands upon her—a brute without a thought save to further his own hellish designs and passions. Virtue, honor and purity to him were things unknown. The frail little woman was but a willow in his hand, a flower to crush, and he, the brute, to besmirch the godliness of nature and the edict of man.

With the demon's arm about her and with his hand over her mouth, she fell lifeless to the mattress on the floor.

Oh, God, draw the veil.

The prediction was self-fulfilling. Sometime after dark, several hundred men gathered outside the jail. With every passing hour, the crowd consumed more whiskey and became more boisterous. Finally, the sheriff came out of the jail to meet with the crowd. He told them he would not turn the prisoner over to them, because they weren't even sure he was the culprit. Taking that as an indication that the sheriff might let the black man go free, the mob stormed the jail. They dragged a cowering Alfred Blount several blocks to the Walnut Street Bridge, where he was hanged.

The second lynching took place in 1897, in the nearby community of Soddy, a place where very few black people lived. A young husky black man named Charles Brown was chased by a group of white men into a wooded area after a teenaged white girl accused him of assaulting her. Brown ran inside a house, where sheriff's deputies finally caught him. Late that night, a band of sixty armed men masked by handkerchiefs and minimal disguises forcibly took the suspect away from the lawmen. After giving Brown a severe beating, they took him to a bridge over the Chickamauga Creek, where they planned to hang him. When their rope broke as the mob hoisted their prey skyward, the men opened fire.

For each lynching that took place, several were thwarted thanks to the efforts of local law-enforcement or religious leaders. Specifically, the Reverend T. H. McCallie and the Reverend Jonathan W. Bachman served as the city's honorary chaplains, using their positions as bully pulpits for social change. Both men were revered in all neighborhoods. Dr. McCallie was a Northern transplant, a Unionist, who preached peace and harmony. Lawlessness would only harm the community, he said. Dr. Bachman was a native Southerner who had fought for the Confederacy during the war. But as pastor of the First Presbyterian Church, he urged local citizens of all races to be united and to resist bigotry and violent tendencies.

The two ministers were of like mind in deploring violence in their community and openly preached against vigilantism. Both agreed that if they ever received word of a lynching attempt they would rush to the scene and attempt to intercept the mob. Together, they created an association of ministers to monitor local race relations, the basic purpose being to promote law and order.

On one occasion in 1892, Dr. McCallie stood face to face with the mob. He preached to them about the law, about mercy, and about hatred. He told them that violence was a product of their own sinful hearts, and that they should go home, read their Bibles, fall on their knees, and beg God for forgiveness. Because they respected him, the men put away their guns and returned to their families.

But on the night of Thursday, January 25, 1906, Dr. McCallie and Dr. Bachman were out of town. The men and women in the jail had to pray that someone else would step forward.

By 8:40 p.m., news of the mob gathering had reached the city police department, which was located only six blocks away, and the Armory, where the state militia was drilling, less than a dozen blocks away. Judge McReynolds had learned about the lynching attempt and called Governor Cox for assistance. In turn, the governor called the captain commanding Troop B of the National Guard of Tennessee. The young men of the militia immediately responded to the governor's orders. They arrived at the jail within a few minutes and split into three smaller teams, with about five officers per unit.

At first, the soldiers tried rushing into the crowd in an effort to disperse them. But the mob had grown too large, and the soldiers were too young. In fact, the soldiers were so young—mostly seventeen to nineteen years of age—that the mob leaders did not believe the militia boys would actually fire upon them, and the men in the lynch mob simply took the bayoneted rifles right out of the soldiers' hands. By 9:00 p.m., the young men had returned to the Armory to regroup, without their weapons.

A handful of Chattanooga police officers were alerted about the same time. They immediately armed themselves and rushed toward the county jail. The officers made their best efforts to move the large crowd. But as soon as they would clear one area of the street, the mob and its observers would simply spill over into another area.

About 9:15 p.m., a police officer ran to the top of the Hamilton County Courthouse to ring the alarm bell. It had been more than ten years since the bell had sounded. The hope was that it would alert other police officers and members of the militia to rush to the jail to help suppress the mob. Instead, it only served to add to the ranks of the crowd and to stir the lynch mob into further frenzy.

By 9:30 p.m., the leaders of the mob had nearly destroyed the steel door to the jail with the sledgehammers. The door was hanging by only a few splinters; its facing and jamb had been torn from the brick wall. The mob leaders could actually see the deputies standing inside, their guns drawn.

Just as the mob was about to finally break through and enter the office of the jail, the deputies made their move. They reached through the holes in the iron-barred door and grabbed the sledgehammers away from the men when they weren't expecting it. The leaders of the mob and the deputies traded profane remarks.

Then, about 9:45 p.m., Hamilton County Criminal Court Judge Sam D. McReynolds arrived at the scene. He had been attending a Chamber of Commerce meeting a few blocks away when he was informed about the mob at the jail. Slowly, he elbowed his way through the crowd.

"Going to help us hang that Negro?" one man asked, as the judge passed by.

"The jury is in, Judge," said another, "and we find him guilty and sentence him to hang by the neck until dead."

"Go home," Judge McReynolds replied.

At age thirty-five, Sam McReynolds was the county's youngest judge. He had been appointed by then-governor J. D. Frazier in April 1903 to fill a newly created judgeship in the state's Sixth Judicial Circuit, which basically encompassed Chattanooga and Hamilton County. A man of ruddy physique and constant vigor, the judge had to approach this situation with diplomacy. He despised mob violence and had a deep passion for the rule of law. However, he was a political creature with great ambitions, soon to face re-election. Appearing weak on crime was not an option.

As the county's highest-ranking officer of the criminal court, Judge McReynolds asked to address the mob. Waving his hands and standing on the same chair that Nevada Taylor's brother had used earlier, he finally gained the attention of the crowd.

"It's time for justice," someone screamed from the crowd.

"Bring the Negro out," yelled another. "His day of reckoning has arrived."

Holding out his arms and hands in a hushing motion to quiet the impatient audience, Judge McReynolds began to speak.

"Who is it that you want?" the judge inquired.

Most shouted that they wanted Ed Johnson. A few said they also wanted other black men who had recently been arrested for serious crimes. Then the judge began to speak.

Men, the Negro suspected of assaulting the young lady at St. Elmo is not here. He has been sent away to Knoxville. You might search the jail all night and you would not find him. I appeal to you as a friend, and I am sure you are all friends of mine, to quietly disperse to your homes and refrain from violence. The accused rapist is not here. He is in Knoxville.

I know you want justice and punishment. I do as well. But this is not the way. We have laws we must follow.

I have called for a special session of the county grand jury for next Saturday to take up the case. Following an indictment, I will give the criminal trial precedence over all other trials. I hope that before week's end, the rapist will be convicted, under sentence of death and executed according to law before the setting of Saturday's sun.

The crowd jeered and hissed. There were a jumble of catcalls and more shrieks for the blood of a black man. They wanted justice, but they were so inflamed that they did not want to wait. And they still didn't believe that Ed Johnson was not inside the jail.

Judge McReynolds explained that he had ordered Sheriff Shipp earlier in the day to move the prisoner to Knoxville for safekeeping until the trial. He said that the sheriff had dressed Ed Johnson in a disguise and taken him by train to the Knox County Jail.

In fact, Sheriff Shipp and two deputies had escorted Johnson and Broaden out of town about four hours before the mob began to gather. The judge and the sheriff feared there would be a lynching attempt. Johnson was handcuffed to the sheriff, Broaden to the two deputies. Even though Sheriff Shipp believed Broaden was not involved in the

St. Elmo attack, he decided to keep the young black man in custody. His motivations were twofold. First, he feared the lynch mob would still kill Broaden, believing he was guilty; ushering Broaden out of town kept him alive. But the sheriff also had plans to use Broaden to get Johnson to confess.

Judge McReynolds himself pulled a quick one that night: his remarks to the mob were intentionally misleading. The sheriff had not taken the two black men to Knoxville, but had escorted them via the Tennessee Central Railroad to Nashville. The ruse was to elude any possible interception.

Seeing that the mob would not be placated, the judge offered the group a proposition. He told them to select a small group of men who would accompany him and the deputies in a tour of the jail.

"You can see for yourself that he is not here," Judge McReynolds said.

Five men were chosen and escorted into the jail by the deputies. They went from cell to cell. In each unit, they searched for Ed Johnson. A news reporter for the *Times* was invited to accompany the group: "When the Negro department was reached, the inmates were found to be in a state of most abject terror. They were nearly all on their knees praying with upturned, ashen faces, and gave every evidence that they believed their hour had come." The forty-minute search of the jail produced no Ed Johnson. The committee of five left the now badly wrecked jail disappointed and addressed the would-be lynchers. The man they had come for was not there. Within minutes, the crowd had dispersed and everything returned to normal. None of the inmates or deputies had been injured. Two members of the mob who were accidentally shot and another man who was stabbed were treated by physicians; none of them were seriously injured. Not a single member of the lynch mob was arrested.

Even though the leaders of the mob went home disappointed that Thursday night, they had put Sheriff Shipp and Judge McReynolds on notice: convict and punish this Negro quickly or they would be back.

CHAPTER FOUR

PRETENSE OF LAW
AND ORDER

DAWN ARRIVED FRIDAY at about 7:00 a.m. to reveal the damage done to the county jail the night before by the angry mob. Every window and lamp was shattered. The assault on the front door had left it in ruins. Bullet holes riddled the building's brick-and-cement walls, as well as the doors and furniture inside.

Speculation abounded that Judge McReynolds planned to ask the same local grand jury considering the St. Elmo rape case also to indict those who had participated in the lynching attempt. The grand jury, which consisted of a dozen local citizens, had been called into special session for Saturday.

More than 100 miles away, Sheriff Shipp learned about the attack on his jail through a handful of telegrams from Judge McReynolds and newspaper reports. In an interview with the *Nashville Banner*, the sheriff expressed outrage at the mob. However, he seemed more upset about the property damage the crowds had caused than about the assault on the inmates and deputies inside the jail. And Sheriff Shipp said he wasn't sure what, if any, action would be taken against the vigilantes.

The rape that has so inflamed the community is a capital offense in Tennessee. It is time for the people to allow the law to do what the mob wants done. The most bloodthirsty of the community can well afford to wait.

The wrecking of the jail was a useless and wanton destruction of public property for which, even as mobs go, there was not the slightest excuse.

Yet the elections were just two months away. Now the sheriff was plagued with a more interesting dilemma:

Should he side with the element in society that believed crime was the community's top problem and employ whatever means necessary to stop the criminal activity? To do so, he would have to ignore the actions of the mob and publicly state that he understood their concerns and frustrations with the criminal-justice system. Such a stance would gain him many votes.

Or Sheriff Shipp could take the high road. He could publicly vilify the mob for adopting uncivilized behaviors that did not respect the basic rights and liberties due every man. He could blast the mob for being racist hate-mongers who the Bible says will spend an eternity in hell. And he could enforce the law by identifying and arresting the people who had taken part in the lynching attempt.

But the sheriff was, above all else, a politician. So he carefully crafted a statement to the newspapers that, he hoped, would satisfy people in both categories. He blasted the mob and defended his protection of the prisoners. At the same time, he said he had been under orders from Judge McReynolds to move the two suspects out of town, thereby shifting the blame or responsibility. And he certainly did not hesitate to promote his own efforts to capture the St. Elmo rapist and his desire that the suspect receive the ultimate punishment for his crime.

I have heard that the fact of my having taken away the Negro Johnson in order to save him from Thursday night's mob would cost me a defeat in my race for re-election. I want to say that when I entered the sheriff's office, I did it under an oath to enforce the law.

PRETENSE OF LAW AND ORDER

Had I let Johnson remain in jail here over Thursday night,
I have no doubt but that the building would now be wrecked.
No one knows how many Negro prisoners innocent and guilty
would have been hanged without authority. I took Johnson
and Broaden away to save their lives until some definite evidence could be gathered as to the guilt of one of them or the
innocence of both of them.

During the interview with the *Banner*, Sheriff Shipp pointed out
that officials in Little Rock, Arkansas, were preparing to execute a
black man for assaulting a white woman. The circumstances were
nearly identical to the St. Elmo case. In the Arkansas case, the crime
had been committed on December 29; the trial took place January 5;
by the end of that day, the suspect was found guilty and sentenced to
die. The hanging was set for February 4. "Justice is quick enough
when it really wants to be. This is not quite so quick as lynching, but it
reads better in the statistics." Sheriff Shipp and Judge McReynolds
wanted the Ed Johnson rape case to move along in the same speedy
manner. The evidence against the defendant was starting to mount,
they contended. Ed Johnson fit the general description that the victim
had given police. Will Hixson identified Johnson as having been near
the crime scene with a leather strap identical to the one used in the
attack. The sheriff also believed he had caught Johnson in some contradictions that indicated he was hiding the truth.

And Sheriff Shipp and Judge McReynolds hoped that Ed Johnson would simply admit his guilt. But the suspect showed no signs of
making a confession. Instead, he became more insistent of his innocence. At that point the sheriff tried one of the oldest tricks in the
law-enforcement how-to book, a tactic that has long since been
banned as unconstitutional: the sheriff had Broaden, the other black
man who had been arrested in the case, put into the same cell as
Johnson in Nashville. In doing so, Sheriff Shipp turned the other
inmate into an agent for the state. The sheriff, who told Broaden
what he wanted, hoped the future preacher would have some sway
over Johnson.

"You should not go to your death with a lie on your lips," Broaden told Johnson. "You should pray with me and confess your sins to God and to man."

In the next cell, the sheriff planted an undercover deputy who could hear if Johnson did confess. Despite many tries, however, they were frustrated. Johnson stuck to his story of innocence. He refused to bend.

There was one more link missing in the evidentiary chain. Sheriff Shipp needed a positive identification from the one person that mattered most: Nevada Taylor.

Sheriff Shipp stayed in Nashville Friday and Saturday to meet with friends and continue questioning the suspect. He also called William Taylor, the victim's father, on Friday morning to say he needed Miss Taylor to travel to Nashville to look at the man they had arrested. The county bought a train ticket for the victim and her older brother for early Saturday morning, January 27.

They arrived at the Davidson County Jail by midmorning. Miss Taylor was nervous, but fully committed to seeing the process through. The sheriff led her into a special room the police used especially for eyewitness identifications. In the far corner, hidden in dark shadow, was a chair. Miss Taylor was told to sit in that chair. Her brother stood behind her, his hands on her shoulders as a calming effect.

A bright light was pointed toward the spot where Johnson and Broaden would stand, so that Nevada Taylor could better see the two men but neither man would be able to get a good look at her. Sheriff Shipp then escorted the two men into the room, with Broaden on his right and Johnson on his left. The sheriff asked both men questions that required them to speak several sentences, to see if the victim could recognize either of their voices. The sheriff also had them walk around the room, to show Miss Taylor their manner of movement and the style of their clothes.

For more than fifteen minutes, she scrutinized the two men. Finally, the sheriff took both men back to their jail cells and then returned to speak with his star witness.

Nevada Taylor told Sheriff Shipp that she had "never entertained a hope" that the man who assaulted her would be caught.

"Does either one of them look familiar?" the sheriff asked.

She responded that the black man who stood to his left was "like the man as I remember him."

"What about how he talks?" the sheriff inquired.

"He has the same soft, kind voice," she said.

"Are you sure that he is the man?" Sheriff Shipp asked again.

"From that Negro's general figure, height, and weight, from his voice, as I can distinctly remember it, from his manner of movement and action, and from the clothing he wears, it is my best knowledge and belief that the man who stood on your left was the one who assaulted me," Miss Taylor stated.

But she had something else to say as well. Miss Taylor wanted to make it clear that she and her family deplored mob violence. She said her younger brother had been angry over the attack. The night of the mob's siege on the jail, her younger brother had participated in "some hot talk." She said he now regretted his statements and involvement that night and he promised never to do it again. Nevada Taylor wanted the sheriff and the newspapers to tell the people of Chattanooga that she did not approve of the attempts to lynch the man accused of raping her.

Her statements were officially recorded and made a part of the case file. At a time when black-on-white crime, especially the attack by a black man on a white woman, was considered so outrageous, Miss Taylor's comments were extraordinary. After all, the mob and its leaders considered its primary purpose to be the protection of the white woman's purity from the black man.

Sheriff Shipp thanked Miss Taylor for courageously going to Nashville and facing her attacker. He said he would take the train back to Chattanooga with them, but he needed to send a telegram first. They agreed to meet at the train station after having a bite of dinner.

TO: Judge S. D. McReynolds
        Criminal Court of Hamilton County
FROM: Sheriff Joseph Shipp
DATE: January 27, 1906

Nevada Taylor has identified suspect.
Proceed with grand jury.

Sheriff Shipp remained worried that Miss Taylor's identification would be interpreted as soft or weak. He didn't really want her to take the witness stand anyway: testifying in open court about being sexually attacked would be very embarrassing, something no woman should ever have to endure.

So, before he left the jail that day, he met one last time with the defendant. If only he could elicit a confession from the suspect, it would eliminate the necessity of calling the victim as a witness and remove any doubt about the case's outcome. The pressure he put on Ed Johnson that day was intense. It would later be revealed that the defendant was slapped several times, that he was denied food and water. The sheriff told news reporters that the defendant was close to breaking. This information, the sheriff believed, would convince people that he had arrested the right man.

But in the end, Johnson did not break, nor did he ever come close to confessing. He remained unwavering in his story. He had not attacked Nevada Taylor, he said.

BACK IN CHATTANOOGA, Judge McReynolds received the telegram from the sheriff and immediately proceeded with the case. Two days earlier, he had sent word to the twelve white men who were then sitting as grand jurors that they should report to the courthouse Saturday afternoon for a special session. The judge didn't indicate why he wanted them there, but each was aware of the St. Elmo rape case.

Then, as now, grand juries in Tennessee sat for about six months. The tribunal consisted of at least a dozen, sometimes as many as sixteen, local citizens supposedly chosen at random from the property and voting records. Only white men had ever served on the panel. No black people, or women of any color, had ever been summoned to serve. Black people weren't specifically excluded by law, but court officials in Hamilton County and across the South frequently employed a clause in the law requiring that grand jurors and jurors be "men of good morals and character." Court officials claimed that they didn't mean to exclude black men systematically from the jury pool or from the grand jury, but that they just didn't know any black men who had passed those strict requirements.

The American grand-jury system was imported by the nation's founding fathers from England, where it was used in colonial times to prevent the British Crown from prosecuting dissidents. In the United States, it also serves as a means of keeping an eye on out-of-control or wayward prosecutors. It was designed to be the citizen's means of supervising law enforcement. The group meets in absolute secrecy to protect the reputations of potentially innocent people who are being investigated or questioned. The rules regarding the grand jury have remained basically untouched in the nation's legal history.

Grand jurors are supposed to review the evidence gathered by law enforcement to see if there is probable cause for the case to proceed to trial. If the panel finds there is sufficient evidence, it issues what's known as a "true bill," or an indictment, that names the defendant and the crimes he or she has been accused of committing. If the grand jury does not believe there is enough evidence to suspect the person of the crime, then they return a "no bill," which prevents prosecutors and police from moving forward in their case against the defendant.

This particular panel of grand jurors had begun their service in January 1906. They were not scheduled to meet again until mid-February. But about 3:00 p.m., they filed into Judge McReynolds's courtroom. He wanted to speak with them before they went behind closed doors to hear from the district attorney and police. Newspaper reporters, many lawyers, and court personnel were present to hear the judge's statement. He began by addressing the Johnson case.

> Such outrages as this must have the immediate attention of the law, that the law may be preserved. It is the "law's delay" that brings about mob spirit. And this court is determined that there shall be no delay in enforcing the law in this instance and the court is equally determined and takes this method to serve notice on this community, that the law shall be respected.
>
> And if in the investigation of this most dreadful crime there is any attempt to interfere with the due process of law,

the law shall and will be preserved at any cost of treasure or human life. These are not idle words, but after deliberate thought and full determination.

Judge McReynolds said the grand jury would also have to investigate the mob's assault on the county jail. He said it was a misdemeanor to wantonly injure, deface, or destroy a public building. More important, he added, it was a felony, punishable by imprisonment from three to twenty-one years, for two or more people to conspire to take human life or to engage in any act reasonably calculated to cause loss of life.

However, the crimes of the mob were not to be considered at that time, the judge told the grand jury. That would come later. Instead, he wanted them to focus on the evidence against Ed Johnson.

The twelve members of the panel filed slowly into their deliberation room. The only person who joined the grand jurors was Hamilton County District Attorney Madison "Matt" Newton Whitaker. The prosecutor would turn forty-six in two days and had hoped to take a few days off to celebrate with family and friends. But, deciding he needed to focus all of his attention on the Johnson case, he postponed his vacation plans.

Once inside the grand-jury room, Whitaker discussed the key evidence against Ed Johnson. He told them about finding the leather strap at the crime scene. He pointed out that the police had a witness named Will Hixson who had told the sheriff he saw Johnson near the spot where the attack took place about 6:00 p.m., about thirty minutes before the rape occurred. Hixson claimed Johnson had such a leather strap wrapped around his finger. And the prosecutor told them that the victim had made a positive identification of Johnson as the man who assaulted her.

The members of the grand jury had very few questions. After two hours, they decided to vote on whether there was enough evidence to establish probable cause to believe that Ed Johnson was Nevada Taylor's attacker. The vote was unanimous: a true bill.

At 5:00 p.m., the twelve men filed out of the grand-jury room and into the courtroom. The grand-jury foreman, J. C. Forstner, handed

Judge McReynolds the ominous single sheet of paper that was the indictment. They took no action regarding the lynch mob. Their work for the day was done. The judge thanked each member of the tribunal for coming to the courthouse on a Saturday, and the dozen men left the courtroom.

Later that afternoon, Whitaker, Shipp, who had just arrived back in Chattanooga, and McReynolds met privately at the judge's home on 9th Street. In modern times, such a meeting would be considered highly unethical: judges are not allowed to meet with either side of a case individually. But this was long before the American Bar Association had issued their "code for professional conduct," which prohibited *ex parte*, or private, communications between judges and prosecutors in a case. Indeed, it was commonplace in 1906 for the judge and the prosecutor to map out the strategy for the trial together. There was much planning to do, and so many questions to answer. How soon should they hold the trial? Should Johnson be tried quickly, to quell the cries of the town, or would it be better to delay any trial for months, praying that tempers would evaporate? What about moving the trial to another county?

If they delayed the trial, Sheriff Shipp said he could leave Johnson locked up in the jail in Nashville for safekeeping. More time would mean more opportunities for the defendant to confess, he said. But Judge McReynolds reminded them of two things: First, it was an election year and the people demanded swift and certain justice. Second, he had promised the mob the trial would take place quickly, and he would not go back on his word. They all agreed the trial would take place as soon as possible, maybe within the week.

"But we must keep all of this in the closest confidences," the judge said. "When the trial will begin must remain among us."

The consensus was that the mob would strike again, especially if people believed that Johnson was back in the local jail. For that reason, all plans for bringing Johnson back to Chattanooga and trying him were not to be mentioned outside of the three of them.

"What is the chance the Negro will plead?" Whitaker inquired.

Shipp said he doubted that would ever happen. If Johnson was unwilling to admit to the crime even privately to a minister, he certainly would never make a public admission of guilt. Besides, no defense lawyer would let his client plead guilty to a crime for which the state was seeking the punishment of death.

"It can be assumed that the state will be asking for a sentence of death by hanging," stated the judge. "I think the people demand it."

The sheriff and the district attorney nodded in agreement.

Which led to another problem. What about a lawyer to represent Ed Johnson? In the United States, a person charged with a crime was not guaranteed a lawyer until 1963. That year, the U.S. Supreme Court, in *Gideon* v. *Wainwright*, determined that every person accused of violating a state or federal law had the right to counsel, and that, if the defendant in a criminal case was unable to hire a lawyer due to poverty, the state must hire a lawyer for him or her.

However, Tennessee was one of the few states in the country that in 1906 already guaranteed a court-appointed lawyer to any person facing the death penalty in a trial. The sheriff told Judge McReynolds that the defendant was very poor, his family had no money, and he could not afford a lawyer. The judge said he would appoint the suspect two lawyers. But who? Any attorney who voluntarily accepted this case would certainly become the scorn of the city. Or even worse: if that lawyer were to win an acquittal, God save his life from the mob.

At first, they discussed the possibility of asking a black lawyer in town to take the case. But Judge McReynolds said that would be too risky—too risky for the court in case of a "not guilty" verdict, and too risky for the black lawyer, who might also face the vengeance of the lynch mob.

With the consent of Sheriff Shipp and District Attorney Whitaker, the judge selected white attorney Robert T. Cameron—an interesting, if not odd, choice. Cameron was not exactly one of the city's best-known trial lawyers. In fact, he had only tried a handful of cases in his entire legal career, and these involved simple no-fault divorces or small real-estate disputes. He had never handled a criminal case in his life, let alone a capital-felony trial. Cameron was basically a "runner" for other lawyers. He would find clients for some of the better trial attorneys. If those lawyers won a case that he had brought to their attention, they would share their purse with him. In essence, he was considered little more than a paralegal.

That evening, Judge McReynolds called Cameron at his home to see if he wanted to work on the case. A young lawyer not short on enthusiasm, Cameron immediately accepted. The judge said he would be naming another lawyer to work with Cameron on the case. However, the judge had not yet decided who that would be.

Finally, there was the issue of security. All three men still feared an attack on the jail by the mob. Sheriff Shipp agreed to tell the newspapers to print that Johnson would remain in Nashville until the time for his trial came. They hoped such an announcement would decrease the chances of an attack. Judge McReynolds said he also planned to travel to Nashville the next morning to ask the governor for support from the National Guard. And the sheriff said he would seek help from the Chattanooga Police Department.

The newspapers certainly played along. Whatever the judge, prosecutor, or sheriff told them, they printed as fact. Seldom did they ever attribute information, and never did they seek a second source for confirmation. The next day, for example, both newspapers told readers that the evidence against Johnson was strong. The *Chattanooga News*, which frequently referred to Johnson as "the Negro brute," printed that "the noose around the Negro's neck is tightening": "In case of the guilt of Johnson being proven, there will be no unnecessary delay in executing the sentence of the court. A gallows stands in the jail, erected months ago to meet an emergency. Hangman's ropes are in possession of the sheriff already stretched with the knot already tied."

Late that evening, Judge McReynolds and his wife drank hot tea and ate pecan pie at one of downtown Chattanooga's finer establishments. As they were finishing, Lewis Shepherd, a former judge and possibly the most prominent member of the local bar, stopped by to say hello. Judge Shepherd, as he was referred to by most citizens and the news media, told Judge McReynolds he had heard that Robert Cameron had been appointed to defend Ed Johnson. The judge acknowledged that it was so.

"This is a very important case," Shepherd told Judge McReynolds. "You need to have one of the older members of the criminal bar involved." The former judge cited several prominent lawyers who would do an excellent job.

Judge McReynolds interrupted. "Why don't I appoint you, Judge Shepherd?"

The offer fed the ego of the seasoned criminal-defense attorney. McReynolds felt the advice from Shepherd was merely a means of soliciting an offer. Shepherd said he would accept the appointment under one condition: McReynolds must convince another prominent lawyer, W.G.M. Thomas, to join the defense team as well.

McReynolds nodded in agreement. "I'll see what I can do," he said. The two men shook hands, and Shepherd left. Mission accomplished. When McReynolds and his wife returned home, he called his court bailiff and asked if he would inform lawyers Cameron and Thomas to be in his office the next day at 9:00 a.m.

Sunday morning found the skies above Chattanooga overcast and the temperature below freezing. Snow was predicted. Robert T. Cameron and W.G.M. Thomas arrived at the judge's chambers on time, neither knowing that the other had also been requested. Both men were dressed in their Sunday best, preparing to attend church. Cameron assumed the meeting was about Ed Johnson. Thomas, on the other hand, was baffled about why the county's criminal-court judge would summon him to his chambers, especially since Thomas, like Cameron, had never handled a criminal case during his career.

Born in Canada, Thomas was a graduate of the Vanderbilt University School of Law. He opened a civil-litigation-and-commercial-law practice in 1882 with his brother, and the two remained together in business for more than forty years. In fact, the law firm he created remains in operation even today, with Thomas's descendants still as partners. By 1906, the forty-nine-year-old Thomas was earning good money defending insurance companies against lawsuits. Different Tennessee governors appointed Thomas to various political positions over the years, including police commissioner of Chattanooga, election commissioner, and a member of the State Board of Law Examiners, the committee that approved and rejected requests for law licenses in Tennessee.

Judge McReynolds wasted no time in getting to the point. He

needed lawyers with solid reputations in the community to represent Johnson in the upcoming trial. He planned to appoint three men and he said he was looking at two of them. Thomas was shocked. He immediately pointed out that they were not criminal-defense lawyers and that such a significant case required nothing less. He told the judge he had his own cases to argue in civil court, and he pleaded with Judge McReynolds to pick someone else.

The judge, though claiming he understood these concerns, was unmoved. It was within his authority to appoint counsel to a criminal defendant in a case, and he was doing so. But there was even more bad news for the two lawyers: They had to get their case ready for trial within a week, maybe less. The judge said he had another important murder trial to complete, that of Floyd Westfield, but it should be finished up by Thursday. The Johnson trial, he said, could begin as soon as Friday.

Cameron and Thomas were dumbfounded. They could not adequately investigate what had happened, learn the criminal law that applied in the case, and develop a defense in less than a week. They needed at least a month. Again, Judge McReynolds said that was impossible. They had a week, and that was it. Besides, he told them, there was little to debate in this case.

Finally, the judge said he would be appointing Lewis Shepherd to join them. A former prosecutor and experienced trial lawyer, Shepherd knew criminal-law procedures better than any attorney or judge in Chattanooga. That announcement seemed to ease the heightened apprehension of the two civil lawyers. Before they left his office, Judge McReynolds reminded the lawyers that they were taking this case *pro bono*, meaning they would receive no compensation for their work. The hint from the judge, one of the lawyers would later admit, was that he did not expect them to invest a lot of time or effort in their representation of Ed Johnson.

Cameron and Thomas walked out of the judge's chambers with the weight of the world on them. Neither man knew exactly what to say to the other as they exited the courthouse. Both realized their first mission was to find Judge Shepherd and develop a game plan.

"Judge Shepherd!" both men said in unison as they walked down the courthouse steps. "Oh boy."

A former circuit-court judge, Shepherd was by far the most flamboyant trial lawyer in the region. He handled civil and criminal cases and was known to represent anyone with money to pay him and a few who were broke. At age fifty, he was the consummate establishment lawyer through his active involvement in the local bar association. Twice he had been elected to the state legislature, only to resign later because he didn't enjoy "serving with men with less intelligence than my wife's mule." Shepherd was frequently appointed by judges to handle the tough cases that other lawyers shied away from. He thrived on the challenge of the unwinnable case and he wallowed—or "wallered," as they say in southeastern Tennessee—in the attention from the newspapers. Two years after being appointed to the position of circuit-court judge, Shepherd resigned; he said he "loved the fight, loved the battle too much" to spend his life "sitting high on a bench in a cheap robe . . . I was born an advocate, not a referee."

Cameron and Thomas knew and liked Lewis Shepherd. Better yet, they knew he didn't mind doing things that were out of the social mainstream. He was highly critical of laws that discriminated against minorities, and he frequently accused police, prosecutors, and judges of not applying the law equally to white people and black people. He didn't mind mixing it up with prosecutors during a trial. They thought it was good that Shepherd frequently represented black people in criminal cases—something neither of them had ever done. And he never hesitated to denounce lawyers who did less than their best in defending their clients. He was, in essence, a liberal trial lawyer—someone they needed on board quickly to tell them what they should do.

It was agreed. Cameron said he would visit with Judge Shepherd to welcome him into the case. The two men decided they would meet later that day to devise a strategy. Judge McReynolds, meanwhile, boarded a train to Nashville to meet with Governor Cox.

In churches across Chattanooga that Sunday morning, pastors, priests, and ministers took to their pulpits with one message in mind. The Pastors' Association, headed by Reverend Bachman and Dr. McCallie, had met in special session that Saturday, to discuss how they should address the racial unrest in their city. After hours of praying together, the religious leaders passed a six-point resolution that each agreed they would strongly endorse before their parishioners. They also agreed to circulate it throughout the city.

> In view of the recent lawlessness in this city, the Pastors' Association, while deploring the horrible crime committed at St. Elmo, desires to place on record its judgment that one crime is not corrected by the commission of another.
>
> There is absolutely no excuse for mob violence in this land where the people rule, make the laws, enforce them, sit on juries, elect their own judges, and administer all of the affairs of state.
>
> One—Mob violence is simply one set of bad citizens endeavoring to overthrow the law in order that they may revel in the blood of another set of bad citizens.
>
> Two—We counsel deliberation, care and patient investigation that the guilty party may be found out and punished and that the innocent may not be condemned.
>
> Three—We desire to extend our most sincere and warm congratulations to the pastor and members of the St. Elmo Baptist Colored Church for their action taken just after the commission of the crime, tendering the cordial and earnest support of the colored people to the authorities and aiding them to find out and punish the wrongdoer. This action of theirs speaks well for them and teaches us all a lesson that we should not condemn a race for the wickedness of one of its members.
>
> Four—We commend the diligence and efficiency of our officials in saving us from the disgrace of a lynching.
>
> Five—We call on all good citizens to give their aid to our officials in suppressing the reign of lawlessness in our city and in meting out just punishment to the criminals in accordance with law and order.
>
> Six—This association tenders its sincere sympathy to this family and others who have suffered from such a brutal and horrible outrage.

W.G.M. Thomas arrived at the Highland Park Presbyterian Church a little after the morning worship service had started. The Reverend T. H. McCallie stepped to the pulpit, with no idea that Thomas was now Ed Johnson's new lawyer. The minister asked the assembly to turn in their Bibles to the book of Romans 13:1–4. He read aloud from the King James Version.

Let every soul be subject unto the higher powers. For there is no power but of God: the powers that be are ordained of God.

Whosoever therefore resisteth the power, resisteth the ordinance of God: and they that resist shall receive to themselves damnation.

For rulers are not a terror to good works, but to the evil. Wilt thou then not be afraid of the power? do that which is good, and thou shalt have praise of the same:

For he is the minister of God to thee for good. But if thou do that which is evil, be afraid; for he beareth not the sword in vain: for he is the minister of God, a revenger to execute wrath upon him that doeth evil.

Without announcement, Dr. McCallie bowed his head and prayed to God Almighty. His invocation was brief, but extremely pointed. He begged the Lord's mercy for the wickedness perpetrated that week by the people of his city. His sermon did not last long: he was an old man and needed the support of the podium to stand for long periods of time. But on this Sunday morning, as Dr. McCallie explored the faces of those who sat before him, tears dribbled from his eyes down his cheeks and disappeared into his beard. He called his message "Mob and Mob's Law."

The old adage says, "There is no use locking the stable door after the horse is stolen. But if there are other horses still in the stable, it will be well to lock the door."

In this instance, the law is the stable, and in its keeping are lives, the safety of our families, our property, and everything we hold dear on earth. The stable has been entered and a human being under protection of the law is being threatened for death. The prevalence of mob law throughout the country demands the most serious consideration of thoughtful men.

Its wrong lies in this fact: That it is murder. . . .

Those of you who make light of it now, will presently find that this lawless spirit is contagious, and it will not be long until it will not be content to put to death supposed criminals, but it will strike at all who oppose its will.

Dr. McCallie then gave ten reasons why mob law should be rejected. He called it murder, pure and simple. He said it was contagious and would lead to other atrocities. "It is cowardly. Its vengeance is wreaked only on the weak and the defenseless, the poor and the humble," he told his congregation. "If a rich man's son, a man of influence and many friends, had committed the crime in St. Elmo, he would not have been sought for death."

By Monday morning, everyone was in motion. Sheriff Shipp and his deputies were revisiting the scene of the crime. With Nevada Taylor at his side, the sheriff retraced every step the victim had taken the night of the attack. As they walked, Miss Taylor narrated the events of that night. The sheriff hoped discussing the assault with him again would help her better organize her thoughts and make her more at ease and better prepared to recite the events of the tragedy to a jury during the trial.

That same day, Chattanooga Police Chief John Mosely, whom Sheriff Shipp had asked to help in the investigation, visited the Last Chance Saloon to check on the list of men who Johnson claimed would verify that he was at the bar at 6:30 p.m. on January 23.

Chief Mosely's visit was not his first to the Last Chance. His appearances were never social. He and Sheriff Shipp had made many arrests at the saloon, usually over fighting or gambling or, every once in a while, a murder. Though black and white people frequently shopped at the same stores, they seldom socialized together. The Last Chance was one of the few places in Chattanooga where people of both races drank and ate together. They just weren't people who were considered respectable.

Chief Mosely questioned every man in the bar about Ed Johnson. Some knew him because he had worked there. Others played pool with him. None had a bad word to share about Johnson. They all expressed surprise that he would or could execute such an attack. The police chief had little interest in the opinions of these men. Most were drunk or well on their way.

What he really wanted to know was if any of them could testify under oath, in a court of law, that Johnson had been there in the saloon with them at the exact time that Miss Taylor was raped. Not a single person stepped forward. The owner of the Last Chance told Chief Mosely that Johnson was there that night. He said he remembered seeing him about 5:00 or 5:30 p.m., and he recalled selling Johnson a glass of gin somewhere around 8:00 p.m. However, the owner said he could not vouch for Johnson during the hours in between.

The criminal-defense lawyers were also starting their effort. As the sole attorney with experience in criminal cases, Shepherd took control. Cameron and Thomas gave his judgment considerable weight. In developing their strategy, Shepherd listed several things the lawyers needed to do immediately:

- They needed to interview their own client. They had to find out from his lips what happened. They needed to know what he had told the sheriff or others.

- They needed to visit the crime scene at the time of evening when the attack took place. The idea was to see what the lighting conditions were, and to try to uncover witnesses who might have seen something.

- They needed to find any alibi witnesses who could testify that Johnson was with them at the time of the attack.

- They needed to learn all the evidence that the sheriff and district attorney had against their client.

But above all, Shepherd told his colleagues, they must create reasonable doubt in the mind of the public. They must use the two newspapers to convince people that Johnson deserved a fair trial, that public condemnation of their client might have developed too quickly, that he actually might be innocent of the crime.

While the other two lawyers searched for evidence, Shepherd went to visit his friend and colleague Noah Parden. Shepherd had high regard for Parden, who had established himself as the city's premier black lawyer. The two had worked together in cases, and their relationship was not only professional but social. But this visit was purely business. By the time Shepherd arrived at Parden's law office, word had spread that he was defending Johnson. And Parden knew why he was there.

"You want to help us in this case?" Shepherd inquired.

"No, thank you," Parden responded. "I like my practice here just fine."

"We need help. We need your help," Shepherd repeated for emphasis. "Johnson may be innocent, I don't know. But this is the kind of case where we need to have some strong evidence to convince a jury that he's not the guilty man."

The two lawyers discussed the case for several hours. They agreed that the evidence against the defendant was less than overwhelming. Under normal circumstances, a jury would not think twice about acquitting the suspect with such shabby evidence against him, Shepherd said.

"But people are very upset," Parden said. "They want someone to die for this, evidence be damned. You need proof of actual innocence. You need solid evidence that Johnson cannot be the guilty man, or evidence pointing directly at someone else."

Shepherd confided that Johnson had given the sheriff a list of a dozen or so men he thought would testify that he was with them at the Last Chance Saloon at the time of the attack. Get the list of those names, Parden told the lawyer, and I will help you find them and help you convince them they must testify. Parden wanted only one promise in return: he didn't want anyone to know he was helping in this case. If word leaked out that he was assisting in the defense of Johnson, it could ruin his struggling law practice. Shepherd understood, and they shook hands.

The defense team soon had another problem. They had become the target of threats and ridicule. Their own neighbors were visibly angry. People at their churches gave them the cold shoulder. Both Cameron and Thomas lost paying clients. Cameron's wife refused to talk to him for days because of the case. She told him that everyone in town "knows the Negro is guilty." And their children were being heckled at school. She couldn't understand why he would be trying to help Johnson go free.

Lawyer Thomas's secretary quit because of the case. She told him she hadn't joined his law practice to defend black men who rape young white women. And Thomas's mother refused to cook dinner for him when she learned he was handling the case.

As for Shepherd, he was used to it. Indeed, he tended to revel in being a rebel. White people were always throwing racist and profane language at him. He seemed to feed on the attention.

But the community's anger was too much for Cameron. After one of his best clients withdrew his business from Cameron's law firm, he called a news reporter for the *Chattanooga Times* to make a statement, which was printed on Tuesday, January 30, saying that he hadn't asked to represent Ed Johnson and that he would not have defended the accused but for the order of Judge McReynolds. He asked the people of Chattanooga not to take their anger out on lawyers defending a criminal defendant, because they were simply doing their job. And he begged the public to keep an open mind regarding the evidence.

When the court first asked me to defend Johnson, I hesitated because I knew the sentiment that prevailed against him at that time and was not satisfied myself of his innocence. Yet, knowing how hard identity is under such conditions, I withheld my judgment and decided not to shift the painful duty to anyone which the court had seen fit to impose upon me.

I have been engaged all day trying to get the true facts in this case and since my investigation, I doubt if the perpetrator of this most heinous crime has been apprehended. Before this investigation shall have been concluded before an impartial jury of the county, the public will be reminded again of the danger of mob law and of judgment passed in too great haste.

I find among the best colored citizens, as well as the whites, expressions condemning the crime and a willingness to assist in bringing the guilty party to justice. The only question that remains to be decided is: Is Ed Johnson guilty or innocent? What more can the public demand than that this question be left to an impartial jury to answer? If he be convicted, so far as the law is concerned, the crime has been revenged, and the public should be satisfied. If he is acquitted, so far as the public is concerned, the public owes an apology for its hasty judgment.

A few days later, William G. Thomas was at home in bed, about to go to sleep, when he heard the sound of crashing glass. He immediately sat up. Then it happened again, coming from his living room. And again, this time from his kitchen. In another room, Thomas's aged mother screamed. He rushed to her bedside and discovered she was unhurt. He quickly led her into the bathroom and bolted the door shut, then grabbed a gun and went to find out what was happening.

At that moment, a rock came crashing through his mother's bedroom window. Glass shattered everywhere. By the time Thomas stepped out on his porch, the vandals were gone. But the message they had sent was clearly designed to frighten Thomas and to discourage him from representing Johnson.

That night, he took his mother to an uncle's house in a nearby suburb for safekeeping. His mother pleaded with him to quit the case. She said that the family couldn't understand why he was defending such an obviously guilty man. He later testified that even his dead wife's father showed him no compassion. His father-in-law, he said, chastised him repeatedly and urged him to drop the case immediately. Confused and frustrated over the lack of understanding shown by even his closest friends and family, Thomas hand-delivered a letter to the newspapers the next morning.

I want the people of my home city and county to know what Judge Shepherd, Mr. Cameron and I are attempting to do in obeying the hard appointment of Judge McReynolds.

I would avoid the task if I could honorably do so. I didn't want it. I didn't ask for it. But the law justly requires that every accused man shall be represented by an attorney, and it became the duty of Judge McReynolds to select some lawyers from the Chattanooga Bar, and this lot has fallen on me, and I shall not dodge or shirk the hard duty thus imposed.

The task given into my hands . . . involves the question whether the prisoner is the right man, whether he is guilty or innocent. If the prisoner is the guilty man, he has forfeited his life under the laws of both God and man, and an outraged law will rightly condemn him to death. If he is innocent, if some other person is the scoundrel, then no one would demand innocent blood. No one would want an innocent man to suffer.

I am trying with all my power to solve that question. I am trying to ascertain the truth. I am not trying, and I shall never try, to free a guilty man. I am doing my best to find if I can whether he is guilty or innocent.

I ask, therefore, that the good people of this city and county withhold their judgment of my associates and I until we can complete a fair and impartial investigation.

W.G.M. THOMAS

That Monday night, large crowds once again began to rendezvous downtown near the jail. Most of them came after patronizing nearby taverns and saloons where they had freely indulged themselves with liquors, wines, and beer. About dusk, they began to move in small crowds, gathering on street corners and participating in loud inflammatory discussions.

There were rumors circulating around town that the sheriff had secretly brought Ed Johnson back to Chattanooga from Nashville. Speculation was wild that the trial might begin the following day. One thing was certain: the people of Chattanooga were extremely disgruntled about the delay in the case.

Many citizens have been heard to express the sentiment that they were willing to wait until Wednesday for the Negro to be brought to Chattanooga for trial, but unwilling to wait longer, regarding the "law's delay" in this matter as explicable.

There have been expressions of concern that the Negro

was enjoying too long a lease of life after his crime. There exists a determination to see that the Negro Johnson shall pay the extreme penalty for his terrible crime.

Chattanooga News, Wednesday, January 31, 1906

But this night, Sheriff Shipp and Police Chief Mosely were well prepared. They had their deputies posted on street corners several blocks around the jail. Squads of sheriff's deputies were ordered to clear the streets directly surrounding the jail. The police officers, meanwhile, were told to keep people moving on nearby streets. No one was allowed to loiter on street corners. Keep the groups small and keep them moving, the officers were told. The deputies near the jail were also provided with high-powered rifles and told to protect the jail and the courthouse using any and all measures. In addition, the Reverend Bachman and Dr. McCallie were asked to be present at the jail in case the other precautions failed.

It worked. What had obviously started as an attempt to riot and raid the jail was completely defused.

THE NEXT TWO days were somewhat peaceful. There was still talk among many of the city's hotheads about raiding the jail, but they agreed they should wait until they knew for sure that Ed Johnson was locked up there.

Sheriff Shipp, District Attorney Whitaker, and defense lawyers Shepherd, Cameron, and Thomas met with Judge McReynolds several times during the week to discuss the case. Their main topic was when to conduct the trial. The state and the judge wanted it to begin quickly, within days. The defense team begged for more time, saying they had many leads to track down. They had yet even to meet with their client.

But McReynolds was adamant. He wanted the trial to take place quickly. A speedy trial was the only thing that would satisfy the demands of the community, he said, and could thus preserve the rule of law and order and prevent further lynch-mob attacks.

The defense lawyers did receive a reprieve that was partially of their doing. The judge had already started the murder trial of Floyd Westfield, and it was taking much longer than expected. Judge McReynolds had thought the case would take only two or three days to complete. It was now into day four and was certainly expected to last until Friday or even Saturday. Shepherd was also involved in that case as the lead defense attorney. There was speculation that he was intentionally slowing down the Westfield case to give his co-counsel in the Ed Johnson case more time to investigate.

The fact that the Westfield trial was taking place as the Johnson trial drew closer only increased the racial tensions in Chattanooga. Many vigilantes wanted to lynch both men at the same time. In the South, there were two taboos that almost always resulted in a hanging: a black man raping a white woman, and a black man killing a white law-enforcement officer. The two cases combined had put the city in absolute racial turmoil.

Westfield was a notorious black gambler accused of killing a white Hamilton County Constable on December 24, 1905. Westfield, his wife, and their two sons had raised the ire of those who lived nearby by shooting off fireworks as part of a pre-Christmas celebration. When the constable confronted Westfield, tempers flared. Westfield ran into his house and locked the doors.

Unable to convince Westfield to surrender, the constable gathered a posse and proceeded to knock down the suspect's front door. Westfield was standing directly behind the door with a loaded single-barrel shotgun, and pulled the trigger when the constable entered the house. Accused of murder and facing a death sentence, Westfield hired Lewis Shepherd to be his lawyer.

MOST PEOPLE THOUGHT Ed Johnson would be brought back to Chattanooga Friday morning to stand trial. The anticipation and satisfaction that the trial would start on this day had helped suppress desires in the community for vigilante justice. The problem was that the Westfield trial was still going on, though it was winding down, and most court officials predicted it would be over sometime late Friday or early Saturday.

The most surprising development of February 2 came in the form of a news bulletin from Nashville. A columnist with the *Nashville Banner* had somehow gotten a personal interview with Ed Johnson.

Was Ed Johnson, the alleged Chattanooga rapist, at the Last Chance Saloon on Whiteside Street between the hours of 6:30 and 8:00 on the night of January 23?

Johnson stoutly maintains his innocence. He denies that he committed the crime. Says he was in the saloon during those certain hours and says he never saw Miss Taylor before in his life before she was brought to the jail and would not know her now if he were to see her.

The Negro talks freely of his movements, protests his innocence and does not hesitate in his manner while telling his story. He does not appear to be a Negro of education, is respectful in manner and has not a mean face.

If he is faking in his story, he is more intelligent than he looks and has rehearsed it until he had it down pretty well.

Shepherd and Thomas learned of their client's statement to the newspaper when they arrived in Nashville that Friday morning to meet him for the first time. Judge McReynolds had given Shepherd the day off from the Westfield trial to meet with his new client. After formal introductions and explanations about their roles in the case, the lawyers wanted to know why he had spoken to a journalist.

Johnson told them that he only spoke with that particular reporter because the columnist had been by to visit him every day and had been nice to him. "Besides, it was the truth what I said," Johnson told them in a slow Southern drawl. "So what does it matter?"

Even so, the two lawyers made him promise that he would make no more statements to the newspaper. They feared that any comments he made might contradict his other statements, and this could be used to undermine his credibility in court. Then they proceeded to review his case. For several hours, the attorneys had Johnson walk them through the afternoon and evening of January 23. He told them his every step and gave them the names of people he remembered seeing and speaking to that afternoon and evening. Those people, he said, would vouch for him.

Shepherd told him he was personally tracking down all of those men. But he warned Johnson that every one of them was black and all had reputations in the community for being derelicts and drunks. They would not make the best of alibi or character witnesses, the lawyer said. Before they left, Shepherd promised that he would vigorously fight for Johnson during the trial.

"What's going to happen?" Johnson asked.

"I don't know," Shepherd responded. "But soon the sheriff will come for you and bring you back to Chattanooga, where there will be a trial. I will be there. So will Mr. Thomas and another lawyer."

"Will I be able to go home and see my mother?" he asked.

"Ed, these are very serious charges," the lawyer said. "You should pray very hard. Your life is at stake. The people of Chattanooga are very mad and they want someone to die for this crime."

"But I don't understand," Johnson continued. "I never done what they say. I swear to God I didn't. I've never seen the woman they brought up here before. I didn't even know where she lived. I just want to go home."

Shepherd put his arms around his client and gave him a strong hug. At that moment, the lawyer knew the authorities had the wrong man. As they left for home, Thomas shook Johnson's hand and promised they would do what they could for him.

THE NEXT MORNING, Saturday, February 3, Ed Johnson was awakened early in his cell by Sheriff Shipp, who had come to get him. They were taking the next train back to Chattanooga. The trial was expected to start later that day or early Monday morning. Johnson simply nodded and dressed. Shipp attached the handcuffs—one to Johnson's right arm and the other on his own left arm. Outside the cell, three deputies from Hamilton County waited to escort the suspect back to Chattanooga. Their purpose was as much to protect the sheriff and suspect from any attackers as to keep an eye on Johnson.

Only Shipp, Judge McReynolds, and District Attorney Whitaker had any advance notice that Johnson was being brought back. The officials didn't even tell the other deputies, who stayed behind. Johnson's own lawyers weren't notified until after the trip had begun. The judge and sheriff continued to fear another attack on the jail.

But when Johnson and his entourage arrived in Chattanooga, they were met with bad news. The Westfield jury had still not returned a verdict. Worse, news had somehow leaked out that Johnson was being brought to town soon. No one knew the prisoner was there yet, but deputies said the speculation around town was that he would be back and in the jail during the weekend. Several officers said they had heard a group of agitators planned to form a mob to attack the jail again in the next day or two.

After Shipp consulted briefly with Judge McReynolds, the two men agreed Johnson should not stay in the Hamilton County Jail during the weekend: it was too risky. The sheriff assigned three of his deputies to rush the prisoner back to Nashville immediately before anyone discovered he was in town. After all, no trial could begin until Monday morning anyway.

That Saturday night, the jury in the Floyd Westfield trial returned with a verdict. For many hours they had been deadlocked, unable to reach a unanimous verdict. Nine men believed he was guilty of murder in the first degree; three thought he should be convicted of a lesser charge. But Judge McReynolds made it clear to the jury that they would not be going home until they reached a unanimous decision. Finally, late Saturday night, the three holdouts conceded. Westfield was found guilty and sentenced to die.

CHAPTER FIVE

"CAN YOU SWEAR IT?"

DAY ONE

RESIDENTS LIVING ALONG 9th Street, a main thoroughfare through the heart of Chattanooga, were awakened about 7:00 a.m. Tuesday morning, February 6, to the sound of horses. People were standing on their porches watching as a city-police patrol wagon with its curtains closed proceeded at a gallop from the train depot on King Street to the Hamilton County Jail, which was adjacent to the courthouse. A platoon of heavily armed police officers and sheriff's deputies surrounded the wagon.

It didn't take long for people to figure out what was going on. Ed Johnson was being brought back to Chattanooga. He was quickly escorted from the wagon into the Hamilton County Courthouse, then rushed upstairs to the second-floor courtroom where Judge McReynolds conducted his trials. Placed in a seat at the back of the courtroom, he was given his breakfast in a basket: a roast-beef sandwich, a pickle, and an apple. Witnesses said that when two deputies asked Johnson to have his picture taken with them he appeared to enjoy the attention. They said he laughed and talked freely.

"That shore was good," a newspaper reporter quoted Johnson as saying after he finished his meal. "I feel good now."

There had been daily speculation in the newspapers and the general public about when the Johnson trial would start. But no one had predicted this particular day. The judge, sheriff, and lawyers did an excellent job of keeping the secret.

That day, District Attorney Matt Whitaker delivered a pre-emptive strike. As potential jurors picked up their morning newspaper, they found several statements from the prosecutor that were clearly designed for them to read. The message was equally unmistakable: no mercy should be shown Ed Johnson.

The prosecutor had invited reporters to hear his closing argument in a case involving minor property damage by a small group of black youths. In his speech to the jury, Whitaker said jurors needed to consider that the public was frustrated with "the Negro crime problem" and that it was the jury's duty to send a message that such criminal acts would not be tolerated.

> I want to say right here, that the officers of the law are not to blame for the reign of crime in your midst.
>
> The fault for the present reign of crime lies not in the officers of the law, not with the judge on the bench, not with the attorney general in the pit, and not with the sheriff at the jail. It lies with the juries of this county, with the men in the jury box.
>
> All of the vigilance of the sheriff, energy of the attorney general, and earnestness of the judge could not rid the community of criminals if the juries continue to acquit or assess light workhouse sentences in felony cases.

Such a statement was not only inflammatory and prejudicial but should have resulted in an immediate postponement of the start of the Johnson trial. It also should have caused Whitaker to be sanctioned for his inappropriate comments. However, neither the judge nor the defense attorneys ever complained or objected to the statement.

Instead, trial preparations proceeded. Security around the courthouse was tightened. The sheriff and others still feared a mob attack once people learned that Ed Johnson was back in the local jail. No one was permitted to walk on the sidewalks that surrounded the courthouse. An armed guard stood at every entrance. Only lawyers, law-enforcement officers, and court personnel were permitted to enter the building. Policemen were stationed at every street corner. Forty uniformed officers walked downtown beats that morning. Extra deputies were sworn in to patrol the streets around the jail and courthouse to help detect and defuse any potential mob gathering. And the governor had promised immediate access to 100 officers in the Tennessee National Guard.

AT 9:00 A.M., JUDGE Samuel Davis McReynolds stepped into his courtroom dressed in his black robe. Everyone immediately stood up. The judge entered the room from a side door that linked his office to the courtroom, and walked hastily toward the bench. His bailiff announced his presence with tradition.

"Hear ye, hear ye, hear ye. This honorable court is now in session. Any persons having business with this court, please step forward that ye may be heard."

At that moment, every head in the courtroom bowed. All but Ed Johnson were familiar with the ceremony of the start of court.

"God save this state, the United States, and this honorable court," the bailiff concluded.

With that, Judge McReynolds rapped his gavel and demanded order in his court. Everyone was asked to be seated. When McReynolds was appointed as a judge in 1903, at the age of thirty-three, he was the youngest person ever to sit as a judge on the Criminal Court of Tennessee. His Irish parents were farmers and stock raisers in nearby Pikeville, Tennessee. McReynolds studied law at People's College in Pikeville, which would later change its name to Cumberland University. Between 1893 and 1895, he served as an assistant district attorney, prosecuting all sorts of misdemeanor and felony crimes. For the next seven years, he operated a small private law firm that handled mostly civil matters and a small portion of minor criminal cases. He was also active in local Democratic Party politics, campaigning for many office seekers.

That McReynolds was a law-and-order judge, there can be no doubt. In his writings and speeches, he let it be known that the law was there as a check on crime. Violence was never to be tolerated. He believed rights and liberties belonged to society, not necessarily to individuals.

A hush came over the courtroom as the judge sat down. The show was about to begin. The courtroom was stuffed with local lawyers, deputies, news reporters, and people who worked at the courthouse—only those involved in the case. Ed Johnson's parents and the pastor of the church he attended were kept out.

The prosecutor and his three assistants sat facing the judge on the left side of the room. They had their documents and evidence neatly arranged on the long wooden table before them. Behind them, on the first row of the gallery, sat William Taylor, the father of the victim. The defense team—Lewis Shepherd, R. T. Cameron, and W.G.M. Thomas—was seated behind an identical table on the other side of the room. Ed Johnson sat directly behind them, with sheriff's deputies on each side.

Judge McReynolds asked if both sides were ready to proceed. Whitaker stood and announced that the state was ready. Thomas also stood, but said the defense was not ready to go forward with the trial. He wanted it to be part of the record, he said, that they had privately been told by Judge McReynolds that any attempt by the defense attorneys to delay the trial or seek a change of venue would be denied.

> Even with the greatest of diligence, we have not been able to investigate every phase of the case or to run down all reported facts. Mr. Cameron and I have worked day and night in the interest of truth and justice. I slept one hour one night and went forty-eight hours without removing my shoes.
>
> Your Honor knows what occurred between us yesterday. As appointees for a man arrested for the worst crime known to men, whose life is involved in the issue, in the fact of law and in the interest of justice, we do not believe we have had sufficient time to develop the facts to our satisfaction.
>
> We do not believe that this is the time or Chattanooga the place, in view of recent happenings, for this trial to take place.

The defendant ought to be tried at a later date and in some other county. We argue this not for the sake of delay, but that justice may be done.

We have understood that your honor does not agree with us on any of these points. We, therefore, bow to Your Honor's view in the matter.

The judge responded that he had "thought all along that the trial should take place in Chattanooga and as soon as possible, and I have not changed my views on that.

"Let's proceed," he said.

Judge McReynolds had issued thirty-six summonses for local citizens as possible jurors. All of them were white men, and all but two of the thirty-six were present. Judge McReynolds was mystified why two local citizens had either ignored his summons or could not make it on this day. He gave a court officer the names of the two men and told him to go to their homes, or their workplaces and find out why they were not there.

The case immediately moved into a phase known as *voir dire*, commonly referred to as "jury selection." Each of the jurors was qualified after proving he was a citizen of the United States and resident of Hamilton County, Tennessee, owned property, and was not a convicted felon. Each potential juror was asked if serving on this trial would produce any serious hardships for him or his family. One juror, a tobacco grower, was excused because having to serve would take him away from his farm during the crucial planting season.

After the judge finished his questioning, it was the lawyers' turn. The prosecutor asked each member of the panel about his view on the death penalty. Rape was a capital offense, he told them, and the state was asking that the defendant be hanged for his crime. "Do any one of you have a personal or religious belief that would prevent you from serving in a case where the state was seeking capital punishment?" Whitaker inquired. A couple of men raised their hands. They were excused.

Shepherd stood for the defense. He was well known throughout the community, and seemed to have a way with jurors. His only line of questioning had to do with race. Shepherd asked each juror if he had biases or prejudices in his mind against black people. A few raised their hands. Then he walked to his client's side, put his hand on his shoulder, and continued addressing the jury: "I ask but one thing of you. I ask that you treat this man throughout this trial and during your deliberations as you would a white man. He deserves no less. The law requires no less."

During the initial questioning, Judge McReynolds removed eight of the potential jurors because they demonstrated so much bias against one side or the other that they could not be fair and impartial jurors. Then the two sides went down the list of jurors. Under the law at that time, the defense attorneys had six "peremptory strikes" and the prosecution had three. These they could use to remove any person they did not like or trust from the panel.

The defense used all six of its strikes, to remove persons who stated that they had already developed a strong opinion about the guilt of Ed Johnson. Prosecutors used their strikes to eliminate those who they thought expressed a little too much sympathy toward the defendant, or who were not strong proponents of the death penalty. An hour after they began, they were done.

Judge McReynolds asked the dozen men selected to stand in the jury box and raise their right hands. He administered the oath given to jurors, requiring that they follow the law and the Constitution. He told the panel they could not read any newspaper accounts of the case, tell any family members or friends about what was happening inside the courtroom, or discuss the case or their feelings about it with other jurors until all the evidence and testimony had been presented to them. At that time, he told them, they would begin deliberations.

With all the formalities out of the way, Judge McReynolds turned to District Attorney Matt Whitaker and told him to begin presenting his case.

Both sides agreed to waive opening statements to the jury and move straight to the production of evidence and witnesses. This was a frequently agreed-upon maneuver at the turn of the century, simply designed to move cases along more quickly.

The prosecutor's first witness was Nevada Taylor. The courtroom filled with quieted whispers as she entered through the doors at the back of the large hall. Young and appearing frail, Miss Taylor walked slowly to the front of the courtroom and onto the witness stand. Johnson had been calm and relaxed throughout the pretrial court proceedings, but the sight of the victim seemed to make him nervous and uneasy.

> A funeral hush pervaded the court. Not only did an air of solemnity prevail as the victim of the most horrible crime ever known entered the room and ascended to the witness stand, but as she detailed the events of the fateful night, tears stood in the eyes of strong men. Brave officers whose daily task puts them face to face with the seamy side of life lost their nerve as the realization of the young lady's embarrassing position dawned upon them.
>
> *Chattanooga Times*, February 7, 1906

Whitaker asked Miss Taylor to put her left hand on the Bible and raise her right hand in the air.

"Do you swear to tell the truth, the whole truth, and nothing but the truth, so help you God?" the prosecutor asked.

"I do," she answered.

Whitaker then asked the bailiff to provide the witness with a cup of water. He thanked her for being so courageous and apologized for requiring her to testify.

"If it were up to me," he said, "I would not require your testimony in such an open forum before so many people. But the law states that every criminal has the right to face his accuser in public court. It is a law that should be amended."

The prosecutor then proceeded to ask the witness a series of questions.

WHITAKER: Miss Taylor, would you state your name for the record?

TAYLOR: Nevada Taylor.

WHITAKER: Tell the jury your age.

TAYLOR: I'm twenty-one.

WHITAKER: Where do you live?

TAYLOR: In St. Elmo. My father is the groundskeeper at the Forest Hills Cemetery. We live in a small house on the grounds.

WHITAKER: What about your mother?

TAYLOR: She died a few years ago.

WHITAKER: Where do you work, Miss Taylor?

TAYLOR: For the past two years, I have been a bookkeeper and stenographer at the W. W. Brooks Grocery Company.

WHITAKER: OK, Miss Taylor, I'm going to ask you now about the night of January 23. Are you ready for that?

TAYLOR: Yes.

WHITAKER: Tell us, the best you can, what happened that night. Walk us through your evening.

TAYLOR: On the night of January 23, I left my work at 6:00 and went to St. Elmo on the car leaving the transfer station at 6:00. I reached what is known as the Cemetery Station at nearly 6:30 o'clock and started home, a distance, if it is measured, of nearly two and one-half blocks.

I heard someone behind me, but I did not think they were following me. I felt the strap around my neck before I thought anyone was going to do me any harm. I was by myself and was going toward the cemetery gate along the sidewalk on the west side of the street, near the broad fence which surrounds the marble yard.

There are no houses along there. I had reached the end of the board fence when I felt the strap about my neck and was close to a place where two telegraph poles are close together. I had my pocketbook in one hand and my umbrella in the other. The man, whoever he was, took my pocketbook.

WHITAKER: What happened then, Miss Taylor?

TAYLOR: I reached up and pulled the strap loose and screamed. He pulled the strap tight.

WHITAKER: Is this that strap?

TAYLOR: I think that strap is the one he used.

WHITAKER: Please continue. What happened next?

TAYLOR: He pulled me back to the fence, a distance of ten or twelve feet, and then threw me over the fence. I swung clear of the boards. I know I didn't touch them.

The Negro, for I could see it was a Negro man, then got over the fence. I pulled the strap loose again and screamed again. Then the Negro put the end of the strap through the hole in the other end and pulled it tight around my neck. He then put his hand on my face to see if my tongue had been forced out of my mouth and then choked me until I was insensible.

Before he choked me with his hand, he waited a minute as if he were listening to find out if anybody were coming. He then told me in a kind, gentle voice that if I screamed again he would cut my throat. I saw him face to face by the dim light cast by the block signal box on the pole owned by the Rapid Transit Company. It is from this light that I got my best view of him.

WHITAKER: And then you blacked out?

TAYLOR: Yes, sir.

WHITAKER: What do you remember when you regained consciousness?

TAYLOR: No one came by that I know of at the time. I reached home after coming to myself about 6:45 o'clock, my home being about one and a half blocks from the scene of the crime.

My father, two brothers, and three sisters were at home when I got there and I told them what happened. They telephoned Sheriff Shipp and Dr. Wilson was summoned to attend me.

WHITAKER: Do you remember anything else about the Negro brute who assaulted you?

TAYLOR: He had on a dark sack coat.

WHITAKER: Miss Taylor, would you know the man again if your were to see him?

TAYLOR: I think so.

WHITAKER: Is that man present in this courtroom today?

TAYLOR: I believe he is the man [pointing to Ed Johnson, the only black person in the courtroom].

The prosecutor then offered the witness the opportunity to take a brief break from testifying to drink some water or collect her thoughts. But Miss Taylor said she was ready to continue. Whitaker asked her to tell the jury about traveling to Nashville and identifying Johnson as the man who attacked her.

TAYLOR: I went to Nashville with Sheriff Shipp and saw two Negroes brought out in the sheriff's office where I could see them. I sat in the obscurity and they were in the light. Sheriff Shipp talked to them, and one of them, from his voice, his size, his face, and everything combined, I thought was the Negro who assaulted me.

He, at first, had the same soft voice he used in talking to me, and later changed it, making it deeper. I looked at the Negroes and listened to them.

Though this Negro tried to change his voice, I believe that I recognized it. His hat, the one he had on the night of the assault, and the one he had on at the Nashville jail, was a soft, dark hat. The brim looked like it had been rolled at one time and had become straightened out.

WHITAKER: Miss Taylor, do you have any doubt in your mind that this Negro is the brute who assaulted you?

TAYLOR: There is no trouble in my mind about this Negro being the right man. I want the guilty man punished and I don't want an innocent man punished.

With that, the prosecutor thanked Miss Taylor for her testimony and told McReynolds he had no further questions for the witness. The judge asked the defense team if they had any questions they wanted to ask the victim. Attorney Thomas rose from his chair and said he had just a few things to ask her.

Before the trial had even begun, the defense attorneys had discussed how they would handle the victim when she took the witness
stand. Shepherd decided that the defense should not attack any part of
her testimony. Nor should they disparage her in any way, he said. She
was the victim in the case, and if they attacked her or even tried to get
her to contradict her own testimony, the jury might hold it against
their client.

Instead, Shepherd suggested that they use the cross-examination
to try to elicit information from Miss Taylor that might be helpful to
their client. They also agreed that Thomas would be the appropriate
person to question her, because he was the least threatening of the
three.

William G. Thomas walked toward Miss Taylor very slowly, asking if she would like to take a short break or needed more water. She
responded that she was fine. The lawyer began by saying that he, too,
appreciated her courage and the obvious pain and humiliation she was
going through. It was painful to ask her even a single question, he
said. No one from the defense would be casting doubt on her statements. What she had been through was horrible, something no woman
should ever have to endure. And he said he agreed with her that the
man guilty of this crime should be severely punished, probably
killed.

The lawyer then asked her what time it was when she stepped
from the trolley car the evening of the attack.

> TAYLOR: About 6:30 o'clock.
> THOMAS: Your house is how far from the station?
> TAYLOR: Two and one-half blocks.
> THOMAS: Are there any buildings or trees blocking the
> line of sight between your house and the train station?
> TAYLOR: There are a few trees between them. But you
> can see my father's house from the depot.
> THOMAS: Could you see your house from the station that
> night?
> TAYLOR: I could see the lights from the house. It was too
> dark to see the house itself.

The defense attorney quickly wrapped up his cross-examination, again thanking Miss Taylor for her cooperation in the case. The prosecutor said he had no additional questions for the witness and asked the judge if she could be excused. Judge McReynolds agreed, and she left the courtroom.

The next witness called by the state of Tennessee was Dr. H. B. Wilson. As the longtime physician for the Taylor family, Dr. Wilson said he had been called by the victim's father just minutes after the attack occurred. He told jurors about the red streak around Nevada Taylor's neck, about two and a half inches in width and bright red on the upper edges.

Dr. Wilson told of watching Sheriff Shipp hold the leather strap that had been found near the scene of the crime up to the red streak around Miss Taylor's throat. "It matched," he said. The elderly physician also said he had examined the victim and believed she had been raped. He was not asked to give proof or additional evidence supporting his claim. It was deemed too much of an invasion on Miss Taylor's personal life.

The defense lawyers asked perfunctory questions, but nothing too inquisitive. For example, R. T. Cameron asked Dr. Wilson if he knew for sure that this particular leather strap was the one used in the assault. The physician said he did not, but that it was either the weapon used or one very similar. When Cameron also asked if he had any firsthand knowledge that Ed Johnson owned such a strap, Dr. Wilson acknowledged that he did not—that he had no evidence directly linking the defendant to the crime.

Whitaker then handed the bailiff a slip of paper with the name of his next witness. The bailiff walked out of the courtroom and into the hallway.

"Will Hixson."

Witnesses in most civil and criminal cases are not allowed to be in the courtroom to hear the testimony of other witnesses. The reason is simple: judges want each witness's testimony to be exclusively his or her own, not relying on or being influenced in any way by the memory of others. It is commonly referred to as the "rule of witness sequestration."

A young white man walked through the courtroom doors and

strolled to the witness stand. This would be a key moment for the prosecution: Hixson was the witness that they hoped would connect the rapist to the weapon.

WHITAKER: Tell us your name?

HIXSON: Will Hixson.

WHITAKER: And how old are you, Mr. Hixson?

HIXSON: Twenty-two.

WHITAKER: Where do you work?

HIXSON: Chattanooga Medicine Company.

WHITAKER: Have you ever seen the defendant in this case, Ed Johnson, before?

HIXSON: I believe so.

WHITAKER: Have you ever seen this strap before?

HIXSON: That one or one like it.

WHITAKER: Tell the jury what you told the sheriff.

HIXSON: At 5:50 o'clock on the evening of the assault, I saw the defendant with a strap in his hand closely resembling the strap you showed me, near the scene of the crime. I know the Negro's face, for I have known him for about a month when he worked on the rock church four or five blocks away from where I saw him that night.

WHITAKER: Wasn't it very dark?

HIXSON: I saw him in the light made by two electric cars which passed each other at the Cemetery Station, where Miss Taylor alighted from the car. I saw his face well and could not be mistaken in it. This defendant here is the Negro I saw.

The Negro looked me full in the face for a minute and then turned away and walked up toward the cemetery gate. I saw him before, on Monday morning, for he asked me for a match at that time.

I looked for the Negro good, for I had heard that on the night before a purse had been snatched from a lady's hand in Mountain Junction.

I helped find Johnson, for I remembered seeing the Negro with the strap on the night of the crime. I hunted for him from

Wednesday morning at 10:00 until Thursday at 1:00 or 2:00. I finally saw him at the rock church talking to a Negro.

WHITAKER: What did you do then, Mr. Hixson?

HIXSON: I telephoned Sheriff Shipp and he came out with some deputies. However, I followed the Negro, who turned and walked away when he saw me. He led me to Red Row [a black residential area], where I lost him.

The sheriff and I found the Negro to whom Johnson was talking, in Red Row, and arrested him. We then went on and found Johnson riding on a wagon in front of Foust's stockyard. Deputy Kirkland arrested him.

If the defense attorneys intentionally avoided attacking or questioning the credibility of Miss Taylor or Dr. Wilson, they took the opposite approach with Will Hixson. R. T. Cameron immediately challenged the witness's testimony and his motivations.

Cameron asked Hixson how he knew it was 5:50 p.m. when he supposedly saw Ed Johnson that night. The witness said that the train station always blew its whistle at that time.

The lawyer then questioned Hixson about the reward. Getting the $375 being offered by the sheriff, the governor, and others was the only reason Hixson had come forward, Cameron shouted. Hixson said that wasn't true.

"So you don't want the reward?" Cameron asked.

"Of course I do," Hixson responded.

Finally, the defense attorney asked Hixson about conversations the witness had had with Harvey McConnell, an older black man who supervised work at a church. This was the first time the jurors and prosecutors had heard McConnell's name. It caused immediate speculation among those in court that he might become a surprise witness in the case. But Hixson emphatically denied he knew or had ever spoken with McConnell about Johnson.

"You are saying you weren't having a conversation with Harvey McConnell the day after the assault in St. Elmo and during that conversation Ed Johnson walked by?" Cameron asked. "You're saying that's not true."

"I did not have a conversation with any man named Harvey McConnell," the witness answered. Hixson also denied that he had ever told McConnell or anyone else prior to Ed Johnson's arrest that he was going to get the $375 reward being offered.

The next witness was Sheriff Joseph F. Shipp. Assistant District Attorney E. S. Daniels conducted the direct examination of the sheriff, who basically gave jurors a play-by-play account of the case, from the moment the attack occurred to Miss Taylor's identification of Ed Johnson as the perpetrator of the crime.

The county's highest-ranking law-enforcement officer started his testimony by officially identifying the leather strap as the one discovered near the scene of the crime. That allowed it to be formally admitted as evidence in the trial. Jurors were allowed to hold the strap.

Sheriff Shipp said the victim had walked him through her steps the night of the attack and pointed out the specific spot where the crime took place. He told of offering the reward, and how the amount had grown quickly. He discussed the tip from Will Hixson that had led to the identification and arrest of Ed Johnson. Shipp also told the panel that he had questioned the defendant several different times and that each time Johnson appeared to give a different story.

> The first story Johnson told me was he had gone to the Last Chance Saloon the night of January 23 about 6:00 and remained there until close up. Later, he said he had gone to the rock church Tuesday morning but it was too cold to work. So he went to the saloon at 12:00 and remained there until it closed at night. In Nashville, Johnson said he went to the saloon at 4:00 and remained there until 10:00.

The sheriff told jurors that Johnson had tried to change his voice when Miss Taylor made her visit to the Nashville jail. He said the defendant "raised his voice to a higher pitch" when he realized that someone was there to identify him.

On cross-examination, Shipp agreed that Miss Taylor's identification of the defendant was not exactly positive. Under repeated questioning by Shepherd, the sheriff conceded that Johnson had remained unwavering in insisting on his innocence. Shipp also expressed surprise and frustration that he had been unable to obtain a confession from the defendant.

The prosecution's final two witnesses were Deputies Charlie Baker and George Kirkland, who had led the sheriff's investigation into the rape. Individually, they told jurors about finding the leather strap and interviewing Johnson. They repeated Shipp's contention that Johnson had given three different stories about where he was the evening of the St. Elmo assault.

With that, Whitaker rose from his chair and announced to the court, "The state rests." With daylight almost gone and everyone in the courtroom appearing physically and emotionally exhausted, Shepherd called the first witness for the defense to testify. It was none other than Ed Johnson.

Ed Johnson is a Negro with a peculiar method of walking, one whose eyes when he is talking to one seem to say that he is thinking of something foreign to the conversation, whose face is one of the strangest that can be imagined.

He told his story in the strange voice which is so noticeable. His nose is sharp and his skin is very dark. His eyes are bloodshot. His nose seems to spring suddenly to its position, making an extraordinarily sharp angle with his forehead. The lower part of his nose and his mouth, including the front portion of his cheeks, protrude from his face in a curious fashion.

He sat in the witness chair and grasped the arms of the chair with his hands, looking straight at his questioner and leaning far toward him as he answered the questions.

Chattanooga News, February 7, 1906

Lewis Shepherd led his witness through the preliminaries in an effort to allow the jury to get to know Ed Johnson. The defendant said he was raised on Missionary Ridge. He now lived with his mother and father on Higley Row, a black residential area in the southern portion of the city limits of Chattanooga. He said he did odd jobs for people throughout the community. Every spring, he said, he worked at a local fertilizer plant. Throughout the fall and winter, he had helped put a roof on a church in St. Elmo. The witness told the jury he had only been arrested once before, and that was several years earlier, for trespassing.

Then Shepherd moved directly to the issues that everyone wanted to know about. Johnson emphatically denied he was the attacker. He asserted his innocence in the strongest terms, saying he had never met or even seen Miss Taylor until she took the witness stand earlier that day. Johnson reiterated his claim that he was at the Last Chance Saloon at the time of the assault. And he adamantly denied the testimony of Sheriff Shipp that he had told inconsistent stories. He said the sheriff and the deputies simply misunderstood what he was telling them about his whereabouts.

SHEPHERD: Tell the jury how you spent that Tuesday.

JOHNSON: I had been working on the rock church at St. Elmo since the day after Labor Day. On Monday, it rained and we did not go to work that day.

On Tuesday, I went out to the church. I got there before 8:00 and left there about 8:00. It was too cold to work. I stayed around home for an hour or better. Then I went up to the Last Chance Saloon and stayed there till about 2:00.

I went back home and came back to the saloon about 4:30 o'clock. I stayed there until 10:00 that night. At noon that day, the saloon owner's son sent me over to his house to water a pony. Then I helped fix some chicken nests until about 12:30, and I came back to the saloon.

At 2:00, I left the saloon and went home and got dinner. I got back at 4:30 and stayed until 10:00 that night.

SHEPHERD: What did you do at the saloon?

JOHNSON: I worked for the porter of the pool room. I kept pool tables there two or three times a week.

SHEPHERD: What did you do that Tuesday?

JOHNSON: When I got there, John Duckworth [a deputy sheriff], Jeff Lee, Mr. Jones [the owner], Uncle Ike Kelley, Joe Graves, and perhaps others were already there. Jeff asked me to fix the fire upstairs because it was getting cold in the pool room. Mr. Jones told me to light the lamps.

SHEPHERD: How much money did you make that night?

JOHNSON: Maybe $1.00 or $1.50.

SHEPHERD: Did you ever leave the saloon that night for any extended period of time?

JOHNSON: Mr. Jones sent me out for firewood a couple of times.

Ed Johnson gave the court the names of nine people who had seen him at the saloon throughout the evening. The witness said he spent the night at his mother's home, at number 3 Higley Row. He said that the next day, Wednesday, he was at the saloon from 7:00 a.m. until 10:00 p.m., because he was told by co-workers that it was too cold to hammer stone at the rock church.

SHEPHERD: Tell the jury everything that happened Thursday.

JOHNSON: I went to work Thursday morning and got there about 7:30 o'clock. I stayed at the church till 8:00. It was too cold to work and we were not getting out again until noon. I went home. After I got there, Johnny McConnell, who drives Schultz Brothers Packing House wagon, came by about 9:30. We drove out to Whiteside, then we went to Sherman Heights, where he delivered his last load.

We were driving back toward home when I was arrested. Mr. George Kirkland, a deputy sheriff, arrested me.

SHEPHERD: Were you still on the wagon when he arrested you?

JOHNSON: He came up to the wagon and stopped the driver and told him to "wait a minute." Then he said to me, "Ed, I want you." I got down and he handcuffed me. I asked him what he wanted with me and he said, "I'll tell you later."

SHEPHERD: What happened next?

JOHNSON: They took me to jail and some men examined me and cut my clothes. I reckon they were doctors. One of them was, as he had treated me before.

SHEPHERD: Ed, did you assault Nevada Taylor?

JOHNSON: No, sir. I never done what they charged me with. If there's a God in heaven, I'm innocent. If that was the woman they brought to the jail there in Nashville, I never saw her before in my life. In jail, I learned she lived at the cemetery. I learned since that the crime took place on a Tuesday, the 23rd.

SHEPHERD: So you are denying that the leather strap found near the crime scene is yours?

JOHNSON: I didn't do it. I never had any strap. I didn't even have any belt, only these suspenders I got on.

Whenever prosecutors made a point in the trial, people in the courtroom cheered. When the defense would object, the pro-prosecution audience hissed and jeered. There was much heckling and booing throughout Johnson's testimony. Not once did Judge McReynolds speak out against the courtroom conduct.

On cross-examination by prosecutors, Johnson said he "didn't notice or remember" changing his voice when Miss Taylor came to visit at the Nashville jail. He did admit that he knew she was there and why she was there—to identify him.

WHITAKER: After Miss Taylor left that day, did you tell James Broaden that you were afraid they had caught you?

JOHNSON: No, sir.

WHITAKER: What did you tell him?

JOHNSON: I told him that I guess they'll lay this crime on me. I told him I don't know what will become of me, so I gave him my ring and ask him to give it to my mother.

Johnson concluded his testimony by saying he had never met Will Hixson. He said he didn't know who Hixson was, and he denied Hixson had given him a match the day before the assault. Johnson stepped down from the witness stand and was escorted by deputies back to his seat behind the defense attorneys.

Most people in the courtroom expected Judge McReynolds to recess for the day. After all, the clock on the back of the courtroom wall read past 8:00 p.m. But the judge had other plans. He asked the jury if they were tired or hungry or if they could handle listening to a few more brief witnesses. The jurors agreed to keep going for another hour or so.

McReynolds told the defense team to call its next witness. They gave the bailiff the name Jeff Lee. He would be the first person to attempt to corroborate Ed Johnson's testimony.

A middle-aged black man who also worked part-time at the Last Chance Saloon, Lee told jurors he was at the saloon from 4:00 p.m. until 8:00 p.m. More important, he said Johnson was there with him the entire time. The witness said he saw the defendant several times throughout the evening, including near or at the precise time when the St. Elmo attack had taken place.

Under cross-examination, Lee admitted that it was possible for Johnson to have left the saloon for as much as thirty minutes without anyone's noticing his absence. Lee adamantly denied he'd told two sheriff's deputies that he "never laid eyes" on Johnson the night of the attack. "That's not true," he said. In all, Lee was on the witness stand no more than five minutes.

John G. Lucas, a young white man, took even less time to testify. He told the court that he had seen Johnson standing in the doorway of the Last Chance about 5:30 p.m. He based this on a clock he saw later on the west side of the saloon. However, he admitted he did not remember seeing Johnson anymore that evening.

Next came Isaac Kelley, an older white man, who had been at the saloon drinking. He told jurors that he had seen Ed Johnson several times between 6:00 and 7:00 p.m. at the bar. Under cross-examination, Kelley said, "The time wasn't fixed in my mind. It might have been a few minutes before 6:00 or a few minutes after 7:00."

The final two witnesses for the day—Ernest Cobb and Charlie Bruce—testified that they had arrived together at the Last Chance Saloon at 6:10 p.m. and that Ed Johnson was there when they arrived. Both men said they knew the time because they saw a clock on the south wall of the saloon when they arrived. They told the court, with only a few insignificant variations in their testimony, that they had chatted with Johnson for several minutes and seen him at different times throughout the evening. Under cross-examination, neither man backtracked or flinched in his testimony.

"We've certainly heard a full day of testimony," Judge McReynolds told jurors as he excused them for the evening. "I think everyone here is a little spent. Go home, have a good meal, and get a good night's sleep. Tomorrow promises more of the same."

Two hours later, Shepherd was sitting in his study at home preparing for the next day when he heard a knock at the door. It was Noah Parden. The two men sipped coffee and talked about the first day. Shepherd thought it had gone well, though he said several jurors had appeared ready to hang his client throughout much of Nevada Taylor's testimony.

Shepherd said the five alibi witnesses who testified at the end of the day had seemed to take the sting out of the state's case. Parden had helped find a dozen of the men Johnson claimed would provide his alibi. A few had simply disappeared or were in hiding, Parden said. Even many of those he found did not want to testify. But Parden told them that they had to, that they would be under subpoena and forced to appear.

"Just tell the truth," Parden said. "Don't be intimidated. Don't just say what you think they want to hear. Just tell the truth."

DAY TWO

THE SECOND DAY of testimony began at 8:30 a.m. Security around the courthouse remained stringent. However, people having business to conduct at the official government offices inside the building were permitted entrance. Those allowed into the courtroom to view the Ed

Johnson trial were still carefully screened. Supporters of the defendant were prohibited.

Seventeen witnesses were called by the defense to testify on Wednesday, February 7. Nine were black people, or "colored," as duly noted in the official court record by the clerk of the court. The newspapers also noted the race of any nonwhite witness.

The testimony focused on a tangle of clocks and time. The witnesses were called to vouch for Johnson, to say that he was at the Last Chance Saloon at the time the rape of Nevada Taylor took place. However, there was considerable confusion over the whereabouts of the clocks the witnesses were basing their testimony on, and whether the clocks even worked.

The first witness of the day was Will Hunnicutt. Court records identify Hunnicutt as a "colored" who worked at the Chattanooga Packing Company. Under direct examination, the witness said he had arrived at the Last Chance at about 6:00 p.m. and that Ed Johnson was there at the time. Hunnicutt said he had only one drink at the saloon and left about twenty-five minutes later, and that Johnson was still there at that time. Asked how he knew the time, Hunnicutt said he remembered looking at the large clock that he saw facing the front door.

On cross-examination, prosecutors asked Hunnicutt why he didn't go downstairs and join Johnson and the others in a game of pool. He replied that he was "too much of an expert pool player to engage in playing with the ordinary Negro. There was no one there in my class," he told the jury. The courtroom erupted in laughter.

George Bailey was the second witness called to the stand. Bailey said he knew Johnson personally and could not believe the allegations. The witness told the jury he had arrived at the Last Chance at about 5:00 p.m the evening of the attack and stayed for more than an hour. He said Johnson was there the entire time.

The third witness, J. G. Groves, who worked at the Ernest Scholze Company, said he was also a good friend of Johnson and a regular at the Last Chance. He had come to the saloon about 6:00 p.m. on the night in question. He said that Johnson was there at that time and that he saw Johnson periodically throughout the next several hours. Groves said he noted the time on the large clock opposite the front door.

Witness number four for the day was John Jackson, described in the official court record as "a Negro of the fun-making variety." Jackson said he had been at the Last Chance Saloon from 5:00 until 7:00 p.m. and that he saw Johnson there the whole time. On cross-examination, the witness denied telling a city patrolman that he did not remember seeing Johnson at the saloon the night of the attack.

The defense team's next witness was W. J. Jones, the owner of the Last Chance. The saloon, which had become pivotal in the trial, sat on the west side of Whiteside Street, smack up against the city limits. It served as the last chance for travelers along that street to get a drink before leaving the city, and the first chance for those arriving in the city.

Jones said that he had seen Ed Johnson at his saloon the evening of the assault. However, he stated that he did not recall seeing the defendant before 8:00 p.m. Jones said he had not gone downstairs into the pool room all evening and did not know if Johnson had been down there. Johnson had approached him at the bar at about 8:00 p.m. to "settle with me for drinks sold downstairs. He paid me three dimes," the witness said. Jones said he did not know what time Johnson had arrived at the bar or when he left.

On cross-examination, Jones added another twist to the case. He said there were two clocks at his establishment on the night of January 23. The first was an old, small clock on the south wall of the saloon, facing the bar. Jones described this as a "crazy clock."

SHEPHERD: What do you mean, a crazy clock?
JONES: Sometimes it works, sometimes it doesn't work.
SHEPHERD: Was it working the night of January 23?
JONES: Maybe. Maybe not. I don't know.
SHEPHERD: Is that the only clock at the Last Chance?
JONES: No, sir, judge. We have a new clock.
SHEPHERD: And where is the new clock situated in the saloon?
JONES: It's on the wall at the west end, directly across from the front door.
SHEPHERD: Is this a crazy clock, too?

JONES: No, sir, judge. It's new. They just brought it for me that day or the day before.

Jones also admitted that he had contributed $1 into a pot of $9 given by his patrons to help pay the legal fees of the lawyers representing Johnson.

The sixth witness of the day was Van Lowe, an employee of the Lookout Boilerworks, who took the witness stand with his lunch basket in hand. He said he had been "run away from Patterson's" saloon the night of January 23 on a threat from its owner that he "would be run in for vagrancy." The witness said he went directly to the Last Chance Saloon, arriving about 6:00 p.m. He said he was there for more than an hour. Lowe testified that Johnson was within his sight the entire time.

On cross-examination, Lowe said he saw the time on the little clock on the south wall of the bar. When District Attorney Whitaker cautioned Lowe that the clock was not working, the witness was adamant. He did not remember seeing a bigger clock facing the front door, he said. But he was absolutely positive that the small clock was running and that it read 6:00 p.m. Lowe said he believed the new clock was not installed until the next night, but he could not be positive. The witness also admitted under oath that he had been convicted of larceny for stealing a hog several years earlier, but that his citizenship had since been restored.

Isaac Dorset was the seventh person that day to testify that he had seen Ed Johnson at the saloon at about 6:00 p.m. and several other times throughout the evening. He timed his own arrival at the bar by the clock opposite the front door.

The next witness called was Cole Foster, a young black man who described himself as "one of the daily hangers-on" at the Last Chance. He told the jury that he had seen his friend Johnson at the saloon several times the night of the attack. However, he was unable to pinpoint a specific time.

Following an hour lunch break, the lawyers representing Johnson shifted gears a bit. There were other alibi witnesses they could call, but they believed they had made their point. The defense had pre-

sented eight alibi witnesses on this day and five the day before—all of
whom swore under oath that Johnson was at the Last Chance Saloon at
or near the time of the attack in St. Elmo. The prosecutors had simply
dismissed the alibi testimony as coming from unreliable sources. They
badgered each of the witnesses and constantly pointed out to the
jurors that the witnesses were black men who were alcoholic gamblers.

The defense lawyers concluded it was time to move on to other
issues. Specifically, they were ready to challenge the testimony of Will
Hixson, the young informant. The defense attorneys called Harvey
McConnell, described by court records as "an old-time Negro," to the
witness stand. The newspapers said he was "a Negro given much
respect" in both the black and the white communities. Everyone in
the courtroom seemed to know McConnell, greeting his entrance with
a hearty hello, a handshake, or a friendly wave. Lewis Shepherd got
right to the point during the direct questioning.

SHEPHERD: Do you know or have you met Will Hixson?

McCONNELL: Yes, judge. I know him.

SHEPHERD: Where do you know him from?

McCONNELL: Well, judge, the morning before Ed was
arrested . . .

SHEPHERD: That also would be the day after the St. Elmo
crime?

McCONNELL: Yes, sir, judge. Will Hixson came to my coal
yard and inquired of me concerning a man working at the
"rock" church. I told him I know the men only by sight and
not by name, except one. That is Ed Johnson. I know Ed
pretty well. That's when Will Hixson told me that Ed was the
man the sheriff wanted for the outrage the night before.

SHEPHERD: And what did you say?

McCONNELL: It can't be Johnson. He's like me. He may
have enough sense to do such a thing, but he isn't brave
enough.

SHEPHERD: What did Will Hixson say?

McCONNELL: He wanted to know what Ed Johnson
looked like and I was describing him when Ed and another

fella walked by the office headed toward town. I pointed Johnson out to Hixson.

SHEPHERD: And then what?

McCONNELL: Hixson left the office and followed behind Johnson toward the city.

McConnell testified that his son, Cicero, was present during the entire conversation with Hixson. The younger McConnell was called to the witness stand. He said he had stopped by his father's coal yard that morning to wait for a car to take him to his work across town. And then he repeated nearly every detail of his father's testimony.

The trial then took a strange twist. Shepherd announced that he planned to call his fellow defense attorneys in the case, W.G.M. Thomas and Robert T. Cameron, as his next two witnesses. Then, as now, it was highly unusual for a defendant's own lawyer to be called to testify.

Thomas testified first. He told jurors how McConnell had told him and the two lawyers his story, which was identical to the testimony he had just given. A few days later, Thomas said he tracked down Will Hixson.

THOMAS: We had a long conference.

SHEPHERD: What did you tell Will Hixson?

THOMAS: I reasoned with the young man concerning the vital part of his testimony and urged him to adhere only to the truth.

SHEPHERD: What was Will Hixson's response?

THOMAS: He denied in toto every part of Harvey McConnell's story. He even volunteered to accompany me to face Mr. McConnell. I accepted his offer, and we went to the coal yard.

SHEPHERD: What happened?

THOMAS: Mr. McConnell and Will Hixson stood face to face and Mr. McConnell repeated the same story we heard here today.

Thomas told the jury that, as Harvey McConnell spoke, Will Hixson "hung his head very low." Hixson never looked McConnell in the eyes. The more McConnell spoke, the lower Hixson's head dropped. "Will Hixson uttered no word of denial," he said.

Shepherd then asked his co-counsel in the case if he had been to Nashville to meet with Johnson while he was housed at the jail there. Thomas said he had. But when Shepherd began asking about those discussions, the prosecutors objected, declaring that such conversations were "hearsay testimony" that should be inadmissible. Shepherd argued that such conversations *were* admissible, since his client had already testified. The lawyer said Thomas's testimony would have indicated their client's state of mind and shown that Johnson had not changed his story about where he was the night of January 23. Judge McReynolds disagreed and told Thomas he could not answer the question.

Robert T. Cameron was sworn in as the next witness. He repeated the same story about meeting Will Hixson and Harvey McConnell. The defense lawyers then called D. W. Thomas, a member of the City Council from the 8th Ward, as a character witness for the McConnells. He told the jury that Harvey McConnell and his son were extremely honorable men and that their testimony should be given full faith and believability. The lawyers also called a prominent local businessman, J. W. Younger of St. Elmo, who said he had known the McConnells for many years. Both men, he said, had good reputations in the community and should be believed under oath.

The final two witnesses for the defense attorneys were also designed to question or cast doubt on Hixson's testimony. A ticket agent and a conductor at the Lookout Mountain Incline Railway station each told the jury that they had worked the night of the attack. Both men specifically stated that it was one of the darkest nights of the year and that it was already dark by 6:30 p.m., the time the rape occurred.

The young conductor said he, too, had had trouble determining if a person was white or black that evening, because the sky was so dark. Their testimony certainly undermined Hixson's statements and identification of Johnson. But it also allowed the defense attorneys to plant a seed of doubt in the mind of jurors as to the already strained identification made by the victim. However, neither Miss Taylor's name nor her testimony was ever mentioned.

And with that, Lewis Shepherd rose to his feet, turned to the judge and jury, and announced, "Your Honor, the defense rests." Day two of testimony in the case of Ed Johnson came to a close.

DAY THREE

THE THIRD DAY of the trial started the same as the first two days, with the jurors filing into the courtroom. None of the dozen jurymen had changed seats in the jury box since they were selected. The next stage of the trial was set to begin, as prosecutors presented rebuttal evidence to the jury. And though this day would produce a certain amount of drama, it started out without fanfare.

The first three witnesses—J. T. Lupton, who owned the Chattanooga Medicine Company; George W. Patton; and R. C. Stewart—testified that they knew and trusted Will Hixson. Each said he believed Hixson was a man of good character who should be believed.

Prosecutors called Donald Smith, a longtime inspector for the Chattanooga Electric Railway, to the witness stand. His testimony was subdued but extremely important: he told the jurors that it took only five minutes for his electric trains to travel from the terminal near the Last Chance Saloon to the Cemetery Station in St. Elmo.

The implication was clear: it wouldn't have taken Ed Johnson much time to sneak out of the saloon without anybody's noticing his absence, journey to St. Elmo, attack Nevada Taylor, and take the next trolley back to the Last Chance. Under cross-examination, Smith did admit that the trolleys only ran every thirty minutes after 6:00 p.m. between the saloon and the cemetery. Shepherd told the jurors that his client would have had to take the trolley before Miss Taylor's trolley and then catch the next trolley back. That would mean that Johnson had to have been gone from the bar for at least an hour to have perpetrated the horrible crime.

The state also made a strong impression on the jury with the clock issue. Even as the alibi witnesses for the defense testified about the time on the new, large clock at the saloon, prosecutors scoured the city for someone who could cast doubt or refute their testimony. They found J. G. Brooks, a salesman and clock repairman for the Anchor Supply Company. His words raised the eyebrows of everyone in the courtroom.

> BROOKS: I put the clock there at W. J. Jones's suggestion.
> WHITAKER: When did you take the clock there?
> BROOKS: January 25.
> WHITAKER: That would be two days after the St. Elmo assault. Are you sure about that?
> BROOKS: I am. While I was there at the Last Chance putting the clock on the wall, three deputy sheriffs were there. I asked them what was the matter and was told they were investigating the St. Elmo outrage.
> WHITAKER: Is the clock still there?
> BROOKS: No, sir. I left it up ten days and I removed it last Tuesday.

Prosecutors now surprised the courtroom by announcing they had found a new witness. Whitaker told Judge McReynolds and defense attorneys that his investigators had only that morning learned of the existence of J. A. Berger. The district attorney said he didn't know much about Berger, except that he was near the scene of the crime the night of January 23 and may have seen something. Over the strenuous objections made by Lewis Shepherd, the judge agreed to call Berger to the witness stand.

> WHITAKER: State your name for the record.
> BERGER: I'm James A. Berger.
> WHITAKER: Where do you work?
> BERGER: I am the superintendent at Wheland Machine Works.
> WHITAKER: I understand you have told deputies that you may have seen something on the evening of the crime?

BERGER: Yes, sir. I was near the Cemetery Station in St. Elmo that night. It was between 5:45 and 6:00 o'clock.

WHITAKER: And what or who did you see?

BERGER: I saw a man, a Negro standing near the station.

WHITAKER: Go on.

BERGER: He had both of his hands in his pockets. He was dancing around. And he wore a hat.

WHITAKER: Judging from appearances, voice, hat, and what you saw, is that Negro the defendant in this case?

BERGER: It looks like him.

WHITAKER: Thank you for coming forward, Mr. Berger.

JUDGE McREYNOLDS: Your witness, Judge Shepherd.

SHEPHERD: Thank you, judge. It was very dark that night, wasn't it, Mr. Berger?

BERGER: I think it was.

SHEPHERD: Wasn't it so dark that you couldn't see?

BERGER: I could see.

SHEPHERD: Can you say for sure that the man you saw that night was Ed Johnson?

BERGER: It looks like him.

SHEPHERD: But you can't say for sure, can you?

BERGER: No, sir.

SHEPHERD: No more questions for this witness, your Honor.

JUDGE McREYNOLDS: You may step down, Mr. Berger.

Needing to reinforce earlier witnesses, the defense attorneys announced they were recalling W. J. Jones, owner of the Last Chance Saloon, to the witness stand. Lewis Shepherd said he had "but one question: was the big clock on the wall the night of January 23?"

"Yes," Jones answered. "I believe it was."

The witness said the clock salesman had installed the new clock either that afternoon or the day before, January 22.

As W. J. Jones stepped down from the witness stand, the whole courtroom appeared to be in turmoil over the contradictions regarding the clock. At that moment, one of the jurors, C. E. Bearden, a well-known architect in the city, threw his hands to his head. Tears streamed down his face.

"I cannot stand it any longer. I cannot stand it," he said.

Judge McReynolds immediately announced a recess and had jurors escorted into a back room. They departed arm in arm, offering each other support. After ten minutes, the judge brought the jury back into the courtroom. As they were being seated, another juror, J. L. Wrenn, got to his feet and asked to address the court. Though such a request was highly unusual, Judge McReynolds agreed.

Wrenn, an employee of the North Carolina and St. Louis Railway, said he had "circulated among fellow jurors" during the break and it was their united request that Nevada Taylor be asked to return to the witness stand. They wanted to review her answers. The victim was not at the courthouse, but Judge McReynolds ordered deputies to find her and bring her immediately.

Less than thirty minutes later, Miss Taylor walked into the courtroom for the second time. The judge reminded her that she was still under oath and that she should tell only the truth. As she was being seated, Juror Wrenn rose again. He asked that Johnson put on the black slouch hat and that he be ordered to stand directly in front of the witness. Judge McReynolds ordered it to be done, over the objections of defense lawyers. Shepherd argued that forcing the defendant to wear the hat would violate his Fifth Amendment right not to be compelled to testify against himself. The newspaper states that Johnson was placed in front of Miss Taylor in such a way that the jury could look at them both. "Johnson's eyes shifted from side to side as Miss Taylor looked at him," the newspaper reporter wrote. "The sight of the young lady face to face with the Negro she accused brought tears to the eyes of many of the jurors." After a few seconds, the same juror again stood up.

WRENN: Miss Taylor, tell us again—is that Negro the one that attacked you?

TAYLOR: To the best of my knowledge and belief, he is the same man.

WRENN: Miss Taylor, can you state positively that this Negro is the one who assaulted you?

TAYLOR: I will not swear that he is the man, but I believe he is the Negro who assaulted me.

JUROR BEARDEN: In God's name, Miss Taylor, tell us positively—is that the guilty Negro? Can you say it. Can you swear it?

Tears streamed down the juror's face and his voice fluttered as he posed the question. Nevada Taylor, her hands trembling, turned to face the jury. She closed her eyes for scant seconds to gather her composure. Then she raised her left hand heavenward. With her voice cracking, her lips quivering, she spoke: "Listen to me. I would not take the life of an innocent man. But before God, I believe this is the guilty Negro."

Even Johnson, who stood before his accuser, bowed his head into his hands and wiped away his tears. Unable to take any more, a juror sitting in the box collapsed from the emotion. Two other jurors leaned forward in their chairs, choking with sobs. Lawyers on both sides were speechless. Another juror suddenly rose to his feet and started to rush toward the defendant, only to be restrained by fellow jurors. Pointing at Johnson, he yelled: "If I could get at him, I'd tear his heart out right now."

District Attorney Matt Whitaker slowly walked to the witness stand as Johnson was escorted back to his chair behind the defense table. The prosecutor apologized to Miss Taylor for making her go through this embarrassing procedure. She was then led out of the courtroom by her father and a bailiff.

Sensing that everyone in the courtroom was emotionally spent, Judge McReynolds announced a ninety-minute recess for lunch. He told the lawyers he wanted them to return promptly and be prepared to begin closing arguments that afternoon. He wanted the case to be in the hands of the jury by nightfall, he said. With that, he pounded his gavel and announced that court would be in recess until 1:30 p.m.

CHAPTER SIX

THE JURY'S VERDICT

AT 2:15 P.M., Hamilton County Criminal Court Judge S. D. McReynolds walked back into the courtroom from the recess. The break had lasted longer than he or anyone else expected.

"Everyone stand," the bailiff shouted. "Court is now back in session."

"Thank you," the judge said. "Everyone be seated. Are the lawyers ready to proceed?"

"Your Honor," began Lewis Shepherd, standing behind the defense team's table, "the defense renews its proposition to give the case to the jury without argument." The cagey trial lawyer realized that closing arguments would only serve to increase the emotion in the trial and give prosecutors the opportunity to inflame jurors further.

"The state declines to accept the proposition," responded District Attorney Whitaker.

"Very well," said Judge McReynolds. "I will not interfere."

The judge then told both sides they had one hour and forty-five minutes each to present their entire closing arguments. They could divide their time any way they wished. The state would be allowed to speak first, then the defense, and the prosecutors would get the last word, because the burden of proving guilt lies with the state.

At that moment, Nevada Taylor, the victim in the case, was

1. The site of Ed Johnson's grave, on Missionary Ridge

2. Ed Johnson's tombstone. The inscription reads: "God Bless you all. I AM A Innocent Man."

3. (OPPOSITE, TOP LEFT) Styles L. Hutchins, Ed Johnson's lawyer and one of the first blacks to practice law in the South

4. (OPPOSITE, BOTTOM RIGHT) W.G.M. Thomas, who represented Johnson during the appeal of his conviction and death sentence

5. (ABOVE) Hamilton County Criminal Court Judge Samuel D. McReynolds, who presided over Johnson's trial in Chattanooga

6. (ABOVE) District Attorney General Matt Whitaker, Ed Johnson's prosecutor, on the campaign trail

7. (OPPOSITE, TOP LEFT) Noah Parden, who represented Johnson during the appeal of his conviction and death sentence

8. (OPPOSITE, BOTTOM RIGHT) Sheriff Joseph F. Shipp, who was accused of conspiring with a lynch mob to kill Ed Johnson

9. The Fuller Court. Clockwise from top left: William Rufus Day,
Joseph McKenna, Oliver Wendell Holmes, Jr., William Henry Moody,
Rufus Wheeler Peckham, David Josiah Brewer, Melville W. Fuller,
John Marshall Harlan, and Edward Douglass White

10. John Marshall Harlan, U.S. Supreme Court Justice from 1877 to 1911

escorted into the courtroom, down the aisle, and into a chair seated directly behind the district attorney. She had requested to be present to see and hear the closing arguments. Her white-haired father sat beside her and held her hand throughout the entire proceeding. Behind her, every pew in the courtroom was full and overflowing. The crowd consisted of mainly local lawyers, several pastors from the city's churches, and several of the witnesses who had testified during the trial. There was not an empty seat in the room. Sheriff's deputies lined the walls, and guards were stationed at every entrance to the building.

Assistant District Attorney E. S. Daniels, who had handled the cross-examination of some of the witnesses, spoke first. He started by reading from a thick dark-green cloth-covered book called the *Tennessee Criminal Code*. He turned to page 183, third paragraph—the state law defining the crime of rape. It was this statute under which Johnson had been indicted for attacking Miss Taylor.

For the next forty-five minutes, Daniels took the jury through the story of this case. He relived the assault, the search for the assailant, and the arrest of Johnson. He reminded them of Will Hixson's identification of Johnson, of the victim's own identification of the suspect, and about the defendant's changing his voice when speaking in the presence of Miss Taylor in the hope that she would not pick him as the attacker.

The prosecutor pointed out the testimony of Sheriff Shipp, who had said that Johnson told three different stories about where he was on the evening of January 23 and what time he arrived at the Last Chance Saloon. And he told jurors they should ignore the witnesses who had testified that Ed Johnson was with them at the saloon playing pool at the time the attack occurred. He said the witnesses were men of "less than honorable character who fabricated an alibi based on a clock that did not exist."

Finally, Daniels returned to the testimony of Hixson, whom he described as the most important witness in the case. The assistant district attorney said Hixson was unequivocal about Johnson's being the man he had seen near the scene of the crime the night of January 23. The reason Hixson could be so sure, Daniels told jurors, was that he had given Johnson a match to light a cigarette only days before.

Lewis Shepherd was the next to stand before the jury. As a lawyer, he was known for courtroom antics that made indelible impressions. As a speaker, he frequently demonstrated his detailed knowledge of history and his love for reading by incorporating either or both into his closing arguments. And he loved to be theatrical—slamming his fist down onto the podium, stomping his feet, running around the courtroom, and alternately shouting and whispering to obtain the desired effect.

On this day, the fifty-year-old trial lawyer began with an hour-long tirade against Judge McReynolds, prosecutors, the sheriff, and the witnesses in the case: "This case wasn't about justice. This case wasn't about finding the truth. This case wasn't about preserving the rule of law. Justice and truth and the rule of law have been trampled on in this court and in this very case." Everyone in the courtroom expected the judge to interrupt, to find the lawyer in contempt or, at the very least, declare Shepherd out of order. But Judge McReynolds sat silent. So did the prosecutors. Shepherd continued:

> I do not flatter myself that by oratory I could paint this great crime in blacker colors than it has been made by the statements of witnesses. Neither could I by oratory or rhetoric convince you of the innocence of this defendant better than can the language of the witnesses.
>
> It was an atrocious crime, and by it a good, a pure young lady has been despoiled of her virginity. But did this Negro commit the deed?

Shepherd accused Judge McReynolds of denying his client a fair trial, claiming that the "rulings of this court have been inimical to my client and biased in favor of the state." He cited the judge's refusal to delay the trial so that the lawyers could better prepare, and the decision to conduct the trial there in Chattanooga instead of changing the venue to Nashville or Knoxville. He accused McReynolds of bias in the case by not allowing Shepherd's co-counsel W.G.M. Thomas to testify about conversations the lawyer had had with Johnson at the Nashville jail. And he charged that the judge had demonstrated his bias in front of the jury by asking one-sided questions of witnesses during the trial.

Shepherd returned to the defense table and picked up a tattered old book written by an English barrister and judge in the seventeenth century. The lawyer turned the fragile pages to a section discussing the proper qualifications of a court and the requirement that all judges should remain pure.

His tirade against Judge McReynolds ended only when he began a similar lambasting of the prosecutors. He accused them of being more interested in obtaining a conviction than in seeking the truth. He said they had ignored evidence of innocence and their minds were closed to any information that pointed away from Johnson as the guilty party.

And then Shepherd got personal. He referred to the assistant district attorney as E. S. Daniels "the quibbler and not Daniels the able, the just, or the honorable lawyer." He said the deputy prosecutor had made too many unneeded objections during the testimony of defense witnesses. He accused District Attorney Matt Whitaker of being a "stooge for the lynch mob." And he said Sheriff Shipp had had only one agenda. "Arresting Ed Johnson may not avenge this despicable crime," he told the jury. "Convicting and condemning Ed Johnson may not achieve justice. But it does get you re-elected."

Shepherd finally turned his attention to the evidence and witnesses. He focused on two issues: Hixson's identification of the defendant and the darkness of the night. The lawyer reminded jurors of the two Incline Railway employees who had testified that there was so little natural light the night of January 23 that they could not tell if people only a few feet away were black or white. And he pointed out that every witness, including Miss Taylor, admitted under oath that it was an unusually dark evening. "This evidence is without dispute," he said.

The meaning, Shepherd told jurors, was that it was impossible for Hixson to have seen and identified Johnson from such a distance. The same was true for Miss Taylor, the lawyer said. "I have no argument that Miss Taylor believes or wants to believe that the defendant was the perpetrator of this crime. But the night was so dark and she states that the crime happened so speedily that the victim of the outrage could not have been cool enough in the hour of the attack to so closely watch the assailant as later to identify him."

Just as the prosecutor had praised Will Hixson, Shepherd decried him. The defense attorney accused the young man of fabricating his identification with the sole intention of collecting the $375 reward. Shepherd reminded jurors of the testimony of Harvey McConnell and his son, Cicero, who said that Hixson had met with them the morning after the reward was announced. They said he had inquired about Johnson's identity and wondered aloud about the possibility that he was the St. Elmo rapist. And he reminded the jury that Hixson had hidden his face when confronted with McConnell's allegations.

Defense lawyer R. T. Cameron followed with a very brief address to the jury in which he also excoriated Hixson, describing the witness as a liar and a perjurer.

The final plea for Johnson's life came from W.G.M. Thomas. Unlike Shepherd, Thomas was remarkably low-key, soft-spoken, and unassuming. He attacked no one. At different times throughout his closing argument, he stood directly in front of Miss Taylor and her father, as if talking to them personally. Instead of speaking with anger in his voice and judgment in his eyes, Thomas stood before jurors crying and pleading for mercy. The newspapers described it as "one of the most remarkable arguments ever delivered in a Tennessee courtroom."

> This is a solemn hour. The most solemn hour that has ever met me in my professional life I feel is here now while I do the last service I can do for my poor client in this case.
>
> Were I not convinced of the absolute innocence of the Negro sitting over there, I would be there silent in my chair or over at the other side aiding the attorney general to fasten the guilt upon him. Log chains couldn't pull me and make me stand before twelve men of my home and say a word for that man did I not believe in his innocence.
>
> I as a lawyer and appointed by the Honorable Court have a sworn duty to perform, and I am determined that if that boy is convicted and sent to the gallows his blood shall not be on my hands.

I repeat, I have done my duty in this case. I have risen from my bed at 4:00 in the morning and started out in my search for the truth. Myself and Judge Shepherd have freely used our own time and money to make a trip to Nashville solely in pursuit of duty. And here I am now doing the last act that can be done in his defense.

Am I not interested in finding the right man—in finding the guilty scoundrel? For years, that old man sitting over there, his sons, and his daughters have had care of the graves where sleep my wife and little baby, the only little family I ever had, and who died a few years ago. I carried a wife and child to that cemetery tended by that old man—and now I say to him and his beautiful daughter that I am ready to do anything I can to help you find the guilty scoundrel.

If Ed Johnson is the man, then hang him. If he is not, don't let an innocent man hang for the deed of a scoundrel.

I am a firm believer in the Book of Books and in the God of the Bible. Only Ed Johnson, my God, and your God know whether Ed Johnson committed that nefarious crime. And I believe there is one other being that knows—that is the real criminal. Where he is, I do not know.

In the face of twelve good men from my own home, all of whom I know and most of whom I know intimately, I could not stand here and ask the acquittal of a man I believed to be guilty. My home is here. Every friend that has ever been a friend to me is here. My old mother lives now on McCallie Avenue and she is there while I am here talking to you. I have two sisters and three little nieces living in this city.

I could not be so false to the womanhood dear to me and to the mothers, wives, and sisters dear to me, as to stand here and ask you to acquit this man if there were any reasonable certainty of his guilt. If I could, I'd help you find the truth in this solemn hour. That's why I'm here. I want to help you.

With that as his introduction, the advocate summarized the weaknesses of the state's case. He said the entire case was built of "flimsy" circumstantial evidence that "does not hold true" when closely examined.

Thomas started his critique of the prosecution's case with the testimony of Miss Taylor. He told jurors that no woman or child should have to endure the tragic events that befell the victim. He said his sympathy and that of the entire city were with her. Then, as delicately as he could, the lawyer described the flaws in her testimony. He pointed out over and over that Miss Taylor had failed to identify Johnson adequately as her attacker, despite repeated opportunities to do so. Using the stenographer's notes, Thomas read back the star witness's testimony to the jury.

"I believe he is the man."

"To the best of my knowledge and belief, he is the same man."

"I will not swear that he is the man, but I believe he is the Negro who assaulted me."

None of this was meant as a criticism of the victim. Far from it. Instead, the lawyer praised her for being truthful. She could not state what she knew was not true. She could not and would not look the defendant in the eye and then look the jurors in the eye and condemn his life, Thomas said. She could not and did not say that Johnson was, without a doubt, the fiend who had attacked her.

Hixson was next on Thomas's list. The lawyer blasted the witness as a liar and a snitch, someone not to be trusted, comparable to Judas.

Thomas also told the jurors not to forget the testimony of all the alibi witnesses. He reminded them that man after man had taken the stand to say that they were at the saloon the night of the rape and that Johnson was there too. As jurors, they could not simply ignore such a staggering amount of evidence that pointed away from the defendant's guilt and toward his innocence.

The defense attorney finished his summary of the case by focusing on the testimony of Johnson. His client was not an educated man, or "a person of wealth or influence." But Thomas said Johnson had never changed his story, despite the incredible pressure to do so from the sheriff and deputies. Maybe he had been confused about the exact time he had arrived at the Last Chance. But he never wavered, Thomas said, about being innocent of this crime.

Thomas concluded his remarks by pleading with the jury to rely on their "logic and reason" in deciding the guilt or innocence of Johnson. When he sat down, the defense was finished.

Hamilton County District Attorney General Matt Whitaker rose from his hardwood chair behind the prosecution table. He turned toward the audience, leaned over the bar, and whispered something in the ear of Nevada Taylor. He squeezed her hand, and then returned to the mission ahead—closing arguments. The next day, the *Chattanooga Times* summarized his arguments.

Nothing short of a reproduction could do justice to the great plea uttered by the Attorney General as he closed the case. It was masterly, almost cruelly denunciatory and most convincing.

He pled for womanhood and girlhood of the country and rebuked the defense for asking the jury to believe the perjured testimony of a lot of "thugs, thieves and sots—the offscourings of hell"—in order to acquit a fiend guilty of despoiling the happiness and clouding the life of one of Chattanooga's fairest daughters.

While he was applying some of his choicest epithets to the Negro witnesses, attorney Cameron arose and objected to the Attorney General's language. The objection was greeted with hisses audible in many directions.

The Attorney General quickly retorted to the interruption: "You shouldn't object to the statement of truth if it's light you're after in this case"—an utterance that was approved by cheers.

Whitaker's final statement to the jury was not lengthy. He didn't rehash the facts of the case or the testimony of the witnesses that jurors had come to know so well. Instead, the prosecutor's remarks were designed to humanize the victim, demonize the defendant and his alibi witnesses, and remind jurors of the brutality of the crime. His intentions were to give the trial one last heavy dose of emotionalism. He ended his remarks by walking to Taylor's side, putting his hand on

her shoulder, and looking directly at each juror as he spoke his final
words.

> Send that black brute to the gallows and prove to the world
> that in Chattanooga and Hamilton County the law of the coun-
> try does not countenance such terrible crimes, has not ceased
> to mete out the proper punishment for such horrible outrages.

At 5:28 p.m., Judge McReynolds charged the jury as to the law in
the state of Tennessee regarding rape. He told the panel they must
find the defendant guilty beyond a reasonable doubt. And he said the
burden of proving the case rested with the state. A few minutes later,
he sent the dozen men into private chambers to select a jury foreman
and begin deliberations.

The jury began its discussions about 5:40 p.m. Twenty minutes
later, they reported to the judge that the verdict would not be produced immediately. They deliberated until midnight, breaking only
briefly for dinner. At the end of the evening, the panel informed Judge
McReynolds that they were split—eight for guilt, four favoring innocence. The judge sent them home for a night's sleep, to return to the
courthouse and continue their work at 8:00 a.m.

The news of a split verdict rocked the court. Judge McReynolds
knew a hung jury would not be accepted well within the community.
Only a verdict of guilt and a sentence of death, as he had promised earlier, would satisfy many of his townsmen. Long after everyone else
had left the courthouse, McReynolds, Whitaker, and Shipp shared a
bottle of whiskey in the judge's chambers. They all agreed that a "not
guilty" verdict could not be tolerated, nor could a mistrial—the city
could not afford, financially or socially, a second trial. What they
decided to do, no one knows. After three drinks each, the judicial leaders of Chattanooga went their own ways.

The next morning, the jurors seemed refreshed and newly determined to tackle their task. And it didn't take them long. As divided
and confused as they had been the day before over the evidence, they
were now quickly united. After a night at home with their families,
their doubt over Miss Taylor's identification and Hixson's motives

evaporated. The four dissenters who had so adamantly argued during the first day of deliberations how insufficient the evidence was against Johnson were now amazingly silent. Unlike the day before, there was no debate over the facts.

At 9:11 a.m., the jury's foreman, A. T. Hooker, opened the door to their deliberating room and motioned for a court officer.

"We have a verdict."

The officer, taken aback by the pronouncement, nodded and said the jurors should remain in their room while he informed the judge. Within minutes, Judge McReynolds called the prosecutors and defense attorneys into his chambers.

"The jury has reached a decision," he told them. He didn't know what the verdict was, but he said they needed to prepare for both possibilities. He had Sheriff Shipp increase security throughout the building. An armed guard was posted at each entrance. Deputies and police officers were once again placed at every street corner surrounding the courthouse. Additional officers were placed in the courtroom as well. And Sheriff Shipp said he himself would stand behind Johnson to protect others from him or him from others.

Word spread like Southern kudzu throughout the courthouse that a verdict had been reached. People quickly headed toward the courtroom. Ed Johnson, handcuffed and in leg chains, was escorted into the room by three deputy sheriffs. Once the defendant was seated, the handcuffs and chains were removed. The officers remained within reach.

"All rise."

Everyone stood. Judge McReynolds walked to the bench placed high in the center of the courtroom.

"The Criminal Court of Hamilton County is now in session," yelled the bailiff.

"Be seated," the judge told the crowd. The room was packed. Police officers, courthouse workers, and local lawyers lined the walls. Those sitting in the pews were crammed in. Yet now the courtroom, which had been buzzing with people trying to predict the verdict, was silent.

"The jury has communicated to me that they have reached a

unanimous verdict," Judge McReynolds said. "Is the state ready to receive it?"

"Yes, Your Honor," announced Whitaker, who displayed no sign of nervousness about the possible decision.

"Is the defense ready to accept it?"

"We are, Your Honor," said Thomas, whose voice and eyes did exhibit the tension of the moment.

Turning to the bailiff, the judge said: "Let's bring in the jury."

At 9:24 a.m., the twelve white men filed into the courtroom. The lawyers in the case stood up as the jury entered the courtroom. The men stepped into the jury box and took the very same seats they had occupied during the trial.

"Members of the jury," Judge McReynolds began, "I understand you have reached a verdict."

A. T. Hooker, the man the jury had chosen as its foreman, spoke up: "We have, judge." He then handed the bailiff the jury form on which they had to mark one of two selections:

NOT GUILTY OF RAPE.

GUILTY OF RAPE.

The bailiff took the single sheet of paper to Judge McReynolds. He opened the folded jury form and studied it carefully but only for a few seconds. Without expressing any puzzlement, approval, or judgment, he handed the note back to the bailiff, who returned it to the jury foreman.

"Will the defendant please rise?" the judge asked.

Ed Johnson, with the same empty, apathetic expression he had brandished throughout the previous three days, stood up. His shoulders slouched. His head bowed slightly. His large eyes darted around the room. Lewis Shepherd, R. T. Cameron, and W.G.M. Thomas also stood by their client. Sheriff Shipp and a slew of deputies surrounded the defendant. The prosecutors also stood.

"Mr. Jury Foreman, what is your verdict?" asked Judge McReynolds.

"On the single count of rape, we, the jury, find the defendant, Ed Johnson, guilty."

Hooker said the jury offered the court no qualifications or recommendations. Under Tennessee law at that time, a person convicted of rape was automatically sentenced to death. However, jurors did have the power to award a lesser punishment if they believed the circumstances warranted it or if they found there were mitigating factors. This was not offered to Ed Johnson by the jury.

A hushed murmur swept the courtroom. The judge told his clerk to poll the jury members individually, to make sure each juror agreed with the verdict. There have been numerous instances throughout legal history in which a juror who believed a defendant innocent voted guilty in the deliberating room because he or she felt intimidated or pressured by other jurors, only to reverse course again in the open courtroom. As the clerk called the names, each juror stood. One by one, the jurors said they agreed with the verdict. There were no surprise dissenters.

With that procedural requirement completed, Judge McReynolds told the jury panel that they had been "one of the finest" ever to sit on a case in his courtroom. He told them he appreciated their diligence, commitment, and service to their state. Then he told them they could go home and see their families again.

In his seat, the seat he has occupied during the trial, sat Ed Johnson, now convicted as the inhuman monster who attacked and outraged a defenseless girl. A slight quivering of the black chin, a slight indrawing of the breath, were the only evidences of the fact that the Negro knew and realized what the statements being made by the jurymen meant to him.

It is now 17 days since the crime for which Johnson was today convicted was committed, and the Court and law officers are receiving congratulations upon the celerity with which the wheels of justice have revolved, in capturing, preserving, trying and convicting the Negro Johnson.

On Friday, that day unlucky for criminals from times long past, that day when English high criminals were sentenced to death, and on which they met their doom upon the scaffold. On Friday, Ed Johnson heard the words which will without doubt bear him to the gallows and witness his legal execution.

Unless some higher power than the Court which tried him intervenes, then those words will send Ed Johnson to the gallows and the hangman's noose.

Chattanooga News, February 9, 1906

As the jurors left the room, the three lawyers representing Johnson huddled together near Johnson at their table. For several minutes, they whispered animatedly. Finally, Shepherd broke from the pack. He told Judge McReynolds that they would be making their official request for a new trial the following day. Such a petition is the first step required in appealing a conviction.

The judge nodded his head and announced that he would give the lawyers on both sides several hours to prepare for the sentencing. He told all parties to be back at the court at 3:00 p.m., then returned to his chambers. Staring out the window, he watched Sheriff Shipp and a squadron of deputies shepherd the defendant, still wearing the greasy old slouch hat, across Walnut Street and into the jail.

At that moment, a knock sounded on the judge's door. It was W.G.M. Thomas. The defense lawyer said he wanted the judge to appoint three additional attorneys to advise him, Lewis Shepherd, and Robert Cameron. The three said they were divided over how to proceed. He wanted some outside independent counsel who could help in making the next decision.

Judge McReynolds agreed to appoint an advisory panel. First, however, he wanted to discuss the request privately with the district attorney. For several minutes, the judge and prosecutor met behind closed doors—an action considered highly unethical. When the two exited from their meeting, the judge announced he would appoint Foster V. Brown, Robert Pritchard, and J. H. Cantrell to assist the defense team in reviewing the evidence presented in the case for flaws or errors. McReynolds would later admit under oath that the district attorney had recommended two of the men.

The three new lawyers, all of whom had attended different portions of the testimony during the three-day trial, accepted. They retired to Cantrell's law office, which was only a block away from the courthouse, to discuss the trial and what to do next. The meeting quickly grew heated. On one side was Lewis Shepherd, who stated that he believed Ed Johnson was innocent and that the case should be appealed. Every defendant in a criminal case has the right to appeal, and it was their duty as Johnson's lawyers to seek a new trial and appeal the verdict.

Besides, he couldn't understand what had happened to those four jurors who just the previous night were so rigid in their belief that Johnson was innocent. What had changed their minds? Had someone tampered with them? This was something that needed to be pursued as part of an appeal, Shepherd said. Cameron agreed with Shepherd on this point.

Thomas and the three new lawyers disagreed. They contended there was no obvious flaw in the trial and they seriously doubted that the Tennessee Supreme Court would reverse the jury's verdict. An appeal would only grant the defendant a few more months of life and would never result in his freedom or an acquittal, they argued.

The other lawyers also attacked Shepherd's contention that it was their duty, as Johnson's lawyers, to seek an appeal. To the contrary. They felt they had done their duty as required of them by the court. They had fought hard for Johnson and represented him well. But they had lost. Now they wanted to end this case and their affiliation with Johnson.

There was yet another reason Thomas felt they shouldn't appeal: the lynch mob. The lawyers had been told over and over that if they tried to delay the trial the mob would raid the jail and kill Johnson and other inmates. If there were a prolonged appeal, Thomas argued, the chances of a mob uprising would only increase. Thomas later expressed this in an open letter he wrote to the newspaper:

> The life of the defendant, even if the wrong man, could not be saved. An appeal would so inflame the public that the jail would be attacked and perhaps other prisoners executed by

violence. The defendant, now that he has been convicted by a jury, must die by the judgment of the law, or else, if the case were appealed, he would die by the act of an uprising of the people.

Shepherd remained unconvinced. He said that the right to appeal belonged not to the lawyers but to the criminal defendant. He argued to his fellow attorneys that their consideration must not be themselves or even the other prisoners at the jail. Their sole concern, he said, must be in defending their client. But the former judge could see that he was making no progress in converting the other lawyers, so he pitched a compromise: leave it up to Ed Johnson. If he wanted an appeal, Shepherd said, then they should appeal. Thomas agreed, with one condition: he planned to tell the defendant that an appeal would be useless.

About 3:00 p.m. Shepherd, Cameron, and Thomas walked to the jail to meet with their client. The conference in the prisoner's cell didn't take long. Shepherd began by explaining the situation to Johnson. He was now convicted, and the judge would soon be sentencing him to die. The lawyer explained to Johnson the options. He could waive his right to appeal, throw himself at the mercy of Judge McReynolds, and probably die. Or he could file for a new trial, which the judge would deny, but could then seek an appeal to the state Supreme Court, which would not be in session to hear the appeal until next fall.

However, the chances of an appeal were not good, Shepherd said. The Tennessee Supreme Court reverses very few criminal convictions, and they would be even more hesitant to overturn such a high-profile, controversial, tragic case as this. At about this point, Thomas jumped in. He warned Johnson about the very real threat of a lynch mob. If they appealed and stayed any execution, there were many rumblings that the people would revolt. Now that Johnson was convicted, Thomas said the sheriff might be less inclined to protect him.

THOMAS: Ed, do you feel we lawyers have performed our duty in defending you?
JOHNSON: Yes, sir. You've done all you could.

THOMAS: Ed, we don't know whether you are the guilty man or not, but you and God know. The jury says you are the man.

JOHNSON: Yes, they have put it on me, and I guess I have to take it, but I ain't guilty.

THOMAS: Ed, your life has been saved up to this time, but the people believe now that the jury has acted more than they ever did before, that you are the right man. They are outraged against you, and even if you are innocent, as you say you are, we do not believe that we can save your life.

JOHNSON: (Nodded his head as if he understood.)

THOMAS: Have you ever heard the story of Old Dog Tray?

JOHNSON: Yes, sir.

THOMAS: Old Dog Tray lost his life because he was found in bad company. Ed, the Last Chance Saloon is bad company. If you are an innocent man, you, like Old Dog Tray, were found in bad company. Old Dog Tray lost his life on that account and it looks like you must lose your life on the same account. The jury would not believe your bad company. If you die, Ed, and you are innocent, your bad company will be the thing that killed you, because the jury refused to believe anything they said.

JOHNSON: Yes, sir.

THOMAS: Ed, there are two choices here. You can accept the verdict of the court and die in an orderly, lawful manner. Or you can die horribly by the hands of the mob. Do you want to die at the hands of the mob? Do you want to die in an orderly fashion or do you want a lynch mob to take you from your cell, drag you into the streets, beat you, and hang you in front of everyone, leaving your body there for all to see?

JOHNSON: No, sir.

THOMAS: Do you want us to do as we think best in deciding on an appeal?

JOHNSON: Yes, sir. I will tell the judge I am ready to die. But I will also say I am not the guilty man.

The clock at the back of Judge McReynolds's courtroom read 3:25 p.m. when Sheriff Shipp and his deputies re-entered with Ed Johnson in tow. The defense lawyers were close behind. A few minutes later, Judge McReynolds and District Attorney Whitaker entered the courtroom from the judge's private chambers.

The judge rapped his gavel and instructed the clerk to call court to order. He then asked Thomas if the defense wanted to make any statements before sentencing. Thomas stood and walked over to Shepherd, who shook his head in the negative. "I have nothing to say," the former judge commented.

Thomas proceeded to the podium, where he addressed Judge McReynolds in a quiet, monotone voice.

May it please Your Honor.

As Your Honor knows, at the request of Judge Shepherd, Mr. Cameron, and myself, made to Your Honor this morning, you appointed Messrs. Foster V. Brown, Robert Pritchard, and J. H. Cantrell as associate attorneys to advise with us and to assist us in this case. Your Honor stated that those gentlemen would meet with us this afternoon at 1:30 o'clock.

These gentlemen met us at that hour, and we spent one and one-half hours together and have just come from that interview. It was the judgment of those gentlemen, in view of all the facts and circumstances, that Judge Shepherd, Mr. Cameron, and I had performed our duty to Your Honor, to this court, and to this defendant, and that, if Your Honor approve the verdict which the jury has rendered, we ought to acquiesce in the finding and the conclusion reached by the twelve men comprising that jury.

We feel, Your Honor, that we have performed our duty as far as we have been able to see it. A jury composed of the citizens of this county, all of whom are known, and many of whom are my friends and acquaintances, have heard all of the proof on both sides, have looked at it and reviewed it impartially, and those twelve men have said upon their oaths that this defendant is the right man.

After this conference with Messrs. Brown, Pritchard, and Cantrell, we feel that we should acquiesce in the action of the jury, if it is Your Honor's judgment that the jury verdict is the correct verdict. We leave that question for Your Honor to decide.

We feel grateful to the people of Chattanooga and this county for the orderly trial through which we have passed. The times have been restless. There has been agitation, but the officers of the law of this county and city have protected this defendant and we have had a quiet, orderly trial. And after we have performed our duty, as we believe we have, and the jury of twelve of our fellow citizens have, upon their oaths, said that this defendant is the right man, we must leave it to Your Honor to say whether that verdict meets with Your Honor's approval.

Prosecutors were astonished. Most people in the audience didn't realize what had just taken place. The defense lawyer had just announced to the judge that they were waiving their client's right to file for a new trial. They would not appeal the verdict. Whatever the judge decided, they agreed, would be acceptable to them. The defense lawyers were accepting defeat.

Meanwhile, Ed Johnson remained seated. The newspapers reported that he exhibited "no sign of fear or emotion" during the proceeding. The *Times* wrote:

Johnson appeared to be in good spirits and seemed to take an interest in every move made by those assembled in the courtroom. He looked to be the coolest man in the crowd. He did not display the least emotion or weakness during the time that he was before the court and seemed to be in a pleasant frame of mind when sentence was passed upon him. The crowd in the courtroom seemed much more impressed by the solemnity of the occasion than did the condemned Negro.

When Thomas had returned to his seat, Judge McReynolds addressed everyone in the courtroom. He briefly summarized the facts of the case. He told how he had ordered the sheriff to send the defendant to the jail in Nashville for safekeeping. The judge discussed the attempt by the lynch mob to raid the jail, and detailed his appointment of the three lawyers to defend the suspect. He also said he had ordered Shipp to provide the names and locations of every witness in the case.

> All the powers of this court and the officers of this court have been rendered the defendant in procuring such witnesses or anyone that might reflect light upon the guilty party.
>
> One of the best juries was selected to try this case that I have ever seen in a jury box. All the witnesses were present and ample time was given for the examination of these witnesses in order that a fair trial might be had.
>
> This jury, compiled of some of the best men in the city, after hearing all the evidence in the case, the argument of counsel and charge of the court, report, upon their oaths, that the defendant's guilty and shall suffer death by hanging. With the verdict of this jury, the court concurs, and I have no doubt from the proof in the case that the defendant is the guilty party.
>
> It, therefore, becomes my duty to pass the sentence of death upon him.

Under Tennessee law in 1906, a person convicted of a capital offense was supposed to be executed in no fewer than thirty days and no more than sixty days. Since Johnson's lawyers had announced that they would not appeal the conviction to the Tennessee Supreme Court, Judge McReynolds's pronouncement of sentence would likely be the final order entered in the case. The judge paused for a few minutes and took a drink from the cup on his desk. He looked directly at Nevada Taylor, who continued to sit behind the prosecutors' table. He noticed that a few of the jurors in the case had decided to come back to court to watch the sentencing. Finally, he turned his attention to the man on trial, Ed Johnson.

JUDGE McREYNOLDS: Will the defendant rise?

You have been convicted of one of the most atrocious crimes known to the criminal law and I now ask you, have you anything to say why sentence of death should not be passed upon you?

ED JOHNSON: No, sir. I haven't anything to say. The jury says that I am guilty and I guess I will have to suffer for what somebody else has done.

JUDGE McREYNOLDS: Do you feel you have been given a fair trial?

ED JOHNSON: Everything I know of has been done for me. I guess I will be punished for another person's crime.

JUDGE McREYNOLDS: You have been ably represented and every effort has been made to find out the guilty party, and as before stated, I am satisfied that you are the guilty party.

It is therefore the judgment and sentence of the law and of this court that the Sheriff of Hamilton County take and safely keep you in the county jail of said county until Tuesday, March 13, 1906, when, within the legal hours and in the manner prescribed by law, he shall hang you by the neck until dead.

May God have mercy upon your soul.

ED JOHNSON: Thank you, sir.

CHAPTER SEVEN

ENTER NOAH PARDEN

MINUTES AFTER JUDGE Sam McReynolds sentenced Ed Johnson to death, the prisoner was escorted out of the city by Sheriff Shipp and two deputies to the Knoxville jail. The local authorities believed they were rid of Ed Johnson and the turmoil his case had caused. They had fulfilled their promise to follow the law by giving the defendant a procedurally correct trial as required by the Constitution and the statutes of Tennessee. But they also had shown the people of the city who thirsted for vengeance that justice through the courts could be swift and punishment severe.

What they didn't count on was Noah Walter Parden.

As a child, Parden dreamed of being the high sheriff, so fast with his pistol no outlaw would dare enter his jurisdiction. In high school and college, he aspired to be a prosecutor or even a judge. Now Parden was about to turn the world of the Hamilton County sheriff and judge upside down. In doing so, he would make legal history.

Parden was born in 1865 in Floyd County, Georgia, a small farming community between Chattanooga and Atlanta. His mother was a former slave struggling to exist in the aftermath of the Civil War. She cooked and kept house for two neighboring families. He knew nothing of his father, though people said his dad was white.

When he was six, his mother became extremely ill. Parden was holding her hand when she died. Unsure what to do, neighbors packed up all of young Noah's belongings—a few toys, clothes, and a Bible his mother had gotten him for Christmas—and took him to a nearby orphanage run by missionaries. There he attended school and did daily chores.

By the time Parden turned nineteen, he was ready for a new adventure. He moved to Chattanooga and enrolled at Howard High School. To support himself and pay tuition, he worked evenings and weekends as a barber. Five years later, he received his diploma. He accepted an offer to study law at Central Tennessee College in Nashville, where he continued clipping hair. While there, he met and married Mattie S. Broyles, who was seven years younger. Though everyone else called him Noah, she preferred Walter.

In 1893, Parden graduated at the top of his class. Many job offers followed—teaching school, editing a newspaper, and pastoring a church. The newspaper proposal interested him tremendously, because he loved writing and he believed knowledge through information was the single most powerful tool in undermining racism. In the end, though, he decided to return to Chattanooga to practice law.

As a young man studying sociology and the Negro's place in America, Parden became a disciple of Booker T. Washington, the leader of the Tuskegee Institute. Washington shunned conflict with white agitators. He believed black people should forgo immediate attempts to secure their full civil rights under the law. Instead, he taught that black people would obtain a greater degree of respect and acceptance from white people by better educating themselves, cultivating farming and industrial skills, keeping out of legal trouble, and working hard. To encourage or invite confrontation with white people, he said, would only deepen their mistrust and prejudices against black people. Washington promoted vocational training for black people, not intellectual pursuits.

Parden was in the audience in 1895 to hear Washington speak at the Atlanta Cotton States and International Exposition. Parden would frequently cite that speech, referred to as the "Atlanta Compromise," in articles he wrote for black newspapers across the South. The lawyer believed that the economics of society would eventually bring the two races together. Washington said the races could be as separate as five fingers in their social lives but had to be as united as the hand in gaining economic prosperity and legal justice.

Parden was also fervent in his religious beliefs. He never missed Sunday-morning worship at his church, prayed before every meal, and spent several minutes on his knees each night before bed. He refused to drink alcohol, use tobacco products, or eat pork. "The body is the temple of the Holy Spirit," he said.

At age forty-one, Parden had built himself a successful, if barely profitable, law practice. He was certainly the most successful black attorney in Chattanooga. He and his partner, Styles Linton Hutchins, represented nearly two-thirds of the black people who got into trouble for stealing, fighting, assaulting, and loitering; defended a few murder suspects; handled the lion's share of the civil cases filed by black people; represented several of the smaller black-owned businesses in town; and executed most of the real-estate transactions within the black community. As a lawyer, his status among Chattanooga black people was rivaled only by certain preachers and his law partner.

Despite having no shortage of clients, the lawyers faced a significant problem: most of their clients had no money to pay them. Poor black clients seemed to expect the lawyers to represent them for free. The black people who did have money would frequently go to a white lawyer if they got into trouble. Though Parden was certainly respected as an attorney in the black community, the general perception was that white lawyers were afforded more respect by white judges and white jurors.

When payment for services did come, it was more likely to be an invitation to a home-cooked dinner at a client's house. Paying black clients were so scarce that one story tells of a black lawyer who actually postponed his wedding when a client ready to pay cash showed up unannounced that morning.

In thirteen years of practice in Chattanooga, Parden had never represented a white man. His many offers to assist white people were always rejected. The fact that black people were systematically excluded from serving on juries in Tennessee and throughout the South only aggravated the problem. Litigants did not want a black lawyer if it might offend the all-white juries. As a result, poor black people would also turn to white lawyers if they were involved in a more lucrative civil lawsuit. To help attract more paying clients, Parden advertised in the local black newspaper, the Blade.

As a trial lawyer, he knew the law as well as anyone else in court. Most attorneys in those days didn't attend law school. Instead, they received their law licenses after studying for three or four years under an experienced trial lawyer. Such a mentoring program was called "reading law." There are a few states, such as Virginia and California, that still offer such programs. Parden was a law-school-trained attorney; his grasp and understanding of common law, the Constitution, state and federal statutes, and previous court rulings were far superior to those of many of his colleagues.

His courtroom skills were equally as formidable. The well-spoken Parden employed simple trial techniques: devise a strategy in a case and never depart from it, he told younger lawyers, and, above everything else, develop a story you can tell to the jury that helps your client's cause and is supported by the facts.

Many of Parden's biggest legal victories were in civil cases. His tenacious attacks on the insurance companies made the plaintiffs' bar extremely proud. Insurance companies made a lot of money selling policies to black families and minority businesses. However, claims filed by black policyholders were systematically denied, because the companies didn't think the owners of the policies would sue them. Parden made them rethink their strategy, and he made some money in the process. Realizing that many of his clients had no money to pay him, Parden became an early contingency-fee lawyer. He agreed to represent people for free. They paid him nothing if he lost, but if he won the case, the clients shared a portion of the judgment with the lawyer—a proposition the clients readily accepted. Parden developed a consistently winning strategy against the insurance companies. He told the all-white jurors to keep in mind that if big insurance firms were allowed to cheat black policyholders, white people would be next.

The civil practice financed Parden's handling of criminal cases. Very few of the people he represented who were charged with crimes

had any money to pay. He accepted more *pro bono* criminal cases than
any other lawyer—black or white—in the city. And he fought hard for
them, frequently appealing to the Tennessee Supreme Court cases
that most lawyers and judges believed were fruitless. That's not to say
that Parden believed all of his clients were innocent. To the contrary.
If he had a fault in the eyes of the local criminal-defense bar, it was
that he didn't vigorously defend the clients he knew were guilty.
Instead, Parden would encourage them to plead guilty and accept
their punishment. In articles he would write for black newspapers
across the South, including the *Atlanta Independent*, Parden frequently
expressed disappointment in the conduct of his own race.

> Achievement and achievement alone will subdue the hate-
> mongering. Many colored complain to me that they are not
> treated equally by the whites. Why should the whites not look
> down on the Negro when he acts as he does? We shame our-
> selves by frequenting the taverns. We shame the Negro race
> through thievery and drunkenness and improper conduct.
> Negroes who violated the law should not seek to avoid punish-
> ment. And law-abiding Negroes should not protect Negroes
> who steal or cheat or violate another person.

As the city's premier black attorney, Parden had watched the
Johnson case unfold. Like the rest of the community, he was outraged
at Nevada Taylor's rape. He felt relief when the authorities made an
arrest. Though he was disheartened when a lynch mob threatened to
storm the jail, his faith was partially restored when local authorities
repelled the mob and took the necessary steps to protect the defendant, especially a black defendant. But dismay set in once again when
he heard that the judge refused to delay the trial and rejected or discouraged the defense attorney's request to move the case to another
city.

Parden was no different from other residents of Chattanooga in
assuming that Johnson was the culprit. If he was guilty, the lawyer
believed, Johnson should probably spend the rest of his life in prison,
or even pay with his life. No one ever accused Parden of being soft on

crime. He was no opponent of the death penalty, and he advocated lengthy sentences for those who committed violent crimes. But Parden also knew the criminal system, especially when it came to a case involving a black man accused of raping a white woman. To white people, there was no greater indignity, no sin more vile.

The first official association Parden had with the Johnson case came when Lewis Shepherd walked into his law office about a week before the trial. He admired the former judge tremendously. Shepherd was the only lawyer in Chattanooga who was not afraid to stand up against the establishment when defending the rights of a client. And he was one of the few white lawyers who welcomed poor black people as clients. For those reasons, Parden had worked to befriend the older lawyer.

Parden had earlier rejected Shepherd's request to join the defense, because the case was too political and too socially divisive. He did help Shepherd track down several of the black alibi witnesses. At the former judge's behest, Parden checked with his sources throughout the black community regarding Johnson's background and character. He also canvassed the community to see if anyone could provide information pointing to the guilt of Johnson or any other person.

Through this limited research, Parden became convinced that the authorities had the wrong man. Every person who knew Johnson said he never raised his voice, never fought, and seldom cursed. No one had ever seen Johnson become violent or even angry.

At the same time, rumors about other suspects permeated the black community. A few names surfaced. Parden passed them on to Shepherd, who gave them to the sheriff. But no additional investigation was ever done. There also was widespread speculation that Miss Taylor's attacker was not even a black man, but a white man who had painted his face black. Parden found two witnesses in the St. Elmo area who said they had seen a man they thought was a Negro washing his face about 7:00 p.m. When they saw the man wash his face and what appeared to be black polish dissolve, they realized he was really white. However, the two witnesses were black; they didn't approach the sheriff, because they believed he would not accept their story.

Parden also had several discussions with Johnson at the jail during the trial. He would arrive at the jail early in the morning to meet with his clients to prepare them for court, and would take a few minutes to chat with Johnson, who initially shared a cell with two of Parden's clients.

Hours after Judge McReynolds condemned Johnson to die, Parden received a visitor at his law office. It was "Skinbone" Johnson, Ed's father. The lawyer brought his guest a chair and a cup of tea. Together, they lamented over the details of the trial. Parden told the elder Johnson that his son's trial had been a sham and that several of his constitutional rights had been violated. The lawyer wondered why Mr. Johnson and Ed's other relatives had not attended the trial to show their support. Speaking very slowly, the older Johnson said he'd wanted to watch the trial and be with his son, but policemen had told him that no visitors were being allowed in the courthouse.

It was at this point that Skinbone Johnson made his intentions known. He had spoken to his son before the sheriff transported him to Knoxville, and he didn't want to die. Ed did want to appeal. And he wanted Parden to represent him.

Parden didn't know what to say. Just a week or so earlier, he had totally rejected the idea of defending Johnson. The defendant had good lawyers, some of the best in Chattanooga. Though Parden certainly believed Johnson had not received a fair trial and was most likely innocent of the crime, convincing the Tennessee Supreme Court that there was reversible error was a far different matter.

The elder Johnson said he didn't have any money to pay for an appeal. Instead, he thought Parden would agree to handle the case simply because he and Johnson were Negroes. Parden said he would think about it, but he warned that he was inclined to turn down the request. His plate was full of tough cases that he was doing for free.

Unbeknownst to Parden, his law partner was in the next room listening to the entire conversation. Styles Linton Hutchins was Parden's alter ego. As quiet and patient and unassuming as Parden was, Hutchins was the exact opposite. His speeches were filled with blistering attacks on the "lily whites" who denied rights to black people. He was a follower of W.E.B. Du Bois. Du Bois believed in developing the intellect of the black man, not just encouraging him to get vocational training. He believed in freedom and civil rights now, not settling for them in the future.

In a society dominated by the Ku Klux Klan, lynch mobs, and Jim Crow laws, Hutchins believed that the means of achieving equal rights under the law was agitation and protest. He filed unsuccessful lawsuits fighting the segregation of the train and trolley systems. He sued the city for refusing to allow young black children to participate in summer athletic programs. And he encouraged other black leaders to speak out and fight against the injustices they suffered, as in this article he wrote for the *Washington Bee*, a black-owned newspaper.

The Constitution says the Negro has all the rights of the white man. Yet, we are afforded none of the white man's protections. The Constitution says the Negroes are a free people. Yet, we enjoy none of the white man's privileges. The Constitution says the Negro is equal. Yet, we cannot ride on the white man's train. We cannot sit as a juror in the white man's court. We cannot send our children to the white man's schools.

The Negro is not equal. The Negro is not even free. The Negro is simply a dark body who is spit upon without any opportunity for recourse.

At age fifty-three, Hutchins was a veteran lawyer and politician who had lived an atypical life for a Southern black man. He was born in Lawrenceville, Georgia, a suburb of Atlanta. His father was a wealthy artist who paid for his son to get a college education at Atlanta University. After teaching school for several years, Hutchins enrolled in the law program at the University of South Carolina. In 1875, he became one of the first black students to graduate from the school.

That year, Hutchins moved back to Atlanta and opened a law practice. Judges and lawyers in Georgia had never before encountered a black attorney. They didn't like it, and wanted to find a way to stop it. The Georgia Legislature took immediate action, passing a law that required lawyers who had received their law degrees in other states to undergo an examination by the county's presiding judge. The law was specifically designed to discourage black lawyers from moving from Northern states to Georgia.

But Hutchins would not be deterred. He vigorously fought the law. After six months of antagonism, he finally convinced an Atlanta judge to admit him to practice in the state-court system. In doing so, Hutchins became the first black person to be admitted to the Georgia bar. Then, in 1881, weary of the repeated personal attacks by judges and fellow lawyers, he moved north to Chattanooga, where he perceived the racial attitudes to be more accommodating. He enjoyed immediate success, becoming one of Chattanooga's prominent and respected lawyers. In 1886, the Republicans asked Hutchins to run for a state-legislative seat against a very popular Democrat, who was white. Hutchins was attacked by the *Chattanooga News* as an "unprincipled, crooked rogue and dishonest."

In a political shocker, Hutchins won 2,742 to 2,734, by a mere eight votes. However, the newspaper never let up on him. Less than a month after he had been elected, the newspaper reported that a group of leading Democrats considered banding together, capturing Hutchins, taking him to a secluded spot, horsewhipping him, and giving him twenty-four hours to leave town. Despite the constant criticism, Hutchins served his district with distinction.

In 1888, Hutchins left politics to focus on his law practice and to become an ordained minister. He loved preaching, and his hellfire-and-brimstone manner was a favorite throughout southeastern Tennessee and northwestern Georgia. He felt no shame in using the pulpit to sermonize against those in government who exhibited racist or segregationist views. By the time the Johnson case arrived, he was one of the oldest black lawyers in the South.

Many people in 1906 believed Parden and Hutchins were a perfect fit. Together, they published a small newspaper called *The Independent Age* which circulated within the black community for a couple of years. And they joined with other black businessmen in starting up ventures that ranged from a grocery store to a barber shop. But the first love of both men was the practice of law. Neither had children, so they referred to their practice as their "firstborn." They believed God had made the law their calling.

ACCOMPANYING SKINBONE JOHNSON to the door, Parden shook the old man's hand and renewed his promise that he would give the appeal serious consideration that weekend. Parden was watching the elderly man walk away when a familiar voice interrupted his concentration. It was Hutchins. He wanted to talk.

"I know, I know," Parden said, according to his federal court testimony. "You think I should take the case."

"I think we should take the case," replied Hutchins, who had overheard the conversation from the next room.

"You get crazier every day," Parden joked.

For four hours that Saturday evening, the two men talked about Ed Johnson and his case. Mainly, it was Hutchins talking and Parden listening. Hutchins made the arguments why they should accept the case; Parden tried to poke holes in each point. They bickered over costs. They debated the negative impact pushing the appeal would have on their law practice and their reputations. And what if the lynch mob came after them?

To Hutchins, none of it mattered. As lawyers, they were bound by the law to defend an innocent man, to right wrongs, to pursue justice, he contended. Besides, Hutchins had experienced all the threats before. Once, a judge threw the lawyer in jail because he had asked the court to reconsider a ruling. Another judge banned Hutchins from his courtroom when he dared to point out that the prosecutor was not following the law.

Parden argued that the defendant already had lawyers, including one of the best in the city, Lewis Shepherd. If those white lawyers couldn't help him, what chance did black lawyers have?

The senior lawyer finally won by employing a Biblical principle. "Much has been given to us by God and man," Hutchins said. "Now much is expected."

Parden hated it when Hutchins quoted scripture to prove a point, mainly because he knew the older lawyer was probably correct. Finally, Parden relented, conceding that representing Johnson was the right thing to do. They agreed to meet the following afternoon to devise a strategy for the appeal. That night, Parden broke the news to his wife, Mattie. They both knew about the threats the white lawyers had received prior to the trial. They could only wonder what they would have to endure. Mattie fixed her husband of thirteen years a cup of hot mint tea, his favorite. Little did they realize how much their life was about to change.

That night, Parden retrieved from his bookshelf the tattered Bible his mother had given him as a child. He opened it to the book of Job. Lying in bed next to his wife, Parden read all forty-two chapters. He had read the story many times before. Each time, it reinvigorated his faith and determination.

According to the Bible, Job was a "man that feared God and shunned evil." As a result, God had blessed Job with ten children and great riches. Unbeknownst to Job, God and Satan were in heaven debating his loyalty. God claimed Job would be faithful to his beliefs regardless of the circumstances that befell him. Satan contended that Job would curse God if his prosperity turned to tragedy. To prove his point, Satan sent Job's enemies to slay his servants and steal 500 yoke of oxen and 3,000 of his camels. Fire fell from heaven and destroyed 7,000 sheep. And a great wind knocked down the walls of his house, killing his only three sons. The second day, Satan "smote Job with boils from the sole of his foot unto his crown." Even Job's wife suggested that he end the suffering: "Curse God and die," she said. But Job refused and remained unwavering in his faith. As a result, God blessed him with twice as much wealth as he had previously had and gave him seven more sons.

"So Job died, being old and full of days," Parden said to his wife, reading the last verse in the book. He prayed that night that he would be so fortunate.

LEWIS SHEPHERD WALKED onto his front porch early that Sunday morning to pick up the newspaper and found Parden sitting on the steps in his Sunday best. Immediately, the former judge knew it meant trouble. After the pleasantries, the two men moved their conversation into Shepherd's study. Parden told him about Johnson's father's visit to him the day before and the subsequent discussion with Hutchins. They had made up their minds that they would file a motion for a new trial on Monday and pursue an appeal.

Shepherd nodded in total agreement. He had been adamantly opposed to waiving Johnson's right to appeal. And for two days, he had regretted not speaking up. There were real problems with how the trial was conducted, Shepherd said. He thought there was a good chance that the Tennessee Supreme Court might find there were errors and reverse the conviction. And he offered his full support and cooperation in their effort.

For the next two hours, Shepherd and Parden relived the entire trial. As Shepherd spoke, Parden took notes. Together, they came up with nearly a dozen points that the lawyers believed could constitute violations of the defendant's rights. There were numerous trial irregularities, not to mention the judge's obvious prejudices. They began drafting a petition seeking a new trial to present to the court.

Nearing the end of their discussion, Parden blurted out that he and Hutchins needed more than just Shepherd's assistance in the case. They requested his direct involvement and leadership. They wanted him to be co-counsel. Shepherd took a deep breath and closed his eyes. He knew if he agreed he would face tremendous criticism from local lawyers and judges and could become a political and social outcast in his own community. But Shepherd had never backed away from doing what he thought was right. And Parden had helped him in previous cases. It was time to repay the favor. The older lawyer simply nodded.

Judge Shepherd grasped my arm and held it tight. Then, he told me that Judge McReynolds and Sheriff Shipp would be very angry at any decision to appeal. He said they would fight our efforts, and he said there would be significant consequences for each involved, and he told me to be certain that I was ready before I formally filed the petition. Only then did I fully realize the difficulty that faced us.

PARDEN in a speech at the Galbraith AME Zion Church

CHAPTER EIGHT

THE APPEALS BEGIN

NOAH PARDEN and Styles Hutchins arrived at the Hamilton County Criminal Court early Monday morning, February 12, to make their move. Judge Sam McReynolds stepped into the courtroom to find the two black lawyers seeking to approach the bench. Unaware of their intentions, the judge invited them forward. Parden stepped up, telling McReynolds that they planned to file a motion for a new trial and, if he permitted, an appeal in the case of the *State of Tennessee* v. *Ed Johnson*. Hutchins said he wanted to "relieve the judge of the burden of the defendant's life" by appealing the case to the Tennessee Supreme Court.

McReynolds was stunned. He didn't know what to say. Parden said he had drafted a one-page request for a new trial. The lawyer asked the judge to authorize the court stenographer in the case to prepare a written transcript of the trial to submit to the state's highest court, as is required by law, if the judge denied his bid for a new trial.

Judge McReynolds sat back in his chair to ponder his next move. The last thing he wanted was to delay the execution of Johnson. He had to find some way to stop the appeal. Then it came to him. The judge called Parden and Hutchins to the side of his bench. He told them to come back the next morning to file their motion formally in open court. That way, he said, the prosecutor could be present and the motion could be properly heard.

"We should file the motion tomorrow?" Parden inquired. "But that would be the fourth day following the verdict, and local court rules say the motion for a new trial must be filed within three days."

"But you're counting Sunday," Hutchins spoke up. "The judge has never counted Sunday against a defendant." The two lawyers looked at Judge McReynolds for a response, but he only raised his eyebrows and nodded in apparent agreement.

The next morning, Parden and Hutchins slipped into court at about 10:00 a.m. just as Judge McReynolds called a recess in the case he was hearing. During the break, the lawyers approached the bench. Parden handed the clerk of the court his petition officially seeking a new trial for Ed Johnson and began to make his plea.

> Your honor, I ask the indulgence of the court and beg permission to file a motion for a new trial in the Johnson case. I have been impressed by the general opinion that a mistake may have been committed when Ed Johnson was convicted.
>
> If there was no question about his guilt, no one would dare to make a motion for a new trial, but public sentiment is divided on this subject. I have had many white people speak to me about the matter, and as the Constitution allows any man, be he white or black, the right of appeal, I do believe that it is our duty to allow the Supreme Court to pass upon this case.

Assistant District Attorney E. S. Daniels jumped to his feet to object. The prosecutor said Johnson had three lawyers and they had waived his right to appeal. How could Parden and Hutchins now come forward and claim to represent Johnson when the defendant was 100 miles away in Knoxville?

Parden said that Johnson's father had authorized them to file the motion for a new trial and the lawyer believed that was sufficient. Daniels countered that Johnson was twenty-three years old and fully capable of making the decision regarding who should represent him.

Then the prosecutor told the judge that the rules of the local criminal court required lawyers for defendants to file motions for a new trial within three days of the verdict. A motion for a new trial was legally essential before an appeal could be made in a Tennessee case. The jury had returned the guilty verdict Friday. This was Tuesday, four days later; the time limit for filing a motion for a new trial had expired. The motion should thus be rejected immediately, Daniels said.

Parden argued that he had been employed by Johnson's father only Saturday and that he was still trying to learn all the facts of the case. He said Sunday had never been included as counting against the three-day rule. Besides, Parden continued, Johnson's lawyers had abandoned their client following his conviction: the "declaration to Johnson by his lawyers that the defendant had a choice of dying at the end of a lawful rope or one applied by the mob is sufficient evidence that he was abandoned." The defendant should be granted the opportunity to seek an appeal because his initial decision was made under duress.

Judge McReynolds interrupted Parden in mid-sentence to say he had "never witnessed a trial that was conducted more fairly." He said Johnson and his lawyers were given every opportunity to defend against the rape accusations.

The judge then blasted Parden and Hutchins for attempting to override the rules of his court. He said there were many men sitting in the state penitentiary who had simply failed to file their motion for a new trial on time. Lawyers had three days to file the petition, he said, and Sunday was included. The only exception was if Sunday was the third day following the verdict, the reason being that the court was closed on Sunday and no filings could be made then. Such was not the situation in this case, McReynolds said.

Finally, the judge laughed out loud at Parden and Hutchins and publicly scolded them in front of the other lawyers.

What can two Negro lawyers do that the defendant's previous three attorneys were unable to achieve? Do you know the law better than this court or the lawyers who represented the defendant? Are you aware of some legal principle that I have never heard of? What can a Negro lawyer know that a white lawyer does not? Do you think a Negro lawyer could possibly be smarter or know the law better than a white lawyer?

Stunned by the judge's spirited rejection of their motion, Parden told the court he understood the ruling. However, he said, since the trial court would not grant his motion, he would file an emergency petition with the Tennessee Supreme Court seeking a stay of the execution. The lawyer said he also desired Judge McReynolds's blessing in obtaining a transcript of the trial. He needed an official transcript to show the appellate court the errors that had occurred during the trial. But the judge said he would do nothing to condone their efforts, which he described as a waste of time and a personal rebuke to himself and to the three attorneys who had defended Johnson.

Outside the courtroom, Parden and Hutchins were dumbfounded. They had been tricked, set up for failure. The day before, when Judge McReynolds clearly told them to return the next morning to file their motion, he had to know that he would reject their petition on procedural grounds. He also knew they had had their petition ready to file the previous day, but he had turned them away. The opposition by the judge would certainly make their task more difficult. If McReynolds had agreed to hear their motion for a new trial, Johnson's execution would have been delayed automatically pending the arguments on the petition and any other appeals. But now the defense attorneys would have to work at a fevered pace to file the appropriate petitions and supporting documents with the Tennessee Supreme Court. Because Johnson was indigent, the judge could have given the lawyers a copy of the transcript of the trial at the state's expense. Now they had to raise money to get the document. It would not be cheap. Time was running out. Johnson's scheduled hanging was only twenty-eight days away.

The lawyers hoped that black churches and business leaders would step forward to donate money to pay for the appeal. They spread the word that this case was not simply about Ed Johnson and his innocence. Nor was it even about race, Parden wrote in an article in the Atlanta black newspaper *Voice of the People*.

For the sake of justice, we take up this cause. Not just because Johnson is a Negro, but because he is a man who has rights God and man have granted him under the law, and because the evidence against Johnson did not satisfy the opinions of many men, white and black, of his guilt.

This is a state and nation of laws and all men by nature are equally entitled to life, liberty and the pursuit of happiness. The laws neither favor the white man nor suppress the Negro. We rise up in righteous indignation against the tyrannical use of those laws against a human being. We fight for Ed Johnson because the declaration of equal rights to all does not apply only to the white man. The Constitution protects all men.

Parden and Hutchins quickly realized the black community would not be offering them much support in their endeavor. The plea to black ministers for money to pay for the trial transcripts resulted in no donations. The case had been so criticized by leading white people in the community that black leaders hesitated to do anything that could be viewed as helping the culprit.

By Thursday afternoon, February 15, the lawyers knew they were alone in their fight. Times were about to get considerably tougher. Many of their longtime white friends and associates shunned them. But their biggest shock was that their neighbors in the black community turned their backs as well.

In forty-eight hours, Parden and Hutchins had become outcasts in their city and from their own race. The word was out: if you're black and charged with a crime, and if you desire leniency from the sheriff, prosecutor, or judge, do not hire either of these black lawyers. Potential clients went elsewhere for representation. Current clients searched for new lawyers. The most devastating blow to Parden came when his pastor, the Reverend W. B. Fleming of the St. James Baptist Church, criticized him.

"Now for these colored attorneys to undertake to reopen the case is calculated to stir up trouble between the races," the preacher told the *Chattanooga News*. "The best element of the colored people do not approve of reopening the case and the colored lawyers who are advocating it are making a serious mistake, not only for themselves but for the community in which they live."

Attempts by Parden and Hutchins to prepare the appeal were being thwarted, or at least delayed, by court officials at every turn. The court stenographer required that the money be paid to him in advance. In previous cases, he had accepted partial payment, with a credit arrangement for the remainder. At the clerk's office, secretaries said the case file was still in the judge's chambers and they could not retrieve it. The lawyers needed the actual court file to confirm dates, read motions filed by the prosecution and defense attorneys, and examine the written orders issued by the judge.

The lawyers finally got enough money Friday morning to pay the stenographer. However, court transcripts filed on appeal must have the signature of the judge certifying that the documents of the proceedings were authentic, true, and accurate. And an hour before the court reporter turned the transcripts over to the attorneys, Judge McReynolds quickly and quietly slipped out of town on a previously unannounced week-long vacation to Florida.

Tuesday morning, February 20, Parden boarded a train to Nashville. The lawyers, working with Shepherd, had prepared a writ of error claiming that Johnson's trial was flawed and that he deserved a new one. They had also drafted a writ of supersedeas, which asked the court to take emergency steps to postpone the execution of their client.

Later that day, Parden hand-delivered the documents to the state supreme court. The writ of error focused on three primary points:

(1) The evidence in the case did not warrant a conviction. Parden argued that the jury should have found Johnson not guilty. The law in Tennessee and most states permitted state appellate courts to reverse a lower-court conviction if the state justices found that the evidence during the trial actually demonstrated the defendant's innocence rather than his guilt. During the trial stage, prosecutors were saddled with the burden of proving the defendant guilty beyond a reasonable doubt. Once the judgment of conviction was rendered by the jury and confirmed by the trial judge, the burden of proving guilt or innocence for the purpose of the appeal automatically

shifted from the state to the defendant. Because it was extremely difficult for defense attorneys in any case to prove from the evidence introduced during the trial that the defendant was really innocent, very few guilty verdicts were overturned.

(2)   A lynch-mob mentality permeated the entire trial and placed undue pressure on the jury to convict the defendant. In the Tennessee Constitution, the "law of the land" clause guarantees every person facing criminal charges the right to a fair trial and to due process. Parden claimed that the lynching attempts on Johnson's life had so contaminated the community, and thus the jury pool, that Johnson could not receive a fair trial in Hamilton County.

(3)   It was improper to allow a juror to rush toward the defendant during the trial and scream, "If I could get at him, I would tear his heart out." The action of the juror, Parden claimed, proved that the jury was biased against the defendant and was being motivated not by the evidence in the case but by emotion. The incident demonstrated just how tainted and unfair the trial was against Johnson.

If the state Supreme Court agreed to review the case, it wouldn't hear the arguments until the September term. That meant Johnson's death sentence would be automatically stayed until the fall. The justices would then only have to find that one of the three claims was applicable in order to reverse Johnson's conviction.

Most lawyers in Chattanooga believed Parden and Hutchins had no chance of prevailing. The Tennessee Supreme Court was very conservative and extremely law-and-order in outlook. The state justices had not reversed a death sentence in a decade. Neither Parden nor Shepherd could remember the last time the court had stopped the execution of a black man. Yet they had to continue preparing their arguments just in case the justices agreed to hear their petition.

On Saturday, March 3, the state's highest court issued its unanimous decision.

STATE OF TENNESSEE V. ED JOHNSON

The record in this case had been presented to the court with a petition for writ of error and supersedeas. Upon examination, we find that though a death sentence was pronounced upon the petitioner, yet, the motion for new trial was not acted on by the trial judge and the record does not contain a bill of exceptions. In view of this, we have given the technical record a most scrutinizing inspection to see if serious errors were there to be discovered, but have been unable to find any.

We are unable to find any error which will authorize the issuance of a writ of supersedeas, as a writ of error would be of no avail without that writ, it is denied. The petitioner, however, can file with the clerk the record and a writ of error will be issued to him by that officer, as a matter of right under the statute.

This cause comes to be heard upon a petition for writ of supersedeas upon consideration where of the court declines to grant said writ and the petition is therefor dismissed.

It is ordered that the court stand adjourned until Saturday morning, March 10, 1906 at 9:30 o'clock.

Tennessee Chief Justice W. D. BEARD

Without the writ of supersedeas, which would have prevented Johnson's execution, the right to pursue the writ of error was useless. Johnson would already be dead. So certain were Sheriff Shipp and Judge McReynolds that Johnson would be executed as scheduled on March 13 that they ordered deputies to begin stretching out the hangman's noose. To do so, the officers tied one end of the rope to the wooden gallows and weighted down the loose end with a 100-pound rock. Their goal was to eliminate all the kinks and slack in the inch-thick hemp.

Parden, Hutchins, and Shepherd had prayed for victory but expected rejection. Even as Hutchins prepared to present the defense's case to the state Supreme Court, Parden and Shepherd worked on an alternative means of saving their client.

Wednesday afternoon, March 7, the sheriff boarded the train for Knoxville to get Johnson and bring him back to Chattanooga. Shipp, sitting in the all-white first-class cabin, didn't realize it then, but Parden was on the same train. The lawyer was seated in the general boarding section for any person who was not white. The train offered no first-class amenities to black passengers.

Three hours later, they arrived in Knoxville. Parden stepped from the train and went to the Knox County Jail to get his client's approval of the petition. From there, Parden walked to the United States Courthouse to ask a federal judge to intervene in the case. In a nine-page document called a "petition for writ of habeas corpus," Parden contended his client had not received a fair trial, was illegally facing a sentence of death, and had been denied several of his federal constitutional rights.

Parden filed the petition under the Habeas Corpus Act of 1867, which Congress passed to allow defendants in state criminal cases to seek relief in federal court under certain circumstances. The law allowed any persons tried in a state court to seek a federal judge's review of their cases if they believed they had been imprisoned in violation of their federal constitutional rights. The U.S. Supreme Court held in 1895 that federal habeas corpus relief was available in any case in which the state court lacked jurisdiction, or in which the state court had deprived the defendant of due process of law or equal protection under the law.

Though it may have been easy for criminal defendants to appeal their conviction under the federal statute, it was nearly impossible for them to win relief. Neither the U.S. Supreme Court nor Congress had set down exactly what federal constitutional rights belonged to individuals. In fact, the justices had declared that the Bill of Rights was not binding on the state-court system in criminal cases. The justices did not recognize a criminal defendant's right to effective counsel, right against self-incrimination, right against illegal search and seizure, or right to a fair trial until decades later. The Habeas Corpus Act followed by Parden also did not permit federal judges to reconsider the evidence in the original trial presented to the jury, and did not allow the jurists to pass judgment on the defendant's guilt or innocence.

As a result, most trial lawyers believed federal habeas petitions were a waste of time. Many attorneys never availed their clients of the procedure, since the petition was almost always denied. In 1906, it was viewed as nothing more than a tactic to delay punishment.

Parden contended that the primary issue in the Johnson case was—as in most criminal cases—whether the defendant had received "due process" under the law. Under the Fourteenth Amendment to the U.S. Constitution, every person is entitled to due process. But in 1906, the federal court's interpretation of the due-process clause was very narrow—a problem Parden knew he had to overcome. A defendant received due process if the criminal charges were based on an existing law, if the trial was conducted as procedurally required under state law, and if the defendant was given the opportunity to be heard during the trial. Law-enforcement tactics such as beating a confession from a witness or defendant, presenting evidence known to be false, or suppressing evidence pointing to the innocence of the defendant were not considered violations of a state criminal defendant's rights in 1906. So weak and ineffective was the due-process clause that Parden could not find a single case over the previous forty years in which the U.S. Supreme Court or the federal courts had reversed a state-court conviction on the basis of it. Even so, Parden was convinced that the facts in the Johnson case would be the exception.

Employing the equal-protection clause of the Fourteenth Amendment was just as difficult and impotent in reversing state-court convictions. Parden could find only one case since the Civil War in which the U.S. Supreme Court had reversed a state-court criminal conviction based on an equal-protection claim. But that one case appeared to give Parden the opening he needed.

In 1886, the high court ruled that states and counties that systematically kept black people off juries by not putting their names into the jury pool were violating the equal-protection clause. Unlike the Bill of Rights, the Fourteenth Amendment specifically did apply to all state courts. And Parden was confident the Johnson case involved the very cause of action the justices had twenty years earlier declared illegal— the intentional exclusion of black people from juries. Of the thirty-six people summoned for jury duty in the Johnson case, not one was black. Neither Parden nor Hutchins nor Shepherd could remember a single instance when a black person had been called to serve on a jury. This was proof that black people were being excluded from the jury pool, they argued. This issue alone should have been enough to encourage the federal courts to review their case.

The petition also claimed the state court had violated numerous other rights belonging to Johnson, including his right to a fair and impartial trial, his right against self-incrimination, and his right to appeal the conviction. However, the lawyers knew that these claims were a long shot. The federal courts had never recognized that people on trial in state court had such rights under the U.S. Constitution. But because the facts were so egregious in the Johnson case, Parden and Hutchins believed that the time could be right for the courts to recognize additional federal constitutional rights to defendants in state criminal cases. The lawyers knew they were seeking what amounted to a legal revolution: they were trying to change how criminal cases would forever be tried in the United States.

SHERIFF SHIPP MADE several stops before making his way to the Knox County Jail to get his prisoner. He visited with old friends from his days in the Confederate Army. He had lunch with a friend of the family. When he arrived at the jail, he expected to find Ed Johnson in handcuffs, ready to be transported back to Chattanooga to be hanged.

Instead, Shipp stood face to face with a United States marshal. Johnson wasn't going anywhere. By orders of the federal judge, the prisoner was being kept in the Knox County Jail. Already confused, Shipp became even more dismayed when the federal agent handed the sheriff a nine-page petition filed by Parden and a one-page order written by U.S. District Judge Charles Dickens Clark.

ED JOHNSON V. STATE OF TENNESSEE

On presentation of this petition, it is ordered that a copy thereof, and of this order, be delivered to or served on the State District Attorney General, the Hon. Matt Whitaker, at once, as notice that he show cause, if he chooses to do so, against the petition and the writ applied for, on or before 12 o'clock, Saturday, March 10th, in the United States Circuit Court Room in the Custom House at Knoxville, Tennessee, until which time action on the petition is reserved. The petition, and especially the charges as to the conduct of the Jury Commissioner, may, and if disputed, must be answered.

Done this March 3rd, 1906
C. D. CLARK

"What does this mean?" Shipp asked.

"It means you may not have the prisoner," responded the marshal. "He is now officially in the custody of the federal courts pending the hearing next week. I am under orders to have him remain housed here until the conclusion of the hearing."

The sheriff was shocked. There had been no speculation that the lawyers would take their case to federal court. These local authorities had never experienced such a legal maneuver by criminal-defense attorneys. This was the first time a state prisoner from Hamilton County had filed a federal habeas corpus petition since Shipp, Whitaker, and McReynolds had been elected to office.

"Can a federal judge do this? Does he have the power to interfere like this?" the sheriff inquired. The Knox County sheriff, in whose jail Johnson was lodged, shrugged his shoulders. The federal marshal remained silent. Shipp took the court papers and shook his head in disbelief. An hour later, he was on the train headed back to Chattanooga without a prisoner.

CHAPTER NINE

WRIT OF HABEAS CORPUS

NOAH PARDEN WALKED into the U.S. District Court in Knoxville on Saturday, March 10, with great confidence. With Styles Hutchins and Lewis Shepherd at his side, the lawyer placed his old leather briefcase on the dark wooden table at the front of the large, majestic courtroom. Every pew was packed. Half of those in attendance were black, and they all sat on the same side of the courtroom—in the rows behind Parden and the defense team. A few white people were scattered in with them.

Seated directly beside the defense lawyers were Hamilton County Assistant District Attorney E. S. Daniels, District Attorney Matt Whitaker, and Criminal Court Judge Sam D. McReynolds. The benches behind them were filled with their supporters, who were exclusively white men. Sheriff Shipp and two of his deputies sat in the first row.

Upon entering the courtroom, Parden approached the prosecution table to say hello. But none of the Chattanooga court officials responded or even looked at the black lawyer. They refused to recognize he was there.

The biggest surprise for Judge McReynolds and the other state officials came when they saw Shepherd join Parden at the defense table. They had no idea the former Hamilton County judge was assisting the black lawyers. Immediately, they suspected Shepherd was behind the entire plot to stall the execution of Johnson. After all, it was

Shepherd who had criticized the judge and prosecutors during the closing arguments of the Johnson trial.

McReynolds was furious. Not only was he outraged that the criminal conviction had been appealed into the federal courts, but he was convinced that Shepherd was doing it simply to embarrass him—that the proceeding was designed to humiliate him as a judge by putting his rulings and his handling of the Johnson case on trial. He regretted the day he had appointed the flamboyant lawyer to the Johnson case, and he vowed never to give Shepherd such courtesies again. The language of the petition was strongly worded and highly critical of McReynolds and Whitaker, and they blamed Shepherd for all of it.

At that moment, the U.S. marshal opened the side door of the courtroom.

> MARSHAL: All rise. Hear ye, hear ye, the United States Circuit Court for the Northern Division of the Eastern District of Tennessee is now in session. The Honorable C. D. Clark presiding. All those having business with this court draw nigh and ye shall be heard. God save the United States and this honorable court. Be seated.
>
> JUDGE CLARK: Mr. Clerk, will you call the case before us?
>
> CLERK: Ed Johnson versus the State of Tennessee and the Criminal Court of Hamilton County.

Judge Clark told the marshals to escort the defendant into the courtroom. Johnson was seated beside Shepherd. With the formalities out of the way, the judge instructed the defense to make any opening remarks. Parden stepped to the podium to deliver a summary of the accusations against the state. The lawyer's statement closely followed the written petition he had filed in the case. His presentation resembled a Sunday-morning sermon more than an oral argument on the law in a federal court. He waved his arms. He pointed fingers. He whispered, then shouted. His voice was filled with outrage and bewilderment. At key moments, he would pause and simply shake his head in disgust. Above all, he told the story of Ed Johnson and how he had been railroaded through the Hamilton County criminal-justice system.

> We contend, Your Honor, that he is illegally restrained of his liberty by the sheriffs of Hamilton and Knox counties.
>
> He was illegally and improperly put on trial for the offense of rape and illegally and improperly convicted thereof and sentenced to death.

In a very theatrical style, Parden told the judge about the lynch mob that had attacked the jail the night of Johnson's arrest. He praised Sheriff Shipp and the deputies for their "hours of bravery and strenuous resistance in beating back the infuriated mob." He praised the lawmen for suppressing two subsequent attempts by the mob to raid the jail.

Parden then surprised the state authorities by telling Judge Clark about a secret meeting called by Judge McReynolds about a week before the trial. Present at this clandestine meeting were Whitaker, Shipp, the mayor of Chattanooga, and two of the defense lawyers appointed by the judge to represent Johnson. The meeting, according to Parden, was to determine what actions should be taken to prevent mob violence.

Judge McReynolds and the other state officials were astounded. How had Parden learned about the meeting? The information must have come from Shepherd. They were outraged and distraught.

> In that meeting, Your Honor, defense counsel informed the judge and the attorney general that the defendant could not get a fair and impartial jury in Hamilton County. The excitement against him was so high that he could not get a fair trial and that it was his duty to apply for a change of venue to another county or they ought to make application to continue the case until the next term of court, trusting that the excitement and prejudice against the prisoner would subside.
>
> The judge informed the petitioner's counsel that he was not going to grant a change of venue and he was going to try the case on the day fixed.
>
> Petitioner's counsel were advised at that meeting that, if they made an application for a change of venue or to continue

the case, the mob would again attack the jail, with more success than had attended their former effort, and would succeed in murdering the petitioner.

Petitioner's counsel were alarmed by the threats made almost ex cathedra and solely on account of the fear aroused by those threats they did not make an application for a change of venue or continuance.

To help calm the lynch-mob mentality, the officials at the meeting had agreed to tell a reporter from the *Chattanooga Times* that Johnson would be put on trial immediately in Chattanooga and that there would be no further delays in the case, Parden told Judge Clark. He said the judge and sheriff hoped these measures would satisfy the agitators. However, this meeting and its results prejudged any motion for a change of venue or a motion for a continuance of the trial. The secret meeting was not part of the open and public trial, and an obvious violation of the defendant's right to due process.

Parden said police officers surrounded the courthouse every day of the trial, preventing people not associated with the case from going into the building. As a result, he said, Johnson's mother, father, sister, pastor, and other friends were shut out. Only a few select members of the local bar and supporters of Judge McReynolds and Sheriff Shipp were permitted in the courtroom during the trial, said the lawyer, his voice rising to a zealous pitch.

The young lady upon whom the rape had been committed testified that she believed the petitioner was her assailant, and thereupon a juror burst out crying, and with a wild gesture towards where the prisoner was standing, said: "If I could just get at him, I would tear his heart out."

At least two of his fellow jurors remonstrated with him, but the presiding judge did not rebuke the juror by word or gesture or disapproving look.

The makeup of the jury was Parden's next target. The lawyer said the Constitution entitled every criminal defendant to be tried by a jury of his peers. Johnson was not afforded that right. Parden reminded Judge Clark that the U.S. Supreme Court had ruled in 1886 that it was a violation of the Fourteenth Amendment's equal-protection clause for states and counties to exclude black people systematically and intentionally from being called as jurors. Yet, he said, that was exactly what had happened in this case and in every case being tried in Hamilton County, a community where one out of every three people was black but where none ever sat as jurors.

> The jury commissioners illegally refused to put the names of Negroes in the jury box, although there were 5,000 Negro males between the age of twenty-one and seventy in Hamilton County, and more than 3,000 of whom are eligible for jury duty in respect to their intelligence, upright character, and property.
>
> The jury commissioners arbitrarily refused to put the names of any of them in the jury box, or if two or three of their names got in the box, it was an accident which was remedied by the commissioners and judge as soon as the fact was discovered.
>
> The names of these 3,000 eligible and qualified persons were excluded from the jury box solely because of the fact that they belonged to the Negro race.

Parden told Judge Clark this was not by chance. Thirty-six men had been summoned for jury duty in the Johnson case; all were white. If there was any jury that local authorities were going to keep black people off of, it was this one, the lawyer said.

Parden's final point may have been the most emotionally charged. He said that the three lawyers appointed to defend Johnson had abandoned their client after the trial. As a result, the defendant was denied his constitutional right to appeal his conviction. The lawyer said the three trial attorneys had done the best they could under the circumstances. However, the attorneys felt the pressure of the lynch mob when they decided not to seek a new trial for Johnson, thereby forgoing his opportunity to challenge the verdict on appeal.

True, the lawyers did give their client the final say, he said. The three attorneys told Johnson he could accept the verdict and be executed by the state of Tennessee. Or he could appeal and the lynch mob would take him from the jail, beat him, and murder him. Plus, the mob might kill other black inmates at the jail while they were there to get him. Parden said those were not real choices.

"Like a lamb being led to the slaughter, he was dumb," Parden told the court.

Believing that Johnson's three court-appointed lawyers had abandoned their client, Parden said, he and Hutchins had stepped forward to take up the appeal. However, he said Judge McReynolds had refused to accept their motion for a new trial. The judge also tricked them into a procedural snafu by telling the black lawyers not to file their petition until the following day and then ruling that the time limit for making a motion for a new trial had expired the day before.

With sweat streaming down his face, Parden thanked Judge Clark for his indulgence and returned to his seat in the courtroom.

Hamilton County District Attorney Matt Whitaker gathered his papers and walked to the podium. After introducing himself to the court, he immediately launched into a full-scale attack on Parden, Hutchins, and Shepherd. He denied every single point in their petition. "These charges are utterly false, without foundation, and made evidently of a desire to misrepresent the judiciary, and made with a malignant purpose and a wicked heart."

In a decidedly spirited tone, the prosecutor told Judge Clark that Johnson had received one of the fairest trials ever performed in Hamilton County. Judge McReynolds had appointed the best lawyers. The defense attorneys were given all of the state's evidence several days before trial and were allowed to call any witness to testify that they desired. Whitaker adamantly denied that the three court-appointed lawyers were ever threatened or intimidated. No one discouraged them from seeking a change of venue or a delay in the trial.

Whitaker said the statement by Parden that a juror had threatened the defendant during the trial was unequivocally false. He said no jurors had to be restrained and the words "If I could get at him, I would tear his heart out," were never spoken. What did happen, the prosecutor contended, was that a juror, in a low-key voice, told another juror, "If I knew he was [guilty], I would tear his heart out."

Finally, Whitaker blasted Parden for making untrue and malicious statements about McReynolds. The judge had done nothing to discourage Parden and Hutchins from filing their motion for a new trial. Whitaker said it was the lawyers' fault they waited too long to notify the court that they wanted to seek a new trial and appeal the verdict. Judge McReynolds, he said, was simply following the rules of the court in denying their motion. Besides, the entire proceeding in federal court was nothing more than a delay tactic designed to give Johnson a few more days of life. The claims made by the defense attorneys had no basis in fact or law, the prosecutor argued, and therefore the petition should be immediately dismissed.

With opening statements out of the way, Judge Clark told the lawyers representing Johnson to call their first witness. He was Foster V. Brown, one of the three Chattanooga lawyers appointed by Judge McReynolds after the trial to advise Johnson's three trial lawyers regarding the merit of an appeal of the conviction and death sentence. Brown said one of the other two lawyers appointed to consult with the trial team believed an appeal would lead to a lynching.

SHEPHERD: What was the statement by the lawyer as to the effect upon Johnson if an appeal was prosecuted?

BROWN: He had seen a man that morning whom he said was a good citizen and opposed to mob violence, but the man said if Johnson took an appeal that he himself would head a mob to lynch him.

SHEPHERD: Did the lawyer say anything about the action of the police in having protected Johnson up to that time, but that they would withdraw their protection from him if an appeal was prosecuted?

BROWN: He said someone in high authority in police matters stated that if Johnson took an appeal the police department would not afford the sheriff the protection which the police had theretofore afforded.

That was the thing that impressed me, because I live near the jail and I saw how powerless everything was unless the police were there.

We were thoroughly impressed that to attempt an appeal meant that Johnson would be mobbed, and the statement was made that it not only involved the lynching of this man, but of others that were in the jail.

Under cross-examination, Brown said the three trial lawyers, including Shepherd, expressed the opinion that there were no errors in the record and that an appeal would most likely be futile. He said the other lawyers depended heavily on Shepherd's guidance and input.

WHITAKER: How much experience do you have in the criminal law?

BROWN: Not very much.

WHITAKER: Judge Shepherd is regarded as the leading criminal lawyer in Chattanooga, isn't he?

BROWN: Unquestionably.

SHEPHERD: The best lawyer of any other kind, too.

WHITAKER: After everything was talked over concerning the case, what had been done by the judge, and the jury and everybody connected with the trial, you all came to the conclusion that it would effect no good purpose if an appeal was taken?

BROWN: Yes, but I will qualify that. Judge Shepherd and I said we did not believe it would avail anything if appealed, but I would not say I would not have taken an appeal but for the peculiar situation of the public mind at that time.

Shepherd's next witness was W.G.M. Thomas, one of his co-counsels during the Johnson trial. Shepherd asked Thomas to tell Judge Clark about the private meeting between McReynolds, Whitaker, Shipp, and others that took place a few days before the trial. Thomas said he had attended such a meeting, during which he suggested to the others that the trial should be delayed so that the defense attorneys could better prepare and the racial tension in the community might settle down.

SHEPHERD: State whether in the meeting we had with Judge McReynolds and the attorney general whether those gentlemen said it would be dangerous to the life of Ed Johnson if we made an application for a change of venue?

THOMAS: Yes. If we made any dilatory move, it would inflame the spirit of the people.

SHEPHERD: State whether you mentioned that you felt it to be your duty to make an application for a change of venue and for a continuance of the case on account of this feeling?

THOMAS: We did not make this move because we were afraid there would be a lynching if we did. The conditions were such that, in my judgment, it was unsafe. If we made a public application for an extension of time or for a change of venue, I understood that the people hearing of this would rise up and we could not avoid a mob.

SHEPHERD: What did Mr. Whitaker say about having had an interview on the Sunday night before the trial with Governor Cox?

THOMAS: He reported to us that troops would not be furnished, that the governor said the case ought not be tried or, if tried, it ought to be tried in Nashville.

SHEPHERD: Tell us about the meeting with the three lawyers Judge McReynolds appointed to advise us.

THOMAS: I wanted to know whether anything could be accomplished by appealing. In other words, was there reversible error in the record and that by taking the case to the Supreme Court whether or not anything could be accomplished by it, or was it merely a question of continuing a human life?

The lawyers present gave their opinion that the lawyers representing a defendant in a criminal case did not owe to him the duty of merely continuing his life, and if an appeal would mean merely a continuance of a human life, without more, that

that was not the duty of a lawyer representing a criminal, and, second, that there was no reversible error as discovered in such a way as to grant a new trial, and in the third place that an appeal would mean a lynching.

SHEPHERD: What was said with respect to whether or not a lynching would occur if we took an appeal?

THOMAS: If we prosecuted an appeal, the jail would be raided and we would have another uprising in the city.

SHEPHERD: State whether or not the lawyers present gave evidence of what they had heard.

THOMAS: One lawyer had heard at least twenty-five men that morning say that an appeal would mean the lynching of this defendant.

SHEPHERD: Was anything said about them going to lynch the lawyers for the defendant if they persisted in an appeal?

THOMAS: Yes. It was said a dilatory movement would wind up lynching the judge, the lawyers, and everyone else.

Thomas told the judge that he had practiced law in Chattanooga for two decades. However, he had never seen a case in which a black person was in the jury pool.

The next witness was J. P. Pemberton, the deputy clerk of the Circuit Court of Hamilton County. He was the person responsible for summoning all jurors for criminal and civil trials in the county. Pemberton said they kept about 4,000 active names in the jury box at all times. However, he could only remember one instance in which a black person had ever been called for jury duty, and he said that man was "almost white."

District Attorney Whitaker was the next to testify. He denied that any threats or statements of intimidation were made against the three lawyers who defended Johnson at trial. No one had discouraged or prevented the defense attorneys from seeking a delay in the trial or a change of venue. Whitaker said he personally knew that three black people had served on juries in Hamilton County during the past several years, though he could not give one name or cite which case. Finally, he said Johnson was an adult who had made the decision not to appeal his conviction, and now the defendant must live with that.

Judge McReynolds was the last witness. From the start, it was obvious that bitter feelings existed between him and Shepherd. As soon as McReynolds stated his name and official position for the record, he turned to Judge Clark and asked to make a statement before answering any questions from Shepherd. The federal judge agreed.

> I hope the court will pardon me but there are some things in that petition that apply solely to me as an official. I want to say that they are statements that are maliciously false.
>
> Anyone can make infamous and slanderous statements like those in the petition, but it is a different matter to prove them.
>
> When they charge that I, outside of my courtroom, said I would deny a continuance or change of venue, they utter an infamous falsehood, and I believe the man that wrote it knew it was false when he wrote it.
>
> It is also charged that I refused Johnson's father and mother admission to the trial. That is also false. At that time, I did not know even that Johnson had any father and mother.

For his part, Shepherd said that none of the claims in the petition were intended to offend Judge McReynolds personally. However, he refused to withdraw or apologize for the allegations. Instead, he continued to ask pointed questions of the criminal-court judge. Specifically, he queried the judge at length about black people's being denied seats on juries. He also explored the judge's refusal to allow Parden and Hutchins to seek a new trial for Johnson.

> SHEPHERD: What about the charge about getting Negroes off the jury?
>
> JUDGE McREYNOLDS: All I know is that I have appointed three good men as I thought we could find as jury commissioners. We have absolutely nothing to do with the drawing of the juries. When we want a jury, we make an order that the jury

commissioners draw so many jurors and I have absolutely nothing to do with it. I want to say that I have heard the report circulated that there was a Negro by the name of Will Campbell on a jury.

SHEPHERD: What about other Negroes?

JUDGE McREYNOLDS: I do not remember seeing any Negro there on the jury, but I think there was one other that asked to be excused on account of being hard of hearing.

SHEPHERD: Why did you deny the motion for a new trial filed by attorney Parden?

JUDGE McREYNOLDS: I never heard anything about any other attorneys getting into this case until Monday morning. At that time, Parden and Hutchins came to my office and said they wanted to relieve me of the responsibility of this man being hung.

Hutchins said, "Judge, you will give us thirty days to make out a bill of exceptions, won't you?" Parden said, "I want to have a talk with you and the attorney general to see if we cannot arrange to appeal this case without bringing Johnson back from Knoxville."

I told them I would not discuss this matter privately with anyone and Mr. Whitaker is not here today. Parden said he didn't care to talk to Mr. Daniels.

I said they must bear in mind that you must give such notice on the first day that a motion for a new trial will be filed, which is within three days thereafter. You must file your notice stating specifically all the grounds to be relied on.

Hutchins then said, "Sunday is not counted, tomorrow will be in plenty of time." I never said a word, as it was not my duty to advise him.

The hearing lasted well into the night. Both sides delivered strong closing arguments. Parden said the testimony of Judge McReynolds and J. P. Pemberton—that they could only remember one or two Negroes serving on juries during the past seven years—was proof that black people were being systematically excluded from jury duty. And he said Thomas had provided sufficient evidence that the original trial team did not file for a continuance or change of venue, or file an appeal, because they felt threatened or intimidated by Judge McReynolds, Sheriff Shipp, and the lynch mob. Those two witnesses provided sufficient verification that Johnson's right to due process and equal protection had been violated, Parden said.

Parden said there was also a basic unfairness in how the crime of rape was prosecuted. Between 1900 and 1906, the lawyer told Judge Clark, seventeen women had come forward to report they had been raped or sexually attacked. Of these, fourteen were black women. In those cases, only four men were ever arrested. Two of those men were released without receiving any punishment, and the other two were awarded short prison sentences. The cases involving the three white women were handled much differently, Parden said. In each case, an arrest was made. All three villains were black men. All three were put on trial. Two of them were sentenced to die, and the third was given a twenty-one-year prison term.

"The law is not being applied equally," Parden argued. "People are being treated differently in Chattanooga because of the color of their skin. And that is a violation of the Fourteenth Amendment's equal-protection clause. The federal government must step in and correct the situation."

District Attorney Whitaker's closing statements focused almost entirely on the separation of powers between the state and federal court systems. The prosecutor argued that there was no evidence that any of Johnson's federal constitutional rights were violated. The prisoner had the chance to appeal to the Tennessee Supreme Court, Whitaker said, but he knowingly waived those rights. The case belonged in state court and the petition should be denied, he said.

After each side had its say, Judge Clark announced he was going to retire to his chambers to consider the matter. Many people thought he would simply issue a ruling within the next day or so. But he told the lawyers and those in the courtroom that he would return with a decision later that evening, because the matter needed to be expedited. The judge suggested everyone get a bite of dinner while he reviewed the law and considered the arguments and testimony presented to him.

For eight hours, the two sides had done battle. This day would cause a rift between McReynolds and Shepherd that would never be mended. The judge perceived the defense lawyer's attacks on how the trial had been handled as a personal attack against him. It was the first time any lawyer had challenged his competence as a jurist. Shepherd felt that he was merely doing his duty as a lawyer in defending a client, and that his ethics required him to pursue this on appeal. He believed Judge McReynolds had made mistakes and Johnson deserved a new trial. Despite attempts by Shepherd to state publicly that he meant no personal criticism of Judge McReynolds, the two men would never socialize together again.

Similarly, Parden and Hutchins realized their future in the legal profession in Chattanooga was bleak. Their relationships with the judge and prosecutors were strained even prior to the Johnson case. Now they doubted they or their clients would ever be treated fairly in court. Unlike Shepherd's, their status within the legal community and power structure might not withstand a feud with Judge McReynolds. They wondered what would happen if their clients learned that the county's judge hated them. They might never be hired again.

Three hours after he escaped into his chambers, Judge Clark returned to the courtroom. The time was 12:47 a.m. Despite the late hour, it seemed not a single person had gone home: every seat in the courtroom was full. The white people sitting behind McReynolds and the prosecutors were confident that the federal judge would rule in their favor and that they would take Ed Johnson back to Chattanooga with them to be hanged. The black people who packed the pews behind the defense attorneys were equally convinced Johnson would be declared a free man that night.

Judge Clark was poised to disappoint both sides.

"There is an implication here of two things," he said, speaking very slowly. "That there was great haste in this trial, and that the trial was had under a kind of species of apprehension on the part of the counsel, and that counsel were to an extent terrorized on account of the fear of a mob."

The judge said he did not think there was sufficient evidence for him to rule that black people were illegally excluded from sitting on juries in Hamilton County. As to the other claims, he said they were beyond his control. Judge Clark said Ed Johnson's trial very well could have been a sham. The problem, he said, was that the Sixth Amendment to the U.S. Constitution, which guarantees a criminal defendant the right to a fair trial, does not apply to state-court cases. The federal judge said that, even if the allegations that the jury was biased, the trial lawyers were intimidated, and Johnson was improperly stripped of his right to appeal were true, he had no authority to intervene. Only Congress or the Supreme Court could give the federal courts the power to take appropriate action in a state criminal case, he said, and they had chosen not to do so.

Just as the Hamilton County authorities were smiling at each other and prepared to erupt in self-congratulatory praise, Judge Clark tempered their victory. He did not have the jurisdiction over the procedural and evidentiary aspects of the Johnson case, but he believed he did have the power to issue a stay of execution in the case to permit Johnson's lawyers to seek an appeal to the United States Supreme Court. The March 13 hanging was postponed until at least March 23, he said. Ten days should be enough time to allow Parden and the other lawyers to prepare a petition for the high court.

CHAPTER TEN

THE SUPREME COURT INTERVENES

DESPITE NOT GOING to bed until well after 2:00 a.m., Sheriff Shipp awoke before dawn that Sunday. He showered, shaved, and put on the same clothes he wore the day before. An overnight stay in Knoxville had not been in his plans. As the sun slowly peeked over the distant Smoky Mountains, Shipp and three of his deputies walked to the Knox County Jail, a few blocks away. Per Shipp's instructions the night before, jailers had Ed Johnson dressed at 6:30 a.m. and prepared to be transported back to Chattanooga.

The sheriff and his entourage met Judge McReynolds, District Attorney Whitaker, and others at the train depot for the three-hour trip home. Although they had won the federal-court battle the night before, none of the men were in a particularly good mood. They still felt the sting of the public charges made against them. And even though Judge Clark had ruled in the state's favor, the public officials were extremely unhappy with his decision to stay Johnson's execution for ten days pending a possible appeal to the U.S. Supreme Court.

The very idea that the U.S. Supreme Court would ever entertain an appeal by Johnson's two black lawyers was considered preposterous. The stay was nothing more than a delay tactic, a maneuver by Parden and Hutchins designed to give their client a few extra days of life, Shipp told the others. But what could be done, the sheriff asked, as he brandished the order by Judge Clark requiring that Johnson remain in Shipp's custody until March 23.

McReynolds was even more upset. The realization that a federal judge had intervened and superseded his order, setting the day and time of execution, left him outraged. He took Judge Clark's order—albeit a mere ten days—as a personal insult, and thought it demonstrated contempt by the federal courts for the authority and jurisdiction of the state-court system.

As the deputies supervised the prisoner in one car, Shipp, McReynolds, Whitaker, and a handful of Chattanooga lawyers huddled around a table in the dining car. Sipping coffee, tea, and juice, the members of the group contemplated their next move. Their options seemed limited. They could accept Judge Clark's order and wait ten days to hang Johnson. Or they could appeal the ruling to the U.S. Supreme Court, claiming a federal judge did not have the authority to intervene in a state criminal case—especially when there was no evidence or finding by the federal judge that the defendant's U.S. constitutional rights had been violated. Their final option was simply to ignore the federal court order, publicly declare that it was illegal, and execute their prisoner as scheduled.

Judge McReynolds said that had happened only a few years earlier, in a murder case in Georgia involving an Indian. He told his colleagues that lawyers for the Indian defendant had appealed to the Supreme Court for intervention after the trial resulted in a conviction. The federal justices agreed with the defense attorneys, ruling that the state should turn the Indian over to federal authorities because the alleged crime had been committed on an Indian reservation. But only days after the Supreme Court order, Georgia officials decided to ignore the federal court mandate publicly by ordering that the defendant be executed immediately, and he was.

Everyone in the train car wanted to know what had happened to the Georgia officials. Did the federal government take action against them for violating the Supreme Court order? Were they punished in some fashion? McReynolds said the federal government offered no response, and the action of the state authorities was never criticized by the justices. Nothing was ever done about the matter. The story raised the eyebrows of every person in the cabin.

But McReynolds said that each possible solution to the Johnson case was problematic. None of the officials minded waiting extra days before carrying out their revenge on the defendant. But they—especially McReynolds—were indignant that the stay was the result of a federal judge's sticking his nationalistic gavel in their state-court system. Besides, it was an unacceptable precedent to accept federal-court intervention in a state-court case. However, appealing Judge Clark's order could take weeks or even months, and would likely cause the execution to be delayed even longer. The idea of ignoring the federal-court order intrigued them, but no one spoke out for such affirmative action.

For Shipp, the problem was more immediate. He held in his hand two separate court orders. One was from Judge McReynolds instructing him to hang Johnson on March 13, which was just two days away. And, of course, there was the contradictory order from Judge Clark telling the sheriff not to execute the prisoner until March 23.

Both Shipp and McReynolds were unsure as to whether an order issued by a federal judge superseded an order from a state judge in a state-court criminal case.

The other lawyers had to develop a strategy. The next morning, Shipp would tell the newspapers of his predicament—having two conflicting court orders. Whitaker and a group of private lawyers would publicly say that Judge Clark's authority to stay the execution was in doubt. A couple of the lawyers even planned to call the federal judge to express their opinion. Once the federal-court order was undermined, Judge McReynolds would step forward to propose that Tennessee Governor Cox was the only true authority that could rightfully delay the execution of Johnson.

That Monday morning, everything went as planned. The two newspapers reported that Judge Clark's stay might not be viable. Even Judge McReynolds publicly disparaged the federal-court order in a statement to the *Chattanooga News*. "We do not concede that Judge Clark had a right to grant a stay of execution in Johnson's case or that he did do it in fact. His order was practically this: 'Johnson is given into the hands of the Sheriff of Hamilton County to be kept for ten days.' "

The most surprising source of doubt on Judge Clark's ruling was the federal jurist himself. Several Tennessee lawyers contacted Clark to express their concern that federal judges do not have the authority to postpone state criminal executions. As a result, Judge Clark expressed uncertainty about his own power. He called Judge McReynolds and the two men agreed they should ask the Tennessee governor to give the prisoner a short reprieve to allow his lawyers to seek an appeal to the U.S. Supreme Court. Following telephone conversations with both judges, Cox did grant Johnson a temporary stay—but only for seven days, not the ten days ordered by Judge Clark.

The action was clearly a political victory for McReynolds, who could claim he had thwarted unnecessary and intrusive federal intervention and interference in a state-court case. He could also claim complete vindication for his own handling of the Johnson case. The governor immediately issued an oral directive to Sheriff Shipp to delay Johnson's hanging, and he promised to send a written order within days.

If Judge McReynolds was triumphant, Parden and Hutchins were befuddled. The reduction of the stay from ten days to seven days meant less time for them to prepare their case for submission to the U.S. Supreme Court. They began working around the clock. Meanwhile, Johnson was kept in solitary confinement on the third floor of the jail. No family members or friends were allowed to visit him. His lawyers were permitted one brief meeting with their client per day.

As the sheriff prepared the gallows in the basement of the jail for Johnson's execution and the defendant's lawyers hurried to spare his life, the Hamilton County Grand Jury reconvened for the first time since it had indicted Johnson for the rape of Nevada Taylor. It was also the last time this particular panel would meet together. Their final order of business was to investigate the attempted lynching of Johnson and the destruction done to the jail the night of January 25. They had earlier been instructed to learn the names of the men involved and indict them with the most serious charges that could be levied.

But the grand-jury probe took an unusual twist. Despite the pres-

ence of a dozen police officers, deputy sheriffs, and leading local officials, no witnesses were able to identify a single person who had participated in the attack on the jail. Interestingly, not even Judge
McReynolds, who had met at length with several members of the
mob, could remember the names of the people he saw and spoke to
that evening. As a result, the grand jury did not indict a single person
for the January 25 incident. However, the panel did issue felony
charges against a white man for stealing a horse, and against three
black men for stealing two mules. The lack of action brought the ire of
the city's black newspaper, the *Blade.*

> The law and its mechanics have made a farce of our sys-
> tem of justice. Lily whites have assaulted our public institu-
> tions with murderous intentions, destroyed our sense of order
> and permitted mob law to rule.
>
> The leaders of this community have violated the oaths of
> their office and their promise to uphold the constitution. The
> whites have once again demonstrated that the life of a black
> man is less valuable than a horse or mule.
>
> How can Judge McReynolds or any of the lawmen who so
> courageously fought the lynch mob suddenly forget the faces
> they saw and the men they talked to? Is it because Judge
> McReynolds and Sheriff Shipp want to be elected again?
>
> There will be more lynch mobs and they will be more suc-
> cessful, because the lily whites now understand that there is
> no penalty to pay for their dastardly deeds.

The harder Parden and Hutchins worked, the more hurdles and
setbacks they encountered. The lawyers split the duties. Hutchins was
in charge of gathering the appropriate paperwork to present to the
Supreme Court. He needed a certified transcript of the federal court's
hearing in Knoxville. To purchase the copy, Hutchins twisted a few
arms within the black business community for money.

Hutchins quickly studied the traditions, rules, and decorum of the
U.S. Supreme Court. Neither lawyer had previously been involved in
a case that went to the nation's highest court, so they had no clue

about its formalities or procedures. They quickly learned that neither of them had the standing to present an appeal to the justices. Only a member of the Supreme Court bar, who has been formally sworn in by a justice, can appear before the Court as an attorney in a case.

This obviously led to another dilemma. Only a handful of black lawyers had been admitted to the Supreme Court bar. Those black attorneys had been co-counsels on cases debated before the Supreme Court; no black man had yet argued before the high court himself. Fortunately, Hutchins knew one of those black lawyers—Emanuel D. Molyneaux Hewlett.

An 1877 graduate of the Boston University School of Law, Hewlett had practiced law in Washington, D.C., since 1883. Not one to shrink in the face of racism, Hewlett handled many of the city's high-profile murder cases that involved black defendants. He frequently blasted police for the unjustified detention of black people simply to improve their arrest statistics. In 1890, President Benjamin Harrison appointed Hewlett justice of the peace. So impressive was Hewlett's knowledge of the law that he was reappointed to the position by Presidents Grover Cleveland, William McKinley, and Theodore Roosevelt. Hewlett was involved in several cases that were appealed to the U.S. Supreme Court and had officially been sworn in as a member of the bar.

Hutchins had met Hewlett in Atlanta during a convention involving black professionals in the late 1890s in which both men were speakers. They became instant friends, united in their support of W.E.B. Du Bois and the civil-rights leader's aggressive and confrontational philosophy. The two lawyers had traded letters in the years since their initial meeting, but they had not seen or talked to each other in more than a decade.

That changed on Tuesday, March 13. Realizing he and Parden needed a member of the Supreme Court bar to join their team, Hutchins telephoned Hewlett at his judicial offices in Washington. After exchanging pleasantries, Hutchins got right to the point. He explained the case, told about the federal court's habeas corpus hearing, and their desire to appeal to the Supreme Court. They had only a week before Johnson would be executed, so expediency was priority one.

Hewlett was astounded to hear about the handling of the case in state court. The conduct of the judge, prosecutors, jury, and even the defense attorneys had been inexcusable. There was no doubt that a violation of Johnson's constitutional rights had taken place, he said, and the case should definitely be appealed to the high court.

Just then, Hutchins heard his friend take a deep breath on the other end of the telephone line. Hewlett's hesitancy served as a reality check. The justices had never agreed to hear a state criminal case on federal constitutional issues involving the right to a fair and impartial trial, Hewlett cautioned.

But Hewlett understood the potential that rested in the Johnson appeal. This case was unlike many of the prior cases in which the Supreme Court had been faced with many of these same issues. The previous appeals before the high court involved alleged procedural errors—all claims that were vigorously disputed by prosecutors as mere technicalities.

By contrast, the Johnson case was replete with many undisputed facts demonstrating the denial of a fair trial. There was an official federal-court record from the hearing in Knoxville detailing the misdeeds and outrages that had occurred during the Johnson trial. Evidence that the defendant had been denied a fair trial was undeniable. But just as important and explosive, Hewlett thought, was the strong proof that Ed Johnson was actually innocent of the crime. This was not a dispute over whether the prosecutors had met their burden of proof. Here was a case in which an obviously innocent man had been railroaded through the state criminal-justice system and now faced death at the hands of the very men who had stripped him of his dignity and rights. It presented a substantial dilemma for the Supreme Court.

"Wow!" Hewlett responded. "I think we may have a chance here."

Hewlett told Hutchins that there had been speculation for many months among prominent black lawyers and like-minded white lawyers that the time might be right for the Court to be presented with

such an argument. There had been rumors that several members of
the Supreme Court had grown disenchanted, even disgusted with the
lack of professionalism in the state courts. Hewlett said certain justices
were known to believe that black people and poor white people were
not being afforded adequate legal protections and due process in state
criminal cases.

"A case with the right facts and the appropriate argument just
might make the difference in persuading the court," Hewlett said.

The two lawyers agreed to talk again the next day. Hutchins
wanted Hewlett to speak with Parden, who would most likely be the
person to come to Washington later that week. Before Hewlett hung
up, he again warned his friend that the chances of victory for their case
were slim.

Parden, meanwhile, was facing another dilemma—this time from a
surprising source. At the suggestion of his law partner, Parden called
W.E.B. Du Bois to seek advice on how they should proceed. Du Bois,
who surrounded himself with some of the brightest black lawyers in
the country, was the first African-American to have received a doctor-
ate degree from Harvard University. A few years after the Johnson
case, Du Bois was to send a group of lawyers around the country to
prosecute and defend cases they believed important to the interests of
African-Americans. He would organize a network of black lawyers,
doctors, religious leaders, and politicians that reached into every state,
fighting for civil rights at the local, state, and federal levels, working to
improve black people's influence in government, and challenging segregation at every turn. The group he helped found became known as
the National Association for the Advancement of Colored People
(NAACP).

Parden hoped to avail himself of some of the expertise gleaned by
Du Bois. He thought the prominent scholar would offer tips on how to
develop their strategy, or possibly give instructions about arguing their
case. He sought guidance and support. Instead, Parden felt his knowledge of the law was being questioned, his motivations under siege,
and his commitment to civil rights attacked.

Du Bois was familiar with the work done by Parden and Hutchins
in Chattanooga. He praised them for fighting for Johnson's life when

everyone else had condemned the defendant to die. However, he was fearful the two lawyers did not have the expertise or the experience to take the Johnson case effectively to the U.S. Supreme Court. The case was much more important than just the life of Ed Johnson, Du Bois told the Chattanooga lawyer. It was a case that could change history. Parden, Du Bois insisted, was not up to the task.

Parden and Hutchins should turn the case over to more experienced lawyers, Du Bois said, or they should find a more prominent white lawyer to present the facts and argument in Washington. A prominent white attorney would be more readily accepted and respected by the federal justices. For the future of the black race, the Atlanta civil-rights leader pleaded with Parden and Hutchins to resign as defense lawyers in the Johnson case and allow white attorneys with more knowledge, experience, and influence to take the lead. If they refused to step aside in the case, Du Bois suggested, this might demonstrate that they were more interested in self-promotion and gratification than in seeking justice.

Stunned by this brief conversation, Parden felt his ability and integrity as a lawyer had been challenged. White lawyers had abandoned Johnson when he needed them most, and they were part of the reason he was days removed from a hangman's noose. Though Parden had promised Du Bois he would immediately discuss the request with Hutchins, he had no intention of stepping down from the case. He told his co-counsel about the conversation, but made it clear he would never agree to be replaced as lead lawyer. He may not have wanted the case in the beginning, but he was determined to follow it through now. Parden also ignored his pledge to Du Bois to call him back later that day. And when Du Bois called numerous times over the next two days, Parden refused to come to the telephone.

For Parden and Hutchins, the days of the week blended one into another. Hutchins didn't eat for three days and slept in his clothes. Parden napped on the floor in his office for an hour or two a night. His eyes would ache in need of sleep, but the adrenaline rush of trying to save his client was more than sufficient as a stimulant.

Late Wednesday night, Parden was alone in the office scouring law books for last-minute inspirations and guidance. He read and reread the federal statute on habeas corpus appeals. He meticulously sifted through prior Supreme Court rulings, hoping to discover some forgotten precedent that would help his case.

About 1:30 a.m., Parden heard a noise outside the four-room wood-frame building he and Hutchins rented for office space. He thought it sounded like people running. Then he noticed the smell of smoke. Grabbing his coat, Parden cautiously opened the back door of the house. With no one in sight, he slowly walked around to the side of the building where he had first detected the smoke. As he rounded the corner, he saw the flames.

At that moment, people came running out of the house next door, screaming and in a panic. Smoke had filled their home, too. Fire streaked along the ground and up the side of the wall. Parden was soon joined by two other men in beating down the fire with blankets and buckets of water. Fortunately, they had discovered the flames quickly; within minutes the fire was extinguished. Nearby, the men discovered a gas can that the arsonists had used to start the blaze. Parden shook his head in utter disbelief and frustration. The vigilantes had come to disrupt his efforts, destroy his work, and discourage his commitment. Instead, they had set fire to the wrong building and nearly killed his neighbors in the process.

An hour later—about 3:00 a.m.—Parden's wife, Mattie, walked into his office in tears, accompanied by two of their neighbors, who were carrying shotguns. While Parden embraced his wife, the two men explained that someone had thrown rocks through the windows of their house and had fired several gunshots inside. This time they had not chosen the wrong house. Mattie was terrified but unhurt. Parden spent the next hour comforting her. The two neighbors stayed until dawn to guard the couple. This experience only made Parden more determined to seek justice for his client.

Unaware of the events of the night, Hutchins made his initial appearance at the law firm about 8:00 a.m. He was all smiles and immediately announced he had raised enough money to pay for the sixty-eight pages of federal-court testimony taken at the hearing in Knoxville. Hutchins said Judge Shepherd and a few other white lawyers who were sympathetic to their cause had given him the money. After receiving a full briefing on the fire next door and the attack on Parden's home, Hutchins suggested that his law partner take his wife to Atlanta for safekeeping and offered to take the petition to Washington himself. Parden said he would find a safe place for Mattie while he was gone, but he intended to see the case through to the end. He would not be intimidated by racist thugs.

By late Thursday afternoon, Hutchins had obtained a certified copy of the federal court's transcript, complete with Judge Clark's signature. The two lawyers put the final touches on the paperwork they planned to submit to the Supreme Court. Lewis Shepherd reviewed the petition for accuracy and thoroughness. The packet included the petition for writ of habeas corpus that the defense attorneys had filed in their petition for habeas corpus before Judge Clark in Knoxville, along with the final order, and the transcript of the hearing Judge Clark had conducted. Parden then took the petition to the jail for his client's approval.

On the official papers that would be presented to the Supreme Court, next to the typed words that spelled his name, Ed Johnson took an ink pen and marked an "X." Parden hugged his client and the two men prayed. Parden asked God to have mercy on his client, to protect him, keep him safe, and prepare him for the future, whatever it might hold. Johnson's prayer was much shorter: he simply requested that God safeguard his lawyers and their families.

Minutes later, Parden boarded a train for Washington. He would be gone four nights—possibly more, if the Supreme Court decided to conduct some kind of immediate hearing on the matter. He left town with the confidence that he and Hutchins had done their best to represent their client. He also felt comforted about the safety of Mattie. The Reverend T. H. McCallie had heard about the incidents at Parden's home and office. That morning, the aging educator and minister visited with the couple to offer his apologies and support. When he learned Parden was traveling to Washington, McCallie suggested that Mattie stay with his family at their farm on Missionary Ridge.

She would be safe there, he said. Heartened by the outstretched hand, the Pardens accepted the offer.

After Parden boarded the train in Chattanooga, it passed through

Knoxville and Johnson City, then steamed into Virginia, to stop in Bristol, Roanoke, and Richmond. He was unable to get any sleep. His mind developed every possible scenario he would face at the Supreme Court. He practiced what he would say over and over again.

When Emanuel D. Molyneaux Hewlett arrived at his law offices early Friday morning, Parden was waiting nervously. The two men had much to discuss. While Parden sipped a cup of hot herbal tea, Hewlett scanned the petition, reading the highlights. The testimony and allegations were as egregious as Hutchins had told him on the telephone. It was obvious that Johnson had not received a fair trial, and equally apparent to Hewlett that the defendant was most likely innocent. This was an important point to assert, Hewlett said.

Parden spent much of the day asking the more seasoned lawyer and judge about the Supreme Court, its rules, decorum, and procedures. How many justices would be present? How much time would they get? Would the justices ask questions? What did they think of black lawyers? Were any of them from the old Confederacy? Would they agree to hear the case? Would they rule right away or wait for a few days? Could one justice make such a decision or did it take all nine?

Hewlett answered most of the questions but confessed they were exploring new legal territory. The Supreme Court had adopted its own set of rules in 1790 and had added to them many times since. The rules ranged from who may file briefs in a case, time limits on filings, and the days and hours when oral arguments would be heard, to the size of paper, number of pages, and even the color of the paper of the petitions and briefs filed with the Court. There were no written regulations about dress, though Hewlett suggested they wear a morning coat or a frock coat, a wing collar, and a dark necktie; he said business attire was expected. Court started at noon on weekdays and sometimes on Saturdays. Each side was allowed two hours to argue its case, Hewlett told Parden, but lawyers could take more time if they asked in advance.

Hewlett gave the younger lawyer a copy of Rule 5, which states that a lawyer seeking permission to present a case to the justices must be licensed to practice law in a state for at least five years. Unlike today, a lawyer in 1906 did not have to file a written application to be admitted to practice before the Supreme Court. Instead, an attorney was sworn in as a member of the Supreme Court bar by a justice only after being recommended by another lawyer who was already a member. The rules also required that lawyers seeking admission to the bar be of good moral character and have no disciplinary penalties on their record. Hewlett had already taken the oath and would make the motion to the court that Parden be accepted—a procedurally routine event. Even so, the thought of being admitted to the Supreme Court bar sent chills up Parden's spine.

Rule 38 of the Supreme Court sets the fees for filing an appeal with the Court, but Rule 39 waives those fees for litigants who are poor and cannot afford to pay. Ed Johnson certainly qualified as indigent. The Court also required lawyers to file twenty-five copies of each brief with the Supreme Court clerk at least six days prior to argument. The briefs had to be submitted on legal-sized paper (eight and a half by fourteen inches). The paper had to be white or a light shade of gray.

In emergency petitions such as this, only the party seeking the immediate intervention would be heard by one of the justices in chambers. The proceedings were described legally as an *ex parte* hearing, because only one side in the case was present; Hewlett said that he and Parden might be asked to offer a brief synopsis of the case, as well as answer any questions the justices would have. A full hearing, in which both sides made extensive arguments to the Court, would not take place for several weeks, or even many months. But with each answer, Hewlett inserted the disclaimer that the Court might choose to deny their request for a hearing.

Parden listened intently as the elder lawyer spoke. He peppered Hewlett with every question he could think of, and jotted down notes of the things he wanted to remember or believed to be important. There was so much to learn in less than twenty-four hours. Parden knew there would be little time to sleep that night.

The approach they should take, Hewlett said, depended upon which justices were in attendance. The bad news was that the Supreme Court seldom agreed to hear a petition for habeas corpus from the state courts. The justices had shown no inclination to interfere in state law-enforcement matters, and they certainly were no friends to criminal defendants. Though the Court had aggressively expanded the federal government's role in the regulation of commerce throughout the country, it displayed no similar willingness to expand individual rights and liberties under the federal Constitution.

Even as Hewlett depicted the dim reality of the situation facing Parden and his client, he also offered a slight hope. The Johnson case had been tried in Tennessee, which in the federal-court system resides within the jurisdiction of the Sixth U.S. Circuit, along with Kentucky, Ohio, and Michigan. In 1891, Congress created federal circuit courts of appeal to review judgments and verdicts from the federal trial courts and habeas corpus appeals from the state courts. The appeals courts were designed to relieve the Supreme Court of the ever-increasing caseload.

The Supreme Court then and now designated one justice to hear emergency appeals from each circuit and to be a liaison between the high court and the lower federal courts. That person for the Sixth Circuit in 1906 was Associate Justice John Marshall Harlan of Kentucky. If Justice Harlan was available, the rules of the court required that he be the justice to whom they would make their initial presentation. However, Hewlett said, another justice could be given the case if Harlan was unavailable or ill. And it was also possible that, because the Court was actually in session hearing cases in March and near the end of its term, all of the justices would be present to decide on their initial request.

In all probability, however, the case would come before Justice Harlan, and that had Hewlett encouraged. The black lawyer knew the elderly justice personally and considered him an honest and open-minded jurist. In addition, he had done a considerable amount of research on Harlan for a class on the Supreme Court he frequently taught at Howard University's law school. Hewlett's analysis was simple: if any of the nine justices would be sympathetic to Ed Johnson and outraged at the state court's handling of his case, it was Justice Harlan.

Harlan was born into privilege in 1833 in Boyle County, Kentucky, a rural community in the center of the state. He was named after the

Supreme Court's first chief justice, John Marshall of Virginia. His father—a lawyer and a staunch member of the Whig Party, which advocated a strong national government—held several elected positions, including state attorney general and member of Congress. Political activist Henry Clay was a close friend of the family.

After graduating from Centre College in his hometown of Danville, Harlan studied law at Transylvania University. He received his law license in 1853 and practiced civil and criminal law several years with his father. Harlan seemed destined for politics, too. However, the Whig Party evaporated following the deaths of Henry Clay and Daniel Webster. After a brief stint with the Know-Nothings, Harlan joined the ranks of the Republicans.

Harlan's family had owned slaves, though the justice would later describe slavery as a "peculiar institution." But when war broke out between the North and the South in 1861, Harlan wore Union blue and became a colonel in the U.S. Army. At the end of the war, he returned home and was elected the attorney general of Kentucky. Twice he ran for governor as a Republican, but the party remained weak in the state and he was soundly defeated both times.

At the youthful age of forty-four, Harlan became the beneficiary of what was obviously a political payback. As a member of the Republican National Convention in 1876, he became a key swing vote that gave Rutherford B. Hayes the presidential nomination. A year later, President Hayes rewarded Harlan with an appointment to the U.S. Supreme Court.

Harlan had been on the Court for thirty years when Noah Parden walked in that day. He was the oldest member of the Court and its longest-serving member. As a politician in the Bluegrass State, Harlan was a critic of Lincoln's Emancipation Proclamation, which he denounced as "unconstitutional and null and void." But by the early 1870s, his public statements on slavery and equal rights had evolved. After he was confirmed to the Supreme Court, which provided the security of a lifetime appointment, he actually became a strong advocate for civil rights. He called slavery the "most perfect despotism that ever existed on this earth." He labeled men who belonged to the Ku Klux Klan a "band of murderers and assassins." When asked about his transformation, Harlan stated: "Let it be said that I am right rather than consistent."

The justice berated the other members of the Court for upholding racial segregation in public facilities—a social principle he contended was nothing more than a "badge of slavery." Harlan believed that the Fourteenth Amendment and the civil-rights laws passed by Congress following the Civil War appropriately granted the federal government the authority to protect and promote the rights of former slaves. However, the elderly justice had been unable to convince a majority of the other members of the Court of his more liberal ideology.

Harlan's views were never stated more clearly than in 1896, when the Supreme Court reviewed the case of *Plessy* v. *Ferguson*. When the high court held that segregation of people by race was constitutional, Harlan issued a scathing dissent. To Harlan, the equal-protection rights granted under the Fourteenth Amendment belonged to the person, not society. "Our Constitution is color-blind," he stated in one of the most quoted Supreme Court opinions of all time.

The arbitrary separation of citizens on the basis of race, while they are on a public highway, is a badge of servitude wholly inconsistent with the civil freedom and equality before the law established by the Constitution. It cannot be justified upon any legal grounds.

What can more certainly arouse race hate, what can more certainly create and perpetuate a feeling of distrust between these races, than state enactments, which, in fact, proceed on the ground that colored citizens are so inferior and degraded that they cannot be allowed to sit in public coaches occupied by white citizens. That, as all will admit, is the real meaning of such legislation.

The thin disguise of "equal" accommodations for passengers in railroad coaches will not mislead any one, nor atone for the wrong this day done.

What many people in 1896 or even 1906 did not realize was that the Plessy case and subsequent cases involving racism were personal to Justice Harlan. He had a half-brother, Robert Harlan, who, like Homer Plessy, was seven-eighths white. Robert was sixteen years older than John and raised in the Harlan home. As a result, John could see and experience firsthand the prejudices and hardships faced by his half-brother. Over the years, he came to believe that it was legally and morally wrong to discriminate against a person on the basis of race.

As a lawyer, Harlan believed that justice under the law was a divine tool given to people by God as a means to regulate or govern themselves. He believed that the law was a part of the fabric of the universe and that God had blessed the court system as the orderly means by which people settled their disputes. Being a lawyer was a heavenly calling, as was being a minister, a missionary, or an evangelist.

Justice Harlan's view of the world was that of an old-fashioned Presbyterian, which was exactly what he was. He saw society and morality in black and white. There were rights and wrongs, and he believed the purpose of the written law was to determine the difference. One of his best friends on the Court, Justice David J. Brewer, once said that Harlan went to bed every night with "one hand on the Constitution and the other on the Bible, safe and happy in a perfect faith in justice and righteousness."

On the personal side, Harlan was equally as colorful. He chewed Burley tobacco and drank Kentucky bourbon. He loved playing golf, watching baseball, and wearing outrageous clothes. Though he would curse at the slightest irritation, he fell to his knees nightly to seek forgiveness, guidance, and perseverance.

To emphasize Harlan's eccentric character, Hewlett told Parden a story that had been repeated around the Capitol many times. It seems that when Harlan was a young man his cousin was charged with murder. Every morning of the three-day trial, Harlan and another cousin sat in the front row of the courtroom, directly behind their relative, with loaded pistols in their holsters and knives in their hands. Harlan and his other cousin feared that friends of the victim would try to kidnap his cousin from the courtroom to lynch him, and they vowed to fight against any would-be lynch-mob members. In the end, Harlan's cousin was acquitted of the charges.

That Friday afternoon, March 16, the two men walked several

blocks to the U.S. Capitol. They passed through security and into the meandering hallways under the great dome. They eventually found their way to the clerk of the U.S. Supreme Court and filed the necessary paperwork with him. The clerk quickly read through the request, scanned the materials to make sure they were complete, and told the lawyers to return the following day. The justices were all in town and hearing cases, he said, but he wasn't sure which one or how many would review their petition. And he couldn't say for sure that the Court would want to hear from them at all. Even so, the clerk told them to be present the next morning in case the Court had any inquiries.

Hewlett and Parden agreed. Hewlett had other business to attend to, and Parden needed to send a telegram home to let his wife and Hutchins know he had arrived safely and that the petition had been filed. The two lawyers agreed to meet the next morning on the steps of the Capitol.

Back in Chattanooga, time was running out. Tensions were high. Sheriff Shipp and Judge McReynolds were trying to calm public restlessness by assuring people that Johnson would die as scheduled on March 20. The chances of the U.S. Supreme Court's intervening, they told their followers, were extremely slight.

> People here are decidedly anxious as to whether Johnson is to suffer death for his crime next Tuesday or escape for an indefinite period of time by reason of intervention by the court at Washington. More unrest on the subject exists than was anticipated when Johnson was brought back to the county.
>
> The condemned Negro has experienced religion. He became pious during his incarceration at Knoxville. He declared on the way home that he was ready to die and would be ready to die now as any other time. In the county jail here he is confined apart from the other prisoners. Only occasional visitors enliven his solitude. He declares that he is alone with his God and cares not for any other company.
>
> Johnson is often reminded of the grim instrument of death that waits in the basement of the jail for the word that fixes the

final hour of his life, but it seems to have no terror for him. Of late the Negro has posed for several pictures. Aside from a restlessness of the eye, the Negro's nerve is keeping up in surprising manner, and officials at the jail are predicting that he will go to his death as calmly as he faced the victim of his crime when she sat with hand raised to heaven and denounced him as her assailant.

Johnson is confined on the second [third] floor of the jail and is yet not provided with a special guard. He is talkative and when any of his guards approach his solitary cell, he persists in chatting with them. He seems little moved by the fate which seems to be unavoidable for him now.

Chattanooga Times, March 16, 1906

CHAPTER ELEVEN

GALLOWS DISAPPOINTED

WITH HIS SCHEDULED execution less than forty-eight hours away, Ed Johnson was in excellent spirits Sunday morning. He chatted with friends, recited his Bible, and ate the biscuits, gravy, and grits served to him for breakfast. Not even the hourly reminder from guards at the jail that the gallows waited for Johnson in the basement of the jail three floors below his cell seemed to disturb him. In 1906, counties in Tennessee, not state officials, had to carry out their own executions, and the legally required method was by hanging.

If his faith in heavenly things had grown, Johnson's hope in the criminal-justice system had completely evaporated. He was resigned to dying. He had accepted the prediction of Sheriff Shipp and other local officials that the Supreme Court would never intervene in his case. When the justices issued no decisions late Saturday or early Sunday, the Tennessee authorities felt secure in their hopes that Johnson would be executed as scheduled on Tuesday, March 20. Many local lawyers doubted that Johnson's defense attorneys would get the opportunity even to present their petition to the Supreme Court.

What no one back in Chattanooga—including McReynolds, Shipp, or even Johnson—knew was that Parden had been allowed to present the case to Justice Harlan late Saturday evening. He had filed the petition with the high court, and Justice Harlan had even granted him ten minutes to argue personally why the Supreme Court should bother with the matter. Now Parden was on the train headed home.

Ed Johnson was oblivious to all that. He was living for the moment, determined to harbor no ill-will in his heart. Sunday morning began with more than a dozen local citizens stopping by the jail to have their picture taken with the condemned Negro. They were not his friends or neighbors. In fact, he had never laid eyes on most of the visitors. To them, the photographs were simply souvenirs. The deputies would parade Johnson out of his cell and force him to pose like an animal in a zoo. But he did it without complaint, according to a reporter for the *Chattanooga Times* who spent the day with Johnson.

> A morbid desire seemed to possess large numbers of white people to see the prisoner. Many of them left him fruit, sweet meats and delicacies, and last night his cell was well filled with the day's offerings.
>
> There were numbers of oranges, apples, cakes and other good things to eat and books and magazines were also left for him to read. He appeared glad to see all who called and talked freely when spoken to.

Even in 1906, prisoners facing death were given one final wish, as long as it wasn't too outrageous. Most condemned inmates chose a favorite meal with family or other prisoners. Some asked to visit a special place, such as Lookout Mountain or their mother's home. One inmate wanted to play an all-night poker game on the eve of his hanging.

Ed Johnson's request was a little different. His only wish was to be allowed to attend a Sunday morning worship service. He had experienced a religious conversion in the Knox County Jail. Now he wanted to be baptized and share his testimony with other Christian believers.

Sheriff Shipp believed Johnson was sincere in his request. He didn't suspect the prisoner was masterminding some elaborate escape attempt. Yet he was reluctant to remove Johnson from the jail. Too many risks; too many things could go wrong; too many people still wanted to lynch the defendant.

At the same time, Shipp wanted to accommodate the inmate's

request. He had not changed his mind about Johnson's guilt, but he was a Christian man of compassion and he understood that granting the final request of a condemned man was traditional. The sheriff also had a second motivation in allowing his prisoner to attend a final church service: God might inflict a deep conviction upon Johnson's soul, so that the defendant would publicly confess his sins, including the attack on Nevada Taylor.

So, although Shipp wouldn't let Johnson go to the church service, there was nothing wrong with bringing the church service to the jail and to Johnson. Shipp contacted the Reverend W. B. Fleming, a prominent black minister in Chattanooga and the pastor of the St. James Baptist Church, which Johnson had requested to attend. The sheriff explained the situation. He said Reverend Fleming would be allowed to bring the church's choir and several parishioners to the jail.

To the great surprise of Shipp, more than 300 members of the black church packed into the eating area of the jail, the largest room in the facility. They overflowed into the jail's lobby and outdoors into the courtyard. Johnson was brought downstairs from his third-floor cell and seated to one side. Sheriff's deputies were placed at each corner and two near the prisoner. They were the only white people in the multitude. Fleming started the service by announcing that they had gathered for the benefit of Johnson. He then led the group in a series of hymns.

Johnson had requested that the congregation sing "There's Power in the Blood." Reverend Fleming readily agreed and started the congregation in song. No one sang louder or with more spirit and joy than Ed Johnson—a great contrast to his normally soft-spoken manner.

> *Would you be free from your burden of sin?*
> *There's power in the blood, power in the blood.*
> *Would you o'er evil a victory win?*
> *There is power in the blood of the Lamb.*

The choir sang "Amazing Grace" and "When the Roll Is Called Up Yonder." Amid shouts of "amen," the minister preached a fervent message of heaven and hell, sin and condemnation, mercy and love.

The singing, preaching, and reaction from the congregation were so noisy that it could all be heard several blocks away.

Throughout the sermon, Johnson sat with his hands folded as if in prayer. Asked by the preacher to address the congregation, the condemned prisoner slowly rose to his feet. Tears on his cheeks and a quiver in his voice, Ed Johnson began to speak.

"I have had a change of heart," he said.

Sheriff Shipp and the deputies immediately perked up. Johnson, with tears in his eyes, took a deep pause. The lawmen looked at each other hoping, thinking the condemned man was about to confess. If he did, there would be much less controversy over the hanging. However, they were quickly disappointed.

> I am ready to die. The change came over me all at once and I can't tell you how it was. Before the change, I hated the people who were against me. I couldn't eat and could only think of the arrest and the trouble I was in. I didn't want to talk or eat and didn't want to see anyone. All at once, I felt different. I didn't hate white people anymore.
>
> I pray every day for Miss Taylor. But I am not the one who did those things to her. I am not that man.

At that moment, an elderly deacon in the congregation spoke up: "I move that Brother Ed Johnson be received into membership of the St. James Baptist Church and be accepted as a proper candidate for baptism, since he has here made a public profession of his faith." Reverend Fleming repeated the motion and asked the audience if anyone objected. There were no votes against.

Before Johnson could be made a member of the church, the minister said he had to be baptized. A jumbo-sized bathtub was located at the end of the corridor near Johnson's cell. Deputies filled it with water. Right there in the jail, the preacher immersed Johnson's head under the water and then lifted him out, proclaiming his spirit to be pure and ready to enter the gates of heaven. "I baptize you in the name of the Father, the Son and the Holy Ghost," the pastor said as part of the Protestant ceremony.

Johnson came out of the water in a paroxysm of emotion. He started down the corridor clapping his hands and with his eyes raised wildly toward the ceiling. His conduct further excited the women in the choir and as they began shouting and singing "In the Sweet By and By," some of the women fell prostrate on the floor, one of them apparently going into a trance.

Chattanooga Times, Monday, March 19, 1906

Late Sunday evening, Noah Parden stepped from the train depot in Chattanooga exhausted from his fifteen-hour trip. After replaying every word and phrase, each expression and argument, Parden was convinced that his meeting with Justice Harlan the day before had gone as well as it could. But he had left Washington without any indication of how the jurist would decide.

The first person Parden saw as the train arrived at the station was Styles Hutchins. Parden had never known his law partner to display much emotion. Yet Hutchins wore the biggest grin Parden had ever seen. He was waving a small sheet of paper in the air.

Immediately, Parden knew the news was good. Before any words were spoken, Hutchins hugged the younger lawyer and congratulated him on a job well done. Parden grabbed the piece of paper from Hutchins's hand and read the brief message intently. It was a telegram from Washington—more important, from the U.S. Supreme Court.

Washington, D.C.—March 18
To Honorable C. D. Clark, U.S. Circuit Judge, Chattanooga,
    Tennessee

Have allowed appeal to accused in habeas corpus case of Ed Johnson. Transcript will be filed tomorrow and motion also made by Johnson's counsel for formal allowance of appeal of court.

Signed: JOHN M. HARLAN, Associate Justice

Parden reread the telegram to make sure it said what he thought it did. The message was in the typical legalese, but the interpretation was clear: Johnson would not be executed as scheduled on March 20 and there would be a lengthy hearing of the defendant's case in Washington. The two lawyers embraced again.

Justice Harlan had notified federal Judge Clark, state Judge McReynolds, and Sheriff Shipp about the stay of execution via telegram. Hutchins and Parden had also been sent a copy. The formal paperwork, the Court said, would follow in a few days. At that time, the justices would also set a date for oral arguments for both sides.

The decision in Washington to intervene in the Johnson matter had not been an easy one. Indeed, it was precedent-setting. In the hours following Parden's presentation to Justice Harlan, the Supreme Court jurist had read the entire transcript of the hearing held before Judge Clark in Knoxville. Many of the allegations made by Parden appeared to be supported by the record and did not seem to be disputed by lawyers for the state. The justice was troubled that this conviction had been the result of a rush to judgment, and he definitely believed the appeal raised important federal constitutional issues.

Justice Harlan decided late that Saturday night to issue a temporary stay of execution. He believed Johnson deserved a full and impartial hearing. Yet the elderly justice remained reluctant to announce his decision formally. He was unsure if he alone had the authority to grant an appeal and delay Johnson's death sentence. He wanted to confer with Chief Justice Melville Fuller and the other associate justices before taking such action.

At Harlan's request, a majority of the Supreme Court met Sunday morning at Chief Justice Fuller's home in the Foggy Bottom section of Washington. Harlan gave each of the justices present a copy of Parden's brief and the accompanying documents. He recited as much of Parden's presentation as he could remember.

To his fellow justices Harlan made an impassioned plea. He said there was little doubt that Johnson had been denied a fair trial, and told them about the lynching attempt and the prejudices that permeated the Chattanooga community. The law, he said, was about justice and doing what was right. Justice had not been served. This was the time for the U.S. Supreme Court to send a message to law-enforcement and court officials throughout the country that they were expected to obey the spirit as well as the letter of the law.

Finally, Harlan told the other members of the Court that he believed the defendant was actually innocent of the crime. If Johnson had been wrongly convicted and would hang as a result, the other justices said, the Supreme Court should intervene. They could not allow an innocent man to die, and they could not allow the U.S. Constitution to be trampled underfoot in a sham state-court trial because of the racial prejudices of court officials in Hamilton County. Such an act by a government could not be tolerated, they agreed.

Associate Justice Oliver Wendell Holmes was the first to speak in favor of Harlan's proposal that they accept the appeal. Though he admitted his reluctance to assert federal-court jurisdiction in a state-court criminal matter, he said there appeared to be substantial evidence that Johnson's constitutional rights had been violated. Holmes, a Harvard graduate born and raised in privileged circles in New England, had been disenchanted with the handling of criminal and civil cases across the South. The Johnson matter only reinforced his belief that state courts in the old Confederacy were another means of suppressing black people.

After an hour-long discussion, Chief Justice Fuller felt a consensus had been achieved. The justices unanimously agreed on the action that needed to be taken. Fuller told Harlan to proceed with issuing the stay of execution and granting the appeal. The case would be moved to the top of the Court's docket, he announced. The chief justice also said that lawyers for both sides should file briefs with the Court within thirty days and be prepared to argue the petition thereafter.

Harlan had not won many of these battles in the past. His usual style was confrontational. In the past, he had argued with the other justices to accept more state-court criminal appeals. Each time, he was rebuffed. The other justices had been extremely reluctant to interfere in state-court criminal cases. But this time was different. On this day, he played the role of coalition builder. The facts were so strong in showing that an injustice had taken place that the other members of the Court knew they must act. This time, the United States Constitution and possibly an innocent man's life were at stake.

The aging justice immediately walked to the Capitol to formalize the Court's ruling. There he took an ink pen to the bottom of the petition filed by Parden and wrote the Court's decision by hand.

The herein named Ed Johnson asks an appeal from the judgment herein rendered in the Circuit Court of the United States for the Northern Division of the Eastern District of Tennessee on March 10, 1906, denying his application in a writ of habeas corpus. Pursuant to the statutes of the United States, the appeal asked for is hereby allowed. Evidence by my hand, as an associate justice of the Supreme Court of the United States.

Signed: JOHN M. HARLAN

Justice Harlan then filled out the formal notice to be delivered to the participants in the case saying the Court had agreed to hear the appeal. The order also told lawyers for the state of Tennessee to prepare to file an answer to Parden's petition within thirty days.

Harlan then instructed the clerk of the Court to send telegrams immediately to Judge McReynolds, Sheriff Shipp, District Attorney Whitaker, and the defense team informing them of the decision. He told the clerk to confirm that the sheriff had received the notice, which officially made Johnson a federal prisoner. And he said that the clerk should make sure that the Chattanooga authorities understood that the Supreme Court was staying the defendant's execution. The clerk agreed to send an additional telegram to the sheriff and judge making clear the Court's order.

All further proceedings be stayed and the custody of the accused retained pending an appeal in Washington.

JAMES H. MCKENNEY, Clerk of the United States Supreme Court

That evening Harlan walked home. He was feeling pretty good about himself and the Court. For three decades he had sat on the nation's highest tribunal. Much of their work involved what he considered big business and government. To Harlan, these cases offered nothing of the heart and soul and compassion for the law that he loved so much. In fact, the commerce controversies represented all that was wrong with the world: they were about greed and power. But on this one occasion, in this single case, Harlan believed the Court had chosen to do the right thing. They had employed the law to save a man's life. To make such decisions was why Harlan served on the Supreme Court.

Such was certainly not the predominant opinion back in Tennessee. The legal community was stunned at the decision. They concluded that, by agreeing to hear the Johnson appeal, the nation's highest court was setting precedent, and they didn't like it. The average person in the city was less analytical but equally perturbed at the intervention—or interference, as they viewed it. Throughout the town, people in taverns and coffee shops, restaurants and drugstores took offense at the Supreme Court ruling. This was their town and state. And they resented having people in Washington, D.C., tell them how to run their court system and how to deal with their criminals. The *Chattanooga News* seemed to encourage vigilantism.

The gallows in the Hamilton County Jail has again been disappointed in the case of Ed Johnson, convicted by the state courts of rape and sentenced to death.

Johnson was told this morning by his jailer of the present status of his case. He said very little, except, "All right," in the same tone which was so much noticed during his testimony in the trial of the case.

It will be at least 30 or 60 days before Johnson can be legally executed.

All of this delay is aggravating to the community. The people of Chattanooga believe that Johnson is guilty and that he ought to suffer the penalty of the law as speedily as possible.

If by legal technicality the case is prolonged and the culprit finally escapes, there will be no use to plead with a mob here if another such crime is committed. Such delays are largely responsible for mob violence all over the country.

CHAPTER TWELVE

GOD BLESS YOU ALL; I AM INNOCENT

STYLES HUTCHINS HAD received the telegram from the Supreme Court at such a late hour Sunday evening that he had been unable to deliver the good news to his client: no visitors were permitted in the jail on Sundays after 6:00 p.m. Judge McReynolds received his notice late that evening while dining at home with his wife. And officials were unable to locate Sheriff Shipp until early Monday morning.

Jailers awakened Ed Johnson with the other prisoners about 7:00 a.m. Hot tin bowls of oatmeal and metal cups of coffee or milk were given to each inmate. Johnson hungrily cleaned his plate. Seconds were not offered. It was not until midmorning Monday that he learned from the jailers that his date with death would be delayed. His lawyers met with him in the afternoon to explain what had happened in Washington and what it meant to him. Parden was surprised, almost perturbed, at his client's lack of excitement.

Parden and Hutchins spent much of Monday celebrating their victory. Numerous friends within the black community congratulated them on their achievement. They received telegrams of praise from black lawyers and activists around the country. Both men were feeling pretty good about their achievements. Lewis Shepherd invited the two lawyers and Parden's wife to his weekend home on the Georgia side of Lookout Mountain for dinner and an evening of well-deserved relaxation. The meandering Tennessee River could be seen from his porch. It was a time of needed isolation for these men, who had worked so hard to overcome so many obstacles. There was no telephone in the home, and no one knew where they were. For dinner, Shepherd's housekeeper cooked a pheasant that the former judge had killed during a recent hunt.

Parden relived in excruciating detail his meeting with Justice Harlan. Hutchins and Shepherd teased Parden about his initial refusal to defend Johnson. That night, they toasted justice for Ed Johnson, as well as Parden's success. And they discussed the future of the case and how it was likely to play out.

Unbeknownst to any of them, rumors were spreading throughout the white community, especially in the suburbs, that there would be another effort to lynch Johnson that night. A frequent phrase was heard from the lips of many white men: "Tonight would be a real good night for a mob." Sheriff Shipp and his deputies quickly learned of the rumors, too.

With the election just over a week away, the sheriff was again feeling political pressure from his supporters. Many of them had complained earlier that Shipp had been too vigorous in his protection of Johnson. They frequently reminded him of what had happened to another former Hamilton County sheriff, John Skillern. In 1892, Sheriff Skillern arrested George Weims, a twenty-five-year-old black man, for the attempted rape of a white farmer's wife. In that case, there was no doubt about the identification of the suspect: the victim had severely bitten her attacker's finger during the assault, and when Weims was arrested, the authorities saw that his finger had been badly bitten.

As Sheriff Shipp had done, Skillern had sent his prisoner to Nashville following several lynching attempts. However, as the sheriff and his deputies were bringing Weims back to Chattanooga to stand trial, the train was boarded by a mob of a dozen white men. In an effort to save their inmate, two of the deputies jumped with Weims from the moving train more than thirty miles outside of Chattanooga. When five members of the mob followed them, the deputies drew their revolvers and held the barrels to the heads of some of them. "We told them if they advanced one step we would kill them," said one of the deputies. "And I certainly would have kept my word." For two days, the deputies and Weims hiked through forests and across Lookout Mountain. Under cover of darkness, they finally sneaked their prisoner into the county jail safe and unnoticed.

When Chief Deputy Brown suggested that the sheriff post extra men around the jail that evening just in case, Shipp shook his head in disagreement. He said the talk of a lynching was nonsense. It was nothing more than "hot talk" from a few men who drank too much.

Not only did the sheriff decide against seeking additional assistance from the city police and National Guard; he told his deputies they had been working too hard and gave them the night off. He said a single guard, Jeremiah Gibson, the elderly nighttime jailer, would be sufficient to guard the inmates that evening. None of the deputies offered an objection, readily accepting a night off from work.

By 7:00 p.m., every deputy except Gibson had left the jail for his home. The prisoners had been fed and were locked down in their cells. Despite assurances from the sheriff that the night would be calm and quiet, the prisoners were noticeably uneasy. Throughout the day, the inmates had kept watch out their cell windows, looking for clues as to what the night would hold. If the others were nervous, Johnson seemed without a worry. After eating the breaded catfish served to him in his isolated cell on the third floor, Johnson lay down on his bunk and drifted into a light sleep.

About 8:00 p.m., a group of men carrying pistols and rifles made their first approach into the jail. A black trusty, who was working on the first floor, saw them enter the jail and immediately tried to run. A few of the men grabbed him and hit him in the face and on the head with their weapons. His nose, apparently broken, bled profusely. However, the trusty was able to escape their grasp and ran from the jail through the kitchen.

Gibson was making his evening rounds when he heard the commotion and voices coming from the first floor. "I guess that's another bunch of prisoners," he said to a few of the inmates. The prisoners weren't so sure. Instead, they begged him to call the city police department or the sheriff or the National Guard for additional protection. But Gibson instantly dismissed their pleas as paranoid. He told his captives that Shipp and the other deputies were sure nothing unusual would happen that night.

Within five minutes, the number of intruders who had invaded the jail jumped from a half-dozen to fifteen or twenty. Their talk was loud and angry. None of them seemed surprised when they found no law-enforcement officers in their initial search of the first floor and office of the jail. In a workmanlike effort, they began their task of seizing Ed Johnson from the facility.

There on the first floor, the mob was confronted with its first barrier—a large steel door with rods extending into the stone-and-cement foundation of the building. The door was fastened shut by a heavy metal lock. Immediately, the leaders of the mob called for a sledgehammer, which was instantly produced. It was as if the vigilantes had been fully informed of the various impediments they would face and had equipped themselves to deal with them.

Grabbing the huge and extremely heavy hammer, the men began taking turns at attacking the blockade. The shrieking sound of metal slamming against metal echoed throughout the jail.

Jeremiah Gibson realized the jail was under attack and knew he was there alone. Rushing from room to room on the second floor, where most of the prisoners were being held, Gibson searched for a telephone to summon help. But he quickly learned it was too late: the telephone lines had been disabled. His next thought was to sneak one of the trusties out of the jail to the police station to get backup. However, he discovered that that, too, was fruitless: the mob on the first-floor corridor had blocked all avenues of escape.

Downstairs, the hoodlums had made quick work of the first two obstacles—the large steel door and a smaller metal door—using the sledgehammers and a crowbar.

Ed Johnson was awakened about 8:30 p.m. by the shouts of fellow inmates who were housed on the floor below. They were shouting his name. The only other prisoner on the third floor was a woman named Ellen Baker from Ducktown, an extremely rural community east of Chattanooga. The deputies had moved the other suspected criminals to the second floor earlier in the day. Johnson didn't know why. Some of the inmates had their suspicions, but none bothered to share these with Johnson. Baker was charged with selling whiskey without a license, also known as bootlegging. She had been arrested several times, mostly for whiskey running. The police arrested her once for shooting a man, but she was acquitted after it was learned that the victim had threatened to kill her if she did not share her bottle of bourbon with him. According to subsequent federal investigative reports and sworn testimony, Johnson asked her what was going on.

"There's a mob gathering, boy, and you're in a heap of trouble," she said. "You better check out that window."

Johnson rose from his squeaky bed and cautiously walked toward the window, which was guarded by steel bars and glass. Peeking outside, he saw about two dozen men gathered in the dusty courtyard in the front of the jail. A few were carrying rifles and pistols. They were huddled in a circle. Most of the men were listening intently while two or three others did the talking. When the group dispersed ten minutes later, six of the men were wearing handkerchiefs on their faces to disguise their identities.

"Why are they doing that?" Johnson asked.

"You stupid nigger," Baker said. "They're here to kill you!"

Johnson could hear the pounding of steel on steel downstairs. The woman in the accompanying cell offered no comfort.

"They're coming to get you," she said. "They may be coming to get us all. But they are definitely going to get you. I wouldn't want to be you."

Johnson could hear the voices of several men downstairs in the jail, yelling for the jailer to show his face and warning Ed Johnson that they were coming for him.

"You better do some more prayin'," the woman said.

Johnson was perhaps the most isolated man in all of Tennessee. His only solace was the cries of the inmates on the floors below, telling him to be strong and to beg for mercy from God Almighty.

Once they had forced the first-floor door open, the men turned to the right and marched up the spiral staircase past the second floor and up to the third floor. At the top of the steps, they were confronted with three more doors—all of them locked. These barriers that had been used to protect the public from dangerous criminals were now gates protecting the prisoners from a violent public. Together, they presented a formidable challenge.

The first, a steel-plated door, was easily removed. This gave the mob access to several rooms on the third floor, but not to the cells. The second door, made up of iron bars, proved more frustrating. It was considerably more sturdy, held in place by five steel rivets. Angry that the door withstood their initial efforts simply to rip it away with their hands, the intruders cursed Gibson, who was not playing along as they had believed he would. A second sledgehammer and an ax were produced, and the men immediately took turns pounding at the lock that fastened the door and the rivets that held the door in place.

After several minutes of avoiding direct contact with the mob, Gibson left his hiding place on the second floor, loaded his pistol, and ran up the stairs to where the mob was at work. Several members of the group quickly recognized Gibson as the jailer.

"We need the keys to open this lock," one of the vigilantes demanded.

"Give us the keys and we promise to do you no harm, old man," said another.

Gibson, his gun drawn but not pointed at the men, said he could not and would not give them the keys. With inmates and news reporters watching, the deputy told the vigilantes he didn't have the keys, and an initial search of his pockets failed to produce the tools to undo the locks. He also warned them that he had called the National Guard Armory for assistance.

The leaders of the mob were at first mystified, then infuriated. They had believed Gibson would be on their side and would help them gain access to Johnson. Maybe he was offering this minimal resistance because he thought he had to as a lawman, they thought. In any case, the raiders were positive that no telephone calls had gone out. They also noticed that Gibson did nothing to hide the key ring hanging from his belt and holster. Within a minute of the confrontation, the bandits had seized the jailer's Smith & Wesson revolver, which he had purchased just a week earlier for $18. "Be careful with that," he told the men who took the pistol. "It's brand-new."

The rioters said they would return the gun if he would give them the keys to unlock the door. Gibson nodded and slowly pulled the key chain from his belt. He selected a long, slender silver key. With the mob members watching, he slid the key into the lock's hole. He struggled for a moment trying to get it in. Finally, it fit. But then, as Gibson attempted to turn it in the lock, an expression of confusion crossed the jailer's face. It wouldn't turn. He was sure this was the key.

Unamused, the intruders cursed Gibson and shoved him aside. They accused him of trying to delay their efforts. However, their attempts to turn the key in the lock also proved fruitless. They tried other keys, thinking the jailer was trying to trick them, but none of the others fit. That's when the frustrating truth set in: they had the right key, but the members of the mob themselves had ruined the locking device by beating on it with the sledgehammer and ax, so that the key would no longer turn the bolt. After making several threats toward Gibson, the men resumed their physical assault on the door. They returned to the awful pounding at the lock and rivets, shaking the jail with each blow.

About 9:00 p.m., Johnson again peered out the window near his cell. The number of people standing around in the courtyard outside the jail had swelled to 250. More joined by the minute. Whispers turned to chants. Speeches mixed vulgarities with Bible verses. The Ku Klux Klan was praised. White faces turned red with anger and hatred.

"Turn the black bastard over to us!"

"Open up or we'll burn down the whole goddamn jail!"

The infuriated voices grew louder and louder. Even the few women in the crowd thirsted for blood. They shook their fists and stomped their feet. Some threw rocks at the barred windows. Their hostility fed upon itself. The words grew stronger, more malicious.

A tall, thin man exited through the front door of the jail. He and others standing around him began waving their arms in an attempt to gain the attention of the crowd. When the audience was sufficiently quieted, the man announced what efforts were being made inside the jail. He informed them of the barriers and of finding the jailer. The crowd booed and hissed. One member of the mob threatened to get some dynamite.

But the man briefing the crowd said dynamite was unnecessary: he was confident they would capture Johnson within the hour, and he told them they would need a rope. This sent the mob into a frenzy.

> Friends, we are here for one reason. We are here for the sake of the purity of our wives and daughters and all the women of the South. We are here to protect them from the savagery of the Negro brutes.
>
> We cannot stand by while Negroes defile and ruin our precious women. We must make an example of this Negro to show the other Negroes that they must leave our women alone.

Of course, most of the people in the crowd did not personally know either Nevada Taylor or Ed Johnson. Nor were they victims of black crime. They could not name a relative or a friend who had ever been raped. They were not there to mete out justice for a crime. Most of them were merely poor and white, and very angry. They had always seen themselves as superior to black people. After all, black people had been slaves. They all believed white men were intellectually superior to blacks. But now, forty years after the Civil War, the economic and social conditions of their world had changed. Black people were not only legally equal to white people, they were increasingly on the same socioeconomic scale, too. In fact, many black people were actually better off economically. Lower-income white men found themselves competing—and frequently losing out—for jobs at the city's factories and textile mills.

One man complained that the court system was too slow, too expensive, and too ineffective. Simply killing the defendant was the best and easiest form of punishment. Besides, he said, this was the community's method of sending a message back to the Supreme Court in Washington to stay out of their business.

Ed Johnson peered down from the window of his cell. People were dancing, laughing, cursing. The revelry might have reminded him of the traveling carnival that came to town once a year. This was a game to the mob below. But these screams, chants, and giggles were not fun to Johnson. The other black inmates were in a state of total terror. They feared the mob might get them by mistake.

Johnson returned to his steel-framed bunk. There was no give in the springs, which dug through the thin mattress and into the flesh of his bare back. He pulled the dirty green wool blanket to his chin, closed his eyes, and tried to concentrate on the 23rd Psalm, a passage of scripture that his mother had read to him as a child every night before bed. Johnson had stopped going to school in the third grade and never learned to read. But we know from Ellen Baker's testimony that he had heard the prayer of David so often that he could recite most of it from memory.

The Lord is my shepherd; I shall not want.

He maketh me to lie down in green pastures: he leadeth me beside the still waters.

He restoreth my soul: he leadeth me in the paths of righteousness for his name's sake.

Yea, though I walk through the valley of the shadow of death, I will fear no evil: for thou art with me. . . .

Outside, the sound of gunshots interrupted Johnson's prayers and thoughts. He couldn't help hearing the venom in the words of the mob as they echoed throughout the nearly empty third floor.

"We know what to do with his nigger ass!" echoed a voice to cheers.

"Ain't no court in Washington going to save him now," yelled another.

Johnson prayed louder, shutting his eyes and holding his hands over his ears. He couldn't remember the rest of the words to Psalm 23, so he started over. He repeated the same four verses again and again.

Peering out the window one more time, Johnson saw that the crowd was continuing to grow. And they were more boisterous. Across the street, he spotted the new opera house that had opened just two weeks earlier. A large sign advertised French actress Sarah Bernhardt's appearance in *Camille* that coming weekend. Johnson had no idea who Bernhardt was or what she did to entertain people. He could not read the sign to understand the program.

One thing he was becoming surer of by the minute: help was not on the way.

Less than a mile away, Sheriff Joseph Shipp was sitting down to a late dinner prepared by his black housekeeper. After he and his wife enjoyed a glass of red wine, they began to eat baked chicken, rice, and homemade bread. But after only a few bites, the telephone rang. The housekeeper answered. It was a reporter for the *Chattanooga Times*.

Initially, Shipp declined to come to the phone, saying he didn't like to be interrupted during dinner. But the reporter insisted, telling the housekeeper he had urgent news that the sheriff would want to know. The elderly black woman who had worked for the Shipps for a dozen years delivered the message. The sheriff nodded, folded his napkin, and walked to the phone.

The reporter apologized for taking Shipp away from his dinner, but he said he had just returned from the jail, where a large mob was gathering. In fact, he said, several members of the mob were inside the jail trying to break through the steel-barred doors that gave access to the third floor and the cell holding Ed Johnson. The reporter told the sheriff that many of the men had guns.

The county's top law-enforcement officer offered very little in response. He thanked the reporter for calling and said he would walk immediately to the jail. After kissing his wife good evening and telling her not to wait up for him, Shipp began the half-mile walk down McCallie Avenue toward the jail. On the way, he passed the National Guard Armory and the city police department. But he stopped at neither. He solicited no assistance.

About 9:30 p.m., Sheriff Shipp arrived alone at the jail. He was winded from the long walk. Members of the mob saw him coming a couple of blocks away and warned the leaders inside.

"It's the sheriff," yelled one man. "He can get the Negro out for us."

As Shipp made his way into the building, members of the mob clapped him on the shoulder. Inside, he found Gibson in the office on the first floor. The elderly jailer explained to him what had happened. A group of vigilantes quickly surrounded the sheriff and asked him for the keys that would allow them to grab Johnson. Shipp insisted he had none of the keys that the men sought. He pleaded with the mob to cease their efforts and allow the law to take its course. However, he offered no physical resistance to the hoodlums. The loaded six-shooter on his hip never left its holster. He did not demand that the armed intruders leave. Not once did he attempt to restrain them physically. Nor did the leaders of the mob require the sheriff to relinquish his weapon.

For several days, Shipp had heard his critics complain that he should not have been so aggressive in protecting Ed Johnson during the first lynching attempt. If he had simply bowed to the will of the people two months earlier and let them have the prisoner then, none of this would have been necessary. Time and time again, he heard people he knew and respected say that having prevented the earlier lynch mob might just cost him re-election.

When the leaders of the mob grew tired of the sheriff's pleas not to destroy his jail, several of the men led him to the jail's bathroom and told him to stay in there. No guard was posted at the bathroom door and nothing was done to keep Shipp from leaving the jail. Even so, he remained in the facility.

The leaders of the mob did permit a reporter for the *Times* to roam freely throughout the jail during their assault. He was there from the beginning and took extensive notes regarding the evening's developments. The identities of the mob leaders were not included in his notes. While the crowd outside the jail grew to a few hundred, the reporter said they were mostly inactive bystanders who were there out of curiosity, to support the leaders of the mob, or simply to watch a man die. Only about twenty-five men played an active role in the attack.

About every fifteen minutes, the leaders of the mob were successful in beating another rivet on the steel door into submission. Every time a bolt fell to the floor, the intruders in the jail would announce it to the ever-increasing crowd outside. At 10:15 p.m., the fourth of the rivets was removed, leaving one final barrier to the mob.

Johnson sat on his bunk without moving a muscle. He prayed and prayed again, realizing the end was near. He no longer sought God's deliverance from the angry mob, but now asked for courage and strength. He just wanted the affair to be over as quickly as possible. He wished he could see his dad and mom and sister just one more time, and worried the mob might go after his family next.

The excitement of the mob outside grew by the minute. It was now obvious that there would be no intervention by law enforcement. If the men could remove the obstacles and get to Johnson, it appeared as if no one would try to interfere with their efforts. The mob had free rein.

For twenty minutes, the men pounded away at the fifth rivet. Finally, a big, broad-shouldered man in overalls took the hammer and stepped up to the steel door in the stairway. Each time he raised the heavy gavel over his head and slammed it down with force, the entire jail shook, and men in the crowd cheered. The lock was strong, but this mountain of a man was stronger. His beard dripping sweat, he reared back again and brought the heavy sledgehammer down with one more mighty chop.

"We're coming to get you, Negro," the hammer wielder shouted. "No damn Supreme Court will save you tonight."

"You'll need all the religion you got yesterday," said another man. "Better be sayin' your prayers."

"Guess now you're sorry you done it, ain't you," added another.

The fifth bolt gave way at last, allowing the determined men to remove the door. Applause filled the courtyard. The leaders of the mob took the keys Gibson had given them and unlocked the large circle door that gave them access to the third floor. Stepping into the third-floor corridor, the vigilantes got their first look at Ed Johnson sitting in cell number 7, to their left.

A wrench was used to throw a lever that opened the final door, and the mob had access to the series of cells where Johnson was being held. Six men appointed by the others stepped forward to get the suspect. One of them pulled Gibson's keys from his coat. The lock on the cell door answered the key, and two men cautiously entered Johnson's cell. They expected him to fight, thought he would curse them or even spit on them. He did none of that. They ordered Johnson to stand up. He obeyed, and spoke not a word as the men tied his hands behind him with a short rope and dragged him from the cell. It was nearly 11:20 p.m. when the thugs forced Johnson out the door for all the world to see.

> There before the leaders of the mob stood the Negro, seemingly unterrified, but his eyes, long, narrow blood-shot, rolling from one to another of his captors.
>
> One of the mob leaders stepped to Johnson's side with a short rope and throwing it over his prisoner's shoulders and drawing it tight, marched him out into the corridor.
>
> Johnson walked well, except when he was pushed by the mob. He held his head in the same lowly position which it is now known is characteristic of the Negro, and went along with the mob with his lips tight closed and his eyes downcast.
>
> The mob hangers-on welcomed them at the foot of the jail stairs and greeted with cheers Johnson's appearance. Then began these cries which strike terror into the heart of the innocent—the cry of one human being thirsty for the blood of another.
>
> Like wild beasts for a moment, the crowd circled the Negro in their midst, but about him stood determined men whose plan of action seemed to have been mapped out long before and who seemed determined that no hitch should occur in their arrangements.
>
> The prisoner was the calmest person in the jail. Not a quiver of the lip or utterance of a sound betrayed the slightest terror.
>
> *Chattanooga News*, March 20, 1906

As the men stood on the jail steps showcasing their prize, Johnson quickly scanned the crowd, looking for a friendly or familiar face. A brief sense of hope came when he spotted a few uniformed police officers in the crowd. Maybe they were here to rescue him, to save him;

maybe they could disperse the mob. Had the sheriff called them? Was the National Guard far behind? But all prospects died when he saw those lawmen laughing and joking with members of the lynch mob. They were part of the horde.

Looking across the courtyard, he saw two men watching from the third-floor window of a building down and across the street. The men looked familiar, very familiar. He was certain he knew them, but as he strained to get a clearer view, the leaders of the mob yanked him from the jail steps and down into the crowd.

"Kill him now!" demanded one man.

"Cut his heart out right here!" howled another.

As the leaders discussed their next move, Johnson was bombarded with verbal assaults. He was called an animal, a brute, a beast, and names much worse. He was spit upon and kicked and slapped and punched. Stones from the courtyard struck his back and his head, leaving small gashes. A few men struck Johnson with their rifles. Eventually, blood trickled from his brow and down the side of his face.

The hatred in the eyes of these vigilantes was like nothing he had ever seen or even imagined. He couldn't guess what had filled the hearts of so many men with hatred and ill-feeling toward him personally and his race in general. Indeed, the grudge held by these men wasn't confined to Ed Johnson. They wanted to kill a black man. Any black man. Johnson's arrest and conviction simply gave them self-justification and made him their target.

Some in the crowd wanted Johnson taken to St. Elmo, the spot where the attack on Nevada Taylor had occurred. That would be the appropriate place to hang the culprit, they argued; that would send the strongest message to the Negro community. But the hour was late and St. Elmo was several miles away. It would have taken more than an hour to drag Johnson to the crime scene, and the mob was too impatient for that.

"To the county bridge!" someone finally shouted.

A tremendous applause erupted. It was agreed. The fifteen-year-old bridge that spanned the Tennessee River, and connected downtown Chattanooga with the residential section to the north, would have to do.

The leaders of the mob gathered around Johnson and slowly walked him to the bridge. They had little to say and made no noise—unlike the crowds surrounding them, who yelled and pushed their way to the river. A newspaperman following the mob described it as a "strange funeral procession."

Near the end of their six-block march toward the bridge, the mob passed an electric trolley car taking passengers home. Realizing that the rope around Johnson's shoulders was not long enough to hang him from the bridge, a leader in the mob ordered the trolley conductor to stop, boarded the electric train, and cut the trolley rope and cords used to ring the bell.

Along the way, individuals in the mob taunted Johnson, telling him if he would just confess they would let him go free. They dragged Ed Johnson across the wooden planks to the first steel span on the bridge. He walked most of the way. A few times, he stumbled and fell. The men would kick him and order him back to his feet.

"To the second span," yelled several members of the mob. The men remembered thirteen years earlier, February 14, 1893, when a mob had dragged Alfred Blount, also a black man, from the same jail to the county bridge. He was lynched from the first span for allegedly attacking a white woman. It was only appropriate that the second man lynched on the bridge be hanged from the second span, the men argued.

The leaders of the mob complied with the request of the crowd and kept Johnson moving another 100 feet, toward the next steel span that acted as a brace for the bridge. As they walked, one of the men tied the rope into a hangman's noose. Most of the crowd stayed a good distance away, like spectators at a sporting event. About fifty armed men pushed their Negro forward. Two men climbed hand over hand up the iron beam. They threw the rope over the metal girder and then looped it around the frame of the bridge.

Task completed, the men dropped the end of the rope with the noose to the men on the ground. Almost comically, the other end of the rope fell to the ground as well. It was quickly put back into place.

"Do you have anything to say?" a man holding the rope asked.

"Confess!" screamed others.

Ed Johnson, with blood dripping from the corners of his mouth, stood absolutely calm. He expressed no emotion even as the noose was placed around his neck. The leaders of the mob told him that nothing he could say would save his life, so he might as well confess. Finally, Johnson spoke up.

I am ready to die. But I never done it. I am going to tell the truth. I am not guilty. I am not guilty. I have said all the time that I did not do it and it is true. I was not there.

I know I am going to die and I have no fear to die and I have no fear at all.

I was not at St. Elmo that night. Nobody saw me with a strap. They were mistaken and saw somebody else. I was at the Last Chance Saloon just as I said.

I am not guilty and that is all I have to say.

His words turned the mob into a frenzy. They cursed his name, they spit on his face. They threatened to find his family and do to them what he allegedly had done to this white woman. Again they demanded he confess. Then Ed Johnson uttered his last words:

God bless you all. I am innocent.

Deciding that time was being wasted, the leaders gave the order to hoist Johnson into the air. Several men grabbed one end of the rope and started to pull. Suddenly, the rope snapped taut, hoisting Ed Johnson's body high into the air, where he swung by the neck more than 100 feet above the mighty Tennessee River. For two minutes, his body jerked with life. A few men in the crowd grew impatient and opened fire. Round after round of ammunition was emptied into Ed Johnson's body.

Johnson's mutilated body abruptly dropped with a thud to the wooden bridge. A stray bullet had severed the rope. With more than 100 spectators looking on, including women and children, Johnson's head moved and his body twitched.

"He's not dead yet," someone spit in disbelief.

A second fusillade of bullets rained into Johnson's torso.

"Be sure he is dead," exclaimed several members of the mob.

A large, bearded man slowly reloaded his revolver and then approached Johnson's body. He put the barrel against Ed Johnson's head and fired five times. Scores of bullets had literally torn pieces of Johnson's body apart.

In a final act of desecration, one leader of the mob stepped forward and pinned a large note to the victim's body. It read: "To Justice Harlan. Come get your nigger now." With that, the scores of men and handful of women involved in the lynching could finally go home, their mission accomplished.

Fifty-three days after he was arrested for the rape of Nevada Taylor, Ed Johnson was dead.

> Peaceful citizens, in their beds last night hearing the shouting which accompanied the line of march from the jail to the county bridge, and the shots which told too well the story of triumph of the mob law, shuddered as they thought of that monster of a thousand feet and a thousand hands and heads, swayed by impulse that was loose in the city and though they knew it was against the Negro branded a brute that their efforts were being directed, yet they were nonetheless uneasy on that account.
>
> *Chattanooga News*, March 20, 1906

CHAPTER THIRTEEN

THE HONOR OF
THE COURT

AFTER EMANCIPATION, LYNCHING was the ultimate expression of racism. During the days of slavery, few slaves were lynched, because they constituted valuable property: no one would destroy his own wealth. Those who lynched another man's slave were prosecuted and severely punished for the loss of property. In addition, if a black slave committed a capital offense and was executed, the state had to reimburse the owner for the fair market value of the slave.

During the first two decades that followed the Civil War, the number of people lynched climbed slowly. By 1892, the number of black men and women murdered at the hands of white supremacists had jumped to a total of 162. An overwhelming majority of those lynchings occurred in Southern states. Indeed, 80 percent of the 3,693 people in the United States killed by a mob between 1888 and 1929 were African-American. Two-thirds of the victims were twenty-one years of age or younger. Half were married with children. Less than 10 percent had previous criminal records. Most of them were illiterate and had very little education.

More than a third of the people lynched had been charged with murder. One-fourth of the victims had been accused of rape or attempted rape. There is no explanation for the lynching of another 25 percent.

Those who made up the lynch mob could be divided into three categories: (1) those who took an active part by breaking into the jail and killing the prisoner; (2) those who were in complete sympathy with the active lynchers and voiced their support for the lynching but took no part in it; (3) and those who were present merely out of curiosity. Not only did the onlookers make it more difficult for law-enforcement officers to stop the mob, but their presence also implied public acquiescence in the activities of the mob and gave police officers second thoughts about interfering with the mob.

People who made up lynch mobs were generally less educated and unemployed, had previous criminal records, did not own property, and were frequent visitors to saloons. They usually came from the suburbs or rural neighborhoods.

The leaders of lynch mobs were almost never arrested and remained relatively safe from prosecution by the courts. Of the sixty-five people murdered by vigilantes in 1906, only three arrests were made. None of the cases resulted in murder charges. In the few cases in other years when the vigilantes were charged with murder, all-white male juries seldom issued harsh punishments.

The men who dragged Ed Johnson's body from the jail the night of March 19, 1906, believed they would never be arrested. From the time the assault on the jail began to the moment Ed Johnson's body was lifted into the air, more than three hours had passed. During that time, not one sheriff's deputy, city police officer, state militia member, or local leader appeared at the jail to attempt to prevent the lynching. They all said later they had been unaware of the lynching effort.

The final bullet pierced Johnson's body at 11:45 p.m. For another hour, his torso lay openly on the Walnut Street Bridge. Even as members of the mob drifted away from the crime scene, curiosity seekers drove or walked onto the bridge for a better look at what had happened. More than a dozen women came by carriage or car or on foot to get a glimpse of the victim.

An elderly black woman approached just as the horrible task had been completed, and elbowed her way to the front of the crowd. As she neared the lifeless body on the bridge's wooden planks, she asked people who the man was and what he had done. Significant pieces of flesh had been ripped from his body by the barrage of bullets.

"Is he dead, white folks?" she asked.

When the leaders of the mob answered in the affirmative, the old woman shook her head in disbelief. "Well, I swear," she said, and walked away.

Jailer Jeremiah Gibson had also followed the mob to the bridge, but he had no intention of trying to stop the men from completing their task. Instead, his primary mission was to recover the new Smith & Wesson the mob leaders had taken from him and never returned.

"Have you seen the man who has my pistol?" he asked of people he passed on the bridge. Gibson did not attempt to interfere with the hanging, or write down the names of witnesses. He did nothing to apprehend those participating in the lynching. And he never did find his revolver.

Not a single person was arrested that night. Additional deputies were never called in to investigate the lynching. No police reports were ever filed. As far as the official police records in Hamilton County were concerned, the lynching never occurred. After the mob dispersed from the bridge, a Chattanooga police officer walked over to Johnson's body and cut off one of his fingers as a souvenir.

Well after midnight, a horse-drawn wagon from a black-owned and -operated funeral home slowly made its way on to the county bridge. Three black men who worked for the funeral home scooped up Johnson's body, threw it in the back of the wagon, and took off.

The newspapers, which had published so many inflammatory articles about Johnson and expressed such outrage at the Supreme Court's interference in the case, suddenly took the moral high road. The *Times* denounced mob violence and declared that those who participated in it should be punished.

In circumstances of this kind, all that the good citizen can do is to bow his head in shame and look for better things in the future. In the presence of the mob spirit rampant in the land, we have nothing to expect but anarchy and ruin. If something is not done to stay the growth of that spirit, who shall say it will not be upon us full before we know it?

It is a time for lovers of law and order and the friends of society and the home to take counsel together and see if something may not be done to check this evil that seems ready and able to run riot at any time its promoters may think it has provocation.

The reaction to the lynching varied widely throughout the city. Black people expressed their outrage by systematically staging a one-day work stoppage. On Tuesday, March 20, manufacturing and textile plants across Chattanooga were idle because black men, who constituted a large segment of the workforce, stayed home.

Most white leaders echoed the sentiments of the newspapers, declaring the lynching an awful event that should never be allowed to happen again. The business community took an especially critical stand against mob rule. They viewed the lynching as a horrible blemish on the city's image at a time when they were trying to position Chattanooga as a progressive, economic stronghold in the South that had none of the racial tensions of the other cities in Dixie.

While nearly everyone condemned lynch law, most leaders in the city also placed the blame for it squarely on the U.S. Supreme Court. They claimed the justices in Washington were just as responsible as the lynchers for Johnson's death, because they had antagonized the mob by delaying the inevitable death sentence. "No lynching would have occurred had the case not been taken from the Tennessee courts into the federal courts," Governor James Cox told the *Nashville Banner*.

Judge McReynolds, District Attorney Whitaker, and Sheriff Shipp made separate statements to the same effect. "Had the federal courts not interfered and delayed the adjudication of this case, the mob violence we so deplore would never have raised its fierceful face," said McReynolds. "As long as this prisoner was in the state court system, we protected him from mob violence and provided him with every benefit due a man."

On this point, the city's two newspapers differed. The *Chattanooga Times* condemned mob rule and said there was absolutely no justification for it. The *Times* encouraged an immediate investigation of the lynching and said there would be no justice without arrests of those who had been involved in the slaying of Johnson. The *Chattanooga News*, by contrast, took the position that the lynching was wrong but understandable. The afternoon paper said Johnson had gotten what he deserved, and they blamed Parden and Hutchins and the Supreme Court for inciting the riot.

The lynching is a direct result of the ill-advised effort to save the Negro from the just penalty of the laws of Tennessee. Had not that effort been made, the Negro would have been legally executed today at the county jail. There was not a scintilla of doubt in the minds of the jury that he was guilty.

The News deems it timely to mention that this community was content to let the law take its course provided there was no unnecessary delay. It was the appeal to the federal courts that revived the mob spirit and resulted in the lynching. This fact should be a lesson in the future.

There is no community south or north which will submit to delay in punishment for this particular crime. The Supreme Court of the United States ought in its wisdom to take cognizance of this fact.

Discussions on the street and in saloons all over town were not so analytical. There were widespread rumors that a group of black men would get their revenge the following night. There was talk of organizing a black lynch mob to storm the jail to take a white man who had recently been arrested for killing a young black girl. And there were those who simply advocated rioting by burning down white businesses and houses.

Leaders in the black church immediately took to the streets and communities to suppress such thoughts. Preachers begged their followers to remain nonviolent in their protests. They applauded their one-day work strike as a sufficient statement of their displeasure. And they asked black people to seek revenge in more lawful ways, including at the ballot box. After all, the county elections were only a week away.

No one was more disheartened or more outraged by the lynching than Noah Parden. Convinced that Johnson was innocent of the rape, Parden had invested his entire soul in the case. If anyone had a right to be bitter and desire revenge, it was he. Yet Parden was among those who pleaded for peace in an article he wrote for the *Chattanooga Blade*.

> An awful event has taken us by surprise. No Negro should be satisfied by what has happened. Justice for Ed Johnson and for the Negro as a people has been denied.
>
> But it does no good for any man to react to injustice with mob violence. We have displayed our dissatisfaction this day by our actions. Let us not ignore the very laws we seek to protect us.
>
> Let us now seek just punishment against those who violated the laws of our state and country.

All day Tuesday, Chattanoogans—black and white, men and women—packed hardware stores to buy weapons and ammunition. Everyone feared a race riot, and no one wanted to be left unprotected. As a safety precaution, the larger department stores and grocery markets closed their doors early to allow the women who worked there to get home before dark.

To help suppress possible disruptions, Sheriff Shipp recruited an additional 200 people to act as temporary deputies to patrol the county. The city police added a few dozen men of their own. And the governor asked the fifty members of the local National Guard to assist the sheriff.

The mayor ordered all the saloons frequented by black people to be closed that Tuesday and Wednesday. He issued no such mandate for taverns visited by white people. The sheriff also issued a curfew exclusively applying to black people. He did not want to see any black people on the streets after 9:00 p.m. Law-enforcement officials also rounded up the habitual drunks and those constantly charged with disorderly conduct and kept them in jail for two days, just as a precaution.

For the most part, the racial confrontations were limited. There were no riots and no group clashes. Most black people stayed in their homes. A few prayer meetings were conducted at black churches throughout the city.

The only violent incident occurred at a local foundry where a white employee was seen slapping a young black boy. When an adult black man sought to intervene, the white man shot him with a .32-caliber pistol. The black man died from the injury, and the white man was charged with assault, but not murder.

Community leaders downplayed the shooting incident as isolated. They insisted that the two races were putting aside their differences and hatred. Most of all, city officials hoped the world would quickly forget the tragic lynching. It was a horrible event that should be left behind and not dwelled upon, they said.

If the people of Chattanooga thought they could simply declare the lynching an event in their history and move on, they were badly mistaken. Other lynchings—indeed, most lynchings—had been executed without consequences, but not this one.

The news of the lynching reached the U.S. Supreme Court the morning after it occurred. Notified by reporters, the justices were stunned. They had never been confronted by such a situation before. The Court found particularly offensive the note pinned to Johnson's body that condemned the Supreme Court for its action.

> The open defiance of the Supreme Court of the United States of the mob that lynched the Negro, Ed Johnson, last night, has no parallel in the history of the Court.
>
> The event has shocked the members of the Court beyond anything that has ever happened in their experience on the bench. They have met in twos and threes today and discussed the matter, and the course to be taken to vindicate the power and authority of the Court.
>
> No justice can say what will be done. All, however, agree

in saying that the sanctity of the Supreme Court shall be upheld if the power resides in the Court and the government to accomplish such a vindication of the majesty of the law.

New York Times, March 21, 1906

The morning following the lynching, Justices John M. Harlan and Oliver Wendell Holmes met with Chief Justice Melville W. Fuller at the chief justice's home. The Supreme Court had officially recessed for the spring. However, they were so furious that they met informally to discuss the matter. At the end of their closed-door session, each expressed outrage to news reporters and condemned the mob actions. All three rebuked the mob and said definite action must be taken. In an interview with a reporter for the *Washington Post*, Justice Harlan expressed "righteous indignation" that his order staying the execution and protecting the defendant had been obviously and intentionally ignored.

The fact was that Johnson was tried by little better than mob law before the state court.

A juror rose in the box and demanded of the young woman who had been attacked if she was sure the defendant was the man who had committed the act and when she said she was not willing to swear that he was, the juror demanded that she should swear that he was the man, and he would get down out of the jury box and cut his heart out.

There was abundant proof that there was intimidation of witnesses and counsel and the reason why the court did not allow an appeal or a plea in abatement was the fear that if any such consideration was shown, the mob would lynch the prisoner.

There was reason to believe that the man was innocent.

But be that as it may, whether guilty or innocent, he had the right to a fair trial, and the mandate of the Supreme Court has for the first time in the history of the country been openly defied by a community.

An even stronger rebuke came from Justice Holmes. He described the state-court trial given to Johnson as "a shameful attempt at justice." He also compared the judge and jury to the lynch mob. "This was not merely a case of a defendant claiming he did not receive a fair trial," Holmes told reporters. "In all likelihood, this was a case of an innocent man improperly branded a guilty brute and condemned to die from the start." Holmes also scolded the lawyers appointed to defend Johnson at his trial for abandoning their client after the jury's verdict.

Chief Justice Fuller agreed with Harlan and Holmes that action needed to be taken. He said there would be immediate consultations with President Roosevelt, U.S. Attorney General William Moody, and federal law-enforcement officials based in Tennessee. The first two goals, Fuller said, were to vindicate the Supreme Court's power under such circumstances and to determine the parties responsible for the lynching. Fuller said the parties should be tried for murder, but he admitted that that was a state crime, so that the federal authorities would have no role in such a prosecution.

President Theodore Roosevelt also condemned the lynching and termed the event as "contemptuous of the court. It is an affront to the highest tribunal in the land that cannot go by without proper action being taken."

By Wednesday morning, thirty-six hours after the lynching, the attention of the federal authorities was already starting to focus on Sheriff Shipp. U.S. Attorney J. R. Penland, whose jurisdiction included Chattanooga, believed that the federal government did have jurisdiction to investigate the lynching, because Johnson was a federal prisoner. Justice Harlan's stay of execution and order to the Chattanooga authorities had made it clear to Shipp and other court officials, Penland said, that Johnson was a federal prisoner and should be kept safe pending his appeal.

Penland, a career prosecutor and an appointee of President Roosevelt, said he planned to investigate the lynching thoroughly, and "if any of the participants can be identified, I will prosecute them to the fullest extent of the law." If the newspaper reports were correct that the mob gathering had been planned early Monday, then Sheriff

Shipp must have known that there would be an effort to lynch Johnson that night, Penland said. If this was true, the prosecutor said there was no excuse why more deputies had not been deployed to defend the jail.

"The lynching of the Negro was downright murder," Penland said, "and somebody ought to pay for it."

MORE THAN 2,000 men and women filled the Primitive Baptist Church sanctuary that Wednesday afternoon for Ed Johnson's funeral. His father, Skinbone, greeted people at the front door. Standing beside him were two black ministers. Parden and Hutchins were there, too, as was Lewis Shepherd. Only a few other white people were present—friends Johnson had known from the saloon where he worked.

One preacher sang and offered prayer. The other gave a quiet, almost introspective sermon. There was no shouting or screaming. The service was devoid of all sensationalism. Johnson was remembered as a soft-spoken man who had worked hard and enjoyed the company of friends. He loved to play pool and hated the cold weather.

Asked to speak, Parden thanked God that his client had made a profession of faith in the days before his death. He said that Johnson represented the courage every man needs to have when facing an unbearable situation. Johnson also demonstrated how much more black and white people needed to strive in order to achieve equality and harmony within the community.

The service lasted less than an hour, and there was no direct mention of the lynching or Johnson's case, no protests or demonstrations. Only tears, hugs and sadness. Johnson's father grasped Parden's hand as the lawyer was leaving the church. "For my son's sake, thank you," he said. "God bless you."

The next Sunday morning, March 25, the lynching and its effect on the community were very much the topic of many pastors around the city, and not just in the African-American churches. Dr. McCallie and Reverend Bachman both preached on the sins of the mob to their Presbyterian followers. But the most unexpectedly critical sermon came from Dr. Howard E. Jones of the First Baptist Church. First Baptist was the city's establishment church for white people, the largest church in this community dominated by Baptist congregations. As a young pastor, Dr. Jones had always tried to dissociate himself from the political bureaucracy of the city. He never got involved in politics and seldom spoke about the social ills that faced the community. Instead, he was a hellfire-and-brimstone preacher who spoke on heavenly things and how to be a better Christian, preferring to concentrate on the functions of his church rather than happenings at City Hall. As a result, his church had grown to be one of the largest in the South: about 2,000 people regularly attended his Sunday-morning worship services.

Dr. Jones had been pastor at First Baptist for only two years, having been educated at Wake Forest University in North Carolina, Washington & Lee University in Virginia, and the Baptist Theological Seminary in Louisville, Kentucky. As a preacher, he was a rising star and an influential figure in the Southern Baptist Convention. As an orator, Dr. Jones was without equal. He had learned his preaching skills from his father, Reverend J. W. Jones, who had been chaplain general of the United Confederate Veterans and personal chaplain for General Robert E. Lee.

But as the younger Jones mounted his pulpit that Sunday morning, a heavy burden lay on his heart. The lynching had terrified his spirit and deflated his soul. That morning, he delivered a sermon that was discussed in every household in Chattanooga for weeks. The bulletin handed to every person who walked through the doors of the church had but six words in large, bold letters:

IS LAWLESSNESS A CURE FOR CRIME?

Dr. Jones's message wasn't lengthy, but it was to the point. He knew it would be controversial, maybe even offensive to many of his parishioners. In fact, he worried that the church's deacons might run him out of town. Even so, he announced from his pulpit that he would not apologize for the sermon he was about to deliver: the people of the city needed to hear the truth as God would tell it to them. He then instructed the congregation to turn in their Bibles to Galatians 6:7, and began to preach a sermon that remains to this day one of the most courageous ever delivered:

> "Whatsoever a man soweth, that shall he also reap."
>
> The white man rules in this community. I am using an old phrase, oft used by you, when I affirm that he always has and he always will. The honor of rule involves a burden of responsibility. If the white man rules and this community is condemned with a charge of anarchy and lawlessness, then the white man must face the responsibility. It is not enough for us to say that the responsibility rests entirely upon the officers of the law, because they are only our creatures. Our votes placed them in office and by our support they hold their positions.
>
> Let us now briefly consider the events of last Monday night. They are not pretty, nor poetic. Some fifty or more men, presuming upon the oft expressed fear of a mob and impatient of law and order went to our jail. With evidence of carefully premeditated program, they took the keys away from the one man who was to defend Chattanooga's honor. But owing to their haste to get at their bloody business, they destroyed with sledges the usefulness of the keys and for two hours, they toiled at the steel bolts which were more loyal to Chattanooga's interest than all of her citizenship. But where are the police and where are the thousands who should have and could have defended us against an unspeakable disgrace?
>
> And so the mob marches by a gallows ready prepared with stretched rope within the precincts of the jail. They are not in pursuit of justice, but lawless revenge. Their business is to brutalize a community. Let the curtain fall upon the rest of that unspeakable scene.
>
> The worst elements among the white men of this community took over the reins of government. Was this disgrace ever rebuked? Has any arrest of those men who unsheathed their keen blades and struck deadly blows at the very heart of our

civilization ever been effected? Does anyone here know of any attempt?

"Ah, Ah," but you say, "we were afraid." Afraid? Afraid of what? Afraid of the most vicious, Godless, ignorant and depraved of the white men of this community. Why did we not stop and consider that anarchy was already reigning in our midst, when a community was terrorized into a weak compromise with its most dangerous citizens.

Ah, no.

"Whatsoever a man soweth that shall he also reap."

We had but sown the wind, and were yet to reap the whirlwind. We had cast pearls before the swine, who were presently to trample them in the mire and turn and rend us. We had given the sacred and holy trust of law to dogs, who, despising the holy thing we had compromised, would presently be fixing their vicious fangs in the throat of our civilization.

Not only a fair trial should have been given to Ed Johnson, but a fair trial should also have been given to every member of that mob who could be apprehended. No arrest has been made. No, don't blame the officers altogether. No great, big, strong man stood up in this community and cried aloud in the name of law and justice for the arrest of those men.

But let me speak plainly to the man who sees no more in the tragedy on the bridge than that Ed Johnson got what he ought to have had. Admit it, but how about the community? Has it gotten what it ought to have had? I maintain that that mob struck more terrible blows at the heart of our civilization than it inflicted upon Ed Johnson. The beam in our eye has prevented us from seeing this. So far as Ed Johnson was concerned, the mob only deprived him of a life which in all probability he would only have possessed for a few weeks longer.

But consider what it has done to our community. It advertised Chattanooga all over this land and in foreign lands as a place where it is unsafe to live. It registered our city among that class of communities which have only attained a very low grade of civilization, a place where intelligence flees with fear and trembling when ignorance clenches its fists and gnashes its teeth. Think of the number of people who today only know us as a city where fifty hoodlums can terrify us into passive submission to lawless barbarism. But the largest injury to the community has not yet been realized. Just as the demoralizing effects of war are felt for generations, so a season of lawlessness such as we have just gone through is as far reaching in its baneful efforts. Whatsoever a man or a community soweth, that shall they also reap. What a lesson for our children!

The minute details of the horrible affair are discussed by groups of small boys on nearly every corner. I, myself, saw a picture the other afternoon which has haunted me like a ghost. A crowd of little boys were playing in a vacant lot, and I was horrified to see that they were in mimicry carrying out the revolting proceedings of the mob on Monday night. They went through with it all. They broke into the jail, they secured the Negro, represented by a large ash can, tied about it a rope, rushed yelling with it to a nearby fence, hoisted it in the air, and then for lack of pistols, took rocks and did their best to riddle the effigy. I walked sadly away, wondering how many "pistol toters" for the future were among those little boys, wondering if they were receiving lessons which would prevent a better civilization.

"Whatsoever a man or a community soweth, that shall he also reap."

Lawlessness begets lawlessness. It always has and always will. Sow an act of lawlessness and you will get a harvest of lawless conditions. If this is not true, civilization is a farce, and anarchy is the best goal to strive for.

The speaker scorns the need of denouncing the crime of which Johnson was accused. I could pile up every adjective, as did Hamlet at Ophelia's grave; I could utter overwrought denunciations which would fall back like cold water upon the fiery indignation which such a crime stirs within me, and yet I should find myself saying, apologetically, as did the sweet

THE HONOR OF THE COURT

Prince of Denmark, "Aye, I can rant as well as thou," but this is not a time for ranting.

I resent the crime on the bridge because of my unspeakable indignation against the crime at St. Elmo. To give over our dealing with this atrocity to lawless procedure means that over and over again, not only the innocent man hangs, but the guilty man remains free, as a threat to the sanctity of our homes. Tell me not, with the pages of history open before me, that a mob ever helps civilization. It is a blind Frankenstein monster, and its only power is force. It cannot think, it cannot reason, the most terrible of all, it cannot love. It is born of the hate of hell and has done more in the history of humanity to degrade civilization, laugh in the face of righteousness and defy the majesty of God, than has any other monster who ever issued from the pit. Blow the dust off your Barnaby Rigby, and let Dickens tell you of the mobs of London. Get down your Carlyle's *French Revolution* and let him show you how France lost her chance among the nations of the world through the mobs of the Reign of Terror.

Take your place in the gray dawn of that fatal Friday outside the Pretorium, where Pontias Pilate stands before the fury of a mob and presents the only sinless one who ever lived, and say, "Behold the Man." Hear the hoarse cry of that awful creature, the mob, as with gathering force it answers back, "Crucify Him! Crucify Him! Crucify Him!" and then stand forth and tell me if you hope by the force and fury of a mob to accomplish anything but to destroy the best and crucify the holiest!

In Washington, D.C., officials were afforded a different view of the Southern attitude than that supplied by Dr. Jones. The very Sunday morning of that amazing sermon, the *Washington Post* published a front-page article written by J. G. Rice, the editor of the *Chattanooga News*. He defended the local court's actions against Ed Johnson, asserting that no one doubted Johnson's guilt and that the defendant was afforded one of the fairest trials ever given in Chattanooga. However, the newsman unashamedly contradicted Judge McReynolds and Sheriff Shipp in regard to the allegation that black people were intentionally kept off juries.

> That allegation is a fact. The South long ago decided this to be a white man's government, and there is no appeal in Hamilton County from that decision. If that is treason, our critics are invited to make the most of it.
>
> It has been an unwritten law in the South, since the memory of man runneth not to the contrary that the black man who assaults a white woman shall die. This law maintains in every southern state, and is higher than any statutory law.
>
> And when once it is made certain that the guilty man has been captured there is not power enough in the United States Army to save him. I hold that the worthless, shiftless, criminal black brute who outrages a white woman has no more rights under the law than a serpent.

Members of the Supreme Court, meeting privately in the home of Chief Justice Fuller, read the article that Sunday morning with great interest. It was obvious to them that the lynching had arisen out of contempt for the Court and its ruling. After a lengthy discussion, they agreed they should take action separate from any charges brought by the state or federal authorities, for the lynching was an affront to the Court's dignity and prestige. They also believed they must take a definite stand against lynch law. The members of the Court agreed that their most likely action would probably involve some sort of contempt charges brought against the sheriff, his deputies, and possibly members of the mob. However, the justices all agreed to study the law and make recommendations the next time they met, which wouldn't be for another two weeks.

ON THE PREVIOUS Wednesday, just two days after the lynching, United States Attorney General William Moody had met with Presi-

dent Roosevelt to discuss it. Both believed the men who had participated in the mob should be punished. At a morning Cabinet meeting,
the president had waved a handful of telegrams from concerned citizens of Chattanooga, begging the president to allow local law enforcement to handle the matter. They promised that the leaders of the
lynching would be dealt with severely, and also claimed that federal
intervention in the matter would only incite a race war in their city.

Moody told Roosevelt that their options were limited. They could
simply ignore the matter, allowing the Supreme Court to do whatever
it wanted and permitting the state authorities to make their own investigation. However, Moody said that in the political and legal climate in
Chattanooga it might be impossible, or at least highly unlikely, for a
local grand jury to indict those responsible for Johnson's slaying. If an
indictment were obtained, it was highly unlikely that an all-white
male jury would convict the perpetrators.

An alternative, he said, would be for the federal government to
conduct its own probe and impanel a federal grand jury in the Eastern
District of Tennessee to bring conspiracy charges against the members
of the mob and the local authorities. He cited a specific law passed by
Congress in 1871 that made it a federal crime for "two or more persons
to conspire to injure, oppress, threaten or intimidate any citizen in the
free exercise or enjoyment of any right or privilege secured to him by
the Constitution or laws of the United States." The law provided that
anyone convicted of the crime would receive up to ten years in prison
and be fined $5,000. That federal statute, Moody said, could be con-
strued to fit the facts in the Johnson case.

A final possibility, the attorney general stated, was to conduct a
federal preliminary investigation, allow the local officials to complete
their inquiry, and support the Supreme Court in whatever endeavor it
might pursue. If later the Justice Department determined it should
proceed with criminal charges, it could do so.

President Roosevelt said the third option sounded most logical,
and ordered it done. That afternoon, less than forty-eight hours after
Johnson was killed, Moody sent a pair of Secret Service agents to
Chattanooga to begin collecting evidence in the lynching. The federal

agents were told to make a preliminary report and file it with the U.S. Department of Justice as quickly as possible. In consultation with the members of the Supreme Court, it was agreed that any federal charges would wait until the local authorities in Hamilton County had completed their investigation.

Back in Chattanooga, city leaders continued to bombard officials in the nation's capital with letters, telegrams, and lobbying efforts. Congressmen from Tennessee made personal visits to the offices of Attorney General Moody and President Roosevelt. Their message was quite clear: Leave us alone.

A week after the lynching, the people of Hamilton County went to the polls. In the weeks leading up to the election, most political observers felt Sheriff Shipp would lose his seat. There was great discontent among the local citizens regarding his handling of the Johnson case. Many people believed he had not complied enough with the community's wishes when he sought to protect Johnson from the mob during the first lynching attempt, that he should have given in to the demands of the mob. In other counties, they pointed out, the sheriff frequently participated in lynchings by handing the prisoner over directly to the mob.

However, public sentiment shifted dramatically in the days immediately following Johnson's lynching. Not only had Shipp not stood in the way of the mob's second attempt, but the federal investigation being conducted made him a martyr. In fact, supporters sought to use the lynching to galvanize white voters in their support for Shipp. The best example came in an editorial in the *Chattanooga News* two days prior to the election.

> Sheriff Shipp ought to be re-elected by the white voters of the county. When we remember that the issue against him is his course in the Johnson case, there ought to be enough Anglo Saxon manhood in the county to elect him. He should be given one of the largest majorities in the history of the politics of the county. His defeat would be entirely too much encouragement to the defenders of such fiends as Johnson was. We repeat that we do not understand how a white man can withhold support from Sheriff Shipp under all the circumstances.

That he will be elected the News has no doubt, but his majority should be large enough to forever bury the crowd that has sought to make capital out of the Johnson case. It should be large enough to show the whole country that this county proposes to stand by a sheriff who believes in protecting the womanhood of the South.

The racially divisive campaign worked. The citizens of Hamilton County re-elected Joseph F. Shipp by the largest margin of victory ever recorded at that time. He was immediately sworn in for a second two-year term as sheriff. Community leaders and the newspapers tried to portray the voters' overwhelming support for Shipp as a message to officials in Washington, D.C., that federal interference in the Johnson case was not welcome.

A month later, Judge McReynolds called the Hamilton County Grand Jury into session to investigate the break-in at the jail and Johnson's slaying. With District Attorney Matt Whitaker handling the presentation of the case, more than thirty-five witnesses were sub-poenaed. The sheriff, all of his deputies, and dozens of others gave statements.

Not one of the witnesses called to testify before the grand jury was able to identify a single member of the lynch mob. Even Sheriff Shipp and Jailer Jeremiah Gibson, who spent more than an hour with the leaders of the mob, were unable to remember a single person who was involved. None of the black witnesses to the raid on the jail and the lynching were called to testify.

In the end, the grand-jury probe was dropped. Shipp, McReynolds, and Whitaker announced that no charges would be brought. There was no credible evidence to indict anyone for the raid on the jail and the lynching, they said. With that, the leaders of Chattanooga sought an end to this ugly chapter in its history.

A few days following the lynching, the Reverend T. H. McCallie had sent word to Noah Parden that he wanted a private meeting with the young lawyer. The two had gained tremendous respect for each other during the past month. Though large segments of the commu-nity did not appreciate Dr. McCallie's sermons condemning their racism and separatist views, he was not easily swayed. He spoke the words that God placed in his soul. The minister feared Parden's life was in danger, and he recommended that the lawyer flee town with his wife until tensions calmed.

Parden's defense of Ed Johnson had made him a hero within black communities throughout the country—after all, he had been to the U.S. Supreme Court. He was flooded with requests to speak at black churches throughout the South. The Tuskegee Institute in Alabama and other educational institutions begged him to talk to the students and faculty. Black-owned newspapers and magazines from across the country pleaded with him to write articles for them. Ida Bell Wells, the prominent black newspaper publisher from Chicago, asked him to write an editorial about lynchings and the law.

At home, it was a different story. The two black lawyers became immediate outcasts in Chattanooga. They were labeled troublemakers. These two lawyers who had represented so many black people for two decades—most of the time for free—now found themselves being blackballed. They had expected white people to cause them trouble, but now black business owners who depended on white customers fired Parden and Hutchins. Black people no longer stood in line outside of their law offices seeking representation. The people of their own race were reluctant to hire them for one reason: the white lawyers and judges in town despised them. No one wanted to hire a lawyer who was hated by the judge. Potential clients feared they would receive a tougher punishment if Parden or Hutchins was their attorney.

The pair had rocks thrown through their windows at home and at the office. There were constant threats against their lives. The sheriff refused to send deputies to investigate when either man called for help. Finally, Parden and Hutchins saw no other path to pursue but to pack their belongings and find a new home. Both men hoped they would be able to return to Chattanooga someday.

The white men of the South claim that the Negro is the only criminal. Yet, in this case, the Negro fought on the higher plain, while the white man depended on his brutality.

As lawyers, we have been threatened and the city is in an uproar against us, as bedlam reigns.

The Sunday following the lynching, Rev. Jones of the white First Baptist Church, preached a very strong sermon against lynching. He was notified through several letters that if he did not retract the statements made in that sermon that the mob would call on him. This he refused to do. The following Saturday night [actually Thursday, April 5], his house was set on fire.

Never before in the history of this country has lynching been brought so plainly within the power of the federal government to punish the perpetrators. Johnson at the time of his death was a federal prisoner.

It is now up to the federal government to deal out justice.

NOAH PARDEN, farewell address to a Chattanooga church, printed in
Voice of the Negro, April 14, 1906

CHAPTER FOURTEEN

SECRET SERVICE MEN

When a brute, white or black, attacks and kills or ruins the life of a white woman, we believe that speedy justice should be meted out to him. If the courts permit indefinite delay and fail to protect defenseless women of the south against such outrageous crimes, there is nothing left for white men to do except to handle the guilty devils as they did in Chattanooga.

The idea of the Supreme Court of the United States interfering in a case infamous as that at Chattanooga seems to us to be an outrage against justice, and puts the courts beyond consideration in such cases. We do not believe in lynching or anarchy, but we do believe in the white men of the south protecting at any cost the white women, when the courts fail to do so.

In the case at Chattanooga the crime was especially brutal and inhumane. The people of that city were justified in punishing the guilty Negro when they saw he might try to escape justice by the unwarranted delay and technicalities of the courts.

Atlanta News, March 22, 1906

In the days immediately following the lynching of Ed Johnson, it became painfully obvious to the members of the U.S. Supreme Court and to U.S. Attorney General Moody that neither Chattanooga nor Tennessee authorities were going to investigate sufficiently or prosecute the members of the mob. In fact, the lack of an aggressive investigation caused Moody and some of the justices to suspect a conspiracy among the local officials.

The image the federal authorities received from Southern newspapers regarding the lynching only added to the disdain or mistrust they had for the leaders of Chattanooga. The papers were filled with editorials and news stories blaming the federal courts and the U.S. Supreme Court for delaying the punishment of criminals, which led to the existence of lynch mobs. Publications quoted elected officials and prominent citizens who discouraged any further action against the members of the lynch mob. Instead, papers like the *Chattanooga Times* and the *Chattanooga News* defended Sheriff Shipp for not doing more to protect Johnson, and they criticized federal authorities for their intervention in delaying the Johnson execution.

Whereas officials in Washington, D.C., could adequately gauge the public attitudes of Chattanooga through the newspaper, they were much more hesitant to rely on the papers for truthful or accurate reporting of the facts. Federal officials were convinced the Tennessee newspapers were biased. The facts gathered by the reporters from the *Times* and the *News* certainly came from tainted sources—Sheriff Shipp, Judge McReynolds, and District Attorney Whitaker.

Convinced he needed an independent analysis of the facts surrounding the Johnson lynching, Moody instructed the Secretary of the U.S. Treasury to send two veteran Secret Service agents to Chattanooga. Their fact-finding mission was simple: keep a low profile, interview witnesses to the lynching, and make a preliminary report on their findings. The two agents, senior investigators for the Secret Service in the South—E. P. McAdams from Birmingham and Henry G. Dickey from Memphis—were dispatched by train to Knoxville.

At age forty-five, Dickey was the epitome of a federal agent. He had earned a college degree and studied law for a year under his father before joining the Secret Service, which was the nation's premier federal law-enforcement authority. His appearance and personality, however, belied his position. A heavyset man of medium height, Dickey had a full head of graying hair. His face was completely shaven—a requirement of all Secret Service men. Yet Dickey possessed none of the arrogance or stuffiness of most federal agents. He could routinely be found making new friends at a neighborhood saloon at night. And unlike most government men, Dickey had many newspaper reporters as friends.

McAdams's personality was the exact opposite of Dickey's. McAdams was a few years older but considerably taller and larger-built than his counterpart. He didn't drink alcohol, avoided any appearances of trouble and scandal, and never trusted reporters. He was the consummate G-man.

Their first assignment upon arriving in Knoxville on the afternoon of March 23 was to meet with J. R. Penland, the United States attorney for the Eastern District of Tennessee. Only four days had passed since the lynching, and the evidence remained scant. Penland briefed the agents on the facts as he knew them. He told them about the rape of Nevada Taylor, the arrest of Johnson, and the subsequent trial. He explained about the agitation of the public, the entrance of Parden and Hutchins into the case, and their appeal to the U.S. Supreme Court. During the several-hour meeting, Penland discussed the lynching, the re-election campaign of Sheriff Shipp, and the halfhearted investigation of the lynching by local officials.

The federal prosecutor supplied the agents with newspaper articles regarding the case as well as personal reports he had received from sources in Chattanooga. He also handed them letters written to him about the lynching. Some of the letters threatened retaliation if the federal government took action against the lynch mob; most of those were mailed anonymously. Other letters were from those sympathizing with the federal intervention. They offered the agents background information and even some evidence. Finally, Penland handed McAdams a list of potential contacts in Chattanooga.

At the top of the list were two names that Penland underlined: Noah Parden and Styles Hutchins.

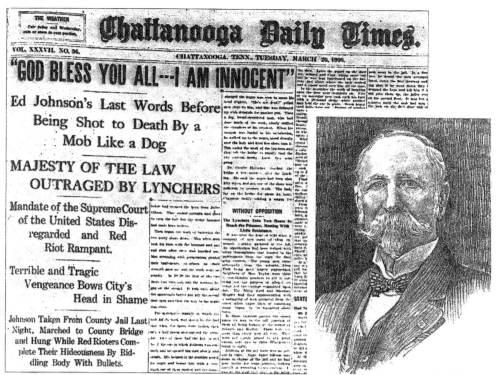

— John Wood/The Chattanooga Times

11. The front page of the *Chattanooga Daily Times* the day after the lynching Inset drawing is of Sheriff Joseph Shipp.

12. Cartoon illustrating Sheriff Joseph Shipp's political ambitions,
The Chattanooga News, Saturday, January 6, 1906

United States of America, ss:

To _The State of Tennessee_

GREETING:

You are hereby cited and admonished to be and appear at a **Supreme Court of the United States,** at Washington, within ___90___ days from the date hereof, _an order allowing an appeal,_ pursuant to ~~writ of error~~ filed in the Clerk's Office of the _Circuit_ Court of _the United States for the Eastern District of Tennessee,_

wherein _Ed Johnson is appellant and you are appellee_

plaintiff in error

~~and you are defendant in error,~~ to show cause, if any there be, why the judgment rendered against the said ~~plaintiff~~ _appellant_ ~~in error as in the said writ of error mentioned,~~ should not be corrected, and why speedy justice should not be done to the parties in that behalf.

WITNESS, the Honorable _John M. Harlan_, Associate Justice of the Supreme Court of the United States, this ___19th___ day of _March_, in the year of our Lord one thousand nine hundred and _Six._

John M. Harlan
Associate Justice of the Supreme Court of the United States.

7 2

13. The order from the U.S. Supreme Court granting Ed Johnson an appeal and stay of execution, signed by Justice John Marshall Harlan

14. The Old Senate Chamber, where the U.S. Supreme Court heard its cases in 1906

15. The courtroom in the Old Senate Chamber where Sheriff Shipp was put on trial

16. St. Elmo and the Lookout Mountain Incline Railway station, the scene of Nevada Taylor's attack and rape in 1906

17. Lewis Shepherd, who defended Johnson during his trial and assisted
Noah Parden and Styles Hutchins in their appeal of Johnson's conviction

18. (ABOVE) Celebration of the opening of the Walnut Street Bridge, on February 18, 1891. The bridge would later become the scene of two lynchings, including that of Ed Johnson

19. (LEFT) The Reverend T. H. McCallie, leading educator and Presbyterian minister in Chattanooga, who openly denounced mob rule and lynching

20. Representative photographs of lynchings

That night, March 23, McAdams, staying at a hotel in Knoxville, penned his first report to his superiors in Washington, D.C. In it, he detailed his meeting with Penland and the strategy that he and Dickey planned to follow in probing the lynching.

On account of the policy of intimidation, which has already begun, I think I had better work incognito. See my witnesses as privately as possible, approach no man whom I have not assurance in advance of sympathy. Let all my talk be absolutely confidential, thus protecting the witnesses against annoyance. So that when the Grand Jury meets I will have my evidence fully on hand for presentation, then have a stenographer or someone take down the evidence given in by each witness so there will be no going back.

Upon arriving in Chattanooga, the Secret Service agents immediately found themselves in hostile territory. At first, no one would talk with them. They located Johnson's father, Skinbone, but he had no reliable information. They met confidentially with some members of the city police department and sheriff's office, but the local lawmen refused to cooperate. Even witnesses the agents believed would be cooperative refused to discuss the matter. White witnesses didn't want to betray their fellow white man, and black witnesses felt intimidated and afraid.

Even as they worked hard to keep their presence secret and their identities unknown, news of their arrival in Chattanooga was published in both local newspapers. As a result, people all over town would see a stranger and wonder if he was a Secret Service man.

The agents' first few days in Chattanooga were only moderately productive. They interviewed people at the telegram office in Chattanooga, confirming that they had received notice from the U.S. Supreme Court that Johnson's execution should be postponed and that the justices had agreed to hear Johnson's appeal. Dickey and McAdams confirmed that the telegrams had been delivered immediately to Sheriff Shipp, U.S. District Judge C. D. Clark, and Hamilton County Criminal Court Judge Sam McReynolds. A clerk for Judge

Clark also verified that he had received his copy of the Supreme Court telegram and immediately informed Chattanooga officials that Johnson was not to be executed.

The agents had a lengthy and friendly meeting with Lewis Shepherd. The former judge told them what he knew, but his information regarding the lynching itself was very limited. He said he had received numerous letters of intimidation during the Johnson trial and during the appeal, criticizing him for his zealous defense of Johnson. The lawyer also informed Dickey and McAdams that he had received several anonymous threats encouraging him not to cooperate with the federal investigation into the lynching.

But Shepherd assured the agents that these threats had no effect on him. His inability to give them evidence regarding the lynching, he said, was simply because he knew nothing. If he did, he said, he would most certainly share it with them. Shepherd suggested they speak with Dr. McCallie, one of the city's most prominent preachers, who had been very outspoken against the lynching. But Shepherd's best recommendation was for the two agents to meet with Parden and Hutchins. They had been collecting names and tips since the day of the lynching, Shepherd said. Unfortunately, both lawyers were visiting colleagues in Atlanta. They were expected to return the next day.

That evening, as Agent Dickey returned to his hotel, three men attacked him by surprise. It was well after dark when the career Secret Service investigator finished interviewing a bartender who he heard had information regarding the lynching. The man had denied he had any knowledge of the slaying. Frustrated, Dickey was walking along the side of the street toward his hotel when he was suddenly approached by two men who asked if he was the Secret Service agent going around intimidating all the townspeople.

When Dickey confirmed he was a federal agent investigating the Johnson lynching, the two men warned him to leave town. As an officer of the law following the orders of superiors, Dickey said he could not do that. While he was questioning the two men, the agent did not notice a third man sneaking up behind him. Just as he sensed the presence of the third man and turned to see who was there, the third man struck him in the side with some kind of stick or pipe. The other two men also took a few swings. The attackers cursed the federal government and told the agent to back off or there would be more trouble.

The confrontation had lasted only a few minutes. Dickey had gotten in a few licks of his own. He believed he had bloodied the nose of one of the attackers and left another of them hobbling from a blow to the groin. The assailants quickly disappeared into the night. The agent shuffled back to his hotel room, where he briefed his partner on the events of the evening.

The next morning, a bruised and sore Dickey and his partner took the eastbound trolley from downtown to Missionary Ridge, the site of the McCallie School. Dr. T. H. McCallie had started the private all-boys school only a year earlier. His goal was to create an educational institution that blended a high level of learning with a strong emphasis on religion, athletics, and morality.

The agents arrived at the school about 9:00 a.m., as the elderly preacher was conducting the daily chapel service. The officers slipped into a back pew of the makeshift auditorium. Chapel was Dr. McCallie's opportunity to impress his Presbyterian beliefs on the teenaged boys. His morning devotion ranged from Biblical truths to impressing the importance of the "honor code" that governed the student body. Boys would be boys, prone to trouble and mischief, according to Dr. McCallie. The honor code—the pledge never to lie, cheat, or steal—was the sole vow that, if broken, would result in immediate expulsion from the school.

"A young man who lies, who cheats, or who steals, displays an absence of the good moral character required to be a respected citizen and a Godly man," he wrote.

Though the officers found a sympathetic figure in Dr. McCallie, there was little direct information regarding the lynching that he could provide. From all he had been able to gather, the minister said he had come to the conclusion that Ed Johnson was most likely innocent of the rape. But he said the community was so inflamed with racial hatred and so outraged by the attack that any black man would have been convicted and sentenced to die.

The Presbyterian preacher and educator told McAdams and Dickey about the threats against Parden and Hutchins. Dr. McCallie said he had been out of town the night of the lynching. He knew very little about the attack on the jail, the killing of Johnson, or who was involved. However, he gave them their best tip yet on whom they should talk to: Dr. Howard Jones of the First Baptist Church. Dr. McCallie told the agents that Dr. Jones was a man of great faith who had bravely denounced lynch law.

That afternoon, the Secret Service agents paid a visit to Dr. Jones at the downtown church, which was less than a block away from the county jail. The Baptist preacher eagerly invited the lawmen into his private study. The story he told them didn't take long, but it was clearly the best evidence the agents had obtained that the lynching was no surprise to Chattanooga authorities and that little had been done to stop the mob.

Dr. Jones stated that he made "an earnest effort to stop the lynching but was met with surprising rebuff." With Agent McAdams taking notes, the minister told about receiving a telephone call at home informing him of the mob's attack on the jail. After confirming from a news reporter that the jail was under siege, Dr. Jones called city police headquarters to see if officers had been sent to the jail.

"I was surprised when the sergeant informed me that the affair of the mob, a vicious violent mob, disregarding law, order, and humanity, was not of concern to police," Dr. Jones told the agents. "I appealed that police be sent to the jail, but I was told that the jail was quite a distance from police headquarters and I was further advised the matter was not of concern to the police."

The preacher said he had heard at least ten hours before Johnson was taken from the jail that there was going to be a lynching attempt, and had relayed the rumor to sheriff's deputies. The minister also said that Sheriff Shipp had told him that a gentleman named Dr. Sutton was a member of the mob and one of the men who had restrained Shipp the night of the lynching. When Dr. Jones urged the sheriff to arrest Sutton, Shipp promised to do so. However, the preacher said no arrests had ever occurred. In fact, he said, Sheriff Shipp was now claiming he did not know the identities of any of the attackers.

Dr. Jones also told Dickey and McAdams about the sermon he had delivered the Sunday following the lynching, encouraging people who had witnessed the event to come forward with their testimony. Several people had warned him against delivering such a message, he said. Others had threatened to burn down his house if he cooperated with federal investigators.

The intimidation tactics had not deterred Dr. Jones. He gave the federal agents the name of the deputies and police officers with whom he had spoken and said he would assist the agents in any manner they needed. Dickey and McAdams thanked him for his courage and cooperation; they said they might just call upon him again as the investigation continued.

On their sixth day in Chattanooga, the federal investigators finally met with the one person they hoped would provide the bulk of the information they were seeking: Noah Parden.

Parden returned home when he received news that Secret Service officials in Chattanooga wished to speak with him. His law partner, Styles Hutchins, remained in Atlanta for a few extra days to speak at a handful of black churches.

Dickey and McAdams quickly found Parden to be a Godsend. Though Parden was not present the night of the lynching and could not offer the agents firsthand knowledge of the crime, he had received scores of tips and leads. He gave them names and addresses of people who he had heard had witnessed the lynching, provided them with the latest rumors about who was involved and why it took place, and also supplied the detectives with his own theory about what happened and why, and the evidence he had to support his position.

Parden told them about a conversation he overheard following the federal habeas corpus hearing in Knoxville, at which Johnson was granted a ten-day reprieve from his execution. Parden had been standing nearby when state Judge McReynolds told U.S. Judge Clark that Johnson "would be hung before the expiration of ten days." According to Parden, Judge Clark replied to McReynolds, "Well, it is up to you."

For nearly three hours, Dickey and McAdams listened to Parden intently. He had already talked with many of the witnesses the agents were trying to track down. In fact, he had spoken with several they had already talked to, but he had gotten much more information from the witnesses than they had.

The lawyer said the hesitancy of the witnesses was understandable, especially given the hostile atmosphere existing in Chattanooga. Black witnesses, Parden said, were especially scared to cooperate. Black people, he said, were afraid local police and leaders of the lynch mob would find out they had given incriminating information to the federal agents and would come looking for them or their families.

"Will they still talk with you?" Agent Dickey asked.

"I know these people," Parden responded. "I've helped them and their families out of trouble many times."

The Secret Service men asked Parden if he would accompany them the next few days to meet with the witnesses. Thanks to a sudden drop-off in business, Parden said he had plenty of time to help, but he wanted a series of stipulations before he would cooperate. First, he wanted the agents to allow him to control the meetings with the witnesses. He did not want the witnesses to be intimidated by federal agents. He also wanted the agents to promise they would not reveal the names of the witnesses to Chattanooga officials before any charges were brought. Finally, Parden did not want to be a witness himself, but he did desire to play a role in prosecuting those involved in the lynching.

Dickey and McAdams said they would certainly defer to Parden in conducting the interviews with the witnesses, and they promised that the names of the witnesses would not be made public unless charges were actually brought in the lynching and the witnesses were needed to testify. As for Parden participating in the federal prosecution, the agents said they welcomed his input. Although a decision on who would be part of the legal team would be made exclusively by the U.S. attorney general in Washington, D.C., the agents promised to lobby the U.S. Justice Department on Parden's behalf.

That was fine with Parden. The trio agreed to meet the next day to begin their quest.

For three days, Parden ushered the federal agents from witness to witness. They spoke to inmates in the jail the night of the slaying, and a couple of black police officers and special deputies or constables who had been working that night. They interviewed a handful of black people who either witnessed the raid on the county jail or the lynching, or had heard about the possibility of a lynching earlier that day.

At first, people were reluctant to tell their stories with Dickey and McAdams present. But with Parden's coaxing, all finally relayed their accounts of things they had seen and heard. The agents briefed Parden on the questions they wanted answered, so they remained silent for the most part during the interview. Once the witnesses felt more at ease, the lawmen would increase their participation in the questioning.

ON APRIL 5, the Chattanooga newspapers reported that Dr. Howard Jones had told the Secret Service detectives about calling the police department for help the night of the lynching. The papers quoted police officials as saying they received no phone calls or tips informing them that a lynching was taking place. That same evening, Dr. Jones arrived at his home to find it on fire. Neighbors and firefighters quickly started spraying water on the blaze, which was contained in a small portion of the house.

To Dickey and McAdams, the incident confirmed that their pursuits were legitimate. Dr. Jones's statement and the subsequent burning of his home were further evidence of a conspiracy to intimidate witnesses into not telling the truth about the slaying of Johnson.

BY THE THIRD week of April 1906, the federal investigators felt they were ready to prepare and file a comprehensive report to their superiors in Washington, D.C. They had sent several progress memos to their bosses, but now enough progress had been made and enough evidence gathered so that they could effectively describe what had happened in the days preceding the lynching, as well as many details surrounding the raid on the jail and the lynching itself. Together, Dickey and McAdams reviewed their notes. They agreed there were certain legal elements they had to include as part of their report.

• Did the notice of the stay of Johnson's execution reach the appropriate parties (Judge Clark, Judge McReynolds, and Sheriff Shipp)?

• Was there any advance warning or obvious signals that a lynching was going to take place?

• Was enough done to protect Johnson from the mob?

• What were the roles of Sheriff Shipp and his deputies in the lynching?

• Was there any way to identify those who had participated in the raid on the jail and the subsequent killing of Johnson?

Dickey and Parden filed their four-page memorandum late Friday in a dispatch to the director of the Secret Service in Washington, D.C.

We can prove by credible witnesses that a guard for the protection of Johnson, of varying length, was maintained at the jail from the time of his arrest, incarceration and trial, up to the eventful night when the mob took the prisoner therefrom, where there seems to have been but one man at the jail, the night jailer Gibson, who was joined later by the Sheriff, Joseph Shipp.

That the granting of the appeal by the Supreme Court was published in both the city papers, the early morning edition of the "Times," and the afternoon edition of the "News," on the 19th of March and was generally known and discussed throughout the day.

There is evidence that the mob was talked of as early as 11:00 a.m. on the 19th of March, that one person, himself a special deputy sheriff, who had served as a guard at the jail since Johnson's incarceration, informed another deputy sheriff that his information was that the mob would move that night.

That during Monday of which day the prisoner Johnson was lynched all the prisoners were removed from the floor occupied by him.

That Shipp on the day after the lynching notified the gun stores that they could sell white men arms but that they must not sell arms to Negroes. We may be able to connect one or more deputy sheriffs as members of the mob.

The action of the Supreme Court was sent to Sheriff Shipp.

I think we will prove that a member of the city police force was actively engaged in the formation and operations of the mob. He it was who cut off one of the fingers of the Negro. A witness stated that he saw him do it.

We will prove that the mob was at least one and one-half hours in forming and getting ready for action. That during the whole of this period, S. D. McReynolds, Judge of the Sixth District Judicial Circuit, who presided at the trial of Johnson and N. M. Whitaker, solicitor general, Sixth Judicial Circuit, who prosecuted Johnson, had knowledge of the mob from its inception to its full development and were discovered in a room in the courthouse enjoying the best point of view of the jail and the formation and full stature of the mob in front thereof.

That at least one hour before the mob began its work, McReynolds and Whitaker left the courthouse and proceeded to the Times office where they notified Mr. Milton Ochs, President and Manager of the Times, of the gathering of the mob and when Mr. Ochs told Judge McReynolds that he (McReynolds) ought to notify Sheriff Shipp, McReynolds replied "No. I will have nothing to do with it since the Supreme Court has butted in."

McReynolds and Whitaker returned to their viewpoint in the courthouse and were observing the mob when Will Allen constable and a reliable man, observing the threatening aspects of the crowd went into the courthouse to ring the "dis-

tress bell" discovered McReynolds and Whitaker in a room
watching the mob. McReynolds asked Allen to go out and see
what the men were doing and come back and report.

Judge McReynolds and Whitaker were in the courthouse
when the mob . . . took Johnson from the jail to his death.
There is no evidence that Sheriff Shipp ever made remon-
strance to the mob or said anything in warning. There is no
evidence that either Judge McReynolds or solicitor Whitaker,
although the "distress bell" was accessible and a phone was
convenient in the room where they sat watching the slow formation of the mob, ever gave notice thereof to any restraining
authority, they had time from this first knowledge of the mob
to have heard from the state executive and probably enlisted
the military arm of the state to prevent the work of the mob.

We have secured evidence against twenty-one members
of the mob and are still gathering evidence.

The truth is, Johnson's death at the hands of the mob was
to Sheriff Shipp, who stands for re-election, a political necessity. Shipp doubtless observing this instead of taking measures to repel the mob rather invited it, at least, did not
suppress it, the mob having done its work, the newspapers
talk of Shipp's imminent prosecution, made a martyr of him,
and his chances for the nomination improved rapidly so that
when the primary came off he (Shipp) was nominated by a
safe majority.

As to the action of McReynolds and Whitaker, aside from
racial prejudice and a desire to be on the popular side, there
were so many errors in the trial of Johnson, neither of the gentlemen, could afford to have the record reviewed.

We have had great difficulty in obtaining evidence, some
witnesses, who could give valuable and convicting evidence
are afraid to disclose anything. All are afraid for their personal
safety.

In view of this condition, we believe it folly to think for a
moment of local prosecutions, it would be simply impossible
to convict in the local United States court, relying on jurors

who would be impressed by the very atmosphere around them and would be subject to local manipulation, besides such feeling would be engendered as would work infinite harm to individuals as well as the community;

Therefore, we prefer that the officers and individual members of the mob be proceeded against for contempt of court, and we feel sure that sufficient evidence will be presented to enable the Supreme Court to administer to the proper persons punishment as the gravity of the cases demand.

The proceedings we recommend would surely, from the evidence, result in convictions, the effect of which would be inestimable to this community as well as to the country at large in preventing a recurrence of such incidents and would also protect the dignity and enhance the respect of the people at large for this high tribunal.

Please advise us at once as to the work at hand.

Very respectfully,

E. P. McADAMS, HENRY G. DICKEY
Agents U.S. Secret Service
April 20, 1906

The agents filed a supplemental report that listed their witnesses and named the people they had determined were involved in the lynching. In the nation's capital, the reports were copied and sent to the U.S. attorney general and members of the U.S. Supreme Court. The two offices were on separate but parallel paths. Each wanted to punish those involved in the lynching, but they had very different ideas on how to accomplish that.

Lawyers at the U.S. Department of Justice preferred to prosecute the vigilantes under a federal statute passed by Congress in 1871. The law read:

If two or more persons conspire to injure, oppress, threaten, or intimidate any citizen in the free exercise or enjoyment of any right or privilege secured to him by the Constitution or the laws of the United States, or if two or more persons go in disguise on the highway or the premise of another with the intent to prevent or hinder his free exercise of any right or privilege so secured, they shall be fined not more than $5,000 and imprisoned not more than ten years.

However, there were definite drawbacks to pursuing the leaders of the lynch mob under the federal criminal laws. The primary obstacle was the very fact that criminal charges must originate and be litigated in the jurisdiction or district where the crime occurred. Many prosecutors in the Justice Department, as well as Agents Dickey and McAdams, doubted that a jury drawn from the citizens of East Tennessee would ever convict Sheriff Shipp or the members of the mob.

A few blocks away, under the Capitol Dome, the members of the U.S. Supreme Court were debating what action they should take in the situation. The justices focused primarily on Section 725 of the U.S. Code, in which Congress defined the power of the federal courts to punish for contempt.

The courts shall have power to impose and administer all necessary oaths, and to punish, by fine or imprisonment, at the discretion of the court, contempts of their authority.

Provided that such power to punish contempts shall not be construed to extend to any cases except the misbehavior of any person in their present, or so near thereto as to obstruct the administration of justice, the misbehavior of any officers of said courts in their official transactions and the disobedience or resistance by any officer, or by any party, juror, witness, or other persons, to any person, to any lawful writ, process, order, rule, decree, or command of said courts.

In the weeks following Johnson's lynching, the Justice Department and Supreme Court feuded over which body would take jurisdiction, each believing it should take charge of the prosecution. As a result, it appeared for several weeks as if the people involved in the lynching might have to face two separate charges—criminal prosecution from the executive branch (the Justice Department) and contempt-of-court charges by the U.S. Supreme Court.

During the second week of May, however, a couple of justices severely undercut the Justice Department's efforts by publicly stating that they had doubts that the Supreme Court would uphold the constitutionality of the federal laws being relied on by the attorney general. In fact, the justices had already declared in a previous case that the statute was unconstitutional when applied to actions taken by individuals. The Court had not spoken about the legality of the law when applied to the action of state authorities, which was exactly what federal prosecutors contended was involved.

Even if the Supreme Court did permit the prosecution under the federal law to proceed, there was no way around the fact that the defendants were entitled to a trial by jury if the case were pursued through the traditional means of indictment. Moody conceded that the jury would most likely have to be drawn from the people of East Tennessee, where the public had become racially polarized and prejudiced over the case. Since the federal-court jury pool also consisted almost exclusively of white people, obtaining a conviction would have been nearly impossible. By contrast, contempt-of-court proceedings required no jury participation.

These circumstances left federal prosecutors with three options:

(1) Ignore the justices' warning and continue to pursue the case under federal statutes, hoping that any conviction would not later be reversed on appeal. This was a risky option, because losing such a case would merely encourage mob rule.

(2) Drop the investigation completely and allow the Supreme Court to continue the unprecedented journey alone. However, Moody recognized that the Supreme Court would need the resources and manpower of the executive branch of the government if it were to undertake such a procedure.

(3) Join forces with the Supreme Court in pursuing contempt proceedings against the sheriff, his deputies, and members of the lynch mob.

On May 17, 1906, Attorney General Moody decided that simply ending the Justice Department's efforts to prosecute the organizers and participants in the lynching was not an option. An unspoken factor in the decision to make peace with the high court was that Moody himself was being mentioned as a possible nominee for an open seat on the Supreme Court. That morning, he met privately with Chief Justice Fuller and Justice Harlan. The two justices confirmed their belief that the federal criminal statute under which the Justice Department was preparing to proceed was most likely unconstitutionally broad.

Over the next hour, the trio reached a historic agreement. Moody agreed to charge the people involved in the lynching with criminal contempt of the Supreme Court. He would prepare the charges, known legally as an "information," and file it with the clerk of the U.S. Supreme Court. In turn Chief Justice Fuller said the Court would cease its own pursuit of the members of the mob, allowing the Justice Department to lead the prosecution.

There was one problem. Members of the Court and Attorney General Moody desperately wanted to bring some kind of action against Hamilton County Criminal Court Judge Sam McReynolds. They all agreed that McReynolds had acted despicably during the trial, allowing Johnson to be railroaded. That the Johnson case was replete with reversible error, there was no doubt. It was evident that Judge McReynolds had talked a great deal about justice under the law but administered very little of it.

What infuriated the justices and federal prosecutor most as they reviewed the Secret Service report was the conduct of Judge McReynolds and District Attorney Whitaker during and following the lynching attempt. Justice Harlan was particularly outraged at the information that the two Hamilton County court officials watched the entire raid on the jail from a courthouse window. That neither man made any efforts to stop the lynch mob or call law-enforcement agencies for assistance was bad enough, Harlan contended, but worse was the fact revealed in the Secret Service report that McReynolds had actually thwarted a citizen's efforts to summon help by sounding the courthouse alarm.

Another disturbing part of the report by Agents Dickey and McAdams involved an interview they had done with editors of the *Chattanooga Times*. According to the report, McReynolds and Whitaker had walked a few blocks to the newspaper offices as the mob was trying to break into the jail. Two different editors at the paper told the agents that they had asked the judge what he planned to do about the mob. McReynolds, they said, responded that he had done all he was going to do to protect Ed Johnson and that he had no plans to stop the mob.

Finally, the justices and federal prosecutor were angered by Judge McReynolds's attitude and public statements following the lynching. They read newspaper reports in which McReynolds blamed the lynching on the U.S. Supreme Court's intervention in the case. They were especially frustrated that the Chattanooga judge had not issued a more forceful public rebuke of the lynching. And they were angry that McReynolds was not more aggressive in demanding that criminal charges be brought against the people involved in the lynching.

Despite all their irritation at McReynolds and disdain for how he had officially handled the Johnson case, Attorney General Moody said he did not think contempt charges could be brought against the state-court judge. He said the order issued by Supreme Court Justice John Harlan only instructed Sheriff Shipp and his deputies, not Judge McReynolds, to protect Johnson. Moody also said that Agents Dickey and McAdams had been unable to find any evidence directly linking McReynolds to the lynching. Pending the development of more evidence against McReynolds or Whitaker, Moody concluded, no charges should be brought against them. Members of the Supreme Court said they were disappointed in the lack of action against the judge, but agreed that the attorney general's decision was appropriate.

On May 28, the U.S. Department of Justice filed the official papers at the Supreme Court. The lengthy document enumerated the details of the Johnson case, the appeal by Parden and Hutchins, the stay of execution by the Court, and the lynching. The "information" included many of the details from the reports by Agents Dickey and

McAdams. For the first time, the filing named the individuals the Justice Department believed were most responsible for Johnson's lynching. They included the following:

- Sheriff Joseph F. Shipp. The accusation said Shipp had failed to provide adequate protection to Ed Johnson, who was a federal prisoner. The petition also charged Shipp with being in sympathy and complicity with the mob.

- Sheriff's Deputies Matthew Galloway, Charlie Baker, T. B. Taylor, Fred Frawley, George Brown, Marion Perkins, Joseph Clarke, and Jeremiah Gibson. The deputies were accused of aiding and abetting the mob by not properly protecting Johnson, as ordered by the U.S. Supreme Court.

- Nick Nolan, a saloon owner; Luther Williams, a saloon owner; Shenie Warner; Paul Poole, a painter who had since moved to Birmingham, Alabama; William Marquette, proprietor of a steam-cleaning and drying company; William Beller, owner of a saloon; Claude Powell, manager of a meat market; Charles J. Powell; Bart Justice, a molder at U.S. Cast Iron Pipe & Foundry; John Jones; A. J. Cartwright, owner of a grocery store; Henry Padgett, a carpenter; William Mayes, a bartender; Frank Ward; John Varnell, a machinist; and Alfred Hammond.

These and a large number of other persons whose names are unknown to complainants, did willfully, unlawfully, and wrongfully combine, conspire, confederate, and agree to break and enter the county jail of Hamilton County for a purpose of taking therefrom the person of Ed Johnson to lynch and murder him, with the intent to show their contempt and disregard for the orders of this Honorable Court made, entered, issued, and published, and for the purpose of preventing this Honorable Court from hearing the appeal of Ed Johnson, allowed by this Court, and for the purpose of preventing Ed Johnson from exercising and enjoying a right secured to him by the Constitution and laws of the United States.

The petition asked the Supreme Court to conduct a hearing that would require the named defendants to show cause why they should not be put on trial for contempt of court. The documents were admitted and stamped with the Court's seal.

Even though the official papers were not served on Sheriff Shipp and the other defendants until three days later, news of the Justice Department's action spread quickly across the country. The Associated Press, the *Washington Post*, the *New York Times*, and dozens of other publications sent urgent bulletins to their readers in every community. They generally heralded the charges as historic and precedent-setting in nature.

> One member of the Supreme Court told *The Star* that such an action has never before occurred or even been contemplated. The justice said the action was necessary to preserve the integrity and honor of the Supreme Court itself and he said that state officials must be educated as to the power and influence of the U.S. Supreme Court.
>
> *Washington Star*, May 1906

CHAPTER FIFTEEN

SUPREME JURISDICTION

ON THE DAY the Justice Department filed the contempt charges, Sheriff Shipp was visiting Birmingham. He and many of the other Chattanooga leaders honestly believed that the threat of federal prosecution would dissipate over time. After all, April and most of May had passed without any official action's being taken. Shipp told friends he believed the Justice Department and the Supreme Court had decided to allow the horrible incident to pass quietly. The sooner it faded from memory, he contended, the better for all involved.

So the news of the contempt charges was met with complete astonishment. Suddenly, Chattanoogans realized that the lynching of Ed Johnson would not be forgotten. The transgressions of the mob would become a much-publicized blight on Chattanooga for years to come.

A news reporter for the *Birmingham News* was the first to inform Shipp of the federal government's action against him. At first, the sheriff didn't believe the reporter. He thought the telegram was a prank. Eventually, reality set in and the reporter asked the sheriff for his reaction.

I have no desire to be considered in defiance of the Supreme Court.

But in my judgment, the Supreme Court of the United States was responsible for this lynching. I had given that Negro every protection I could. Nevertheless, I must be frank in saying that I did not attempt to hurt any of the mob and would not have made such an attempt if I could.

Had not the Supreme Court of the United States interfered, we would have been able to set an example for the maintenance of law and order and a speedy trial in cases of this kind that would have been of great value throughout this country.

I regard it as very unfortunate that this case had not been left to the state authorities where it originated.

It was not until it was known that the Supreme Court had granted a hearing in this case and it had been stated it would probably be from two to five years before the case would be disposed of that the public showed any disposition to interfere in the matter.

I am thoroughly conscious of having discharged my duty in this case and under most trying circumstances and shall wait the result with the confidence of a complete vindication.

Sheriff Shipp's defiant statement was republished in newspapers in Chattanooga, Atlanta, Washington, D.C., and New York City. Federal prosecutors and members of the Supreme Court took special notice of his comments, which seemed to indicate disgust for the federal courts and a sympathy for those who had lynched Johnson.

On May 31, federal marshals served the contempt papers on twenty-six of the defendants (one, Paul Poole, could not be found). Each was required to post a $1,000 bond with federal-court officials in Chattanooga. The bond was necessary to guarantee that the defendants would appear in court to face the charges. If they refused to pay the bond, the defendants would have been jailed pending trial. However, all were able to post it or had family members pledge properties valued at $1,000 or more.

Dozens of lawyers volunteered their legal services to Sheriff Shipp, whose political popularity only increased when the charges were announced. In the end, he chose to hire Chattanooga attorney

Robert Pritchard and Cincinnati lawyer Judson Harmon. Pritchard was one of the more prominent criminal-defense lawyers in Tennessee, and he specialized in federal criminal-court cases and federal appellate law. As a longtime friend and faithful supporter of Shipp, he was someone the sheriff confided in and respected. It was at Pritchard's recommendation that the sheriff also asked Harmon to represent him. Harmon had served as the U.S. attorney general during Grover Cleveland's presidency. As a young lawyer, he had been a prosecutor in the state and federal court systems. Now he was an established criminal-defense attorney and a highly rumored Democratic presidential candidate in 1908.

To help defray the costs of the legal expenses of Sheriff Shipp and his deputies, a group of Chattanooga citizens created a legal-defense fund of sorts. In an open letter printed in the newspapers in early October, the group pleaded with residents who believed Shipp and his comrades were innocent to contribute money to pay lawyers' fees and other expenses. By October 12, more than $5,000 was raised.

On October 15, 1906, eight justices of the U.S. Supreme Court filed into the grand old courtroom on the second floor of the Capitol Building. There were only eight because of the vacancy created in May 1906, when Justice Henry Billings Brown retired after sixteen years on the Court; President Roosevelt had yet to name his successor. On this particular day, the Court had only one item on its calendar: *United States* v. *Shipp.*

U.S. Solicitor General Henry Hoyt stood up and announced that the federal government was ready to proceed. The lawyers in the case were asked to step forward to be sworn in as members of the U.S. Supreme Court bar. The attorneys gathered around an ancient Bible, raised their right hands, and promised to protect the United States Constitution. The Court's clerk administered the oath. Just two years earlier, lawyers had been required to kiss the Bible as part of the ceremony. However, as more and more black lawyers sought admission to the bar, white lawyers complained that they did not want to kiss anything that had previously touched the lips of a Negro. The justices agreed to cease the requirement, though lawyers still touched the Bible as they took their oath. The lawyers also had to pay the clerk a $10 filing fee.

Among the cadre of lawyers who stepped forward within the oak bars of the Court's inner circle were Noah Parden and Styles Hutchins. They occupied front-row seats next to Agents Dickey and McAdams and directly behind Hoyt. While Hutchins had spent the summer in Atlanta, Parden had toured the northeastern coast lecturing on the case to large audiences—black and white. Just the day before, Parden had spoken on the constitutional issues to a gathering of lawyers at the Cooper Union in New York City. The mere presence of the two black lawyers at the Supreme Court gained the attention, as well as the ire, of many of the Chattanoogans who had traveled to Washington, D.C., to watch the court hearing, according to the *Chattanooga Times*.

Both Negroes were well groomed and looked the picture of prosperity. A satisfied smile rested on the countenance of each when they heard the contempt case called. Visions of public justification of their course caused them pleasant anticipations.

With extraordinary powers as an orator, Parden holds large crowds spellbound for hours by his stirring recital of the alleged crime, the conviction on insufficient evidence, the staying of the execution by the Supreme Court of the United States, and the lynching of Ed Johnson.

Parden's recital of the stirring events were received with repeated cries and groans from the Negro portions of the audiences.

Hutchins talks like an alien, an exile from home.

"I tell the people where I lecture," said this relic of reconstruction days, "that I love the south and its people. I was born there. I am one of its products. I was a judge and a senator in South Carolina, and Chattanooga honored me by sending me to the legislature. I am going back and stay where I feel at home."

Parden and Hutchins have been assisting the Department of Justice lawyers in their preparation of the case against Sheriff Shipp and the others. Parden said he is confident that they will win the case in the Supreme Court.

One by one, lawyers for the defendants stepped forward to announce the plea of their clients. Judson Harmon told the justices that Sheriff Shipp and his deputies pleaded not guilty. He handed the clerk of the Court a twenty-two-page legal brief that detailed their official defense. Harmon told the Court his central argument was that the Supreme Court itself did not have jurisdiction to determine the guilt or innocence of the law-enforcement officers. It was clear he was going to make the case a debate about state versus federal rights. Harmon made no comment regarding his client's involvement in the raid on the jail or the lynching. His defense was based strictly on legal procedure, not the facts of the case.

The next lawyer to stand before the Court was none other than Lewis Shepherd. Even though he had represented Johnson during the trial and had assisted in the appeal to the U.S. Supreme Court, Shepherd now spoke in favor of some of the men accused of actively participating in Johnson's lynching. "Our answer is that we were not members of the mob, were not there and are not guilty of the charge. We deny every allegation in the Attorney General's information and move this Honorable Court that we be at once discharged." Shepherd told the justices that all of his clients could provide irrefutable evidence that they had not participated in the raid on the jail or the lynching of Johnson. Each claimed to have alibi witnesses to support his contention that he was someplace else the night of March 19.

The remaining defendants had their own lawyers. Each entered a plea of not guilty. All but one of the suspects claimed alibis or mistaken identities. Only Luther Williams admitted in his legal pleadings that he had been present during the lynching; he said he had only been an observer, not a leader.

As the hearing came to a close, a black man named Wesley Garrett, who worked for the Southern Railway, approached the bar of the Supreme Court seeking to be heard. Chief Justice Melville Fuller asked the man what he wanted. Garrett said he had been notified two weeks earlier by a stranger that he was supposed to appear before the Supreme Court on October 15 as a witness in the Shipp case. The man said he had borrowed money and ridden the train to Washington to be present. Only as Garrett finished his story and the courtroom filled with laughter did he realize he had been bamboozled, the subject of a prank.

With all the "not guilty" pleas officially on the court record, Chief Justice Fuller said the justices would review the legal briefs filed by all parties. If oral arguments on any issues were needed, he said, the lawyers would be notified. With that, the first phase of the only contempt proceedings ever held before the U.S. Supreme Court came to a close.

Since the proceedings were completed before noon, Sheriff Shipp, Judge McReynolds, and more than a dozen people from Chattanooga decided to tour the nation's capital. The group had not planned to return to Chattanooga until the next afternoon. Their first stop: a surprise visit to the White House. The group was immediately admitted into the home of the first family, where President Theodore Roosevelt was meeting with guests. Both Shipp and McReynolds had been big political supporters of the president. They had welcomed and escorted him during an earlier visit to southeastern Tennessee.

As the Chattanooga gang entered the main greeting room, President Roosevelt was dealing with an insistent New Yorker who wanted navy-yard employees given an extra holiday each year. The newspapers reported that the president was "evasive and finally bowed out without committing himself." Shipp's visit to the White House caused outrageous speculation and rumors about the staff's reaction. One report had it that all the Negroes employed at the White House fled, fearing there would be a lynching right there in the heart of the capital. Someone else mentioned that the force of the Secret Service had been doubled when it was learned that the executive office would be invaded by a dozen or more Tennesseans. None of the reports were ever verified.

President Roosevelt, wearing a gray Prince Albert suit and the ever-present eyeglasses and smile, immediately recognized Sheriff Shipp and called him by name. The chief executive reminded the sheriff of his recent visit to Chattanooga, thanking Shipp and McReynolds for campaigning for him.

Not once during the brief conversation did the president mention the contempt charges or the lynching. He kept the meeting short and filled with handshakes, smiles, and light chatter. President Roosevelt was, Judge McReynolds would later comment, "quite engaging and always politicking."

A few weeks following the hearing, the Supreme Court announced it would conduct oral arguments in the Shipp case on Tuesday, December 4, 1906. The justices said the merits of the case would not be discussed. Instead, the Court said it wanted to conduct a hearing and listen to arguments on a very narrow legal issue: whether the U.S. Supreme Court itself had legal jurisdiction in the contempt case against Shipp and the twenty-six other men.

Usually, lawyers in a case before the Supreme Court had a limited amount of time to argue their positions. But because this was a first-of-its-kind case, the justices granted both sides as much time as they needed to make their points.

The importance of the jurisdiction issue to be decided by the Court was not lost on the major news media from around the country. The *Washington Post* described the hearing as "monumental." The *Atlanta Constitution* said the debate "provides the federal justices with the best opportunity yet to voice their opposition to lynch law." Several newspapers, including the *Chattanooga News*, republished an editorial first printed in the *Boston Transcript* on Saturday, December 1, 1906—three days before the hearing.

The decision which the United States Supreme Court is to render in this matter will affect the rules of jurisprudence in both state and federal practice. It is a question of jurisdiction.

If the court of last resort decides that it has jurisdiction in the case of Ed Johnson, the condemned assaulter who paid the penalty for the crime for which he was charged at the hands of the mob, it will set a precedent in such cases, for it is the first time a similar case has gone to the court of last resort.

In the event the United States Supreme Court decides that it has jurisdiction in the Johnson case, it will mean similar cases may hereafter be appealed to the court of last resort, and it may revolutionize the whole system of jurisprudence in the practice and execution of laws touching such matters in this country.

If it develops, however, that the United States Supreme Court should decide that the matter is only one in which the state is concerned, the contempt cases would be dismissed and this will end one of the most remarkable cases in history.

At 2:00 p.m., December 4, the official crier of the U.S. Supreme Court emerged from behind a door near the front of the courtroom. The man was short and balding, but his shrill voice echoed throughout the chambers.

"Hear ye, hear ye, hear ye.

"This Honorable Supreme Court of the United States is open pursuant to adjournment.

"God save the United States and this Honorable Court."

Led by Chief Justice Fuller, the eight justices appeared from behind two thick wooden doors that were partially hidden by heavy drapes. The judges filed into the courtroom. As the older white men sat down, the crier announced that those in the courtroom should also be seated. Sheriff Shipp and twenty-five of the other men charged sat in the hard wooden pews behind their lawyers.

Seated at the lawyer's table on the opposite side of the court was Solicitor General Henry M. Hoyt, who spoke for the U.S. Justice Department, and for the United States government in all legal matters before the Supreme Court. With him were three other seasoned federal prosecutors. As at the October 15 hearing, directly behind Hoyt were Agents Dickey and McAdams, as well as Noah Parden.

Parden and Shipp sat directly across the aisle from each other. Neither man had a good word to say about the other. Parden viewed the Southern lawman as a racist, pure and simple. Shipp had used his powerful position, Parden contended, to suppress and demean black people. In speech after speech, the black lawyer would mention that Shipp had been a captain in the Confederate Army and detail numerous punitive measures the sheriff had arbitrarily taken against black people. Parden told how Shipp would issue curfews during times of racial unrest but enforce them only against black people, how Shipp would shut down saloons frequented by black people but allow the white bars to remain open, and how Shipp had fired or run off most of the black deputy sheriffs and constables who had been in office prior to Shipp's election. In their place, the sheriff had hired only white officers. Furthermore, he prohibited the few black deputies who remained from arresting or even questioning white citizens.

Shipp was equally bitter toward Parden. The sheriff considered the black lawyer a troublemaker who unnecessarily stirred the emotions of black people. Shipp frequently complained that Parden was more interested in legal procedure than in punishing criminals or doing the right thing.

Over the next three days, the two men completely ignored each other, even though they were most assuredly aware of each other's every move. But on this day, neither man was the center of attention. That honor belonged to the eight men dressed in black robes and sitting high on the bench.

Recently retired justice Henry Brown had written the Court's opinion in the infamous case of *Plessy* v. *Ferguson*, in which the justices had legalized segregation. President Roosevelt had nominated Attorney General William Henry Moody to replace Brown. The U.S. Senate was in the process of confirming Moody to the Court, but it did not do so until December 17, 1906. Even if Moody had been confirmed earlier, he would not have participated in the Shipp case. As soon as he was sworn in by Chief Justice Fuller, he announced he would recuse himself from sitting in judgment in the case of the sheriff and the accused lynchers. His decision was viewed as the ethical thing to do, since he had initiated the contempt charges as the top lawyer at the U.S. Justice Department.

The justices sat in deep leather chairs behind an elevated solid oak panel that provided the members of the Court with desk space to spread out their legal briefs and make notes. Seated in the center chair was Chief Justice Fuller, one of the longest-serving and most loved leaders in the Court's history. By tradition, the associate justice who has served the longest on the Court sits to the chief justice's right. The next-most-tenured member sits on the left. That pattern continues to the ends of the bench.

At five feet six inches, Fuller was by far the shortest member of the Court. He sported a thick silver mustache, as did four of his fellow justices: historians named them the "Great Mustachioed Court." At age seventy-three, Fuller had been chief justice since President Grover Cleveland had appointed him to the Court in 1888.

Politically, he was a Democrat who actively supported Stephen Douglas in the race against Abraham Lincoln. Fuller's small stature belied the respect he commanded from other judges, as well as the executive and legislative branches of government. He worked to improve the Supreme Court's reputation and its influence among the public. And he also demanded congeniality among the justices—even when they bitterly disagreed with each other.

"No man has ever more completely realized the impartial, impersonal, integrity and dignity of the Court in its splendid aloofness from prejudice and passion," the *Philadelphia Public Ledger* wrote of the chief justice. A Detroit newspaper added that he "was absolutely fearless of president or mob."

When it came to intellectual leadership, Fuller bowed to the other members of the Court. Instead, he preferred to focus on the management of the Supreme Court. When Fuller became chief justice, the Court was so besieged with cases that it was four years behind in its work. He effectively lobbied Congress in 1891 to add the federal Circuit Courts of Appeal to act as intermediary appellate courts to review the federal trial courts for errors. By 1895, the justices were actually reviewing cases within a year of their being filed.

Fuller's opposition to high tariffs and his opinion that the Fourteenth Amendment did not provide minorities with massive protections from discrimination made him attractive to President Cleveland. Once on the Court, Fuller was not entirely predictable when it came to issues involving race. In cases involving government-forced segregation, the chief justice comfortably turned a blind eye to the racially prejudiced conduct. And he voted with the majority of the justices in the Plessy decision in 1896, in which the Court upheld the social policy of racial segregation under a legal doctrine described as "separate but equal."

In spite of the chief justice's vote in the Plessy case, Justice John Marshall Harlan, the Court's most liberal member, considered him a friend and ally. As the then longest-serving member of the Supreme Court, Harlan sat just to the right of the chief justice. The two judges may have been the same age, but their perspectives on life were at the opposite ends of the legal and social spectrum. If Harlan supplied the middle-class view on the Court, Fuller could only relate to his experiences in elite circles. If Harlan felt comfortable eating and socializing with Negroes, Hispanics, and Chinese, Fuller was more at ease dining with bankers, lawyers, and people of wealth. Yet Harlan believed Fuller's soul was filled with compassion and understanding for the less privileged and people of color.

Sitting directly to the chief justice's left was David Josiah Brewer. Justice Brewer's parents were missionaries to Smyrna, in Asia Minor (modern-day Turkey). Considered an intellectual, Brewer, a native of Kansas, strongly opposed government intervention in economic affairs and was an ardent believer in capitalism. However, the sixty-nine-year-old justice also demonstrated on occasions a deep compassion for the poor and people of color. Brewer had previously served on the Kansas Supreme Court and the Federal District Court.

Seated next to Justice Harlan was Edward Douglass White from Lafourche Parish, Louisiana. At age sixty-one, Justice White was in his twelfth year on the Supreme Court. As a soldier in the Confederate Army, he had been captured by the Union military. His father was a Louisiana governor and congressman. After serving for three years in the U.S. Senate, White was appointed to the bench by President Cleveland in 1894. As a Supreme Court justice, he led the movement to allow more federal-government involvement in private business matters. However, White's idea of judicial activism and federalism did not extend to civil rights or individual liberties.

Justice Rufus Wheeler Peckham occupied the chair next to Brewer. A native of New York State, the sixty-eight-year-old judge was in his eleventh year on the Supreme Court. He had served almost a decade on the highest state appellate court in New York before being nominated by President Cleveland to the U.S. Supreme Court. Peckham, also considered a legal intellectual, was the Court's strongest advocate of the free-market system. He once described a law regulating grain elevators as "vicious" and "communistic." Justice Peckham had demonstrated no interest in judicial activism when it came to issues of individual rights and segregation.

To the right of Justice White was Joseph McKenna, a sixty-three-year-old former U.S. attorney general appointed to the Court by President William McKinley in 1898. Born in Philadelphia, the son of an Irish immigrant, Justice McKenna was a strong believer in an active federal government in the regulation of business and the economy. He had previously had a law practice in California, served as a federal trial judge, and been elected to Congress.

Seated on the ends were Justices Oliver Wendell Holmes and William Rufus Day, the two newest members of the Court. The two lawyers had been appointed by President Roosevelt. Both had previously served as judges—Holmes in his home state of Massachusetts and Day on the Sixth U.S. Circuit Court of Appeals in Cincinnati.

Just as the sixty-five-year-old Justice Holmes was distinctly New England with the traditional liberal streak often found in Northeasterners, Justice Day's Midwestern roots revealed his centrist views. At fifty-seven, Day was in his third year of service and was frequently the swing vote that tilted the Court to the right or left. He preferred to allow the regulation of commerce by state governments. But he would approve federal intervention if Congress or the executive branch could demonstrate that the states were doing an inadequate job. When it came to issues of race, Justice Day voted to strike down laws that prevented black people from voting. By the end of his career, he had generally shifted to the more liberal wing of the Court.

It was this eclectic—and sometimes dysfunctional—group of legal minds that listened to the lawyers for both sides argue the case for two days. As the justices settled comfortably in their black leather-backed chairs, Solicitor General Hoyt rose to his feet, buttoned his coat, approached the wooden lectern, and began to speak on the issue of whether the Court had the power even to hear the contempt charges brought by the Justice Department.

All the seats in the intimate courtroom, including the balcony, were occupied by news reporters and people concerned about the outcome of

the case. Lawyers who understood the importance of the matter lined
the walls two deep. Three U.S. senators and five congressmen were present. Eleven U.S. District judges from the East Coast and three from the
South had seats reserved for them. Nothing less than the integrity and
authority of the United States Supreme Court was at stake.

Hoyt began his argument by reminding those in the courtroom of
the reason for the hearing: to decide if the Supreme Court had jurisdiction in hearing the contempt charges against Sheriff Shipp, his
deputies, and the accused members of the mob.

The answer to that question, the solicitor said, could be found in
the origins of the litigation—the trial and appeal of Ed Johnson. Hoyt
told the justices that Johnson's case had made its way on appeal to the
U.S. Supreme Court only because his state-court criminal trial had
been devoid of fairness and justice. He briefly summarized the claims
Johnson's lawyers had made in their appeal, especially the "state of
terror" that had permeated the case in Chattanooga.

> When I say that a state of terror existed, I don't want to be
> understood as implying that they were personally afraid, but
> they felt that if this man dared to pursue his rights there was
> no telling what would be the result. The state of public feel-
> ing was very grave. There was much excitement, there was no
> telling how many men would be killed if such a course was
> followed.
>
> With his rights under the state law gone, one by one, in
> whatever way and whatever reason . . . it is not strange that
> Johnson challenged that process and result by invoking his
> federal rights, whatever they were.
>
> His appeal to the federal court was in good faith; it was his
> only recourse to save his life. If it was technically frivolous and
> without merit, it was for this Court finally so to determine. If
> Johnson was entitled to be heard in the Circuit Court on his
> application for habeas corpus, and then in this Court on
> appeal, those are rights secured by the Constitution and laws
> of the United States.

Hoyt spent the next two hours citing and discussing numerous Supreme Court opinions to support his contention that the federal courts had the right to intervene in the Johnson case. He specifically reminded the justices of a recent decision in which the Court had said that federal-court efforts to meddle in state cases "should be sparingly exercised, and should be confined to cases where the facts imperatively demand it." Indeed, he argued, federal judges should seldom intrude in state-court matters.

However, the solicitor said, no case that had ever come to the attention of the Supreme Court included such egregious facts that so "imperatively demand federal interposition" as the Johnson case. Besides, Hoyt said, the federal courts and the U.S. Supreme Court "are empowered to take any case." Only the Supreme Court had "jurisdiction to decide that it has no jurisdiction. The Court takes and retains complete jurisdiction until it concludes that it has none." That authority, Hoyt argued, was broad enough to protect petitioners in either the state or federal court system.

Besides, this Court has yet to determine that the Circuit Court rightly refused to issue the writ or had no jurisdiction to do so, and even if it did so determine, that could only be upon the assumption that it had jurisdiction of the case on appeal. In other words, lack of jurisdiction in the Circuit Court to issue the writ would not mean lack of jurisdiction in this Court to entertain and act upon the appeal.

The files of the Court are full of cases, civil and criminal, ranging in importance from capital cases to small money demands, from the pleadings and judgments of which it is evident that when a claim under the Constitution of the United States is properly alleged, however unfounded it may turn out to be, this Court proceeds deliberately and considers that claim and retains that case in its grasp and under its power in all respects, until this Court had rendered its final decision and judgment to dismiss, or to affirm, or to reverse.

We stand on the single proposition that under the author-

ity cited the Circuit Court and this Court had full jurisdiction
of Johnson's case.

Hoyt said the Court was backlogged with civil and criminal cases,
some of them involving claims of obvious violations of constitutional
rights, others completely devoid of any legitimate legal argument. But
only the justices held the power, he argued, to render a final judgment
in those cases. Only the Supreme Court had the authority to dismiss, to
affirm or to reverse each of those disputes. Even so, Hoyt readily
admitted that the contempt charges against Sheriff Shipp, the
deputies, and the alleged members of the mob were precedent-setting.

> This appears to be the only original proceeding in contempt
> ever filed in this Court.
> This is the first time in the history of the country and of
> the Court that an order of the Court has been disobeyed and
> its authority condemned. This Court pre-eminently repre-
> sents and effectuates the judicial branch of power under our
> government, and it is more important to sustain its paramount
> authority and dignity than that of any other judicial authority.
> It is to be certainly assumed, then, that the Court will
> apply in the vindication of its own authority the doctrines
> which it has laid down in cases coming within its appellate
> jurisdiction as to the authority of the lower federal courts over
> contempts.
> Flagrant contempt.
> Of course this shocking occurrence, conceived in lawless-
> ness and revenge, carried on by violence and ending with mur-
> der at the hands of a mob, was an offense against the state as
> well as against the United States and this Court.
> But the same act may be a crime both against a state and
> the United States, and the United States has full power to
> punish whether the state does or not.
> This Court may and should inflict due punishment for that
> disobedience.

Henry Hoyt's argument spilled over into the second day of the hearing. He spoke with authority, frequently impressing the audience with his deep knowledge of federal law and Supreme Court decisions. As the solicitor general, Hoyt had argued dozens of cases before the high court. Yet he told the *Washington Star* that none would have the lasting impact of this one: "This proceeding is about nothing less than establishing and protecting the rule of law."

After completing his argument and gathering his notes from the lectern, Hoyt returned to his chair. Not once during his argument had any of the eight members of the Supreme Court interrupted or questioned the solicitor about the case.

Following a short recess, Judson Harmon, the Cincinnati attorney who represented Sheriff Shipp, slowly made his way to the lectern. He politely introduced himself and his client to the Court and thanked the justices for their patience and consideration. Harmon knew his task would be difficult. In reality, he was asking the same eight men who had unanimously agreed to issue a stay of execution for Ed Johnson and hear his appeal to decide now that their former decision had been improper. Yet the attorney had a definite strategy. Realizing that six of the eight justices had previously served as state-court judges or been elected to other state political positions, Harmon wanted the judges to frame the argument in terms of states' rights. He also wanted to avoid discussing his client's conduct on the day and night of the lynching. Instead, he wanted to retry Johnson and put the actions of Parden and Hutchins in the spotlight. And he wanted to emphasize how a decision against his client would encourage other criminal defendants to seek federal relief from state charges.

Harmon wasted no time in tackling the subject of jurisdiction. He told the justices that Johnson's appeal to the Supreme Court had contained no proof that the construction or application of the United States Constitution had been violated. If there was no evidence that Johnson's federal constitutional rights had been breached, then Johnson had no right to have his case heard by the justices; therefore, his appeal and the stay of execution were improperly pending before the Supreme Court. If the Supreme Court had no jurisdiction in the Johnson case, then technically it could not find anyone who violated the voided orders from the original case in contempt.

> If an order be made without jurisdiction, there can be no punishment for contempt.
>
> When a proceeding is strictly and solely punitive like this, and the penalty may include imprisonment, we submit that this Court, whose standards of personal liberty are so high, should not be controlled by any general theory of discipline or dignity, but only by the result of the inquiry that was made in a case in which its jurisdiction, as limited by law, extends.
>
> The only question is whether Johnson's proceeding in habeas corpus in the Circuit Court did or did not in fact constitute a case that involves the Constitution or application of the Constitution of the United States.
>
> If it did, this Court had appellate jurisdiction of it and should proceed to inquire whether its orders have been disobeyed. If it did not, this court has no jurisdiction of it, and should now so hold for the purposes of this proceeding, just as it would have done if the state of Tennessee had raised the question on the attempted appeal.

Before Ed Johnson's lawyers could petition the federal courts for relief, Harmon contended, they had to assert that their client's federal constitutional rights had been denied in the court of original jurisdiction—the state criminal court in Hamilton Country, Tennessee. However, he said, no such claim had ever been made by Johnson or his lawyers before or during the trial in the state court. If the issue was not properly raised and litigated in the state court, how and why should Parden and Hutchins have been allowed to seek an appeal based on those allegations?

Under the law, Harmon said, they shouldn't have been allowed to go to federal court, and the U.S. Supreme Court should have rejected their petition for emergency relief. The lawyer cited numerous Supreme Court decisions that he contended supported such a conclusion.

The habeas corpus petition filed by Parden and Hutchins, Harmon said, did not dispute the jurisdiction of the state court either to put Johnson on trial or to adjudge the sentence under which he was in custody. Nor did the two lawyers contend that any of the state laws used to prosecute Johnson had violated the federal Constitution. Instead, Harmon noted, the alleged denial of Johnson's constitutional rights by state officials had first to be reviewed by the Tennessee Supreme Court on a petition called a "writ of error" before being appealed to the U.S. Supreme Court. Because Parden and Hutchins failed to do that, the defense attorney said, they could not then seek the same relief through a habeas corpus petition in the federal courts.

Harmon then proceeded to examine the specific aspects of Johnson's federal appeal. He told the justices that the claim by Johnson's lawyers that their client was denied the right of a public trial was unequivocally incorrect. He said the testimony taken in the federal-court hearing in Knoxville showed without dispute that, at the request of Johnson's own counsel, precautions had been taken to prevent the attendance of disorderly persons in the courtroom during the trial. Harmon said those measures were withdrawn following the first day of the trial. The former U.S. attorney general also dismissed as inflammatory the charge that Johnson's father, mother, and friends had been prevented by sheriff's deputies from attending the trial. "There is not a particle of proof to this effect," he said. "The evidence shows it was a mere pretense."

Equally inane, Harmon told the eight justices, was Johnson's allegation that he had been denied a trial by a fair and impartial jury. Harmon said the official record revealed that neither Johnson nor his attorneys had ever objected to the character or disposition of the jury panel. He said the claim that Hamilton County officials discriminated against Negroes when summoning people for jury duty was without foundation. In fact, he said, there was testimony at the federal-court hearing that "the names of coloreds were known" to be included in the jury box.

At that point, Justice Harlan interrupted.

"What about this situation where a juror made threatening moves and statements during the trial against the defendant?" Harlan asked.

"Doesn't that demonstrate the clear prejudice of the very people who swore to be impartial?"

Harmon appeared caught off guard by the question—or maybe it was just that any question had been asked that caused him trouble. He paused for a few seconds, took a drink of water from the glass provided him by the federal marshals who secured the courtroom.

The actions by the juror, though possibly inappropriate, constituted harmless error and had no impact on the final result of the verdict, Harmon contended. When the juror jumped to his feet and lunged toward Johnson screaming, "If I could get at him right now, I would tear his heart out," the trial had been essentially over, all of the evidence already presented. Harmon noted that the juror had apologized to the court for his actions.

That's when the Cincinnati lawyer received his second jolt. Chief Justice Fuller, who seldom spoke from the bench, asked how the actions of the juror could be harmless to Johnson if the juror was demonstrating his own personal animosity toward the defendant.

"How can that be?" Fuller inquired.

"It was treated by all, including the prisoner and his counsel, as merely the effect of the proof on an emotional nature and not as evidence that the juror was prejudiced when accepted and sworn," Shipp's lawyer told the chief justice. "The record is clear that neither the prisoner nor his counsel made any kind of exception or objection in consequence of the incident."

As Harmon answered Fuller's inquiry, the members of the Court looked at each other. A few traded whispered words. It was obvious to those present that the justices did not accept the lawyer's contention that the juror's actions should simply be disregarded as some trivial emotional matter. Indeed, Harlan would later write to a fellow justice that the statement of the juror was "all the evidence needed" to determine that Johnson had not received a fair trial from an impartial jury.

Realizing there was no reason to belabor the point, Harmon moved on to Johnson's contention that he had been denied effective representation during the trial and abandoned by his lawyers following the jury's verdict. Harmon told the justices that Johnson "himself admitted in his petition" that the lawyers appointed by the state to defend him during the trial did so "with ability, fidelity, and zeal."

Besides, Harmon said in a louder voice for emphasis, "it is well settled that the first ten amendments to the United States Constitution apply only to federal courts and federal-government actions and are not applicable to state actions or state criminal-court proceedings." These claims, he argued, had been brought in Johnson's federal habeas-corpus petition under the Sixth Amendment clause that provides individuals in exclusively federal cases with a fair trial and the right to a lawyer.

Once again, Justice Harlan surprised the lawyer.

"What of the argument that the Fourteenth Amendment [incorporates] the Bill of Rights on state courts?" the elderly justice asked. "If we determined that it did, would that make a difference?"

"Well," Harmon cautiously responded, "that is not the law. This Court has ruled repeatedly that state courts are not duty-bound to follow the Bill of Rights in the federal Constitution."

"But you would agree that this Court has the authority to determine that the Sixth Amendment is binding on the state courts, do you not?" Justice Holmes asked.

Harmon was literally dumbfounded. As a legal scholar who had studied the Supreme Court, he knew Harlan wanted state courts to abide by the specific legal principles put forth in the first ten amendments. He expected such a question from Harlan. But not from Holmes. It was at this moment, Harmon would later acknowledge, that he looked into the faces of all the justices and realized just how personally outraged they were at the state court's handling of the Johnson case. Could they actually be considering such a decision? he wondered.

After a lengthy pause, Harmon finally responded that he did not know how to answer that question, since such was not the law of the land. At least not yet. The answer brought a few chuckles and raised eyebrows from the justices.

For the next hour, Harmon attacked the appeal presented to the Supreme Court by Parden as completely without basis in fact or law. He said Johnson had not been denied a request for a change in venue, because no such request was ever made. The same was true, he said, of Parden's claim that Johnson had been illegally denied the opportunity to appeal his conviction. Harmon said Johnson's lawyers had never filed a request for a new trial, nor did they file a bill of exceptions containing the evidence presented during the state trial.

"You say they never sought a change of venue or filed for a continuance." Chief Justice Fuller spoke up. "But isn't it true that the trial judge informed petitioner's counsel that he was not going to grant a change of venue, and did he not advise and inform counsel that, if they made an application for a change of venue or a continuance, that a mob would attack the jail and succeed in murdering the petitioner?"

"There was no evidence whatever to that effect," Harmon answered. "If his counsel saw fit not to take the necessary steps to secure a change of venue or postponement of the trial from the day they themselves had agreed upon, as the record shows, this certainly constituted no invasion of constitutional rights by the state of Tennessee or any official thereof."

Harmon told the court that Johnson had not been denied his right to appeal his conviction, but had voluntarily waived that right. He said Johnson's trial lawyers had intended to file a motion for a new trial; however, they decided against it after realizing that there were no justifiable grounds for such an appeal.

> This conclusion being presented to the petitioner, he submitted to it. He says he did so to avoid being killed by a mob. But surely it will not be contended that this gave the federal courts jurisdiction in habeas corpus.
>
> It is nowhere suggested that the state authorities were unwilling to protect him, as they had already done, nor that the power of the state was insufficient to enable them to do so. Even if this were not so, the fact would not give the federal judiciary jurisdiction.
>
> The conference of counsel, six in number, unanimously decided that Johnson had a fair trial; that no error had been committed; that an appeal would therefore be useless except merely to prolong the life of a man found guilty of a most infa-

mous crime, which they did not consider it their duty to attempt, especially in view of the probable result upon public feeling.

The subsequent effort of other counsel ignorant and reckless of the facts about the trial have put the Court unwittingly in a false position and misled the attorney general.

In short, the record shows that this Court was imposed upon with respect to the true nature of this case, and so grossly that it is hard to resist the conclusion that this was purposely done. There was not even the color of a case involving any real question of constitutional rights.

Harmon then concluded his argument by saying that the Court should set aside its "false pride" in feeling that its authority had been impugned and concede that the federal courts had no business interfering in a state case such as that involving Ed Johnson. The issue, he insisted, was not about whether Sheriff Shipp properly protected Ed Johnson or whether Judge McReynolds provided Johnson with a fair trial. The whole thing, Harmon said, was about states' rights, about the federal courts allowing the states to manage their own court systems.

The people of the South are struggling with a task the like of which was never known before. It is one which nobody but themselves can work out, and they must do it unaided, save by friendly sympathy. The provocations for attempts at irregular justice, which are too common in all parts of the country, are more numerous and frequent there, where apprehension stands at every man's door to quicken his indignation at outrages committed upon the families of his neighbors.

The attorney general [Whitaker] in his testimony said: "I feel like the law's delay engendered whatever mob spirit existed throughout the country on account of offenses like this. If we could have speedy trials rather than delay, then it would have a good effect on the public with reference to allaying in the future any such mob spirit as generally existed in cases of this kind."

That this is true there can be no doubt. There may be cases where haste overleaps the precautions with which the administration of justice must always be guarded, but the courts of the states do not lack the power or the will to correct such errors. When to mere error is added the sacrifice of rights secured by the federal Constitution, this Court has always been and always will be prompt with its ample power of redress which is limited only by precautions against premature or needless interference with state tribunals to which the Constitution is as sacred as itself.

The case here presented involved neither a denial of justice, whether by the laws or Tennessee or by the mode in which they were administered, nor the invasion of a right secured by the federal Constitution.

Following a two-hour lunch break, Lewis Shepherd stepped to the podium. His remarks were focused on three areas: his personal defense of Ed Johnson, his response to Judson Harmon's comments, and the defense of his nine new clients.

The former Republican judge told the Court how upset the community had been in the hours and days following the rape of Nevada Taylor; many of the townspeople had thirsted for blood. But he said there were many who had simply wanted the right man caught and punished. Shepherd made it clear he didn't agree with many of Judge McReynolds's rulings in the Johnson case. Even so, he acquiesced in the decision by the other trial lawyers to convince Johnson to waive his right to appeal his conviction. He said it was decided that appealing the case would only further agitate the public.

Shepherd said he did disagree with his co-counsel Judson Harmon on one significant issue. "The United States Supreme court," he told the justices, "has the authority to take jurisdiction in any case it so desires. And only the United States Supreme Court can decide what cases it can and should take jurisdiction over."

The case of Ed Johnson, he said, was certainly one that had needed and deserved the attention of the federal courts. He thought the justices had made the correct decision in issuing a stay of Johnson's execution and agreeing to hear his appeal.

Regarding his own clients, nine men accused of raiding the county jail and leading in the lynching of Johnson, Shepherd said they were absolutely innocent. His clients entered a complete denial of the charge of participating in the murder of Johnson. Each had alibi witnesses ready to testify. The feisty old lawyer then invoked an ancient technical rule from the Chancery Courts of England. Shepherd said the rule provided that the very terms of his clients' sworn answers to the charges "automatically purged them from contempt accusations and entitled them to discharge without further proceedings."

Throughout the remainder of the afternoon, a handful of different lawyers representing different individuals accused of participating in the lynch mob made their arguments to the Court. Most of the attorneys repeated or paraphrased the legal arguments already made by Harmon or Shepherd.

The final presentation for the defendants was made by Robert B. Cooke. A Chattanooga criminal-defense attorney, Cooke declared that if the lower federal court had completed its record and responsibility in the case its decision would have been that it had no jurisdiction. Hence, he said, there was no jurisdiction in the Supreme Court. But even during his closing remarks, the justices seemed dissatisfied with the arguments.

> COOKE: Is sending a telegram to Shipp such due process of law as would result in the transfer of the prisoner from the jurisdiction of the state court to that of this Court?
>
> We submit that it was not, and that therefore interference with him was not contempt of this Court.
>
> The record will convince you that every right Johnson had was jealously guarded. The jury deliberated from one day to the next. The only thing that occurred was the incident of the emotional outcry of one juror.
>
> Then, suddenly, in the nighttime, the mob sprang up and took Johnson and lynched him.

CHIEF JUSTICE FULLER: After an appeal had been granted to this Court.

COOKE: Yes, sir.

FULLER: Was that what was the matter?

COOKE: No, sir. It could not be attributed to that. Many of these defendants had no knowledge that any order had been issued by this Court.

Chief Justice Fuller thanked Cooke for his presentation. Leaning back in his chair, Fuller asked Hoyt if he had any recommendations on how they should continue procedurally in the case. Standing at his desk, the solicitor spoke with a soft but determined tone that emphasized the underlying significance of the Court's actions.

"Probably there is no case like this in the books," Hoyt said. "I can find none."

The chief justice asked Harmon and Shepherd the same question, and they issued the same response. For the next few minutes, the eight members of the Supreme Court engaged in a rather unique discussion—what would happen next. The group finally decided that each party could have three days to write and file any additional written arguments. Once those had been reviewed by each justice, Fuller said, the Court would again confer and issue a ruling. However, Fuller gave no indication how soon such a decision would be rendered.

With that, the chief justice announced that the Supreme Court of the United States was adjourned for the day.

Outside, dozens of newspaper reporters gathered around the lawyers as they left the Capitol. Each lawyer gave his personal opinion on the case and what he thought the Court's decision would be. The most highly quoted of the lawyers was none other than Lewis Shepherd, partially because he felt so at ease with members of the media and partially because his comments were so straightforward.

I believe that the Court will hold that it has and had jurisdiction in the Johnson case from the time that the case went into the United States Circuit Court. Anybody who watched this hearing and listened to the interruptions made by the chief justice could not but see that he was in sympathy with the action.

It is a fact that this was the most important case that has yet been heard by the Supreme Court of the United States and the Court so indicated this all the way through.

For eighteen days, Sheriff Shipp and the other defendants, their lawyers, and the people of Chattanooga awaited the decision by the Supreme Court. Many believed the justices would not rule until after the New Year. After all, it took them several months to dispose of most cases after they had been argued and briefed.

It was snowing in Chattanooga on Christmas Eve, Monday, December 24, 1906. Shipp was spending time with his children and grandchildren, making last-minute preparations for the holidays. It was an annual tradition for him to dress in a full red coat stuffed with pillows and don a fluffy white beard to play Santa for the little ones.

But his morning jollies were interrupted by an unexpected visit from his lawyer Pritchard. Shaking his head, Pritchard said he held bad news in his hand. The document was several pages long. Shipp took it, sat back in his rocking chair, and began reading. He paid no attention to the legal citations in the opinion. Pritchard had highlighted the most important parts.

UNITED STATES V. SHIPP.

No. 12, Original.
SUPREME COURT OF THE UNITED STATES
December 24, 1906, Decided

Even if the Circuit Court of the United States has no jurisdiction to entertain the petition for habeas corpus of one convicted in the state court, and this court has no jurisdiction of an appeal from the order of the Circuit Court denying the petition, this court, and this court alone, has jurisdiction to decide whether the case is properly before it, and, until its judgment declining jurisdiction is announced, it has authority to make orders to preserve existing conditions, and a willful disregard of those orders constitutes contempt.

After an appeal has been allowed by one of the justices of this court, and an order entered that all proceedings against appellant be stayed and his custody retained pending appeal, the acts of persons having knowledge of such order, in creating a mob and taking appellant from his place of confinement and hanging him, constitute contempt of this court, and it is immaterial whether appellant's custodian be regarded as a mere state officer or as bailee of the United States under the order.

As to the jurisdiction of this court. An appeal may be taken to the Supreme Court in the case of any person alleged to be restrained of his liberty in violation of the Constitution.

The appeal here is matter of right. The court was bound to allow it. When a claim under the Constitution of the United States is properly alleged, however unfounded it may turn out to be, this court deliberately considers the claim and retains the case in its grasp and under its power in all respects and for all purposes until final judgment dismissing, affirming or reversing has been rendered and the mandate thereon executed. If an appeal is technically frivolous, it is for this court to say so.

A case which ultimately goes out of this court on that ground is completely here within the jurisdiction until it does go. The proposition that when the question of jurisdiction is doubtful, individuals and communities need not respect the court's orders and mobs may do as they please is self-destructive.

Power to punish for contempts is inherent in all courts for the purpose of enforcing judgments and orders and compelling submission to lawful mandates, as well as for the purpose of preserving order and imposing respect and decorum in the presence of the court.

The power and dignity of this court are paramount. This court is preeminent as speaking the last word for the judicial power, and looks to the Constitution, not only for its origin in general, but for its express creation, while the inferior Federal courts look to Congress for their actual being, functions and jurisdiction. It may be doubted whether Congress could limit the authority of this court over contempts. This court had expressed that doubt. An act of Congress controls the courts of its own creation, but not this court, if thereby its organic authority and jurisdiction under the Constitution are curtailed. The vital matter of refusing to obey the court's command is as serious in the remotest corners of the country as in the courtroom.

This was murder by a mob, and was an offense against the State as well as against the United States and this court; but the same act may be a crime both against the State and the United States, and the United States has complete power to punish, whether the State does or not.

This contempt was the crime and sin of murder, but because the proceeding is by contempt and not by indictment, a criminal may not deny his crime and then be liable to the bare possibility of the lighter charge of perjury. A contempt committed by a crime is none the less a crime because it is a contempt.

Whether the court's order constituted the sheriff an officer pro hac vice of this court, is not material. The order went to the sheriff with sovereign force in whatever capacity he is regarded, having in fact the legal custody of the prisoner. A state officer having prisoners committed to his custody by a court of the United States is an officer of the United States.

These preliminaries being settled, the trial of the case will proceed.

Signed,

JUSTICE OLIVER WENDELL HOLMES, JR.

There was no good news in any portion of the decision, Pritchard told his client. The decision was unanimous, eight to nothing with Justice Moody abstaining. And the tone of the opinion was extremely unfriendly to the defendants.

The Supreme Court was making an example of Shipp, his deputies, and the alleged members of the mob. Through this case, the justices were informing every lawyer, every judge, and every sheriff in the country that its authority was supreme. Defiance of the Supreme Court's orders by individuals, whether members of a mob or law-enforcement officials or agents of the court, would not and could not be tolerated. The rule of law depended upon it, they said.

As important as this decision was, the case against Sheriff Shipp and the others was only beginning. The case now had to be tried on the merits. Both sides began immediate preparations for a historic and contentious trial.

That same night, in Indianapolis, Indiana, Noah Parden stood before parishioners at a small black church. He told them the good news of the Supreme Court's decision, which was greeted with applause and much excitement.

But on this subfreezing night, Parden found it difficult to rejoice in seeing the fruits of his labor materialize. After reading excerpts of the Supreme Court's opinion and explaining what it meant, the black lawyer lifted another document he held in his hand. The Supreme Court's decision represented some future hope for the end of racism and terrorism in America, but this second document represented reality.

It was a list of every lynching that had occurred in 1906. There had been sixty-five. All but three of the victims were black men. He then read them state by state, name by name.

Ed Johnson's was the last name he read.

CHAPTER SIXTEEN

SHERIFF SHIPP ON TRIAL

THE FIRST WEEK of 1907 found Noah Parden on a train headed for Washington, D.C. The new United States attorney general, Charles J. Bonaparte, had just been appointed to replace William Moody, who was now a member of the Supreme Court. Bonaparte quickly realized the Shipp case might be the most important and certainly the most visible litigation he would supervise as the nation's top law-enforcement officer. He gathered his senior staff and the lead investigators in Washington to discuss their legal strategy in the case. In attendance were U.S. Attorney J. R. Penland of Knoxville and Secret Service Agents Dickey and McAdams.

As a trial lawyer, Bonaparte knew the importance of having a field general lead the trial team. He started off the meeting by introducing his choice for the position—Edward Terry Sanford, a forty-one-year-old lawyer from East Tennessee. Sanford, a trial attorney who had been recruited to the U.S. Justice Department by Moody, had taken the title of "special assistant attorney general," prosecuting high-profile federal criminal cases throughout the country.

In every respect, he was the perfect person to handle the Shipp case. He was born during the closing days of the Civil War into a wealthy Southern family. After graduating from the University of Tennessee, Sanford received a law degree from Harvard. For the next few years, he taught and practiced law in Knoxville. Most important, Sanford was a big believer in equal rights under the law for people of color. He cited Justice Harlan as the justice he admired most, and adopted Harlan's view that the rights listed in the first ten amendments of the U.S. Constitution should be afforded to people in state as well as federal courts.

Once Sanford had finished speaking, Bonaparte introduced Parden to the group. The attorney general explained that no lawyer knew the facts in the Shipp case better than Parden, and he had invited Parden to participate in their discussion of how to proceed against the sheriff, his deputies, and the alleged members of the mob.

This was virgin territory for all parties involved, including the Supreme Court. Never before had a criminal trial taken place before the nation's highest court. Never before had the justices been asked to sit as a jury in determining the fate of an individual. And never before had the federal government attempted to prosecute a person involved in a lynching.

The justices asked both sides to propose a trial plan to the Court, recommending how the case could proceed. Because the Supreme Court is an appellate court and not a trial court, it does not hear live witnesses or examine direct evidence. Its courtroom has no witness stand. Instead, the justices normally decide issues based upon a summary of testimony and arguments made in the lower federal and state courts.

U.S. Solicitor General Henry Hoyt, who had argued the jurisdiction issue before the Court, briefed Parden on the trial structure the Justice Department planned to submit. Hoyt said the proposal allowed the Court to avoid spending weeks and weeks listening to live testimony. The justices did not want to be burdened with the procedural task of conducting an evidentiary trial. As an alternative, Hoyt suggested that the Court appoint a commissioner to preside over the evidentiary hearings, listen to witnesses, and make an official record. Once the record was completed, it would be reviewed by each member of the Court. The justices would then, after consulting with each other, reach a decision in the case.

The Supreme Court quickly approved Hoyt's trial plan. Both sides submitted names of people they wanted for commissioner. In the end, the justices selected someone recommended by neither side—James D. Maher, a lawyer and deputy clerk of the U.S. Supreme Court. Maher was a familiar face to most of the lawyers in the case. He had been the very person who collected the $10 fee the lawyers had to pay to become members of the U.S. Supreme Court bar only months earlier.

At age forty-eight, Maher had brown hair that was thinning. His mustache was peppered with gray. Wire-rimmed spectacles provided him a quite distinguished look. Maher's accent offered no evidence that he had been born and raised in Ireland. He always wore a smile, eagerly shook the hand of every man he met, and looked people in the eye when he talked. He was the kind of man who made friends everywhere he ventured.

Both sides in the litigation announced that they were pleased with the Supreme Court's choice. They called him a lawyer of great character and honesty and declared their confidence that he would be fair to all parties and faithful to the law.

Maher's first order of business was to set February 12, 1907, as the date to begin accepting evidence in the already infamous case.

With the court date so near, Sanford needed Parden's assistance once again to ensure that the government's witnesses would testify at the trial. Parden said most people would willingly tell their stories, but some would definitely be intimidated, especially if the trial were conducted in Chattanooga. Even almost a year after the crime, he said, some of the witnesses would feel pressure from locals to taint their testimony in favor of the sheriff. To avoid such a situation, Parden asked if there was any way for the case to be conducted in Washington, D.C.

Agents Dickey and McAdams wholeheartedly agreed with Parden. They believed several witnesses would never testify if the trial were held in Chattanooga. Most Tennesseans remained extremely loyal to Sheriff Shipp. The attitude of most citizens was decidedly racist, the agents contended, and threats against certain key witnesses should be expected.

Federal prosecutors received the message loud and clear. On January 25, the solicitor general asked the Supreme Court to allow the government to present its witnesses in Washington, D.C., rather than in Chattanooga. In their motion, prosecutors said they had obtained confidential information that their witnesses would be subjected to danger and undergo substantial coercion.

In Chattanooga, lawyers for Sheriff Shipp and the other defendants readily accepted and approved of the government's suggested trial format. However, the request to move the trial to Washington was taken as an absolute insult. Defense attorneys vigorously opposed the petition. They claimed that moving the trial to the nation's capital would add unnecessary cost by requiring the defendants, their lawyers, and witnesses to travel such a long distance and stay in hotels.

In their legal response, the defendants' lawyers, led by Lewis Shepherd, told the Supreme Court that there was no substantial evidence provided by federal prosecutors that demonstrated the need to move the trial from Chattanooga to Washington. They said all witnesses would find Chattanooga safe and without intimidation.

The city's government and business leaders also expressed outrage at the federal prosecutors' contentions. Judge McReynolds said the Justice Department's petition was a direct attack on the character of the people of Chattanooga. District Attorney Matt Whitaker said the government's position would actually hinder witnesses from testifying, because they would not come forward if they knew they had to journey several hundred miles to tell their story. In a front-page editorial titled "An Official in Contempt of Chattanooga," the *Chattanooga News* blasted the nation's highest-ranking law-enforcement officer for demeaning the honesty and self-respect of local citizens.

> If there is any good reason why the Attorney General of the United States should not be called to account for contempt of this community, the Chattanooga News would like for some advocate of black heels on white necks to point it out.
>
> The attorney general of the United States is hereby advised that there is not the least danger to his witnesses in Chattanooga, unless some of them march forth under the

cover of darkness and commit a crime similar to that for which
Ed Johnson was lynched.

This community, like all other communities in the South,
respects the personal oath on the witness stand, no matter how
damaging the evidence may be to white people.

There is no more excitement in Chattanooga over this
matter today than there is over the fact that the Sultan of
Turkey caused one of his servants to empty the ash can in the
back yard this morning before breakfast.

The Chattanooga News does not lift its voice in behalf of
Sheriff Shipp, his deputies or any member of the mob that
lynched Johnson. Its voice is merely raised in behalf of this
community. It submits that even so high and mighty a person
as the Attorney General of the United States has no just cause
to hold this community up in contempt of the world and in
effect publish it abroad as lawless and firmly set against the
enforcement of law.

In the end, the Supreme Court ruled in favor of the defendants by
ordering that all testimony be heard in Chattanooga. However, the justices gave wide discretion to Commissioner Maher to move the hearing
if the circumstances suggested by federal prosecutors ever developed.

As the date of the trial neared, lawyers representing the defendants met frequently to prepare their cases jointly. Harmon, Pritchard,
and Shepherd met almost daily to develop their strategies and prepare
their witnesses and clients to testify. Each attorney met with the alibi
witnesses who would supposedly swear under oath that one of the
defendants could not have participated in the lynching because he was
with them that night, miles away. Character witnesses were also lined
up, to testify that the defendants were really good citizens who should
be believed under oath.

One evening, after several hours of working on the case, a group of
the lawyers sat around a law office drinking whiskey. Many drinks into
the night, the attorneys decided to conduct a comedy. With Lewis
Shepherd leading the way, they gathered around a table, dimmed the

lanterns, lit a few candles, and announced they were conducting a séance. The whole thing was designed to poke fun at Ed Johnson and his claim of innocence.

With an audience that included a newspaper reporter, several local residents, and a handful of visitors from West Virginia, the lawyers sat around a table, held hands, closed their eyes, and began chanting. Within a few minutes, the people in the room heard a whisper.

"I want to speak to Judge Shepherd," the voice supposedly said. Those present claimed the voice was that of a well-known policeman who had died several months ago.

"I know everybody in the room except three," said the whisper. But before the voice could say anything more, another, stronger voice chimed in. This second alleged spirit also wanted to talk to the lawyer.

"I am Ed Johnson," said the man's voice. "I want to talk to the Judge [Shepherd], too. I want to tell you all that I was guilty, and that they hanged the right man."

A few seconds later, the whispering spirit of the police officer supposedly interrupted, denouncing Johnson's spirit and commanding him to depart.

"Skidoo!"

"Fly you away!"

"Get you back, you evil spirit, whence you came. How dare you?"

"I repeat to you, Skidoo!"

And with that, witnesses said, the spirit of Ed Johnson disappeared into the night and his voice was never heard from again. Everyone in the room received quite a laugh from the skit. Shepherd would later contend that the entire episode was unplanned and unstaged. But, then again, Shepherd was a known prankster who would never be handicapped by the truth.

This very attitude was the primary reason Parden said he would never return to Chattanooga. That Lewis Shepherd, a lawyer whom Parden respected and loved, would participate in such inappropriate shenanigans greatly disappointed him. The event demonstrated how even liberal-minded people like Shepherd would do certain things and act in different ways to remain politically and socially popular in a racially prejudiced community.

The much-publicized incident convinced Parden that it was a mistake to conduct the trial in Chattanooga. Citing that and other, personal reasons, he ended his official involvement in the case. He decided he would not travel back to Tennessee to assist federal prosecutors in the trial. Parden did provide the Secret Service agents with names and addresses of the key witnesses, and he wrote letters to many black witnesses encouraging them to testify for the government. In return, prosecutors promised the lawyer they would not call him as a witness during the trial.

Neither Noah Parden nor Styles Hutchins would ever journey to Chattanooga again.

The week before the trial was scheduled to begin, Agents Dickey and McAdams scampered about Chattanooga seeking out many of the key witnesses. They needed to locate about three dozen individuals, conduct final interviews, and prepare them for their testimony. They also had to serve official federal-court subpoenas on the potentially hostile witnesses. Most of the witnesses would probably have testified without a subpoena. But several—including the friends and associates of Sheriff Shipp and a handful of black witnesses—needed the threat of jail if they did not show up as a necessary encouragement. The Supreme Court had ordered that a special subpoena form be prepared specifically for this case.

SUPREME COURT OF THE UNITED STATES

THE UNITED STATES OF AMERICA, COMPLAINANT, vs. JOHN F. SHIPP, ET AL., DEFENDANTS, OCTOBER TERM 1906.

The President of the United States to (<u>witness</u>).

You are hereby commanded to appear as witness for the United States of America before James D. Maher, Commissioner, at the United States Courtroom, in the city of Chattanooga, Tennessee on the 12th day of February, 1907, at 10:00 a.m., and not depart without leave.

Witness the Honorable Melville W. Fuller, Chief Justice of

the United States, the 11th day of February, in the year of our Lord, 1907—Seal of the Supreme Court of the United States

Signed JAMES H. McKENNEY, Clerk of the Supreme Court
of the United States.

The trial of Sheriff Shipp and the other defendants opened in the United States Custom House, in the U.S. Circuit Courtroom, at 2:00 p.m. on Tuesday, February 12, 1907. No one knew how long the trial would last; some people speculated ten days and others a month. The proceedings were open to the public. More than 200 people—most of them black—arrived at the courthouse three hours early to be assured a seat. Every pew in the second-floor courtroom was full. Spectators lined the walls, eagerly awaiting the testimony. Members of the local bar association were given seating preferences, filling about twenty of the best seats. Because there were so many defendants in the court-room (twenty-six, to be exact), they and their families occupied the first two rows on the defense side of the courtroom.

Maher took his spot sitting atop the high wooden bench so long occupied by U.S. Circuit Judge C. D. Clark. Directly in front of the commissioner sat two government stenographers, who transcribed every word of testimony and catalogued every piece of evidence intro-duced. Immediately facing Maher and the stenographers was a long table that stretched across the entire courtroom. On the right side sat U.S. Attorney Penland of Knoxville. Next to him was Terry Sanford, the assistant U.S. attorney general. Seated behind the two prosecutors were Agents Dickey and McAdams. The defense lawyers were shoul-der to shoulder on the left side of the table. Next to the prosecution lawyers was a small table and chairs for the press. A witness chair was placed on a raised platform situated between the news reporters and the judge's bench.

Exactly one year after Noah Parden and Styles Hutchins sought to intervene and appeal Ed Johnson's conviction, Commissioner Maher pounded his gavel and called the court to order. He announced the case, *United States* v. *John F. Shipp*. Assistant Attorney General Sanford immediately rose to his feet and told the court that some preliminary matters needed to be resolved before the case could proceed.

One thing, he said, was the very style of the case. The official charge listed "John F. Shipp" as the defendant. However, the defendant's correct name was "Joseph F. Shipp." John Shipp, the prosecutor said, was the sheriff's brother, and not a defendant in the case. The mix-up was not a problem: Commissioner Maher ordered the court clerk to make the appropriate correction in the record.

After several other procedural matters were resolved, Sanford called his first witness: J. L. Chivington, a news reporter for the *Chattanooga Times*. The young journalist raised his right hand, kissed the Bible, and swore he would tell the truth. Chivington had covered the entire case: the attack on Nevada Taylor, the subsequent arrest of Ed Johnson, the trial and Johnson's conviction, the efforts of Parden and Hutchins to appeal, and the U.S. Supreme Court's ultimate intervention. And he was present when the mob stormed the county jail, dragged Johnson to the county bridge, and lynched him. His articles the next morning had detailed every aspect of the horrible event.

At Sanford's direction, Chivington spent more than two hours telling the court the story of the case. He was never asked his opinion, nor did he ever offer it. However, the news reporter made two key points for federal prosecutors.

First, he testified that Sheriff Shipp usually had several deputies on duty at the jail during the late-evening hours.

"I think there were normally six or seven deputies on guard every night and I had seen them there as late as midnight," Chivington said.

This was important testimony, because, hours before the lynching, Shipp had given most of his deputies the night off from work. Prosecutors contended that the sheriff knew there would be a lynching attempt that night and wanted to provide the mob with the minimal amount of resistance. Several other witnesses would also testify that a handful of deputies were known to be at the jail at night.

Second, Chivington testified that "the feeling was high at about the time of the lynching." The reporter's statements supported the government's contention that the sheriff and his deputies should have known that a lynching attempt was likely.

SANFORD: What effect did the news of the appeal have on the minds of the people?

CHIVINGTON: There were hotheaded people who made hotheaded remarks.

SANFORD: What do you mean?

CHIVINGTON: I think the general feeling was one of disappointment at the action of the Supreme Court.

SANFORD: What did people say?

CHIVINGTON: I heard people say they might do something. I think there was some danger of a mob.

The next two witnesses called by Sanford were on the witness stand for only a few minutes each. Neither provided much controversy. However, they offered key elements in proving the government's case. A. W. Brazelton, who had been the private secretary to federal Judge C. D. Clark, testified he had received the telegram from the U.S. Supreme Court on March 18 informing him of the decision to delay Johnson's execution and hear an appeal of the case. Brazelton said he had immediately called Sheriff Shipp and informed him of the telegram. He told the court that he had received a second, more detailed telegram from the justices the next afternoon, which he said he hand-delivered to Shipp. Defense attorneys had no additional questions for Brazelton.

The third witness was Edward Chaddick, the manager of the Western Union telegram office in Chattanooga. Chaddick said his records showed that he had received a telegram from the U.S. Supreme Court the afternoon of March 19 and that it was hand-delivered to Sheriff Shipp. He provided the court with a copy of a delivery slip signed by "J. F. Shipp." Under a brief cross-examination, Chaddick admitted he had not delivered the telegram to the sheriff himself and said it was possible that someone had signed Shipp's name to the delivery slip.

The final witness of the day was by far the most explosive: Ellen Baker of Ducktown, the only other prisoner on the third floor the night of the lynching. She gave a detailed accounting of the mob's efforts the night of March 19 and Johnson's reactions to them.

The newspapers said Baker testified in "the language of a child of the mountains." She admitted she could neither read nor write, didn't know the difference between being acquitted and convicted, couldn't remember if she was twenty-seven or twenty-eight years old.

However, her testimony was nonetheless dramatic and helpful to the government's case. Under questioning by Sanford, Baker said deputies had placed a white man in the third-floor cell next to her so he could write letters for her. She said that the afternoon of the lynching deputies had moved the white man and the other prisoners to a more secure cell on the second floor, leaving only her and Ed Johnson housed on the third.

> BAKER: I asked Mr. [Jeremiah] Gibson about it and he said that a mob was coming at night and they took the white prisoner down fearing that the mob might kill him.
>
> SANFORD: Did you say anything to him [Mr. Gibson] about whether you would be hurt? Were you scared or not?
>
> BAKER: Well, he said they wouldn't hurt me; for me to go on back up there and go to bed. He said there was going to be a mob that night.
>
> SANFORD: Was there any unusual disturbances going on at that time, that you could tell?
>
> BAKER: No, sir.
>
> SANFORD: What did you do then?
>
> BAKER: I went back upstairs and went to bed as directed.
>
> SANFORD: When did you see or speak to Jailer Gibson next?
>
> BAKER: It was after dark. Mr. Gibson told me that a mob was coming.

It was much later, she testified, that she began hearing the members of the mob trying to bust down the doors of the jail. She said she started crying and yelling for help. When she became too loud, Baker said, Gibson and a couple members of the mob told her to be quiet.

SANFORD: What did Mr. Gibson say to you?

BAKER: Why, he told me to hush hollering, there warn't nobody going to hurt me.

SANFORD: While this was going on, did anybody threaten you in any way?

BAKER: When that was going on there was a man poked his gun through the bar and told me to quit hollering.

On cross-examination by Pritchard, Baker said the gun only made her more scared. And when she heard the men talking about getting some dynamite to blast the cell doors down, she admitted, she had become hysterical.

PRITCHARD: When he poked his gun through the bar, you quit hollering, did you not?

BAKER: Yes; it scared me. I quit hollering.

PRITCHARD: How long was it after you had lain down before you heard this noise of the mob?

BAKER: It warn't but a little while.

PRITCHARD: How long had you been married at that time?

BAKER: We have been married along since the first of March.

PRITCHARD: The first of what March?

BAKER: Last March.

PRITCHARD: You were just on your bridal tour when you were in jail, then?

BAKER: I just had been married a few days, three days.

PRITCHARD: What did you say your name is?

BAKER: Ellen.

PRITCHARD: Are you known by the names of Elmina, or Elminer?

BAKER: Yes, sir; that is my name, too.

PRITCHARD: Are you what they call a lady moonshiner?

BAKER: I guess.

PRITCHARD: Are you the same Ellen Baker who was tried before a federal jury, found guilty as charged, and the court

fined the defendant $200 plus costs, sentenced to five months
in jail? Are you that Ellen Baker?

BAKER: I guess that's me.

PRITCHARD: But the judge suspended your sentence,
didn't he, because you are a woman and because you are poor?

BAKER: He cleared me.

PRITCHARD: What do you mean, he cleared you? Do you
mean you were acquitted?

BAKER: Quit what?

PRITCHARD: No more questions.

Defense lawyers tried to undermine Baker's credibility by focusing on her lack of education and her criminal record. Yet, though the
courtroom audience and the lawyers had many laughs at her expense,
Baker's story never changed. She repeatedly told how deputies had
warned her hours in advance that a mob was going to raid the jail that
night. This testimony contributed significantly to the prosecutors'
contention that Sheriff Shipp and his deputies had known there
would be a lynching attempt that night but did nothing to prepare to
stop it.

The historic first day of the case concluded with brief testimony
from two more witnesses. Carl Rowden told the court that he lived not
more than thirty feet from the county jail. He was sitting on his front
porch the night of the lynching and watched the entire raid on the jail.
His statement was graphic and detailed. He never saw any police officers or deputies make any effort to disperse the mob or stop them from
taking Johnson from the jail. However, he was unable to identify any
of the members of the mob.

The final witness was J. Perry Fyffe, a captain in the Chattanooga
troop of the Tennessee Militia and editor of a smaller city newspaper.
Fyffe made it clear from the beginning that he was a friend of Sheriff
Shipp and believed the contempt charges were nonsense. However,
he testified that feelings were "so high" that "a lynching could reasonably have been expected" following the Supreme Court's decision to
stay Johnson's execution.

The second day of the trial began with a surprising and explosive witness. Julia Wofford, a twenty-six-year-old black woman, had been Sheriff Shipp's cook for the better part of two years, including at the time of the lynching. Defense attorneys turned to Shipp for any tip on what she might say, but the sheriff shrugged his shoulders in bewilderment. As Sanford asked Wofford to identify herself for the record, Pritchard asked Commissioner Maher to have the record reflect "the complexion of the witness—colored." Sanford then continued his questioning.

> SANFORD: Did you ever hear Captain Shipp say anything in reference to any delay in the proceedings in the Ed Johnson case? If you did, just state what you heard.
>
> WOFFORD: I heard him say one day at the dinner table that if the execution would be stayed Ed Johnson would be mobbed.
>
> SANFORD: Did you hear Captain Shipp, on the day that Ed Johnson was lynched, say anything in reference to whether the Supreme Court had taken any action or not? If so, state what he said, and the time.
>
> WOFFORD: I heard him tell his wife that afternoon that he was going to get a hearing—he would get a trial, or something like that. I don't know exactly the words.
>
> SANFORD: That who was going to get a hearing?
>
> WOFFORD: That Ed Johnson was.
>
> SANFORD: That was in the afternoon?
>
> WOFFORD: That was Monday, and Ed Johnson was mobbed that night.

Wofford's testimony was especially significant along two lines. Shipp's lawyers had announced that they were going to fight the contempt charges on a key procedural point that the sheriff was never properly informed or notified that the Supreme Court had ordered Johnson's execution postponed. If Shipp didn't know that Justice Harlan had intervened in the Johnson case and stayed the execution, then the sheriff could not be held in contempt. However, Wofford's testimony clearly demonstrated that Shipp did know about the Supreme Court's actions.

The witness also made it clear that Sheriff Shipp believed a mob would try to lynch Johnson if his scheduled hanging were delayed. Wofford said she heard Shipp tell his wife and guests during dinner that he was sure a mob would try to kill Johnson. The statement directly contradicted the sheriff's public claim that he had no idea there would be a lynching attempt.

Pritchard introduced himself to the witness and began his cross-examination, which he hoped would cast doubt on Wofford's credibility and testimony.

PRITCHARD: How long did you cook for Captain Shipp?

WOFFORD: I cooked for him, the last time I was there, about two months.

PRITCHARD: When did you leave?

WOFFORD: I left there the week they lynched Ed Johnson.

PRITCHARD: The same week?

WOFFORD: Yes, sir.

PRITCHARD: Before Ed Johnson was lynched or afterwards?

WOFFORD: After he was lynched.

PRITCHARD: Did you tell him you were going to leave?

WOFFORD: No, sir.

PRITCHARD: You just pulled up and left?

WOFFORD: Yes, sir.

PRITCHARD: That is the way you generally do, is it?

WOFFORD: No; that ain't the way I always do. I never did it before.

PRITCHARD: You say you heard two conversations about this matter. The first time was when you heard Captain Shipp say at the dinner table something about it. What was it he said about it at the dinner table?

WOFFORD: He said at the dinner table if Ed Johnson's execution would be stayed he would be mobbed.

PRITCHARD: If his execution would be what?

WOFFORD: Stayed.

PRITCHARD: What do you mean by that?

WOFFORD: He meant if he got a trial.

PRITCHARD: Got a trial where?

WOFFORD: In the Supreme Court.

PRITCHARD: In what Supreme Court?

WOFFORD: Of the United States. I don't know of but one.

PRITCHARD: Did he say the Supreme Court of the United States?

WOFFORD: Yes.

PRITCHARD: Who put these words in your mouth about a stay of execution?

WOFFORD: There didn't anybody put those words in my mouth.

PRITCHARD: Did you ever hear or know anything about a stay of execution?

WOFFORD: There was something in the paper that way.

PRITCHARD: You read it in the paper instead of hearing Captain Shipp say it, did you not?

WOFFORD: No, sir; I hear him say it.

PRITCHARD: Or you talked it over with somebody? Who did you hear say that?

WOFFORD: I didn't talk it over with no one.

Pritchard tried several traditional cross-examination techniques in an effort to shake Wofford's testimony. But no matter what he tried, Wofford never wavered from her story.

Day three of the trial brought equally dramatic testimony. John N. Stonecipher proved to be one of the most important witnesses summoned by the government. A builder and contractor from Cohutta, Georgia, Stonecipher was on the witness stand for more than three hours, becoming the first person to connect some of the defendants in the case officially to the lynching. Under oath, Stonecipher implicated William Mayes, Henry Padgett, Frank Ward, and Alf Handman.

Stonecipher said he had known some of the defendants just a few days and some for many years, but had talked with three of them at a saloon just a few hours before the lynching took place.

SANFORD: Did you have any conversation with them that related to a lynching in any manner? If so, state what it was.

STONECIPHER: Mr. Padgett asked me if I had heard what the Supreme Court had done in the Johnson case. I told him I had understood that they had stayed the execution. He said yes, that is what he had understood, and it was a damned outrage.

SANFORD: Go ahead. Keep right on. Just tell the conversation.

STONECIPHER: Then Mayes said, "We'll see to that ourselves."

SANFORD: Was that in Padgett's presence?

STONECIPHER: Yes, sir. They were both together.

SANFORD: Did you see Ward that evening?

STONECIPHER: Yes, sir. I saw Ward that same evening.

SANFORD: Where did you see Ward?

STONECIPHER: I saw him in front of Muellery's saloon, on Market Street.

SANFORD: What was said? Did you have any conversation with him?

STONECIPHER: I stopped on the curb, waiting for a car to go home, and Ward called to me. He says, "Ain't you from Georgia?" I says, "I used to live there." He says, "We want you to help us lynch that damn nigger tonight."

SANFORD: What was that?

STONECIPHER: He says, "We want you to help us to lynch that damn nigger tonight."

SANFORD: What did you say?

STONECIPHER: I says, "I don't believe it would pay. I believe Sheriff Shipp would shoot the red-hot stuff out of you."

SANFORD: What did he say?

STONECIPHER: He says, "No, it is all agreed. There won't be a sheriff nor deputy there." I said, "Ward, I believe you are lying." That is just what I told him.

SANFORD: How long had you known these men?

STONECIPHER: I have known Padgett and Mayes, I guess, fifteen years.

SANFORD: How had you known them; in what way? What was their business?

STONECIPHER: I have worked with them on several jobs, on carpenter work.

SANFORD: How long had you known Ward?

STONECIPHER: About two years.

SANFORD: What is Ward's business?

STONECIPHER: Bricklayer.

SANFORD: Did you see any of these gentlemen later, after the night of the lynching?

STONECIPHER: Yes, sir.

SANFORD: Which one did you see first?

STONECIPHER: I saw Mr. Padgett first, at Ransom's saloon.

SANFORD: What conversation occurred between you at that time?

STONECIPHER: I went in and Padgett had the *Morning Times*, and the first word he said, he said: "This damn paper has printed a lie about this lynching." I said: "How do you know it is a lie, Henry?"

SANFORD: What did he answer?

STONECIPHER: He told me he was there. And just as he said that Alf Handman come in and Henry just turned his shoe up. He says: "Why, I haven't got the mud off my shoes yet." Alf, says: "I cleaned mine before I come."

SANFORD: Was anything further said between you at that time?

STONECIPHER: And Henry says, "We did the nigger up all right, didn't we?" Alf, says: "You bet we did." That was all that was said.

Stonecipher told the court that, less than ten hours after the lynching, he saw William Mayes walking downtown in front of the Stag Hotel. The witness said the left side of Mayes's nose was "skinned up pretty bad."

SANFORD: Did you have a conversation with him?

STONECIPHER: I says, "Hello, Bill, what is the matter with your nose?" He says, "I skinned it last night breaking that damned jail door down and getting the nigger out."

SANFORD: Did you see Mr. Ward?

STONECIPHER: I saw Mr. Ward that evening.

SANFORD: What conversation did you have with Mr. Ward?

STONECIPHER: He come out of Jack Price's saloon, and was standing in the vestibule, and he says, "You are the first damn man from Georgia ever I saw that didn't have nerve enough to kill a nigger." I told him I didn't have much nerve when I had to buck up against the government.

Lewis Shepherd cross-examined for nearly forty minutes in an extraordinary effort to discredit the witness. Here was a white man testifying against other white men accused of complicity in the lynching of a Negro. He exposed that Stonecipher had been sued because he owed another man money and had refused to pay. Shepherd also showed that Stonecipher seldom stayed in one town for more than a few months before moving. The witness said he simply went where there was business for him. Apparently unshaken in his statement, Stonecipher was dismissed.

Later that night, Stonecipher received an anonymous handwritten letter instructing him to pack up his family and leave Chattanooga within forty-eight hours or his house would be blown up by dynamite. The letter was signed, "The Lynchers." As a precaution, federal prosecutors helped Stonecipher move his family to Georgia.

The day's second witness was on the stand for only ten minutes. Press W. Walker had been a deputy under Sheriff Skillern, the man who preceded Shipp. However, Shipp had demoted Walker to the

position of cook at the county jail because he didn't want any black
people as deputies. In fact, Walker had cooked the meal for the inmates and deputies the night Johnson was lynched.

Walker told the court that several deputies usually lingered
around the jail until the late hours of the night. On the night of March
19, he said, some of the deputies had dined early at the jail—eating
ham sandwiches and drinking beer. He said they discussed receiving
the telegram from the Supreme Court delaying Johnson's scheduled
hanging. And Walker testified that soon thereafter all the deputies left
the jail for the evening, except Jeremiah Gibson.

The final witness on the third day of testimony was Dr. Howard E.
Jones, minister of the First Baptist Church in Chattanooga. The
preacher told the court that he had called city police headquarters
when he heard that a lynching attempt was under way. He said he was
outraged when the sergeant on duty acknowledged he knew about the
attack on the jail but said he would do nothing to stop it.

Dr. Jones also testified that the community was extremely excited
and angered by the Supreme Court's decision to delay Johnson's execution, and that a lynch mob should have been expected. The minister
said he had rushed down to the jail the night of the lynching to see if
he could help stop the vigilantes. But when he arrived, the mob had
already left for the county bridge with Johnson. However, he said, he
did find Sheriff Shipp at the jail, and he testified that there were no
restraints on the sheriff and that no one was preventing him from chas-
ing after the leaders of the mob.

"I suggested to him that we go and try to identify some of the
members of the mob," Dr. Jones told the courtroom. "He [Shipp] said
that would be a very dangerous thing to do, that they were very desperate men. While we were talking a fusillade of shots were heard
from the bridge."

Sanford thanked Dr. Jones for his courageous testimony and
announced that he had no additional questions. The prosecutor knew
how powerful it was for one of the city's leading religious figures to
testify against the sheriff and the other defendants. To demonstrate
ultimate contempt for Dr. Jones's statement, Pritchard simply stood
up and said, "The witness may stand aside." The defense attorneys

knew there was no effective way to cross-examine the preacher, so they said they had no questions for him.

The next morning, federal prosecutors called Robert K. Lyons to testify. Identified in the court record as "a Negro who worked at Sam Light's Saloon on the night of the lynching," Lyons said he had heard from a customer that there was going to be a lynching, so he ran toward the county bridge. When he got there, he saw Luther Williams coming from the direction of Johnson's body. Lyons said he saw two or three police officers on the county bridge that night, too, but he did not know who they were.

Will Tarpley, a black man who had been an inmate at the county jail the night Johnson was murdered, was the next witness. The seventeen-year-old told about the raid on the jail and the terrified reaction of the prisoners. He said he had been able to peek through a crack between the wall and the cell door and had seen a man he knew named Bart Justice actively participating in the raid on the jail. Asked if the man he had seen was in the courtroom, Tarpley pointed to Bart Justice.

On cross-examination by Shepherd, Tarpley admitted that the crack he had looked through was not even an inch wide.

"Don't they ever call you 'Bad Eye Tarpley'?" Shepherd inquired.

"No, sir. They call me Keen Eye," the witness responded.

"You had a keen eye when you saw Bart Justice, didn't you?" Shepherd asked sarcastically.

"Yes, sir."

The rest of the government's case was less than exciting. They introduced three witnesses, including the head of the National Weather Service office in Chattanooga, to show that it had rained heavily the night before the lynching. This corroborated Stonecipher's testimony that some of the men claimed to get mud on their shoes while walking from the jail to the county bridge.

By Saturday evening, thirty-one witnesses had been called to testify for the federal government. A few had identified various members of the mob who had allegedly participated in the lynching of Johnson. Others told how the sheriff had ordinarily encouraged deputies to spend nights at the jail and how unusual it was for him to give them all a night off from work at the same time. Several witnesses testified that the Supreme Court's stay of execution had caused a tremendous amount of anger and resentment in the community. They said there was much talk about a possible lynching throughout the city several hours prior to the raid on the jail. And prosecutors introduced the widely reprinted article from the *Birmingham News* in which Shipp admitted that he had done nothing to physically stop or otherwise prevent the lynching.

With five days of evidence completed, lawyers on both sides and Commissioner Maher realized the trial was going to take much longer than anyone had expected. Further complicating the matter was that several of the government's witnesses had suddenly disappeared. Sanford said he needed more time to locate and interview additional witnesses before proceeding in the case. Explaining that he had other chores to complete in Washington, D.C., Maher announced he was recessing the trial until June. This was not a problem for either side, especially since there was no jury involved.

Prosecutors and Secret Service agents spent the next four months solidifying their evidence and rounding up a few more witnesses. The defense attorneys viewed any delay in the trial as beneficial to them. After all, it allowed them additional time to dig up dirt on the government's witnesses and apply pressure to other witnesses to keep them from testifying.

The two sides finally came back together on June 10, 1907, in the same Chattanooga courtroom. Spectators were equally plentiful. The scene was every bit as dramatic and contentious.

The initial witnesses called by Assistant Attorney General Terry Sanford took only a few minutes to say their piece: city engineers and others who told the court how the streets between the jail and the Walnut Street Bridge "were torn up and muddy for a while." That further supported Stonecipher's testimony that Henry Padgett's shoes were muddy the morning following the lynching.

The first significant testimony of the week came from A. J. Ware, a justice of the peace in Chattanooga. Ware said he had finished work a little after 10:00 p.m the night of March 19 and started walking down Market Street. Within a minute or so, he was confronted by a small group of black youths who told him a lynching was taking place at the jail. A few minutes later, he bumped into a deputy sheriff who confirmed the boys' report.

The most devastating testimony was yet to come. Ware said he had arrived too late to offer any assistance to Sheriff Shipp in protecting Ed Johnson, but had chased the mob down Walnut Street toward the bridge and watched the events unfold. Saying he was less than twenty-five feet away from Johnson, Ware gave a graphic description of what had happened.

SANFORD: Did you see who placed the noose around Mr. Johnson's neck?

WARE: I did.

SANFORD: Who was it that adjusted the noose around Johnson's neck?

WARE: Nick Nolan.

SANFORD: Do you know Nick Nolan?

WARE: I do.

SANFORD: Who is Nick Nolan?

WARE: He is a barkeeper in South Chattanooga.

SANFORD: Was there any shooting on the bridge that night?

WARE: Yes, sir. The bullets must have cut the rope but Johnson's body fell to the bridge.

SANFORD: Did anyone step forward from the mob when Johnson fell and shoot him again?

WARE: Yes, sir.

SANFORD: Who was that man?

WARE: I believe it was Luther Williams. He fired five shots into Johnson's body.

Sanford proceeded to read the names of the men listed as defendants in the contempt case.

SANFORD: Do you remember seeing any of these men at the jail or at the county bridge that night?

WARE: Yes, sir. I saw Matt Galloway at the bridge.

SANFORD: What was Mr. Galloway doing?

WARE: He was carrying a Winchester rifle on his shoulder and walking around the bridge. I asked him, "What are you doing with that gun?"

SANFORD: What did he say?

WARE: Galloway replied, "I came up here to defend the men who took the Negro out. I heard the Negroes were coming up."

The government's next witness was Mose Stokes, a black man who had lived in Chattanooga for twenty-one years. Stokes said he happened to be walking downtown on the night of March 19 when he came across the mob raiding the jail. He watched the developments of the mob for several minutes while hiding behind some trees across the street from the jail. Asked by prosecutors if any of the men he saw that night were in the courtroom, Stokes pointed to Henry Padgett.

Both Ware and Stokes escaped the witness stand without any serious cross-examination or damage to their credibility.

On Thursday, June 13, Sanford announced he had one final witness to present. He called the name Joe Franklin. A former constable in Hamilton County, Franklin had disappeared from the city at the time of the first hearing in February. Secret Service Agent Dickey had tracked him down in St. Louis and brought him back to Chattanooga with a subpoena. Federal prosecutors hoped the black former police officer would be a star witness for them. The information he had given the investigators earlier was explosive and damning. However, defense attorneys were well prepared for his testimony.

Franklin had been appointed to the position of constable three times by the justice of the peace in his district of the city, even though he had very little formal education. He had lived in Chattanooga since 1883 and knew just about every lawyer, judge, police officer, and elected official in the city. As he walked into the courtroom, he stopped and shook hands with most of the defense lawyers. He called them each by name, and they all smiled and welcomed him as well.

Franklin testified that the county jail was used as a "loafing resort by the sheriff and his deputies and that rarely a night passed without some of them being there." He said it was the custom for several deputies to sleep at the jail overnight. The former officer testified that he had gone by the jail the night of the lynching and found Matt Galloway and Joe Clark, two deputy sheriffs, participating in the raid on the jail. He also told the court that he had seen Bart Justice grabbing Ed Johnson's arm as they led him to the county bridge. And he said he had seen Nick Nolan actively involved, too.

However, Franklin's credibility was seriously tarnished during the cross-examination by defense attorney Robert Pritchard. It was obvious the sheriff's lawyers were prepared to attack the witness.

> PRITCHARD: You say you served three full successful terms as constable?
>
> FRANKLIN: Yes, sir. I tried to make an honorable constable. I got arrested several times and didn't get in the penitentiary.
>
> PRITCHARD: You got arrested several times yourself and didn't get in the penitentiary?
>
> FRANKLIN: No, sir; and I didn't kill anybody.
>
> PRITCHARD: And that is what you call being successful?
>
> FRANKLIN: And I didn't steal anything from anybody, and that is a successful constable.
>
> PRITCHARD: Your idea of success in an official position is to keep out of the penitentiary?
>
> FRANKLIN: Yes, sir.

Pritchard introduced evidence that Franklin had been indicted numerous times for theft, larceny, and felonious taking. Pritchard also accused the witness of running off with a woman other than his wife in February—the time when he was supposed to be in Chattanooga testifying for the government in the Shipp case. Franklin denied he had ever stolen from anyone and claimed the indictments were fabricated by white men trying to ruin him.

Despite the disappointment in their final witness, federal prosecutors announced they were ready to rest their case. Outside the courtroom, Sanford told news reporters he thought the government had undoubtedly proved its case against Sheriff Shipp, some of his deputies, and a handful of those involved in the mob. However, he readily admitted that he did not yet have reliable evidence against some of the defendants. If additional evidence did not surface, he said, the charges against those men might be dismissed. Part of the problem, Sanford said, was that some witnesses the government had relied on to testify were too afraid to come forward and say what they had seen or heard.

On Saturday morning, June 15, defense attorneys began the tedious task of disproving the government case against their clients. In all criminal trials, the burden of proving a case is solely on the government; it is the prosecutors who must prove beyond a reasonable doubt that a defendant is guilty. But the defense lawyers found themselves in a strange predicament. Though the burden of proof still rested with the government, because Sanford was refusing to dismiss any of the charges immediately, the defense attorneys felt pressured to present evidence establishing their clients' innocence. Even though they believed the government had not proved its case, Shepherd, Pritchard, and the other lawyers agreed that it was in their clients' best interests if the official record sent to the Supreme Court included testimony pointing to the innocence of all the defendants.

For two weeks, lawyers for those accused of participating in the lynching introduced witness after witness who supplied supposed alibis for the defendants. Most of the alibi witnesses were family members, some were drinking buddies, others co-workers.

The defense attorneys called witnesses who vouched for the defendants' credibility and high moral character. And they provided testimony that the *prosecution's* witnesses should not be believed because their general character was bad.

Every couple of days, one of the defendants took the witness stand. Bart Justice proclaimed his innocence. He claimed he was at home in bed at the time of the lynching. His wife and daughter swore under oath that he was telling the truth.

Will Marquette, another defendant, testified that he was sick the night of March 19, 1906. He said he went to the doctor about 9:00 p.m. and had a prescription filled twenty minutes later. From there, he stopped by the grocery store for some sugar, and then went straight home. He was nowhere near the jail that night and played no role in the lynching of Johnson, he said. Again, his family took the witness stand and corroborated his story.

Less convincing in his testimony was William Mayes, a mechanic, who testified that he had been "quite intoxicated" the night of the lynching. Mayes told the court he didn't remember what he had done that night but he was not at the jail and had not attended Johnson's slaying. He also denied telling John Stonecipher that he had participated in the lynching. Mayes's wife testified on his behalf, saying her husband was home the entire evening of March 19.

Henry Padgett also denied any role in the lynching. He claimed he hadn't known about the lynching until the next morning, when he read the account in the newspaper. He also said Stonecipher was lying about the conversations the two had had the day of and following the lynching. Padgett's lawyer introduced six witnesses who testified that Padgett was a good man and should be believed.

The only defendant who offered a different story to the court was Luther Williams. Several witnesses had identified him as being part of the lynch mob. Under oath, the saloon owner admitted he was there, but only as a spectator. Williams also denied having a conversation with Stonecipher the afternoon before the lynching or the morning following it. Under cross-examination, Williams said he could not identify any of the people involved in the lynching.

Nick Nolan decided not to testify. However, his lawyer introduced seven witnesses, including his brother, who claimed that Nolan was with them at various times the night of the lynching.

One by one, the sheriff's deputies took the witness stand. They adamantly denied they were at or near the jail the night of the lynching. And they remained steadfast in their claim that they had no idea that a lynching would take place.

Jeremiah Gibson's testimony lasted the better part of an entire day. The night jailer told the court that he had had no advance knowledge of a lynching attempt on March 19. And he denied telling Ellen Baker, the inmate in the cell next to Johnson, that he thought a mob was coming that night. Gibson gave a detailed accounting of the raid on the jail. At first, he said he could not identify any of the leaders of the mob. Later, he said he "thought" he recognized Nick Nolan as one of the leaders.

Under cross-examination, Gibson admitted he had made no effort whatsoever to seek outside help in stopping the mob. He also testified that he had never attempted to use his loaded pistol in defending Johnson. When Sanford asked the jailer why he had not tried to shoot the intruders as they made their way up the stairwell, Gibson just shook his head but gave no verbal response.

The final witness to be called by the defense team was Joseph F. Shipp, the sheriff of Hamilton County. His lawyer Robert Pritchard led the county's top lawman through his testimony, making the key points required in defending the sheriff against the contempt charges.

> PRITCHARD: I will ask you to state whether or not you conspired with your deputies, or any one of them, or anyone else, looking towards the lynching of Ed Johnson?
>
> SHIPP: I never conspired with any living man, my deputies or anyone else; and I had no knowledge, not the slightest, that there would be any effort on my part or anybody to interfere with Johnson.
>
> PRITCHARD: I will ask you, Captain, if you remember Julia Wofford and her testimony here in regard to the conversation she says she heard at your dinner table, and whether any such conversation as that took place?
>
> SHIPP: Yes, I heard her testimony. I know Julia Wofford. She was a domestic in my family. But there was no such conversation. The truth was that, on account of the fact that my wife was very much worried and in constant dread of all of this trouble and excitement that we had passed through, I scrupulously avoid talking of it and speaking of it in my family; and if I had anticipated anything, she was the last person on earth that I would have related it to.

PRITCHARD: I will ask you when you first heard or knew that there was a mob at the jail the night this lynching took place.

SHIPP: Well, I had gone home that night, I think, about half past six. My office work had been greatly interfered with; the criminal court was in session; I was making preparations to hang this man the next day, and I had a campaign on at the same time. I was seated at a table when the telephone bell rang. I went to the phone and I recognized Attorney General Whitaker's voice. He wanted to know if I knew what was going on at the jail. I told him I did not. "Well," he said, "you had better get down there."

PRITCHARD: Then what did you do?

SHIPP: I hung up the telephone just as quickly as I could, so that I might get another connection. I wanted to call the jail. I then tried to get the jail immediately after disconnecting with him, and I could not get the jail. I at once anticipated what was the matter as soon as I did not get an answer. I anticipated that if there was a mob there the telephone had been torn out. I hung the telephone receiver up at once, rushed around the room, and got my hat and coat, started for the jail, running most of the way and walking rapidly the balance of the way, going down Georgia Avenue to 6th Street, and by 6th Street to Walnut Street, and to the jail. Just as I got opposite the jail and just before turning into the walk leading up to the office, I saw five or six men standing out in the middle of the street; and without stopping, going rapidly, I made the remark, "What is the matter." No one answered at all, and I then went up the walk and found quite a number of men in the walk and on the steps leading into the office. I made my way through the crowd, shoving them to one side, and got into the office. As soon as I got in I saw that the iron door, the outside door, was open. I entered rapidly, and just as I reached the inside of the door I saw Mr. Gibson sitting back against the wall with three or four men standing around him. I had started over to make some inquiry of him, and just at that time I was seized from behind by several men—I do not know how many. When they seized me I did not know but what they were going to do me some violence, and I reached back for my gun, which I had in my pocket. They assured me that they did not intend to hurt me. I was somewhat indignant, and stated to them that I was not afraid of their hurting me. They rushed me up the steps and carried me into the hallway that is above the level of the floor Johnson was on, and through which there is a drag that we feed the prisoners by, and stood over me there with a guard during the progress of the work. They were hammering; I heard them hammering on the door when I entered the office.

PRITCHARD: State whether or not you were kept a prisoner there by these people 'till after they had got Johnson and left the jail with him.

SHIPP: Yes, sir; I was.

Shipp testified that he had done everything within his power to protect Ed Johnson. He reminded the courtroom how his deputies had heroically turned away the mob during the first lynching attempt in January. He pointed out that he had moved Johnson to Knoxville and Nashville to keep the inmate safe. And he forcefully denied he was involved in any conspiracy or even sympathy with the leaders of the mob to allow them to take Johnson from the jail and kill him.

The sheriff had been a good witness for himself. But, just as the defense lawyers had been anticipating Joe Franklin's testimony, Assistant Attorney General Terry Sanford was prepared for Sheriff Shipp. For the next two hours, the seasoned federal prosecutor grilled the sheriff on his actions and inactions the night of Johnson's lynching. In order to obtain a conviction, Sanford knew he had to pry some admissions from Shipp, or at least trap the sheriff in some contradictions.

SANFORD: There was a great deal of race feeling in this community at that time [the time of Johnson's sentencing] that all these matters had engendered, was there not?

SHIPP: Well, yes, sir; I would say that there was some race feeling.

SANFORD: Did you make any special effort to get your deputies, or to have any special guard at the jail that night [the night of the lynching] for Ed Johnson?

SHIPP: I did not.

SANFORD: Captain, did you recognize any of those men who were surrounding Mr. Gibson?

SHIPP: No, sir, I did not.

SANFORD: Did you recognize anybody in there that night until that mob had left; and if so, whom did you recognize?

SHIPP: I did not recognize anybody that was breaking into the jail.

SANFORD: How long were they with you?

SHIPP: Well, I think I was there about thirty minutes.

SANFORD: And did you recognize a single man?

SHIPP: No, sir.

SANFORD: Did you ask them their names?

SHIPP: No, sir; I did not.

SANFORD: Were they calling each other by name?

SHIPP: I did not hear any names called among them.

SANFORD: Did you call a posse there to relieve you or help protect that prisoner?

SHIPP: No, I did not. I did not think there was anybody there that would have responded to my call if they had been called upon.

SANFORD: You did not make any effort at all?

SHIPP: No, sir; I did not. I made no effort except that I remonstrated the mob.

SANFORD: You used no force?

SHIPP: No, sir.

SANFORD: You did not pull your gun?

SHIPP: I had no adequate force, and knew that the pulling of a gun would be useless.

SANFORD: Were you sheriff of the county?

SHIPP: Yes, sir.

SANFORD: And you did not pull your gun?

SHIPP: No.

SANFORD: You had strength enough to have pulled the trigger, I suppose?

SHIPP: Oh, I guess I could have pulled the trigger.

Sheriff Shipp was on the witness stand for two days. Though Sanford certainly scored several victories during his cross-examination, the sheriff remained unwavering in his basic contentions. Shipp invoked the old cliché about "twenty-twenty hindsight" and said he would have done things differently if he had a second chance. But in the end, the sheriff remained indignant at allegations that he had not done his sworn duty to protect Ed Johnson. On Saturday, June 29, the defense attorneys announced that they rested their case. Both sides awaited further instructions from the Supreme Court.

CHAPTER SEVENTEEN

"GUILTY, GUILTY, GUILTY!"

JOSEPH SHIPP CELEBRATED his sixty-third birthday in 1908 with his wife and seven adult children. He told friends he was in good health and excellent spirits. The federal contempt charges pending against him were frivolous, the sheriff told supporters. He was confident the Supreme Court would hand him a victory, pointing out to friends that his lawyers had filed legal motions with the Justice Department and the Supreme Court asking that the charges against him be dismissed.

"I think they're going to end up dropping this whole mess," Shipp told his friends. "Nothing will ever come of it."

The sheriff was equally upbeat about his political future. He had easily captured the Democratic Party's nomination to run for re-election. Though he faced competition from the Republicans in the fall election, he shrugged the opponent off as a nuisance.

Instead, Shipp was spending some time in Nashville with Criminal Court Judge Sam McReynolds, lobbying the state legislature and governor to implement new laws that would severely limit the right of criminal defendants to appeal their convictions. The sheriff told members of the Tennessee House of Representatives and Senate that criminals found guilty by a jury and sentenced to die sat in his jail for up to six months appealing the verdict and unnecessarily extending their life.

Judge McReynolds and the sheriff asked the legislators to strip condemned criminals of most of their legal rights to appeal their convictions. They argued that once criminals are sentenced to die they should be allowed only thirty days to present to the Tennessee Supreme Court evidence that their conviction was in error, or that the state law under which they were prosecuted was unconstitutional.

"The public demands speedy justice," Shipp told the lawmakers. "Once criminal brutes have been afforded a trial, their sentence of death should be carried out as quickly as possible."

The "get-tough-on-crime" mentality was politically popular even in 1908, but it was obvious that the case of Ed Johnson lingered in the minds of Tennessee legislators. Several judges and criminal-defense lawyers, including Lewis Shepherd, privately counseled their elected representatives against restricting the appeals of people accused and convicted of crimes. The state's General Assembly decided to leave the criminal-justice system untouched.

Johnson's case was also on the minds of Chattanoogans as they went to the polls in the fall of 1908. Fueled by a large protest vote from the black community, Shipp was crushed in his bid to be re-elected Hamilton County sheriff for a third term. The federal contempt charges that had made him a martyr two years earlier now became ammunition for his political opponents.

Two weeks after being booted from office, Shipp received a call from a friend who said he had heard that the contempt charges had been dropped. But the former sheriff quickly learned the bad news. Though the Supreme Court had indeed dismissed the charges against seventeen of the twenty-seven defendants accused in Johnson's lynching, Shipp's case was not among them. (The charges against one of the defendants, Paul Poole, who authorities claimed was part of the lynch mob, were never dismissed or adjudicated, because he was never found or arrested.) Attorney General Charles Bonaparte had filed a motion stating he did not have sufficient evidence to proceed against those seventeen individuals. However, federal prosecutors argued that the testimony taken during the trial weighed heavily toward the guilt of Shipp, Deputy Sheriff Matthew Galloway, Chief Jailer Jeremiah Gibson, and six members of the lynch mob—Bart Justice, Frank Ward, Nick Nolan, Luther Williams, Henry Padgett, and William Mayes.

In agreeing with Attorney General Bonaparte, the Supreme Court announced it wanted to hear oral arguments from both sides before rendering a verdict in the remaining nine cases. On March 2 and 3, 1909, the lawyers gathered in Washington to make their final pleas. The Court gave attorneys on both sides as much time as they wanted to make their presentations. Newspaper reporters and lawyers from across the country packed the courtroom.

At 10:00 a.m., Attorney General Bonaparte approached the lectern and formally identified himself to the Court for the record. He also introduced U.S. Attorney J. R. Penland, who he said was one of the lead prosecutors in the case. The other member of the team, Edward Terry Sanford, had stepped down from his position at the Justice Department to accept a federal judgeship in his hometown of Knoxville, Tennessee. He had replaced Judge C. D. Clark, who had died in office. Even though Sanford and Penland had handled all previous aspects of the trial, Bonaparte said he felt the case was so significant, and would have such an important impact on American law, that he had decided to deliver the final arguments himself. Chief Justice Fuller welcomed Bonaparte and the other lawyers and asked that the hearing proceed. Bonaparte began to speak:

Thank you, Mr. Chief Justice.

This proceeding is unique in the history of courts.

Its importance cannot be overestimated.

Lynchings have occurred in defiance of state laws and state courts without attempt, or at most with only desultory attempt, to punish the lynchers.

Perpetrators of such crimes have heretofore been censured only by public opinion; courts have remained silent. Powerful as such opinion always is, severe as it has been in its rebuke of such deeds, it has been inadequate to check these outbreaks of lawlessness.

Only recently lynchings became so numerous that the whole country was aroused to earnest discussion of mob violence and a remedy for it. It is indeed useless to seek relief unless the judiciary can punish those who snatch and kill the men it has imprisoned. The arm of justice fetters men for years. It strikes death to the murderer. It can take property and life. Must it confess it is too weak to protect those whom it has confined?

The arm can destroy. Can it not protect? If the life of one whom the law has taken into its custody is at the mercy of a mob the administration of justice becomes a mockery.

Over the next two hours, Bonaparte told the story of Ed Johnson. He described how the public pressure on Sheriff Shipp to make an arrest was heightened by the sheriff's upcoming re-election bid. He said that there was no suspicion that Johnson was the culprit until an informant seeking a $375 reward stepped forward to point the finger at Johnson, and that Johnson's court-appointed lawyers were so intimidated by the state trial judge and scared of a lynch mob that they did not adequately defend their client.

The attorney general recapped many of the details of Johnson's trial. The jury had consisted of all white males, and no black people were in the jury pool. He told how the victim had refused to make an absolute or positive identification of Johnson as the man who attacked her: she "believed" he was the man. He named the dozen alibi witnesses Johnson called to testify. And he described for the justices how one of the jurors had rushed toward the defendant screaming, "If I could get at him, I would tear his heart out."

Bonaparte told how Johnson's lawyers had abandoned their client after he was convicted and sentenced to die. The trial judge had even approved of the lawyers' decision to persuade Johnson to waive his rights to appeal his conviction under clearly coercive circumstances. Were it not for Noah Parden and Styles Hutchins, the farce of a trial provided to Johnson would never have been made known, he said. It was that pair who faced the brunt of the terror inflicted by their fellow citizens of Chattanooga and fellow members of the bar in appealing Johnson's conviction to the state Supreme Court. Parden and Hutchins felt the violence of the community when they sought legal protections for their client from the federal courts.

And when the U.S. Supreme Court agreed to intervene, Bonaparte said, it was the justices' turn to realize how little respect the rule of law commanded in Chattanooga and across the South.

> When this Court granted a stay of execution upon application of Johnson, it became its duty to protect him until his case should be disposed of.
>
> It matters not with what crime he was charged. It is immaterial what the evidence was at the trial. Sentenced to death, Johnson came into this Court alleging that his constitutional rights had been invaded in the trial of his case, and upon this, the Supreme Court said he had a right to be, and would be, heard.
>
> From that moment until his case should be decided, he was under the protection of this Court. And when its mandate, issued for his protection, is defied, punishment of those guilty of such contempt must be certain and severe.

Following an hour-long lunch break, Bonaparte took the Supreme Court through a detailed account of the lynching, as given by the many witnesses who had testified before Commissioner Maher. Using the soft yet determined tone of a Sunday-school teacher instructing his pupils, the attorney general said the case was unlike any previous suit before the Court. Normally, he said, the justices decided cases based on theories of law or differing interpretations of the Constitution. This case was not about ideology or some new legal theory, but it did require the justices to put themselves in an uncustomary position: acting as jurors, judging and weighing evidence for its veracity.

> The question now before the Court is one of fact: Has the United States in the evidence which has been taken by the commissioner under order of this Court proved the allegations

of the information? Most of those allegations are established by agreement or undisputed evidence.

The only issues are:

(1) Were the sheriff and his deputies informed of the Supreme Court's decision to hear Johnson's appeal and did they have every reason to believe that an attempt would be made in the evening of March 19 by a mob to break into, and take Johnson from, the jail for the purpose of lynching him?

(2) Did the sheriff and his deputies commit acts and do things manifesting a purpose and disposition on their part to render it less difficult and less dangerous for the mob to lynch Johnson and aid and abet the mob?

(3) Were defendants, excepting Shipp and Gibson, members of the mob which lynched Johnson, or did they participate in the conspiracy?

(4) Did defendants in the things they did intend to show contempt of the order of this Court and to prevent it from hearing Johnson's appeal?

The answer to each of those questions, Bonaparte said, was unequivocally yes. He recited the testimony of each witness to support his points. Some witnesses had told the Court that Shipp and his deputies were notified of Justice Harlan's decision to grant Johnson an appeal and the stay of his execution. Bonaparte named person after person who had testified under oath that a lynching attempt on Johnson's life was expected. He cited several examples from the official record to prove conclusively that Shipp and his deputies had intentionally left the jail unprotected the night of March 19 to allow the mob to do its task unmolested. And he quoted witness upon witness who had identified various defendants as leaders of the lynch mob.

Finally, the attorney general said the trial record was replete with evidence demonstrating contempt for the Supreme Court and all federal courts by Sheriff Shipp, his deputies, and the members of the mob. Most obvious, he said, was the Birmingham newspaper article that quoted Shipp as bragging that he had done nothing to prevent the mob from murdering Johnson, nor would he have stopped them if he could have done so.

> Never in its history has an order of this Court been disobeyed with such impunity.
>
> It is not surprising that in the early history of this country, when the jurisdictions of the federal and the state governments were not clearly defined or well understood, states should have resisted the orders of this Court.
>
> But it is remarkable that individuals should now undertake to defy the mandate of this great tribunal.
>
> Justice is at an end when orders of the highest and most powerful court in the land are set at naught. Obedience to its mandates is essential to our institutions.
>
> Contempts such as this strike down the supremacy of law and order and undermine the foundations of our government. Recurrence of such acts must be prevented. The commission of the offense has been established, and punishment should be imposed in accordance with its gravity.
>
> Where a riot and the lawless acts of those engaged therein are the direct result of opposition to the administration of the law by this Court, those who defy its mandate and participate in, or who knowingly fail to take the proper means within their official power and duty to prevent, acts of violence having for their object to, and which do, defeat the action of this Court are guilty of, and must be punished for, contempt.

The attorney general of the United States spoke for six hours. Chief Justice Fuller thanked Bonaparte for his "concise" argument and the restating of the facts. However, he said, the justices were rather exhausted. He announced that the Court would adjourn for the day and would begin hearing the defense attorneys the following morning.

To counter Bonaparte's skills, passion, and influence, the defense
team agreed that Judson Harmon, lead counsel for Sheriff Shipp,
should start their presentation the next day. A former U.S. attorney
general, Harmon had appeared before the Supreme Court many times,
including once before in this case. His style favored that of a lecturer
or college professor trying to impress certain thoughts on the minds of
his observers. A skilled trial lawyer, Harmon knew that the first few
minutes of every argument were the most important. For that reason,
he wasted no time in presenting the heart of the defense's argument to
the justices.

The testimony shows that Sheriff Shipp did not conspire, aid,
or abet the lynchers and did not fail in his duty to take proper
precautions to guard him.

It is alleged that the prisoner had been heavily guarded
until the night of the lynching and that the guards were purposely withdrawn in order to permit the lynching. The record
shows that the jail had not been guarded with extra guards
after Johnson's conviction on February 9.

The government seems to bring a wholesale indictment
against the whole citizenship of Chattanooga and Hamilton
County. The undisputed testimony of dozens of witnesses is
swept aside by the simple announcement that it is absurd and
ridiculous. The testimony of gray-haired ministers, of veteran
physicians, of merchants, manufacturers, and officials, is all
treated in the same manner. To all of these, counsel for the
government say:

"It is absurd for the defendants and their witnesses to say
that the community was in a state of peaceful repose on March
19 or preceding days. It is idle for them to say that they did not
apprehend mob violence to Johnson."

Judge McReynolds and Attorney General Whitaker are
also severely criticized by counsel for the government. Just
why, it is hard to understand. These gentlemen first sounded
the alarm on the night of the lynching. Walking the streets
about nine o'clock and noticing a suspicious gathering at the

jail, they went to the office of the *Chattanooga Times* and notified the editor and reporters of what was going on—called the
sheriff and requested him to go to the relief of the prisoner—
phoned to the office of the chief of police—and, in fact, did
everything that could have reasonably been expected of any
citizen under the circumstances.

After Johnson was lynched, Judge McReynolds delivered
a strong charge to the grand jury, instructing that body to
indict all those engaged in the lynching. Both he and Attorney
General Whitaker did everything possible to procure indictments. That the grand jury failed to indict any of the lynchers
is not strange in view of the difficulty that the government,
with all of its agents and detectives, have had in establishing
the identity of those engaged in the lynching. These splendid
officials need no defense at our hands.

It is possible that Captain Shipp acted with poor judgment
on the night of the lynching. It is easy to see now that he
should have had the jail guarded and should have been prepared for a mob. But if he had done so, he would have been
wiser and would have shown more foresight than any other citizen of Chattanooga.

It is easy to see now, looking back over events as they
occurred on that night, that Captain Shipp, instead of going to
the jail, should have gone to police headquarters or the
Armory, where the militia were drilling, and organized a posse.

It must be remembered, however, that Captain Shipp did
not have time to carefully consider the situation and coolly
decide the best course to pursue. He was called up in the night
and told by the prosecuting attorney that he should go at once
to the jail.

Certainly Captain Shipp cannot be convicted for contempt
of this Court simply because, in the performance of his duties,
he exercised bad judgment. He says himself that if he had the
thing to do over again he, perhaps, would know better what to
do, and would act differently, but at that time he acted on the
spur of the moment and had gone to the jail for the purpose of

seeing what the trouble was and to do what he could to protect the prisoner.

Captain Shipp denied, in his testimony, all the charges in the information with reference to a conspiracy with those engaged in the lynching.

He denied any intention to aid or abet, in any way, those engaged in the killing of Johnson. He denied that he anticipated or had any reason to anticipate or expect a mob on the night of March 19.

He insisted that he had the very greatest respect for this honorable Court and had done no act, and omitted no duty, from which a contrary conclusion could be drawn.

Captain Shipp has lived in Chattanooga since 1874. He was a Confederate soldier, and has, for many years, been a member of the Confederate Veterans' organization, and is quartermaster general of the entire organization. He was on the staff of the late General John B. Gordon and the late General Stephen D. Lee. He has been a Mason for over forty years and a member of numerous other secret societies.

His splendid character is testified to by every witness whose testimony has been referred to in this brief. Old men and young men, political friends and political adversaries, ministers of all denominations, veterans of the Civil War who wore the blue and who wore the gray, men of all classes and all persuasions who have known Captain Shipp during his long life in Chattanooga, all, in one voice, say to this Court that he is a truthful, law-abiding, honorable gentleman.

Can this Court say that a man with such a character and such a record would suddenly, without any motive whatever, betray his trust, sacrifice the life of a prisoner in his keeping, become a perjurer and a murderer, in order to show his contempt and disregard for the orders of this, the highest and greatest court in the world?

Harmon's closing statement lasted nearly two hours. He quoted many of the same witnesses that Bonaparte had cited the day before—

only with a completely different spin. In some respects, the former sheriff was admitting fault and simply pleading for mercy and sympathy from the justices. Yet he was also seemingly defiant in his continuing refusal to accept the federal government's right to intervene in state criminal cases.

The remainder of the day was occupied by brief arguments from all the lawyers for the other defendants. James J. Lynch, who represented Jeremiah Gibson, said the jailer was surprised when the jail was attacked by the mob. Gibson had no avenue of escape after the mob arrived, and no chance to communicate with the outside world, Lynch told the justices.

Lawyers for Deputy Matt Galloway said their client vehemently denied having any advance knowledge of a lynching or playing any role in the slaying of Johnson. "When we take into consideration the manner in which this defendant exposed himself and his life for the protection [of Johnson] and to prevent the first attempt to mob Johnson, it seems preposterous that the able attorneys for the government should ask this honorable Court to convict or hold this defendant to be in contempt of the orders of this honorable Court," his lawyer told the Court.

The attorneys who represented Bart Justice, Frank Ward, Luther Williams, Henry Padgett, Nick Nolan, and William Mayes said their clients were either not present during the lynching or were simply bystanders who had not actively participated in the killing of Johnson.

Unlike the previous Supreme Court hearing regarding the issue of jurisdiction, the justices asked very few questions and never interrupted any of the lawyers during their arguments. Some on Sheriff Shipp's side thought that this was a positive sign, that the Court's anger had mellowed. Others believed that the silence was a bad sign, that the justices had made up their minds and were simply letting the legal procedure take its course before handing out severe punishments.

When the lawyers asked if the Court wished any additional briefs filed by the parties, Chief Justice Fuller graciously said no: "I think we have enough to read, thank you."

No one knew how long the justices would take to make their decision. There were no time limits under the law for the Supreme Court to render a judgment. The Court has been known to pontificate upon the weightier legal and social issues for up to a year before issuing an opinion. And cases have been known to languish at the Court for as long as three years while a case was argued and later reargued.

For three weeks, the justices pored over more than 2,200 pages of testimony taken during the trial in Chattanooga. The decision was complicated by the fact that there were nine defendants. In reality, they were nine separate cases. Each defendant deserved to have his own case examined separately and individually. The evidence was certainly stronger against some than it was against others.

The Court gathered during the third week of April to discuss the case. As chief justice, Fuller presided over these "decisional conferences." Such sessions have taken place since the founding of the Court, but Fuller was the first chief justice to require that the members of the Court shake hands with each other at the start of each conference. He also demanded that the justices remain cordial even in disagreement, forbidding cursing or yelling. He would go around the table asking each member of the Court his opinion. Custom required Fuller always to start with Harlan, their most senior member.

Everyone knew Justice Harlan's position. He believed in the defendant's innocence. It was the stay of execution he had issued for Johnson that had been defied by the mob. He had been the person who had pushed the Justice Department so strenuously to investigate the lynching.

"The sheriff is guilty," Harlan pronounced. "Any opinion to the contrary is preposterous."

For hours, the justices argued over the facts and the law. The debate lasted into a second day. And a third. And a fourth. Whereas the Court had been unified in its earlier ruling that the Supreme Court did have jurisdiction in the Shipp case and did have the legal authority to bring contempt charges against the sheriff, his deputies, and members of the mob, this decision was different. It was a judging of the merits. The justices were definitely divided. In any ordinary trial in which the jurors were split, the judge and lawyers would probably declare a mistrial. New jurors would be brought in to study the evidence and make a decision. That was not an option in this litigation.

Because the Court was basically acting as a jury by determining facts and guilt or innocence, some of the justices suggested that the Court had to be unanimous before finding any of the parties guilty. But that notion was quickly dismissed. A simple majority was all that was required for the Supreme Court to reach a decision in any case, no matter the nature of the dispute or the parties involved.

The justices also differed on the importance of the case. Chief Justice Fuller and Justice Holmes contended that the case was exclusively about enforcing the integrity of the Supreme Court. Justice Harlan also wanted to use the case to send a message to the country that lynch law should not be tolerated and that local law enforcement should do everything within its power to prevent mob rule.

Even as the Court debated the issues and facts, a telegram arrived from Oxford, Mississippi, detailing how U.S. Senator W. V. Sullivan had led a lynch mob to kill a black man accused of cutting a white woman's throat. "I led the mob which lynched Nelse Patton and I'm proud of it," Sullivan told newspaper reporters. "I directed every movement of the mob. I wanted him lynched. I saw his body dangling from a tree this morning and I am glad of it. I aroused the mob and directed them to storm the jail. I had my revolver but did not use it. I gave it to a deputy sheriff and told him to shoot Patton and shoot to kill. I suppose the bullets from my gun were some of those that killed the Negro."

The article went on to say that no charges were being brought against any person who had participated in the lynching. This news infuriated Justice Harlan and probably helped him win votes on the Court to use their decision to denounce lynch law.

On the fifth day, Chief Justice Fuller believed one side appeared close to having five votes, with three justices equally hardened in their opposing position.

Justice Oliver Wendell Holmes asked to write the Court's opinion, since he had authored the previous jurisdictional decision in the case. However, Chief Justice Fuller told the group that the entire country was watching this case. Normally, he would gladly allow, even encourage, one of his fellow justices to write the opinion. But because of the importance of this case, Fuller believed it was best if the chief justice spoke for the Court. The other members of the Court quickly agreed.

On Monday, May 24, 1909, the Supreme Court met in open session to announce the various decisions it had reached. Chief Justice Melville Fuller announced that the Court had reached a final determination in the matter of the *United States* v. *Shipp*. In his typically soft, almost inaudible voice, Fuller began to read his lengthy opinion. He recited the facts of the Johnson case, the defendant's appeal to the Supreme Court, and the subsequent lynching. Interspersed throughout the narrative were Fuller's attitudes and evaluation of the importance of the case.

> It is apparent that a dangerous portion of the community was seized with the awful thirst for blood which only killing can quench, and that considerations of law and order were swept away in the overwhelming flood. The mob was, however, willing at the first attempt to accept prompt administration of the death penalty adjudged at a trial conducted according to judicial forms, in lieu of execution by lawless violence, but delay by appeal, or writ of error, or habeas corpus was not to be tolerated. . . .
>
> In this instance an appeal was granted by this court, and proceedings specifically ordered to be stayed. The persons who hung and shot this man were so impatient for his blood that they utterly disregarded the act of Congress as well as the order of this court.

Chief Justice Fuller said statements by Sheriff Shipp and his deputies that they had no idea there would be a lynching attempt the night of March 19 were ludicrous. The nation's highest-ranking judge cited a *Chattanooga News* article printed the afternoon that Justice Harlan had issued the stay of Johnson's execution.

> "All of this delay is aggravating to the community. The people of Chattanooga believe that Johnson is guilty and that he

ought to suffer the penalty of the law as speedily as possible. If by legal technicality the case is prolonged and the culprit finally escapes, there will be no use to plead with a mob here if another such crime is committed. Such delays are largely responsible for mob violence all over the country."

The assertions that mob violence was not expected and that there was no occasion for providing more than the usual guard of one man for the jail in Chattanooga, are quite unreasonable and inconsistent with statements made by Sheriff Shipp and his deputies, that they were looking for a mob on the next day. Officers and others were heard to say that they expected a mob would attempt to lynch Johnson on the 20th. There does not seem to be any foundation for the belief that the mob would be considerate enough to wait until the 20th.

The Supreme Court also took special note of Sheriff Shipp's statement to the Birmingham newspaper—a statement Chief Justice Fuller contended was clear evidence of Shipp's contempt for the Supreme Court's decision to hear Johnson's appeal. Fuller quoted Shipp's statement directly in his opinion (albeit with a few changes of wording):

" ' . . . *I am frank to say that I did not attempt to hurt any of them, and would not have made such an attempt if I could.* . . .

" 'The Supreme Court of the United States was responsible for this lynching. . . .

" 'In my opinion the act of the Supreme Court of the United States in not allowing the case to remain in our courts was the most unfortunate thing in the history of Tennessee. . . .

" 'The people of Hamilton County were willing to let the law take its course until it became known that the case would not probably be disposed of for four or five years by the Supreme Court of the United States. The people would not submit to this, and I do not wonder at it.' "

[Shipp] evidently resented the necessary order of this court as an alien intrusion, and declared that the court was responsible for the lynching. . . . In other words, his view was that because this court, in the discharge of its duty, entered the order which it did, that therefore the people of Hamilton County would not submit to its mandate, and hence the court became responsible for the mob. He took the view expressed by several members of the mob on the afternoon of the 19th and before the lynching, when they said, referring to the Supreme Court, that "they had no business interfering with our business at all." His reference to the "people" was significant, for he was a candidate for re-election and had been told that his saving the prisoner from the first attempt to mob him would cost him his place, and he had answered that he wished the mob had got him before he did.

It seems to us that to say that the sheriff and his deputies did not anticipate that the mob would attempt to lynch Johnson on the night of the 19th is to charge them with gross neglect of duty and with an ignorance of conditions in a matter which vitally concerned them all as officers, and is directly contrary to their own testimony. It is absurd to contend that officers of the law who have been through the experiences these defendants had passed through two months prior to the actual lynching did not know that a lynching probably would be attempted on the 19th. . . .

In view of this, Shipp's failure to make the slightest preparation to resist the mob; the absence of all of the deputies, except Gibson, from the jail during the mob's proceedings, occupying a period of some hours in the early evening, the action of Shipp in not resisting the mob and his failure to make any reasonable effort to save Johnson or identify the members of the mob, justify the inference of a disposition upon his part to render it easy for the mob to lynch Johnson, and to acquiesce in the lynching. After Shipp was informed that a mob was at the jail, and he could not do otherwise than go there, he did not and in fact at no time hindered the mob or caused it to be interfered with, or helped in the slightest degree to protect Johnson. And this in utter disregard of this court's mandate and in defiance of this court's orders. . . .

Although Shipp was in the midst or near the members of the mob for about an hour when they were in the jail, he did not seek to obtain information so that he could identify any of them, and he testifies that he does not know any member of the mob.

Only one conclusion can be drawn from these facts, all of which are clearly established by the evidence—Shipp not only made the work of the mob easy, but in effect aided and abetted it.

The chief justice concluded that Gibson was "involved in the same condemnation" as Sheriff Shipp, "though under less responsibility." The jailer had to know that a mob would attack that night, Fuller said.

However, the opinion completely dismissed the contempt charge against Deputy Galloway. Fuller wrote that there simply was not enough evidence to indicate he played a role in the lynching, nor was there enough to convict Justice and Ward.

The chief justice and a majority of the Supreme Court, however, found the evidence against four of the members of the lynch mob— Williams, Nolan, Padgett, and Mayes—to be sufficient to convict.

In our opinion . . . this lamentable riot was the direct result of opposition to the administration of the law by this court. It was not only in defiance of our mandate, but was understood to be such. The Supreme Court of the United States was called upon to abdicate its functions and decline to enter such orders as the occasion, in its judgment demanded, because of the danger of their defeat by an outbreak of lawless violence. It is plain that what created this mob and led to this lynching was the unwillingless of its members to submit to the delay required for the appeal. The intent to prevent that delay by defeating the hearing of the appeal necessarily follows from the defendants' acts, and if the life of anyone in the custody of the law is at the mercy of a mob, the administration of justice becomes a mockery.

The bottom line: Sheriff Joseph Shipp, Jeremiah Gibson, Nick Nolan, Henry Padgett, William Mayes, and Luther Williams had been found guilty of contempt of the Supreme Court. Galloway, Justice, and Ward were declared not guilty.

Four associate justices—Harlan, Holmes, Brewer, and Day—had joined the chief justice's opinion, giving him the majority and controlling opinion. It also made his words the law of the land and the law of the case. When Fuller had finished speaking, he turned to Justice Peckham, who had written a dissenting opinion.

Joined by Justices McKenna and White, Peckham wrote that there was not a single particle of evidence to sustain the view that Sheriff Shipp had done anything less than his official duty. He described the sheriff as "an invalid old man" who had been held to a level of responsibility far beyond any reasonable limit. As for the other defendants, the three dissenting justices took the position that there simply wasn't enough evidence to warrant conviction.

FOR FIVE MONTHS, the justices privately debated what punishment should be imposed upon the defendants. Peckham's group thought a verbal reprimand and maybe a small fine would be sufficient. To them, jail time was definitely not warranted. Of course, the other five justices, led by the chief justice, gave the dissenters less input in the decision.

Justice Holmes wrote an internal Court memo stating that nothing short of a year would be appropriate, for the case involved a murder. He also argued that a stiff penalty, such as a $25,000 fine and a one-year prison sentence, would go a long way toward encouraging local sheriffs, prosecutors, and judges to deter lynch law. It was once again left to Chief Justice Fuller to establish a coalition and consensus within the Court. The justices agreed he would officially pronounce the Court's judgment and sentence on the defendants. They ordered the U.S. marshals to arrest Shipp and the other five defendants found guilty and bring them to Washington for an official sentencing.

On November 15, 1909, Sheriff Shipp and the five other defendants watched as the nine members of the Supreme Court of the

United States filed into the old courtroom. The clerk called the case for the final time.

"The *United States* v. *Shipp et al.*"

Chief Justice Fuller peered down at the defendants and ordered them to rise. They stood to their feet and faced the Court.

> You, Joseph F. Shipp, Jeremiah Gibson, Luther Williams, Nick Nolan, Henry Padgett, and William Mayes, are before this Court on an attachment for contempt. You have been found guilty.
>
> Sheriff Shipp, Luther Williams, and Nick Nolan are hereby sentenced to ninety days imprisonment. Jeremiah Gibson, Henry Padgett, and William Mayes are hereby sentenced to sixty days imprisonment. All sentences are to be served at the United States Jail in the District of Columbia.
>
> This Court is adjourned.

Shipp, who had been depressed since his election defeat a year earlier, accepted the Court's judgment without exhibiting any emotion. He was now sixty-four years old. He had lost the confidence of the public. The Supreme Court had publicly denounced him as an inadequate sheriff. And now he was going to spend Christmas in jail.

Jeremiah Gibson refused to look at the Court as the sentence was read. Instead, the seventy-six-year-old former jailer gritted his teeth, stared down at the hardwood floors, and mustered all the strength he could not to lash out at the justices. Several of the other men cried as Chief Justice Fuller spoke to them. They would not see their families until after the New Year.

The Supreme Court's actions received mixed reviews across the country. State judges, prosecutors, and sheriffs cursed the Court for intruding into traditionally state matters. Black leaders praised the decision, hoping it would reduce the number of lynchings encouraged by local law enforcement. Lawyers believed the Court's action was a first step in providing greater constitutional protections to minorities and people charged with crimes. But back in Tennessee, the public and the newspapers remained defiantly supportive of Sheriff Shipp.

The Supreme Court of the United States is not a popular body in Chattanooga today.

On every hand, indignation is being expressed against the decree by Chief Justice Fuller against Captain Joseph Shipp. Every shade of indignant expression was expressed.

The Court erred in intervening in the state's business involving Ed Johnson and Johnson paid with his life. The Court has erred once again, and we pray the sentence does not cost any more lives.

Chattanooga News, November 15, 1909

Asked by news reporters for his comment on the judgment, Noah Parden praised the justices for their courage. He hoped the Court would intervene in more cases as they had for Ed Johnson. But he said the Court's actions sent a broader, more significant message to the nation's citizens.

The very rule of law upon which this country was founded and on which the future of this nation rests has been enforced with the might of our highest tribunal.

We are at a time when many of our people have abandoned the respect for the rule of law due to the racial hated deep in their hearts and souls, and nothing less than our civilized society is at stake.

NOAH PARDEN, *Atlanta Independent*, November 1909

EPILOGUE

LED BY JOSEPH Shipp, the six defendants hugged their relatives and said their goodbyes. One by one, they were escorted from the courtroom by federal marshals. Placed in a horse-drawn wagon, the group was transported to the federal prison in Washington, D.C.

The prison warden, an older gentleman called Captain McKee, met the celebrated prisoners upon their arrival. As he approached, Shipp noticed a button in the lapel of the warden's coat. It read "GAR," symbolizing "Grand Army of the Republic." A former Union officer taking a former Confederate officer into custody. Most might think this would have made Shipp nervous. Instead, it had the opposite effect.

"Boys, it will be all right," the former sheriff told the other defendants. "At least we are in the hands of a soldier."

Captain McKee promised Shipp and the five others that they would be treated with the utmost respect. They were housed on the fourth floor, which had previously been used to quarter female prisoners. The six Tennessee prisoners shared a large room, twenty feet wide and thirty-five feet long. There were beds for all the inmates. A large table and chairs sat at one end. Here the convicts would eat their meals, served by trustees, and play cards. They also had complete access to an adjoining bathroom, which they shared with no one. Four large circular windows opening to the south and west provided an excellent view of Washington. So nice were the facilities that Shipp instructed his lawyers to withdraw their earlier request to the Supreme Court to have the prisoners transferred to the Atlanta Federal Penitentiary because it was closer to their relatives.

Days following the Supreme Court's sentencing, several Southern civic groups and politicians began a campaign to have President Roosevelt grant Shipp a full pardon, or at least probation. The former sheriff quickly put an end to these efforts by proclaiming that he would seek no consideration that was not afforded to all of his co-defendants, including those who had been members of the lynch mob. However, the six defendants were released earlier than their sentences had indicated, because each received some time off for good behavior.

JOSEPH F. SHIPP

On Sunday evening, January 30, 1910, about 6:00 p.m., the train from Washington, D.C., pulled into Terminal Station in Chattanooga. More than 10,000 people were there to greet Shipp. As the train pulled into the station, bands immediately struck up the soul-stirring tune of "Dixie." The crowd went into a state of frenzy.

Men wept, shouted, and laughed almost in the same breath. Women became frantic as they made desperate efforts to touch the grizzled veteran. So dense was the mass of humanity that there was imminent danger of panic and possible injury to women and children.

As Shipp stepped from the train, the band played "Home, Sweet Home." Shipp was so moved by the reception in his behalf that he was unable to speak a word. He raised his hat and bowed right and left to his admiring friends as officers opened a way for him to pass through to a waiting carriage. The newspapers described it as a "hero's welcome." A monument was erected in his honor.

There were rumors that Shipp would run for sheriff again, but he never did. He was appointed to several prestigious state positions by governors and state leaders, and spent his later years promoting the history of the Confederacy. He was frequently seen wearing his old gray uniform. On his fifty-sixth wedding anniversary, he was given a huge wedding cake designed like the Confederate flag. Shipp, wearing his uniform, drew the same sword he had used in battle to slice the first piece of cake.

Joseph Shipp died on September 18, 1925, at the age of eighty. His illness was short. A week before dying, he left his downtown office complaining of a sore foot. Soon it grew worse, and his entire right leg was affected. A blood clot had formed when an artery broke. A few days later, another blood vessel burst and ended his life. At his funeral, Confederate veterans in uniforms formed an honorary escort. Captain Shipp was laid to rest wearing his uniform of gray. He was buried in the prestigious Forest Hills Cemetery in Chattanooga—the very same cemetery near which Nevada Taylor had been raped and Ed Johnson arrested.

Though ninety days in prison may not appear to be much of a punishment for conspiracy involving a murder, the Supreme Court's actions against Shipp and his deputies obviously had an impact across the country. In 1909, the year when the justices found Shipp guilty and sent him to jail, the number of lynchings in the United States dropped from ninety-seven to eighty-two. This number would continue to decline over the next decade.

Equally important, the number of attempted lynchings that were thwarted by local law enforcement significantly increased in the years following the Shipp case. Tuskegee University, which kept records of every reported lynching and lynching attempt in the country, reported that only six people were saved from the mob by sheriffs and police in 1906. By contrast, authorities prevented nineteen lynchings in 1910, and the number continued to grow annually throughout the next decade.

NEVADA TAYLOR

Following the lynching of Ed Johnson, Nevada Taylor took the advice of friends and returned to work as a means of alleviating her distress. However, the young woman would never be the same. She was always sick and nervous. In March 1907, Miss Taylor and her father returned to Findlay, Ohio, to visit family. This was her birthplace. Three of her sisters—Jeanette Taylor, Alice Taylor, and Mrs. Harvey Cramer—still lived there, as did her older brother, Guy Taylor.

Friends in Findlay reported that "she seemed at that time wholly recovered from the effects of the assault." However, other reports indicated that shortly after the assault "her health began to fail, and it continued to fail up until the time of her death."

Nevada Taylor died in Findlay, Ohio, on Tuesday, May 14, 1907, at the age of twenty-three. The Findlay newspaper, the *Morning Republican*, the next day wrote: "Death was ascribed to nervous prostration incidental to the crime committed under the very shadow of the historic Lookout Mountain." Another report simply claimed that she had died "of a broken heart." She was buried in the Maple Grove Cemetery in Findlay, Ohio, where her father had worked for many years as keeper before moving to Chattanooga.

LEWIS SHEPHERD

The dean of the Chattanooga bar, Lewis Shepherd practiced law for fifty-one years: he had won his first case at age twenty-one and his last case at seventy-two. He published his personal memoirs in April 1915. The most respected civil and criminal trial lawyer of his time in eastern Tennessee, he demonstrated great courage and skill representing the poor and downtrodden. His clients including many African-Americans charged with crimes against whites.

There was no place on earth that Shepherd preferred being to the courtroom. On May 14, 1917, he was in court defending a client. As Shepherd was arguing a legal point, he suddenly collapsed. He lost consciousness standing before the bar of justice, and never opened his eyes or spoke another word.

The attack that he suffered at the courthouse was due to Bright's disease, from which he had suffered for more than four years. Reportedly, he had twice before been at death's door. The immediate cause of death was said to be "uremia consequent to the deep-seated chronic disease." The courthouse was closed the next two days to honor him.

The *Chattanooga Times* article written the day following his death proclaimed: "The long and active career of Judge Shepherd as advocate before the bar ended just as he had frequently expressed the wish—going to his reward straight from the courtroom."

EDWARD TERRY SANFORD

In March 1908, Federal District Judge Charles Dickens Clark of Chattanooga died. Terry Sanford, the lead prosecutor in the case against Shipp and the others, was his replacement. Sanford was liked and respected by President Theodore Roosevelt, probably because both men were Harvard Law School graduates. Justice Sanford had also been recommended by Justice John Marshall Harlan, who wrote to the president: "I see that Judge Clark of Chattanooga is dead. Could you do better than put in Sanford?"

Sanford served as a federal judge until President Warren G. Harding appointed him to the United States Supreme Court on February 20, 1923. Even today, scholars say he was one of the best-educated individuals ever to sit on the Supreme Court.

Sanford's record in almost fifteen years on the Federal District Court bench proved him to be "gentle and courteous, but firm," and not "theatrical or dogmatic." It was said that "he was the most impartial Judge in the South." As a Supreme Court justice, Sanford wrote 130 opinions, though few had any constitutional importance. However, he continued to advocate in his opinions the ideals of Justice Harlan, particularly that the federal Bill of Rights governed state-court proceedings—a legal theory that would not become law for several decades.

Justice Sanford died unexpectedly on March 8, 1930. He had stopped at his dentist's office to have a tooth pulled that morning. Following the extraction, he became dizzy, collapsed, and never regained consciousness. Cause of death was listed as uremic poisoning. He was brought back to Knoxville for burial.

Justice Oliver Wendell Holmes had the following to say about Justice Sanford: "On Saturday, just as we were expecting him at a conference of the Justices, we were informed that our brother, Mr. Justice Sanford, had become unconscious pending a slight operation. Five minutes later we received word that he was dead. Thus, suddenly the light of a faithful worker, who was born also to charm, went out."

MADISON (MATT) NEWTON WHITAKER

Matt Whitaker died at the age of seventy-eight on October 6, 1938, after a short illness. He had served as a prosecutor for sixteen years. In 1929, his former law partner, Governor Henry Horton, appointed him as judge of the Second Division of the Criminal Court of Hamilton County, Tennessee.

In January 1936, Matt Whitaker was honored by the Chattanooga Bar Association with the hanging of his portrait in Division II of the Criminal Court of Hamilton County. The portrait is still prominently featured in one of the courtrooms there today.

SAMUEL D. McREYNOLDS

Following the lynching of Ed Johnson in 1906, Sam McReynolds remained as judge of the Criminal Court of Hamilton County until 1921, serving on the bench for eighteen years. In 1921, he was elected to the United States Congress from the Third Congressional District of Tennessee, where he served another eighteen years. In 1938, the Chattanooga Bar Association hung a portrait of McReynolds in Division I of the Criminal Court of Hamilton County. It still hangs there today.

McReynolds died of a heart attack on July 11, 1939, in Washington, D.C. At the time of his death, Congressman McReynolds was serving as chairman of the powerful House Foreign Relations Committee. In Washington, he was frequently seen with another Tennessean, Secretary of State Cordell Hull.

Over 150 people gathered at the train station to meet the body of

Sam McReynolds on a special train from Washington, D.C. Many dignitaries attended his funeral, including some twenty fellow congressmen and six U.S. senators. One was a senator from Missouri by the name of Harry S. Truman. In addition, there was a senator from the state of Texas by the name of Tom Connally. Among the U.S. congressmen present was Albert Gore, Sr., of Tennessee.

As a congressman, McReynolds had played an important role in securing the establishment of the Tennessee Valley Authority and the Chickamauga Dam at Chattanooga. In 1932, McReynolds accompanied President Franklin D. Roosevelt through the TVA area. On December 16, 1960, a plaque was placed at the Chickamauga Dam, honoring him and his efforts in securing authorization for the project.

Sam McReynolds was buried in the Forest Hills Cemetery.

JUSTICE JOHN MARSHALL HARLAN
AND THE FULLER COURT

Until his death in 1911, Justice Harlan argued that people with cases in state courts deserved the same protections of the federal Constitution and the Bill of Rights as individuals with cases in federal courts. When Ed Johnson's case came before him, Harlan had the perfect opportunity to achieve his ideals—but that opportunity evaporated the day Ed Johnson was lynched. Although many of Justice Harlan's views were later adopted by justices on subsequent Supreme Courts, never again did a case with such outrageous circumstances come before Harlan's Court.

Nearly every single federal constitutional issue raised by Noah Parden and Styles Hutchins in their appeal of the Johnson case became legal precedent in the decades that followed. Most notably, the Fourth, Fifth, and Sixth Amendments of the U.S. Constitution are applicable in state-court cases—a position argued by Parden and Hutchins, and supported by Justice Harlan. In decision after decision spread out over fifty years, the justices have endorsed and implemented Parden's original arguments into the law of the land. For example:

• In 1923, the Court, in an opinion written by Justice Holmes, said that a trial in which a lynch mob puts undue pressure on the judge, the lawyers, or the jury, or otherwise improperly influences the outcome of a case, is a violation of the defendant's constitutional rights of due process under the law.

• In 1932, the justices ruled in a case from Scottsboro, Alabama, that people accused of capital crimes in state or federal cases must be afforded the effective assistance of a lawyer. That right has since been extended to include all criminal cases, including misdemeanor charges.

• The Supreme Court decided in 1948 that all criminal trials in state or federal courts must be open to the public. To close them would be a violation of the defendant's rights.

• In 1963, the Court, in an infamous case called *Miranda* v. *Arizona*, ruled that it is a violation of a person's Fifth Amendment right against self-incrimination for the state or other law-enforcement authority to question a suspect in a crime without allowing the suspect's lawyer to be present. The justices also declared it illegal for police or other government officials to use force or other coercive means in obtaining a confession.

• The Supreme Court ruled in 1967 that an individual does have the right to have an effective attorney when he appeals his conviction, but his attorney cannot make a determination on whether the defendant's appeal has merit. Only the appellate court can make such a decision.

• That same year, the justices ruled that a defendant has the right to have an attorney present when police conduct a witness-identification lineup.

• In 1970, the U.S. Supreme Court ruled that local courts may not systematically exclude black people from jury service. The Court said that judges may look at statistics to establish a *prima facie* case to prove that black people are being discriminated against.

• The justices ruled in 1972 that the death penalty could no longer be used as a punishment in rape cases.

Although they are Supreme Court precedents that stand to this day, the case of the *State of Tennessee* v. *Ed Johnson* and the subsequent case against the sheriff, *United States* v. *Shipp*, had never previously been told or had their importance thoroughly examined. Like Johnson himself, the case that bears his name has been forgotten, buried. Even most legal scholars and federal judges are unfamiliar with it. Yet the issues this case raised and ultimately settled are just as historic and embedded in the American system of jurisprudence as more famous cases, such as *Roe* v. *Wade*, *Miranda* v. *Arizona*, or *Brown* v. *Board of Education*. Indeed, the rule of law and America's respect for it were established or certainly grounded in the Johnson litigation.

"In countries all over the world, the United States is helping develop legal systems similar to ours. But the one thing that has been most difficult to teach is respect for the law," says Thomas Baker, an expert on the Supreme Court and a professor of law at Texas Technical University. "We had to learn it the hard way. There is no better example, there is no clearer symbolic precedent of establishing and enforcing the rule of law than this case."

"In the Johnson and Sheriff Shipp cases, we have the dignity of the Supreme Court being impugned by a rogue sheriff, thugs and a sympathetic state court system," says Professor Baker. "This is the only instance in our nation's history where the Supreme Court enforced its own ruling. It could easily be argued that we have the respect for the law today because of this case. What if the Court had not punished the sheriff? What if cities and counties and states realized they didn't have to obey federal-court orders or the U.S. Constitution? This case is the clearest example of the Supreme Court preserving its place in history and the integrity of the law."

"This case has had a ripple effect throughout legal history," Professor Baker adds.

The Johnson case demonstrates how politically and racially biased the state courts were in 1906. Many people would argue that they are equally political today, and that racial prejudice within the legal system has not been eliminated. But in this instance, Sheriff Shipp and the court officials were in a conflict over the very essence of the criminal-justice system. Was the primary purpose of the court system to punish people for wrongdoing, reducing criminal activity and thus making society a safer place to live? Or was the criminal-justice system designed to protect people's rights, to keep law enforcement honest and within the boundaries of the law, and to make sure innocent people were not punished for crimes they did not commit?

The sheriff, prosecutor, and judge gave every public appearance of following the law and providing Ed Johnson with a fair trial. Yet these officials tilted the court rules and the law against Johnson to such a degree that the outcome was predetermined to their liking. In essence, the legal process was nothing more than a phony show, a demonstration to themselves and the rest of the world that they were a law-abiding community.

It was that very injustice combined with irrefutable evidence of Johnson's innocence that led the Supreme Court justices to agree to stay the defendant's execution and hear his appeal. Unfortunately, we will never know what decision—how far-reaching or narrow—the Court would have made in this case. Because of the lynching, the justices never decided the case on its merits. The issues were rendered moot by brute violence.

"This would have been a wonderful case for the Supreme Court to take up on its merits," says Eugene Wilkes, a law professor at the University of Georgia and an expert on federal death-penalty appeals. "The factual arguments in the Johnson case were so compelling in favor of the defendant, the facts were so egregious, that I believe they would have re-evaluated their entire concept of due process under the U.S. Constitution. This case touched on so many important legal issues that would not be debated for another fifty years. It dealt with ineffective assistance of counsel. It focused on a defendant's right to a fair and impartial trial. The poisonous attitude of the community and how it impacted the jury pool was an issue—the right to appeal a conviction."

"What's incredible in the Johnson case is that the Court knew something was wrong here, they knew an injustice was being committed, and they took action to correct it," Wilkes adds.

Professor Wilkes and many other legal experts agree that the Johnson case was an important "seed of federalism" that grew over the next sixty years. It marks the first glimpse of the federal-court system's exercising its power to protect an individual's rights from wayward state authorities. Now, nearly a century later, there are efforts to curtail these rights. Congress is trying to limit the federal court's authority in overseeing how states treat or mistreat their prisoners. Some politicians want to make it easier to get rid of federal judges who make rulings that are not politically popular. And even the U.S. Supreme Court itself has taken steps to limit the federal court's authority over state-court criminal cases. The story of Ed Johnson and Sheriff Shipp reminds us why this federal intervention was needed and established in the beginning.

The "Fuller Court" officially ended with the death of Chief Justice Melville Weston Fuller on July 4, 1910, seven months after the sentencing of Shipp and his co-defendants.

Justice Oliver Wendell Holmes retired from the Court in 1932, after serving thirty years.

Justice David Brewer died in office in 1910.

Justice Rufus Peckham left the Court in 1909 and died later that year.

Justice Joseph McKenna left the Court in 1925 and died in 1926.

Justice William Day left the Court in 1922 and died in 1923.

Justice Edward Douglass White was appointed chief justice to replace Fuller; this marked the first time that an associate justice was elevated to the position of chief justice.

History does not boast of the Fuller Court's record on civil rights or civil liberties. In fact, records show that the number of state death-penalty verdicts the Court overturned during its two decades can be counted on one hand—Ed Johnson's case included, even though his conviction was never actually reversed.

That being said, the Court's courage in taking punitive action against a politically popular Southern sheriff was a significant step in the maturity of jurisprudence in America. This case occurred at a time when lynch law dominated the entire South. If the people didn't think the justice system was moving fast enough, or if they didn't like a verdict, they formed a violent mob to carry out their wishes.

As the popularity of vigilantism grew, so did the threat to the rule of law, or the public's respect and willingness to obey the law voluntarily despite disagreements. It is America's obedience to the rule of law that separates it from every other country in the world. In this country, courts have little enforcement power of their own. Instead, judges rely on the persuasiveness of their reasoning to convince the executive branch of government to enforce their rulings and the public to abide by their opinions.

Lynch law presented the first and only direct attack on the nation's judiciary. And the contempt proceeding against Shipp was the only proactive step the U.S. Supreme Court has ever taken to combat mob rule directly and demand that the public respect its authority and the authority of the written law.

NOAH PARDEN AND STYLES L. HUTCHINS

According to the Supreme Court curator, the first black lawyer admitted to practice before the Supreme Court was John S. Rock on February 5, 1865. By 1906, there were more than two dozen black lawyers, mostly from the Northeast and the Washington, D.C., area, licensed to handle a case before the Supreme Court. However, Parden was the first African-American lawyer to serve as lead counsel in a case. In the other instances, the black attorneys were associated with white lawyers who argued the cases before the Court. When Justice Harlan agreed that the Court would hear the Johnson appeal, he listed Noah Parden as the lead lawyer and the person who would make the arguments before the Court. Parden never got the opportunity. The first African-American attorney eventually to argue a case before the justices was J. Alexander Chiles, who stood before the Court on April 18, 1910.

Not surprisingly, there was no massive welcome-home party for

Noah Parden and Styles Hutchins. Neither man ever returned to Chattanooga. Friends and relatives sent the lawyers messages that if they did come home they would most likely be killed by a mob instantly.

Instead, they toured the North for a period of time, lecturing on events involved in the Johnson case. They eventually moved to the Oklahoma Territory. There is no evidence that either man ever practiced law again. It is believed that Parden started a small newspaper in Oklahoma. However, no copies of that publication exist today.

Though Parden and Hutchins were not successful in saving their client's life, they did arouse public attention to the fact that black people in the South accused of crimes seldom received a fair trial. They fought for rights never before granted to a black man. They publicly decried the state-court system as unjust and convinced the U.S. Supreme Court to take the unusual step of intervening in a state death-penalty case. Their efforts in the face of violent threats were nothing short of heroic. They risked their careers, their place in society, their homes, even their lives, to protect the rights of one young black man they did not know.

Yet there is no statue in Chattanooga honoring Parden or Hutchins, no memorial to their contribution to civil rights. Their names are not taught in law schools. Despite their marvelous achievements, they have been forgotten by history. If Sheriff Shipp has a statue in his honor that stands to this day, isn't it time to recognize Noah Parden and Styles Hutchins?

ED JOHNSON

Nearly a century ago, Ed Johnson was buried in an African-American cemetery located on the eastern slope of historic Missionary Ridge in Chattanooga. From time to time, it has been known as Pleasant Garden Cemetery and Eastview Cemetery. The present condition of the cemetery is a disgrace. It has been neglected for decades and has become overgrown by trees, vines, bushes, and briars. Tombstones from the turn of the century have been dislodged, tipped over, and badly damaged. Graves have sunk several feet.

Many years ago, as a result of a legal suit, the Hamilton County Chancery Court ordered that the cemetery be donated to a charitable and public trust for its preservation. To this day, nothing has been done to maintain or repair it. Pleasant Garden Cemetery is a blight upon the community and disrespectful to our ancestors. We hope this book will encourage the whole community to restore the site.

Of course, it would be impossible at this late date and time to prove the innocence of Ed Johnson. However, in our system of justice, a person is not supposed to have to prove his innocence. He is presumed innocent until proved guilty beyond a reasonable doubt. The fact that Ed Johnson was convicted by a jury does not end the matter, because it is a certainty that Ed Johnson was not afforded a fair trial, and it is also a certainty that he was denied due process of law. In our system of justice, the presumption of innocence is not rebutted by the kind of trial provided to Ed Johnson, and the judgment is certainly not final when his appeal was denied without due process of law.

Under all of these circumstances, the governor of the state of Tennessee and the president of the United States, be they Democrat or Republican, should issue a posthumous pardon of Ed Johnson. There is precedent for such a posthumous pardon. Roger Mudd, the TV journalist, was able to obtain a posthumous pardon signed by the president of the United States for his great-great grandfather, Dr. Samuel Mudd, who had been wrongfully convicted and imprisoned by a military court in Washington, D.C., as an accessory after the fact to Lincoln's assassination. He had set John Wilkes Booth's leg after Abraham Lincoln's assassination, without realizing what his patient had done. The military sentenced Dr. Mudd to life imprisonment, and he served as much as four years in prison.

A similar effort was successful for Leo Frank in 1986. A Jewish man living and working in Georgia, Frank was improperly accused and railroaded through the state's criminal-court system, which sentenced him to die. Fearful that the governor would commute his sentence, a lynch mob killed Frank in 1915. Seventy-one years later, lawyers in Atlanta, including prominent immigration attorney Dale Schwartz, successfully sought a pardon for Frank.

A posthumous pardon serves the purpose of clearing the name of a person denied a fair trial and denied due process of law. In this case, it would serve as an official government apology to the African-American community for failing to provide due process of law to an African-American citizen. It would also act as a clear reminder to us all of why people accused of committing crimes deserve a fair and impartial trial, as well as a thorough review of their case by the appellate courts.

The tombstone of Ed Johnson cries out from Missionary Ridge in grief, hope, and brotherhood. The statement GOD BLESS YOU ALL. I AM A INNOCENT MAN demonstrates grief over a failure of justice. But also of significance is the carving on the other side of the tombstone, which offers hope. Two hands are clasped together in brotherhood. An inscription reads: FAREWELL UNTIL WE MEET AGAIN IN THE SWEET BY AND BY.

APPENDIX 1

LYNCHINGS BY STATE, 1882–1944*

STATES	WHITES	NEGROES	TOTAL
Alabama	47	299	346
Arizona	29	0	29
Arkansas	59	226	285
California	41	2	43
Colorado	66	2	68
Delaware	0	1	1
Florida	25	255	280
Georgia	38	483	521
Idaho	20	0	20
Illinois	14	18	32
Indiana	33	14	47
Iowa	17	2	19
Kansas	35	19	54
Kentucky	64	141	205
Louisiana	56	334	390
Maryland	2	27	29
Michigan	7	1	8
Minnesota	5	4	9
Mississippi	41	532	573
Missouri	51	71	122
Montana	82	2	84
Nebraska	52	5	57
Nevada	6	0	6
New Jersey	0	1	1
New Mexico	33	3	36
New York	1	1	2
North Carolina	15	84	99
North Dakota	13	3	16
Ohio	10	16	26
Oklahoma	82	41	123
Oregon	20	1	21
Pennsylvania	2	6	8
South Carolina	4	155	159
South Dakota	27	0	27
Tennessee	47	203	250
Texas	143	346	489
Utah	6	2	8
Virginia	16	83	99
Washington	25	1	26
West Virginia	21	28	49
Wisconsin	6	0	6
Wyoming	30	5	35
Total	1,291	3,417	4,708

SOURCE: Tuskegee University

*There were no reported lynchings in this period in Connecticut, Maine, Massachusetts, New Hampshire, Rhode Island, Vermont, or Washington, D.C.

LYNCHINGS BY YEAR, 1882–1944

YEAR	WHITES	NEGROES	TOTAL
1882	64	49	113
1883	77	53	130
1884	160	51	211
1885	110	74	184
1886	64	74	138
1887	50	70	120
1888	68	69	137
1889	76	94	170
1890	11	85	96
1891	71	113	184
1892	69	162	231
1893	34	117	151
1894	58	134	192
1895	66	113	179
1896	45	78	123
1897	35	123	158
1898	19	101	120
1899	21	85	106
1900	9	106	115
1901	25	105	130
1902	7	85	92
1903	15	84	99
1904	7	76	83
1905	5	57	62
1906	3	62	65
1907	2	58	60
1908	8	89	97
1909	13	69	82
1910	9	67	76
1911	7	60	67
1912	2	61	63
1913	1	51	52
1914	3	49	52
1915	13	54	67
1916	4	50	54
1917	3	35	38
1918	4	60	64
1919	7	76	83
1920	8	53	61
1921	5	59	64
1922	6	51	57
1923	4	29	33
1924	0	16	16
1925	0	17	17
1926	7	23	30
1927	0	16	16
1928	1	10	11
1929	3	7	10
1930	1	20	21
1931	1	12	13
1932	2	6	8
1933	4	24	28
1934	0	15	15
1935	2	18	20
1936	0	8	8

YEAR	WHITES	NEGROES	TOTAL
1937	0	8	8
1938	0	6	6
1939	1	2	3
1940	1	4	5
1941	0	4	4
1942	0	5	5
1943	0	3	3
1944	0	2	2
Total	1,291	3,417	4,708

SOURCE: Tuskegee University

ALLEGED OFFENSES OF LYNCHING VICTIMS, 1882–1944

YEAR	MURDER	ASSAULT	RAPE AND ATTEMPTED RAPE	THEFT	INSULT TO WHITE PERSONS
1882	54	0	33	16	0
1883	71	0	27	4	0
1884	62	0	36	10	0
1885	91	2	28	1	0
1886	70	1	32	8	0
1887	54	0	41	6	0
1888	62	0	31	3	4
1889	73	1	40	10	1
1890	35	0	33	5	0
1891	58	14	41	12	1
1892	93	3	61	15	1
1893	60	2	38	8	2
1894	75	1	49	5	1
1895	68	0	47	7	0
1896	39	6	41	6	0
1897	67	2	35	14	2
1898	68	7	21	8	2
1899	43	2	26	7	1
1900	43	5	37	7	1
1901	51	7	25	10	0
1902	37	6	30	2	0
1903	50	7	23	0	1
1904	37	1	22	0	2
1905	32	3	18	2	0
1906	25	7	26	2	1
1907	16	7	24	4	1
1908	35	8	29	3	1
1909	46	5	19	3	4
1910	41	3	23	4	2
1911	36	3	13	3	4
1912	34	2	14	4	3
1913	25	4	10	1	1
1914	30	7	7	2	1

YEAR	MURDER	ASSAULT	RAPE AND ATTEMPTED RAPE	THEFT	INSULT TO WHITE PERSONS
1915	26	9	17	9	3
1916	21	7	12	8	2
1917	7	3	15	1	6
1918	27	3	16	5	2
1919	29	8	19	1	7
1920	23	9	18	0	3
1921	19	8	19	0	3
1922	15	5	19	4	2
1923	5	5	7	1	2
1924	4	2	7	0	3
1925	8	1	6	0	1
1926	13	3	5	1	1
1927	7	2	5	0	0
1928	5	2	3	0	0
1929	1	3	3	0	2
1930	5	0	10	3	0
1931	5	3	5	0	0
1932	1	2	2	0	1
1933	8	4	6	1	1
1934	2	2	6	1	3
1935	8	1	6	0	1
1936	1	0	6	0	1
1937	4	2	1	1	0
1938	3	0	1	0	1
1939	2	0	0	0	0
1940	0	0	1	0	1
1941	0	0	1	1	0
1942	1	1	3	0	0
1943	1	0	0	0	1
1944	2	0	0	0	0
Total	1,934	201	1,999	229	84

SOURCE: Tuskegee University

APPENDIX 2

UNITED STATES OF AMERICA, COMPLAINANT
V.
JOSEPH F. SHIPP ET AL.
[NO. 5, ORIGINAL.]
ARGUED MARCH 2, 3, 1909,
DECIDED MAY 24, 1909.

Information charging a contempt of the Supreme Court of the United States in murdering a prisoner under sentence of death in the Criminal Court of Hamilton County, in the State of Tennessee, after his appeal to the Federal Supreme Court from an order of the Circuit Court for the Northern Division of the Eastern District of Tennessee had been allowed and a stay of proceedings ordered. Rule discharged as to a part of the defendants and made absolute as to the others.†

The facts are stated in the opinion.

Attorney General Bonaparte and Solicitor General Hoyt argued the cause, and, with Mr. Edwin W. Lawrence, filed a brief for complainant.

Messrs. James J. Lynch, Moses H. Clift, and Robert B. Cooke argued the cause, and, with Messrs. Judson Harmon, Robert Pritchard, and William D. Spears, filed a brief for defendant Shipp.

Mr. G. W. Chamlee argued the cause, and, with Messrs. J. A. Hood, W. H. Cummings, and W. F. Chamlee, filed a brief for defendant Ward.

Mr. T. Pope Shepherd argued the cause, and, with Messrs. Lewis Shepherd and Martin A. Fleming, filed a brief for defendants Nolan, Justice, Padgett, and Mays.

Messrs. G. W. Chamlee, W. H. Cummings, and W. F. Chamlee also filed a brief for defendant Williams.

Messrs. Moses H. Clift and Robert B. Cooke also filed a brief for defendant Galloway.

Messrs. James J. Lynch, Robert B. Cooke, and William D. Spears also filed a brief for defendant Gibson.

Mr. Chief Justice Fuller delivered the opinion of the court:

This was an information filed by the Attorney General of the United States against Joseph F. Shipp and twenty-six other defendants, which was dismissed

†Leave granted June 1st, 1909, to present petition for rehearing, see infra, p. 1056

as to eighteen of them and heard as to defendants Shipp, Galloway, Gibson, Nolan, Williams, Justice, Padgett, Mayes, and Ward.

The information charged, in substance, that February 11, 1906, Ed Johnson, a negro, was convicted of rape by the criminal court of Hamilton county, Tennessee, held in Chattanooga, and was sentenced to death; that on March 3, following, Johnson filed a petition for the writ of habeas corpus in the United States circuit court sitting in Tennessee, alleging that, in the trial, he had been deprived of constitutional rights; that on March 10 the petition was dismissed and the writ denied, petitioner being remanded to the sheriff of Hamilton county, to be detained in his custody for ten days, in which to enable petitioner to prosecute an appeal, and, in default of such appeal, to be further proceeded with by the state court under its sentence; that, on March 17, Mr. Justice Harlan, of the United States Supreme Court, allowed an appeal from the decision of the circuit court, and on March 19 an order was made by the Supreme Court allowing said appeal; that defendant Shipp, sheriff of Hamilton county, then was at once notified by telegraph of said order, which stayed all proceedings against Johnson, and required Shipp to retain custody of Johnson pending determination of the appeal; that before 6 o'clock in the evening of March 19 a full account of this action of the Supreme Court was published and circulated in the evening papers in the city of Chattanooga; that defendant Shipp was the sheriff of Hamilton county, and defendants Matthew Galloway and Jeremiah Gibson, among others, were his deputies; that the deputies as well as the sheriff were fully advised of the action of the Supreme Court, and were informed and had every reason to believe from current reports and rumors conveyed to them, that an attempt would be made on the evening of the 19th or early in the morning of the 20th, by a mob composed of a large number of armed men, to force an entrance into the county jail for the purpose of taking Johnson therefrom and lynching him; that notwithstanding said information and said reports the sheriff withdrew from the jail early in the evening of the 19th the usual and customary guard, and left in charge thereof only the night jailer,—defendant Gibson—and committed other acts and did other things evincing a disposition on the part of said sheriff to render it less difficult and less dangerous for the mob to prosecute and carry into effect its unlawful design and purpose of lynching Johnson; that about 9 o'clock in the evening of said March 19 defendants and others conspired to break into the jail for the purpose of taking Johnson therefrom and lynching him, with intent to show their contempt and disregard for the above-mentioned order of this court, and prevent it from hearing the appeal of Johnson; that pursuant to this conspiracy, and in order to show their contempt and disregard for said order of this court, between 9 and 12 o'clock in the evening of said March 19, at Chattanooga, Tennessee, defendants, excepting Shipp and Gibson, assembled with others, broke into the jail, took Johnson out by force, and lynched him; that Gibson was the only officer at the jail when the mob broke in, and that, while the mob was in possession of the jail, defendant Shipp arrived, but made no effort to prevent the mob from taking Johnson from the jail; that defendants Shipp and Gibson were in sympathy with the mob while pretending to perform their official duty of protecting Johnson, and that they aided and abetted the mob in prosecution and performance of the lynching; that all of these acts were committed by defendants with the intent upon their part to utterly disregard the above-mentioned order of this court, and to prevent the court from hearing Johnson's appeal.

The answers on questions of fact consisted of a general denial, and, except in the cases of Shipp, Gibson, and Williams, the setting up of an alibi by each defendant. Williams, admits that he was at the jail a short time before and at the time Johnson was taken from it by the mob, and that he followed the mob and witnessed the lynching, but denies participating in the acts of the mob.

Certain preliminary questions of law were raised by defendants and passed upon by the court. 203 U.S. 503, 51 L. ed. 319, 27 Sup. Ct. Rep. 165, 8 A & E. Ann. Cas. 265. It was held that the complaint sufficiently set forth a contempt of this court; that it was unnecessary, for the purposes of this proceeding, to determine whether or not the circuit court had jurisdiction of the habeas corpus proceedings, or whether this court had jurisdiction to entertain the appeal, as those were questions for this court to determine, and for no other tribunal; and that the answers of the defendants, under oath, disavowing intent, did not purge them.

The case then came on to be heard on the question whether the allegations of the information were made out.

The following is a sufficient résumé of the facts admitted or undisputed:

January 23, 1906, a rape was committed upon a white woman in or near Chattanooga, Hamilton county, Tennessee.

At that time and at all times hereinafter mentioned, defendant Shipp was the duly elected, qualified, and acting sheriff of Hamilton county, Tennessee, and as such sheriff had and exercised full charge and control of the county jail located in Chattanooga, and was the legal custodian, under the laws of Tennessee, of all persons duly committed in said county under the laws of the state to confinement and imprisonment within the jail, and the defendants Matthew Galloway and Jeremiah Gibson were duly appointed, qualified, and acting deputy sheriffs under Shipp.

January 25 Shipp and his deputies arrested Ed Johnson, a negro, in or near Chattanooga, charged with the crime.

Late in the afternoon of the same day Johnson was, by order of the judge of the state criminal court, taken by Sheriff Shipp to Dayton and from there to Nashville, where he was kept until the day of his trial, February 6. Johnson was removed and kept away from Chattanooga during this period because of fear that he would be lynched.

The night of January 25 a large mob attacked the jail at Chattanooga, where Johnson was supposed to be confined.

Three of Shipp's deputies were at the jail, and, with the assistance given them by the police, the chairman of the safety committee, and others, prevented the taking of any prisoners from the jail.

At the suggestion of the deputies the mob appointed a committee to go through the jail and satisfy itself that Johnson was not there.

Even after this committee had reported that the persons whom the mob sought were not in the jail, it was necessary to use force to put the mob out of the jail yard.

The dangerous character of this committee and the mob and their anger at not being able to find Johnson is shown by the testimony of the prosecuting officer for Hamilton county, the judge of the criminal court of that county, and defendant Galloway.

One other night, about the same time, the officers though[t] there was to be a mob. The militia was called out twice about that time to protect the jail against a mob which sought to take Johnson's life.

January 20 a special grand jury was convened, and the next day indicted Johnson for the crime above referred to.

February 6 Johnson was brought to Chattanooga from Nashville, and his trial commenced that day in the criminal court of Hamilton county. February 9 he was convicted and sentenced to death.

The date of execution was originally fixed as March 13, but, on or about March 11, was changed by the governor to March 20.

No appeal to the supreme court of the state was taken by the lawyers appointed by the court to defend Johnson.

Two daily papers were published in Chattanooga,—the Times, a morning paper, and the News, an evening paper, both having a large circulation. Three competent and leading attorneys had been appointed by the court to defend Johnson, and one of them made a statement, which was published in the Chattanooga Times of February 10, as to the reasons why an appeal was not prosecuted in Johnson's behalf. He depicts the mental strain that he and his associates had been under, and the weight of the burden of the responsibility upon them. He says that when the jury brought in a verdict of guilty "we, as the attorneys, had to settle the question whether the case would be appealed to the supreme court." He asked the trial judge to appoint three other lawyers to counsel and advise with them and help to share the responsibility, and three well-known lawyers were designated, who met with the three counsel for the petitioner and considered the matter.

"We discussed the recent mob uprising and the state of unrest in the community. It was the judgment of all present that the life of the defendant, even if the wrong man, could not be saved; that an appeal would so inflame the public that the jail would be attacked and perhaps other prisoners executed by violence. In the opinion of all of us a case was presented where the defendant, now that he had been convicted by a jury, must die by the judgment of the law, or else, if his case were appealed, he would die by the act of the uprising of the people.

. . .

"In view of all the conditions, it was the unanimous vote that the law ought to be allowed to take its course if Judge McReynolds were satisfied with the verdict, and if he were to approve it and pass judgment of death on it."

He then relates an interview had thereupon with the accused. His right of appeal was explained to him, "that the supreme court met in September next; that an appeal would stay the judgment until that time; that we did not see any reasonable ground to suppose that the supreme court would reverse the sentence, and that we feared an appeal would cause mob violence against him."

. . .

"Without giving all that occurred at the jail, he said to us that he did not want to die by a mob; that he would do as we thought best. He said he would go over to the courthouse and tell the judge that he did not have anything more to say than that he was not the guilty man.

"I want the people to know that the foregoing facts moved us to allow the law to take its course under the verdict of the jury and the judgment of Judge McReynolds. Six lawyers settled it in this way after the calmest reflection and under the keenest sense of the great responsibility.

"In view of the awfulness of the crime committed, I beg that the sheriff and every peace officer of Chattanooga and Hamilton county will still try to get all possible further light; and if any person anywhere knows anything whatever tending to show or reflect light on either the guilt or innocence of the defendant, I beg that such person make known all that he may know to us or to Attorney General Whitaker."

On the afternoon Johnson was convicted he was secretly taken from Chattanooga to Knoxville because of fear of mob violence to him.

From the time the crime was committed until after Johnson's trial the people of Chattanooga were greatly excited over the crime and Johnson's alleged connection with it, and there was great apprehension on the part of the people as well as the officers that attempts would be made to lynch Johnson.

It was because of this intense excitement and the feeling that speedy execution of Johnson might prevent his being lynched that Johnson was so quickly indicted and tried.

While the trial was in progress extra deputies were sworn in and an unusual number of guards were kept around the courthouse and at the jail at night.

Guns to be used in protecting the jail against a mob were purchased.

March 3 Johnson filed a petition for a writ of habeas corpus in the United States circuit court for the northern division of the eastern district of Tennessee.

March 10, 1906, the petition was denied, the circuit court ordering that Johnson be remanded to the custody of the sheriff of Hamilton county, Tennessee, to be detained by him for ten days in which to enable petitioner to prosecute an appeal from said order, and, in default of the prosecution of said appeal within that time, to be then further proceeded with under the sentence.

This order was made public through the press.

Johnson was at Knoxville, where he had been kept since his conviction, for hearing upon his petition, and was taken back to Chattanooga, March 11.

Saturday, March 17, application was duly presented by Johnson to Mr. Justice Harlan of the Supreme Court of the United States (circuit justice of the sixth circuit), at Washington, asking that an appeal be allowed to that court from the order of the circuit court, denying Johnson's petition for a writ of habeas corpus. This appeal was allowed by Mr. Justice Harlan on the same day.

March 18, the Chattanooga Times published notice that application for said appeal had been made.

The same day Judge Clark, of the United States circuit court, received a telegram from Mr. Justice Harlan, which was communicated to Sheriff Shipp on the afternoon of that day, that he had allowed appeal to accused in habeas corpus case of Ed Johnson; that the transcript would be filed the next day, and motion also be made by Johnson's counsel for formal allowance of appeal by the Supreme Court.

March 19, the Chattanooga Times published news of the allowance of the appeal by Mr. Justice Harlan, in which it said, among other things:

"From those authorities it was learned that the granting of an appeal in a case like this acted to supersede all process in the state courts. No stay is necessary, according to the authorities, and the statute is self-operative. Pending a decision of the appeal there can be no execution by any state authority."

March 19 an order was made by the United States Supreme Court, allowing an appeal to that court from the final order of the circuit court, denying petition for writ of habeas corpus, and directing that all proceedings against the appellant be stayed, and that the custody of appellant be retained pending the appeal.

About 1 o'clock in the afternoon of said March 19 the following telegram was delivered to a telegraph company for transmittal to the addressee:

Washington, March 19, 1906.

To Sheriff of Hamilton county, Tenn., Chattanooga, Tenn.

Supreme Court of United States has allowed Ed Johnson appeal from Judge Clark's order, and directed all further proceedings stayed, and custody of Johnson retained pending appeal here. See § 766, Revised Statutes of the United States.

JAMES H. McKENNEY,
Clerk Supreme Court, U.S.

This was received by the telegraph office at Chattanooga about 3:30 on the same afternoon, and delivered between 4 and 5 o'clock on that afternoon.

About 2 o'clock on the afternoon of the 19th, Judge McReynolds told Sheriff Shipp that the Supreme Court had granted a stay in the Johnson case, and that thereafter Johnson was a Federal prisoner.

Between 2 and 4 of the afternoon of March 19 the following telegram was received by Judge Clark, and by his secretary communicated to Sheriff Shipp, at the jail, about 5 o'clock that afternoon, with a copy of the statute therein referred to:

Washington, D.C., March 19, 1906.

Hon. C. D. Clark, United States Court, Chattanooga, Tenn.

Court has just allowed appeal in Johnson's case, and ordered all further proceedings against him delayed and custody retained pending appeal here. It will be well to call attention of state officers immediately to § 766 of Revised Statues, U.S. Comp. Stat. 1901, p. 597.

JOHN M. HARLAN.

The statute referred to reads (including the proviso added March 8, 1893 [27 Stat. at L. 751, chap. 226]):

"Pending the proceedings on appeal in the cases mentioned in the three preceding sections, and until final judgment therein, and after final judgment of discharge, any proceeding against the person so imprisoned or confined or restrained of his liberty, in any state court, or by or under the authority of any state, for any matter so heard and determined, or in process of being heard and determined, under such writ of habeas corpus, shall be deemed null and void.

"Provided, That no such appeal shall be had or allowed after six months from the date of the judgment or order complained of."

Shipp understood that thereupon Johnson was held as a Federal prisoner.

There was published and circulated in Chattanooga, in the evening paper published in that city, on March 19, about 4 o'clock, an account of said action of the Supreme Court, under the headlines, "An Appeal Is Allowed. Ed Johnson Will Not Hang Tomorrow." This reads, in part:

"The gallows in the Hamilton county jail has again been disappointed in the case of Ed Johnson, convicted by the state courts of rape, and sentenced to death. The hanging will not take place to-morrow morning, as scheduled."

The news of the action of the court was also posted on a newspaper bulletin.

After hearing of the stay, Shipp says that he made no effort and gave no orders to have deputies or others guard the jail, but left the night jailer, defendant Gibson, there alone.

The county jail at Chattanooga, in which Johnson was confined on the 19th, consisted of four stories, two above ground and two below ground. Entrance to the jail was on the third floor, counting from the bottom. In the front part of the building, on this third floor, was an office section. An iron door led from this section into the jail proper; that is, the protected part of the building, where the prisoners were kept. Johnson was confined on the top floor. To reach him from outside the jail it was necessary to go through the offices, through the iron door between the offices and the jail proper, up a flight of stairs, through a steel-barred door, right behind which was a circular door consisting of heavy steel bars several inches apart, which revolved so as to make a passage. Passing through this circular door one came into a corridor around which were cells having iron doors which could be locked. It was in one of these cells that Johnson was confined.

The jail was located in a populous neighborhood and there were houses around it. In the evening of the 19th a white male prisoner was removed from the upper floor of the county jail in Chattanooga, leaving only Johnson and a white woman on that floor.

This same man had been removed in the same way at the time of the first attempt to lynch Johnson.

About half-past 8 or 9 that night a number of men entered the jail and went directly and without resistance to the door leading to Johnson's corridor. There is a conflict of evidence as to whether the door leading from the offices to the jail proper was locked during the evening, but, if it was locked when the mob came, it was easily broken down.

Gibson was the only officer there at the time, and he was on the top floor with Johnson.

Keys were obtained from him without resistance, but, as the lock on the door leading to the corridor where Johnson's cell was located had been broken by a member of the mob, the keys would not work.

The mob, with sledge and ax, then began to break the bolts on the corridor door.

About twelve men were actively engaged in breaking down the door and in all subsequent events of the lynching. Some of these men were masked.

A crowd of spectators began to gather around the jail soon after the mob reached it, and continued to gather in and around the jail until Johnson was taken out. This crowd was variously estimated from a few to 150 or more.

It took over an hour to break the bolts on the corridor door.

Two men then went through the circular door and in a few minutes brought Johnson out with his arms tied with a rope.

When Johnson was thus brought out, the dozen men or so composing the mob grabbed him.

This mob took Johnson from the jail to the county bridge over the Tennessee river, which was about six blocks from the jail.

Johnson was taken from the jail a little after 10 o'clock.

From the foregoing it is apparent that there was no interference or attempted interference of any consequence with the mob before it left the jail, and there was none after it left.

The crowd which had gathered around the jail followed the mob down to the bridge.

When the bridge was reached, the mob took Johnson a little beyond an arc light, put a rope around his neck, throw it over a beam, and swung him up.

At the bridge the mob actively engaged in lynching Johnson were close to him and separated by a space from the crowd of spectators.

The first time Johnson was swung up, the rope broke or slipped and he fell. He was swung up a second time and shot. After some shots were fired, Johnson again fell, and while lying on the ground was again shot. It was about ten minutes after the mob had reached the bridge until Johnson was killed.

It is apparent that a dangerous portion of the community was seized with the awful thirst for blood which only killing can quench, and that considerations of law and order were swept away in the overwhelming flood. The mob was, however, willing at the first attempt to accept prompt administration of the death penalty adjudged at a trial conducted according to judicial forms, in lieu of execution by lawless violence, but delay by appeal or writ of error or habeas corpus was not to be tolerated.

Under then-existing statutory provisions appeals might be taken to this court from final decisions of the circuit courts in habeas corpus in cases, among others, where the applicant for the writ is alleged to be restrained of his liberty in violation of the Constitution or of some law or treaty of the United States, and, if the restraint was by any state court, or by or under the authority of any state, further proceedings could not be had against him pending the appeal. Rev. Stat. §§ 703; 764, 766, U.S. Comp. Stat. 1901. pp. 594, 595, 597; Act of March 3, 1885, chap. 353, 23 Stat. at L. 437, U.S. Comp. Stat. 1901, p. 595.

In this instance an appeal was granted by this court, and proceedings specifically ordered to be stayed. The persons who hung and shot this man were so impatient for his blood that they utterly disregarded the act of Congress as well as the order of this court.

As heretofore stated, the defendants to the information remaining to be dealt with on the facts are Shipp, Galloway, Gibson, Nolan, Williams, Justice, Padgett, Mayse, and Ward. Of these, Shipp was the sheriff, and Galloway and Gibson two of his deputies. The others are charged with active participation in the lynching. It is contended that the lynching was not expected to occur on the 19th, and the evidence of the United States district judge and some clergymen and others was given to the effect that they had no such anticipation. The event showed that they were wrong, and it is plain the danger might be very great and yet remain unperceived by the adherents of order and peace.

It will be remembered that the crime was committed on January 23, and Johnson was arrested January 25. That night a mob attacked the jail in which he was supposed to be, and ascertained that he was not there. Johnson was kept in Nashville from that day until his trial commenced, February 6. On his conviction, February 9, he was taken away from Chattanooga, and kept away until March 11, the day after his petition for habeas corpus was denied.

It must be admitted that intense feeling against Johnson existed from the time of the commission of the crime until after his conviction, and that this feeling frequently manifested itself, although Johnson was not in Chattanooga from the time of his arrest until his trial began. The intensity of this feeling, and the great apprehension of the officers of mob violence, is shown in the testimony of defendants' own witnesses, describing the precautions and secrecy exercised by them in the way they took Johnson in and out of Chattanooga, as well as by the fact that they kept him away from Chattanooga from the day of his arrest until March 11, two days before the time set for his execution, with the exception of the three days he was there attending his trial. Undoubtedly the public believed that Johnson would be executed on March 13, until the reprieve to March 20 was granted on March 11; and, after the petition for habeas corpus was denied by the circuit court, believed that Johnson would then be executed on the 20th.

Sheriff Shipp testifies that inflammatory reports of the habeas corpus proceedings and efforts to appeal the case to the Supreme Court were sent out by the newspapers on March 11, and because of that he had fear of mob violence to Johnson. The efforts made by Johnson's attorneys to obtain an appeal were kept before the public by the newspapers.

March 16 the Chattanooga Times published a statement that a negro attorney had gone to Washington to obtain an appeal from the order denying the petition for habeas corpus. The article said:

People here are decidedly anxious as to whether Johnson is to suffer death for his crime next Monday or escape for an indefinite period by reason of intervention of the court at Washington. More unrest on the subject exists than was anticipated when Johnson was brought back to the county.

. . .

"During the recent days of suspense as to his execution, the desire for information has been feverish, and telephones at localities where information has been thought to be obtainable have been kept busy by inquirers."

In the News, published the evening of March 19, there was an editorial reviewing the local proceedings, which concluded:

"All of this delay is aggravating to the community. The people of Chattanooga believe that Johnson is guilty, and that he ought to suffer the penalty of the law as speedily as possible. If by legal technicality the case is prolonged and the culprit finally escapes, there will be no use to plead with a mob here if another such crime is committed. Such delays are largely responsible for mob violence all over the country."

The assertions that mob violence was not expected, and that there was no occasion for providing more than the usual guard of one man for the jail in Chattanooga, are quite unreasonable and inconsistent with statements made by Sheriff Shipp and his deputies, that they were looking for a mob on the next day. Officers and others were heard to say that they expected a mob would attempt to lynch Johnson on the 20th. There does not seem to be any foundation for the belief that the mob would be considerate enough to wait until the 20th. If the officers expected a mob at all, as they say that they did, they cannot shield themselves behind the statement that they expected it on the 20th, the day that had been appointed for Johnson to die, and did not expect it the night before. But no orders had been given and nothing had been done up to half-past 8 o'clock on the night of the 19th to protect Johnson from the mob which was, according to their present statements, expected the next day.

Testimony was given by a servant in Shipp's house that, a week before Johnson was lynched, Shipp was heard to say that if the execution were stayed Johnson would be mobbed. This was, however, disputed by Shipp and relatives of his who were there at the time.

On May 28th, at Birmingham, Alabama, defendant Shipp himself, in an interview reported and printed the next morning in the Birmingham Age-Herald, said:

" 'The first I knew of the mob was through a telephone message I received from the Chattanooga Times office, for they had cut the wires at the county jail immediately upon their arrival. I dressed as quickly as possible and went to the jail, and found a crowd of about seventy-five people around it, most of them being in disguise. I made my way through the crowd into the jail and began remonstrating with them against taking any drastic steps. They seized me and took me upstairs, locking me up in a bath room. The members of the mob told me they meant no violence to me. I argued with them against doing anything at all, since the law had so far taken its proper course. *I am frank to say that I did not attempt to hurt any of them, and would not have made such an attempt if I could.* In the first place, I could have done no good, as I was overwhelmed by numbers.

" 'The Supreme Court of the United States was responsible for this lynching. I had given that negro every protection that I could. For fourteen days I had guarded and protected him myself. The authorities had urged me to use one or two military companies in doing so, but I told them I would land the negro in jail, which I did, individually.

" 'Many nights before the lynching there had been a sufficient guard around the jail. *I had looked for no trouble that night, and, on the contrary, did not look for it until the next day.* That night no one was on duty except the jailer, which is the usual guard at our jail, as well as in other counties.

" 'In my opinion the act of the Supreme Court of the United States in not allowing the case to remain in our courts was the most unfortunate thing in the history of Tennessee. I was determined that the case should be put in the hands of the law, as it was. The jury that tried the negro Johnson was as good as ever sat in a jury box.

" 'The people of Hamilton county were willing to let the law take its course until it became known that the case would not probably be disposed of for four or five years by the Supreme Court of the United States. The people would not submit to this, and I do not wonder at it.

" 'These proceedings in the United States Supreme Court recently appear to me to be only a matter of politics. I do not wish to appear in the light of defying the United States court, but I did my duty. I am conscious if it, thoroughly conscious of it, and I am ready for any conditions that may come up.' "

The testimony of the reporter that Shipp made these statements was corroborated by the evidence of another reporter who interviewed Shipp on the following day regarding them, and is not denied by Shipp except in an immaterial particular. From this it appears that defendant Shipp looked for trouble on the 20th, but, as he says, not that night; that he did not attempt to hurt any of the mob, "and would not have made such an attempt if I could."

He evidently resented the necessary order of this court as an alien intrusion, and declared that the court was responsible for the lynching. According to him, "the people of Hamilton county were willing to let the law take its course until it became known that the case would not probably be disposed of for four or five years by the Supreme Court of the United States." "But," he added, "the people would not submit to this, and I do not wonder at it." In other words, his view was that because this court, in the discharge of its duty, entered the order which it did, that therefore the people of Hamilton county would not submit to its mandate, and hence the court became responsible for the mob. He took the view expressed by several members of the mob on the afternoon of the 19th and before the lynching, when they said, referring to the Supreme Court, that "they had no business interfering with our business at all." His reference to the "people" was significant, for he was a candidate for re-election, and had been told that his saving the prisoner from the first attempt to mob him would cost him his place, and he had answered that he wished the mob had got him before he did.

It seems to us that to say that the sheriff and his deputies did not anticipate that the mob would attempt to lynch Johnson on the night of the 19th is to charge them with gross neglect of duty and with an ignorance of conditions in a matter which vitally concerned them all as officers, and is directly contrary to their own testimony. It is absurd to contend that officers of the law who have been through the experiences these defendants had passed through two months prior to the actual lynching did not know that a lynching probably would be attempted on the 19th. Under the facts shown, when the sheriff and his deputies assert that they expected a mob on the 20th, they practically concede the allegation of the information that they were informed and had every reason to believe that an attempt would be made on the evening of the 19th or early on the morning of the 20th.

In view of this, Shipp's failure to make the slightest preparation to resist the mob, the absence of all of the deputies, except Gibson, from the jail during the mob's proceedings, occupying a period of some hours in the early evening, the action of Shipp in not resisting the mob, and his failure to make any reasonable effort to save Johnson or identify the members of the mob, justify the inference of a disposition upon his part to render it easy for the mob to lynch Johnson, and to acquiesce in the lynching. After Shipp was informed that a mob was at the jail, and he could not do otherwise than go there, he did not and in fact at no time hindered the mob or caused it to be interfered with, or helped in the slightest degree to protect Johnson. And this in utter disregard of this court's mandate, and in defiance of this court's orders.

Let us recapitulate the facts bearing immediately on defendant Shipp.

About 9 o'clock on the night of the 19th the judge before whom Johnson was tried, and the attorney who prosecuted him, communicated with Sheriff Shipp at his house, saying that there were persons around the jail who looked suspicious, and suggesting that the sheriff had better go down to the jail.

At that time a report was generally circulated in the city that a mob was at the jail to lynch Johnson.

Shipp lived only a few blocks from the jail. He reached the jail about 9. He was alone. A number of people were in the jail and outside of it when he arrived. He anticipated a mob was inside.

Without stopping to speak to any of these people, he rushed inside of the jail to the foot of the stairs leading to the floor Johnson was on. There he was taken hold of by five or six men and carried upstairs. The men who took hold of him had no firearms.

At first he was put in a bath room, and then was released and stood around near the corridor door, where the mob was at work, with three or four unarmed men around him. He made no effort to get away or use force in opposing the mob. He did not attempt to use his pistol or call for help. After the corridor had been broken in, either Shipp or defendant Gibson told the mob which cell Johnson was in. When the mob left the jail with Johnson, Shipp did not follow or make any effort to rescue Johnson or get others to help rescue him. He was not locked up when the mob left the jail, but was left entirely free.

When the crowd following the lynchers was about two blocks from the jail, Shipp came out of the building alone and unguarded. To a request made by a man at that time to go and identify members of the mob, Shipp replied that it would be dangerous and foolish. This request was made before the shooting occurred.

A special deputy met Shipp at the jail just after Johnson had been taken out and before he was shot. Shipp told him that the mob had Johnson. Shipp was quiet, and made no effort to go after the lynchers, or to reach the police or militia or others.

When he reached the jail he could have gone about three blocks to the police station and got the police.

No alarm bell was rung at the courthouse that night, although it was rung the night of the attempted lynching, January 25, and it drew out a big crowd. No attempt was made by Shipp or others to summon a posse. He sent no one after deputies. He made no effort to send anyone for help.

It is testified that some time after the mob had left the jail for the bridge, Shipp sent Galloway and Clark down to the bridge, but he made no effort to go himself.

There was in the crowd around the jail and at the scene of the lynching a substantial number of law-abiding men of good character.

That assistance in suppressing the mob might have been easily obtained if effort had been made is shown by the testimony of the chairman of the board of safety, who testifies that, at the time of the first lynching, in going four or five blocks to the jail, he gathered about 16 men to help put down the mob.

The militia was drilling on the night of the 19th between 8 and 10:30 in the armory, a well-known place, three blocks from the jail. It was not called upon to assist in suppressing the mob, although it had been called out twice before by the governor, and was bound to respond to another call by him.

The governor had given assurances that any help asked for would be given, and we have no doubt he would have responded, for he would have had the honor of Tennessee in his keeping.

Numerous witnesses testify that no firearms were displayed by the mob except that one of their number was in the office of the jail with a Winchester rifle, and one pistol was exhibited to a reporter when the door was being broken open.

No deputies put in an appearance while the mob was at the jail or during the lynching, except Frank Jones, who approached the jail with a prisoner, but, upon seeing the mob, immediately left with the prisoner, and excepting Matt Galloway, who was seen in the crowd.

From the time he reached there, about 6 o'clock, until the mob came, Gibson was the only officer in charge of the jail. But there was much evidence that customarily many deputies were there nightly, and that several were present on the night of the 19th until just before the irruption of the mob.

Heavy iron chains were sometimes used as additional guards upon circular doors in the jail, such as that leading to Johnson's corridor. These were locked by the prisoners on the inside. During the trial of Johnson these chains were used on the circular doors. But none were on the circular door leading to Johnson's cell on the 19th. It also appears that Johnson's cell door was not locked.

Winchester rifles which were kept to defend the jail against mob violence were, at the time the mob attacked the jail on the 19th, in a show case in the office. Those were taken out of the show case by the mob and unloaded.

Although Shipp was in the midst or near the members of the mob for about an hour when they were in the jail, he did not seek to obtain information so that he could identify any of them, and he testifies that he does not know any member of the mob.

Only one conclusion can be drawn from these facts, all of which are clearly established by the evidence,—Shipp not only made the work of the mob easy, but in effect aided and abetted it.

Gibson is involved in the same condemnation though under less responsibility. We think belief on his part that a mob would attempt to enter the jail and lynch Johnson on the night of the 19th must be presumed.

The day jailer left the jail some time after six o'clock, and transferred the keys to Gibson, the night jailer. Gibson's 15-year-old boy was with him, but went to the opera house at 8:30. Gibson was in charge of the jail more than two hours before the arrival of the mob, and he made no effort to summon assistance to repel the attack, although necessarily he must have known that he alone could only offer slight resistance. Mrs. Baker, a white woman, confined on the same floor with Johnson, testified that Gibson, soon after arriving at the jail, when she had gone down stairs to get a letter written, said to her that a mob was coming, and directed her to go to her room, and when the mob was at the jail came to her door and told her that no one would hurt her. Gibson admits the last statement, but denies the first.

He testifies that when he heard the mob he went into the hospital cell, located on the top floor, and sat down on a lounge, and as soon as the mob got upstairs he handed over to them his pistol and the keys, including a key to the door of Johnson's cell; that he did not try to use the pistol, or to resist the mob by force; that from the top floor he could have gone through the kitchen into the yard and back of the jail, but he made no effort to do so, although it took the mob some ten minutes after he knew they were there to break through the door between the outer door and the jail proper; that he just gave up and made no effort at all to resist the mob or rescue Johnson after they had left the jail; that although the men were bold in their work, he failed to recognize anyone excepting Nick Nolan.

Galloway was a deputy sheriff from the time Johnson was convicted until after the lynching, and was told by the sheriff after the mob had left for the bridge to go down there, and did so, but Johnson was then dead. He was criminal court deputy, and served criminal court papers and made arrests. But he had no charge of the jail or keeping of prisoners except when officially so assigned. He had no connection with the jail or the prisoners at any time after Johnson was brought from Knoxville on the 10th or 11th of March. He testified that he had heard nothing while attending to his duties that made him think Johnson was in danger; was a member of the Eagle Club, and was there on evening of the 19th, at 7:45, not having heard prior thereto anything about any impending lynching. His first information of the lynching was after 10 o'clock, when he went to the jail at once. There he met the sheriff, who asked him to go to the bridge, which he did, but Johnson was dead. We think Galloway must be acquitted of the charges in the information.

This brings us to a consideration of the case in respect of the six defendants who are charged as members of the mob and participants in its action.

As to Williams and Nolan, there is direct testimony to their participation in the lynching, and we do not think that the evidence relied on to weaken that conclusion is sufficient to do so.

As to Padgett and Mayse, there is testimony of statements on their part on the afternoon of the 19th and the morning of the 20th, which, if believed, demonstrates their guilt, We have carefully examined and analyzed the evidence to impeach the principal witness to these conversations, and also to make out a[l]i[b]is, but we cannot accept it as convincing.

We hold that the case as to Justice and Ward fails on the evidence.

In our opinion it does not admit of question on this record that this lamentable riot was the direct result of opposition to the administration of the law by this court. It was not only in defiance of our mandate, but was understood to be such. The Supreme Court of the United States was called upon to abdicate its functions and decline to enter such orders as the occasion, in its judgment, demanded, because of the danger of their defeat by an outbreak of lawless violence. It is plain that what created this mob and led to this lynching was the unwillingness of its members to submit to the delay required for the appeal. The intent to prevent that delay by defeating the hearing of the appeal necessarily follows from the defendants' acts, and, if the life of anyone in the custody of the law is at the mercy of a mob, the administration of justice becomes a mockery. When this court granted a stay of execution on Johnson's application it became its duty to protect him until his case should be disposed of. And when its mandate, issued for his protection, was defied, punishment of those guilty of such attempt must be awarded.

The rule will be discharged as to the defendants Galloway, Justice, and Ward, and made absolute as to the other defendants.

Rule discharged as to defendants Galloway, Justice, and Ward, and made absolute as to defendants Shipp, Gibson, Williams, Nolan, Padgett, and Mayse. Attachments to issue, returnable on Tuesday, June 1.

A NOTE ON SOURCES

The following sources have been used to reconstruct various scenes and conversations in *Contempt of Court*.

PAGES 30–32

Chattanooga Times, January 24, 1906
Chattanooga News, January 24, 1906
Knoxville Journal, January 24, 1906
Sworn testimony of Sheriff Joseph Shipp, February 6, 1906
Sworn testimony of Nevada Taylor, February 6, 1906

PAGES 75–76

Nashville Banner, February 4, 1906
Sworn testimony of Robert Cameron, March 10, 1906
Personal memoirs of Lewis Shepherd, privately published in 1950
Lewis Shepherd's statements to Secret Service agents, March 31, April 7, and
  April 20, 1906

PAGES 124–125

Detailed letter of the meeting by Thomas, one of Johnson's lawyers, February
  10, 1906
Sworn testimony by Thomas in federal habeas corpus proceeding on March 10,
  1906
Chattanooga Times, February 10, 1906
Chattanooga News, February 10, 1906
Personal memoirs of Lewis Shepherd
Lewis Shepherd's statements to Secret Service agents, March 31, April 7, and
  April 20, 1906

PAGE 153

Knoxville Journal, March 8, 1906
Knoxville Sentinel, March 8, 1906
Shipp's sworn testimony in federal investigation
Secret Service investigative reports dated March 31, April 7, and April 20, 1906

PAGES 200–214

Chattanooga Times, March 20 and 21, 1906
Chattanooga News, March 20 and 21, 1906
Knoxville Journal, March 21, 1906
Nashville Banner, March 21, 1906
Chattanooga Blade, March 22, 1906
Atlanta Independent, March and April 1906
Sworn testimony of Deputies Gibson and Brown in the federal investigation
Sworn testimony of Ellen Baker, an inmate in the cell next to Ed Johnson's
Sworn testimony of two other unidentified inmates at the jail the night of the
    lynching
Secret Service investigative reports dated March 31, April 7, April 20, May 8,
    May 17, June 20, July 1, July 25, July 30, and September 19, 1906
Tuskegee Interview Report, May 1906

BIBLIOGRAPHY

PRIMARY SOURCES

COURT AND HISTORICAL RECORDS

Transcript of Record in U.S. Supreme Court in the Contempt Case of *U.S.* v. *Shipp*, Docket No. Original No. 5.

Consisting of 1,275 pages, it contains all of the evidence and legal briefs submitted to the United States Supreme Court, located in National Archives, Washington, D.C.

Record in Habeas Corpus Proceedings of Ed Johnson in U.S. District Court at Knoxville. Docket No. 1469. It consists of 72 pages and contains pleadings and testimony connected with said proceedings. Record was filed in appeal of Ed Johnson in U.S. Supreme Court. Located now in National Archives, Washington, D.C.

Secret Service Investigative Reports Concerning the Lynching of Ed Johnson. The reports are dated as follows: March 23, 1906; March 31, 1906; April 7, 1906; April 20, 1906; June 20, 1906; July 1, 1906; July 25, 1906; July 30, 1906; September 19, 1906; September 21, 1906; September 23, 1906; October 4, 1906; October 8, 1906; October 14, 1906; November 27, 1906; December 5, 1906; December 24, 1906; December 27, 1906; January 3, 1907; January 28, 1907; February 18, 1907; February 24, 1907; June 3, 1907; July 6, 1907; October 18, 1908. Also includes Report of Penland to Justice Department. Located in National Archives, Washington, D.C.

Letters and selected writing of T. H. McCallie and his children, 1905–1910, The McCallie School in Chattanooga.

Selective writings, letters, and memos written to and by U.S. Supreme Court Justice John Marshall Harlan, University of Kentucky and University of Louisville.

Selective writings, letters, and memos written to and by U.S. Supreme Court Justices Melville Fuller and Oliver Wendell Holmes.

U.S. Bureau of the Census, 1890, 1900, 1910.

NEWSPAPERS

CHATTANOOGA TIMES

1886–July 14, ed. page; October 23, ed. page; October 25, ed. page; October 27, ed. page; October 30, ed. page; October 31, ed. page; November 1, ed. page; November 2, ed. page; November 3, ed. page; November 5, ed. page; November 7, p. 5; November 9, page 6.

1892–May 2, p. 4; May 7, p. 3; May 9, ed. page; May 12, p. 4; May 13, ed. page; May 21, p. 1; May 22 ed. page and p. 5; May 24, p. 1; May 25, ed. page and p. 6; May 26, ed. page, p. 5, and p. 8; May 27, p. 2, ed. page, and p. 5; May 29, p. 6 and ed. page; May 30, p. 5; June 1, p. 4 and p. 8; June 13, ed. page; June 14, p. 5 and ed. page.

1893–February 15, p. 1; February 16, ed. page, p. 5, and p. 8; February 17, ed. page and p. 5; February 20, p. 5; February 28, p. 1 and p. 5.

1894–December 18, p. 1.

1897–February 26, p. 2; February 27, p. 5.

1906–January 24, p. 8; January 25, ed. page and p. 3; January 26, p. 1 and ed. page; January 27, ed. page and p. 5; January 28, p. 10; January 29, p. 8; January 30, p. 10; January 31, ed. page and p. 1; February 2, p. 2; February 4, ed. page; February 5, p. 1; February 7, ed. page and p. 1; February 8, ed. page and p. 5; February 9, p. 5; February 10, ed. page, p. 1 and p. 5; February 11, p. 4; February 12, ed. page; February 13, ed. page; February 14, p. 5; February 16, ed. page; February 19, ed. page; February 20, p. 5 and ed. page; February 26, ed. page; March 4, p. 1; March 5, p. 1; March 8, p. 1; March 10, p. 1; March 11, p. 1; March 12, ed. page and p. 1; March 13, p. 1; March 14, p. 1 and p. 5; March 15, p. 1; March 16, p. 1; March 17, p. 5; March 18, p. 1; March 19, p. 1; March 20, p. 1 and ed. page; March 21, ed. page, p. 1, and p. 5; March 22, ed. page and p. 1; March 23, p. 5; March 24, ed. page, p. 1 and p. 4; March 25, ed. page and p. 10; March 26, ed. page and p. 5; March 28, p. 1; March 29, ed. page; March 30, p. 1; March 31, ed. page; April 6, p. 5; April 19, p. 1; May 15, p. 4; May 24, p. 4; May 26, p. 5; May 27, p. 5; May 30, ed. page and p. 1; June 9, p. 1; June 20, p. 4; June 23, p. 5; July 2, ed. page; July 23, ed. page; July 29, p. 10; July 31, ed. page; August 2, ed. page; August 3, p. 1; August 4, ed. page and p. 5; August 17, p. 5; August 20, ed. page; August 22, ed. page; August 28, ed. page; September 4, ed. page; September 7, ed. page; September 8, p. 8; September 14, p. 10; September 24, ed. page; October 8, p. 5; October 11, p. 5; October 12, p. 1; October 15, p. 1; October 16, p. 1 and 2; October 17, p. 2; October 18, ed. page and p. 10; October 19, p. 1; November 8, ed. page; November 11, p. 1; November 27, p. 5; November 30, p. 4; December 5, p. 1; December 6, p. 1; December 8, p. 1; December 11, p. 8; December 25, p. 1 and p. 2.

1907–January 4, p. 5; January 6, ed. page; January 8, ed. page; January 10, p. 12; January 15, p. 1; January 16, ed. page; January 17, p. 8; January 20, p. 4; January 22, ed. page and p. 5; January 25, ed. page; January 26, p. 1; January 27, ed. page; January 30, ed. page; February 5, ed. page and p. 9; February 8, p. 9; February 9, ed. page; February 12, p. 5; February 13, p. 5; February 14, p. 5; February 15, p. 5; February 16, p. 5; February 17, p. 13; March 24, p. 5; April 21, p. 11; April 22, p. 8; June 7, p. 7; June 11, p. 5; June 12, p. 10; June 13, p. 5; June 15, p. 7; June 16, p. 4 and p. 26; June 17, ed. page; June 18, p. 8; June 19, p. 3 and ed. page; June 20, ed. page; June 21, p. 5; June 22, p. 7; June 25, p. 10; June 26, p. 8; June 28, p. 5; June 29, p. 5; June 30, p. 3; September 8, ed. page; October 15, p. 3.

1908–April 23, p. 8; July 1, p. 5; July 5, p. 6; August 7, ed. page; October 14, p. 1.

1909–November 15, p. 5; November 16, p. 1, p. 2, and ed. page; November 17, p. 5; November 18, ed. page; November 19, ed. page; November 20, p. 5; November 21, p. 4 and ed. page; November 28, p. 1; December 2, p. 10; December 3, ed. page; December 27, p. 1.

1910–January 3, p. 4; January 28, p. 8; January 30, ed. page; January 31, p. 5; February 4, ed. page.

1915–September 16, p. 3.

1917–May 15, p. 3.

1922–August 13, p. 9.

1923–April 19, p. 5.

1925–September 19, p. 3.

1931–January 16, p. 5.

1936–July 20, p. 4.

1938–May 29, p. 1 and p. 2; October 7, p. 1.

1939–July 9, p. 1; July 12, p. 1; August 1, p. 5.

1941–August 18, p. 5.

1942–March 2, p. 5; May 17 ed. page.

1960–December 7, p. 4; December 17, p. 4.

CHATTANOOGA NEWS

1892–February 20, ed. page; May 19, p. 1; May 20, p. 1; May 21, p. 1 and p. 4; May 22, p. 1; May 24, p. 1; May 25, p. 1, p. 6, and ed. page; May 26, p. 1; May 27, p. 4; May 28, p. 6; June 3, p. 4; June 13, p. 1.

1893–February 11, p. 1; February 15, ed. page and p. 1; February 16, ed. page; February 23, ed. page; February 27, p. 4.

1897–February 26, p. 5.

1906–January 24, p. 5 and ed. page; January 25, p. 4; January 26, p. 1 and ed. page; January 27, p. 1; January 29, p. 4 and ed. page; January 30, ed. page and p. 4; January 31, p. 10; February 1, ed. page and p. 5; February 2, p. 4; February 3, p. 1; February 5, p. 3; February 6, p. 1; February 7, ed. page and p. 1; February 8, p. 1; February 9, p. 1; February 10, p. 1 and ed. page; February 13, p. 1; February 14, p. 4; February 15, p. 5; February 17, p. 1; February 21, ed. page; February 22, p. 4; February 26, p. 5; March 8, p. 1; March 9, p. 1; March 10, ed. page; March 12, p. 1; March 13, p. 1; March 14, p. 4; March 19, ed. page and p. 1; March 20, p. 1, ed. page, and p. 10; March 21, ed. page and p. 1; March 22, ed. page; March 23, ed. page; March 24, ed. page; March 27, p. 5 and ed. page; March 30, ed. page and p. 1; April 2, p. 4 and ed. page; April 3, ed. page; April 18, p. 1; May 28, p. 1; May 29, ed. page and p. 12; May 31, ed. page; June 8, p. 1; June 9, p. 4 and p. 10; June 15, ed. page; June 16, ed. page; June 27, ed. page; July 18, ed. page; July 28, p. 4; August 1, ed. page; August 3, ed. page; August 4, p. 4; August 14, ed. page; September 5, p. 3; September 15, p. 12; October 4, p. 10; October 8, p. 5; October 12, p. 4; October 13, p. 5; October 15, p. 1 and p. 2; November 10, p. 4; December 1, p. 1 and ed. page; December 5, p. 1 and ed. page; December 6, p. 1; December 7, p. 4; December 11, ed. page; December 24, p. 1; December 25, ed. page.

1907–January 4, ed. page; January 10, p. 4; January 14, p. 1; January 21, p. 1; January 23, p. 4; January 24, p. 1; January 26, ed. page and p. 5; January 28, p. 4; January 29, p. 1; February 4, p. 1; February 5, ed. page; February 7, p. 4; February 9, p. 3; February 11, p. 3; February 12, p. 1; February 13, p. 3 and ed. page; February 14, p. 3; February 15, p. 4; February 16, p. 1 and ed. page; February 22, ed. page; May 4, p. 3; May 13, p. 3; June 10, p. 1; June 11, p. 3; June 13, p. 1; June 14, p. 1; June 15, p. 4; June 17, p. 3; June 18, p. 3; June 19, p. 4; June 20, p. 4; June 21, p. 2; June 22, p. 4; June 24, p. 4; June 25, p. 3; June 26, p. 2; June 27, p. 4; June 28, p. 3; June 29, p. 3.

1908–July 1, p. 4; July 2, p. 3; July 3, p. 4.

1909–March 5, p. 1; May 24, p. 1; May 25, p. 1 and ed. page; May 26, p. 1; May 28, ed. page and p. 1; May 31, p. 4; June 1, p. 1; June 2, p. 1 and ed. page; November 13, p. 1; November 15, p. 1 and ed. page; November 16, p. 1, ed. page, and p. 7; November 17, p. 1, p. 2, p. 7, and ed. page; November 19, ed. page; November 20, p. 7; November 22, p. 3; November 25, ed. page; November 29, p. 3; December 1, p. 1; December 6, p. 3; December 13, p. 1; December 21, ed. page; December 27, p. 1; December 31, p. 1.

1910–January 3, p. 1; January 4, p. 1; January 5, p. 1; January 6, p. 1; January 26, p. 1; January 29, p. 1; January 31, p. 1; February 3, p. 1.

NASHVILLE BANNER

1906–January 26, p. 1; January 27, p. 1; January 29, p. 1; February 1, p. 3; February 6, p. 1; February 8, p. 1; February 9, p. 1.

CHATTANOOGA FREE PRESS

1938–October 31, p. 3; October 7, p. 1.

1939–July 11, p. 1; July 13, p. 1.

WASHINGTON POST

1906–March 20, p. 1; March 22, p. 5; March 23, p. 1; March 24, p. 5 and p. 1; March 29, p. 1; December 5, p. 1.

1909–November 6, p. 3; November 17, p. 1.

KNOXVILLE JOURNAL

1906–January 24, p. 1; January 26, p. 1 and p. 12; January 28, p. 9; January 30, p. 4; February 3, p. 4; February 4, p. 8; February 6, p. 1; February 7, p. 6; February 8, p. 4; February 10, p. 6 and p. 1; February 12, p. 4; February 13, p. 8; February 25, p. 8; March 8, p. 6; March 9, p. 3; March 10, p. 8; March 11, p. 5 and ed. page; March 12, ed. page and p. 8; March 13, p. 1 and ed. page; March 20, p. 1; March 21, ed. page and p. 1; March 22, p. 4 and p. 8; March 23, p. 1 and p. 4; March 24, ed. page and p. 8; March 25, p. 6; March 27, p. 10; March 30, p. 9; April 1, p. 6 and ed. page; April 6, ed. page; April 7, p. 1; April 8, ed. page; May 25, p. 1.

1909–November 16, p. 2.

1910–January 31, p. 1.

NEW YORK TIMES

1906–March 21, p. 1; March 22, p. 6; March 27, p. 1; April 2, p. 1; December 5, p. 10.

1907–May 14, p. 2 and p. 8.

1909–May 25, p. 2; November 16, p. 2; November 17, ed. page.

1911–December 3, Magazine Section, pt. 5.

1912–February 3, p. 1.

KNOXVILLE SENTINEL

1906–January 27, p. 1; January 30, ed. page; February 7, p. 1; February 13, p. 1; February 14, ed. page; March 5, p. 3; March 7, p. 9; March 8, p. 3 and p. 10; March 10, p. 11; March 12, p. 9; March 13, p. 1; March 19, p. 1; March 20, p. 5; March 21, p. 1 and ed. page; March 22, p. 1; March 23, p. 1; March 24, ed. page; March 26, p. 1; March 27, p. 3; March 28, p. 1 and ed. page; March 29, p. 3 and ed. page; March 30, p. 3 and ed. page; March 31, ed. page.

1907–January 3, ed. page; January 18, ed. page; February 12, ed. page; February 13, p. 4; February 14, p. 1; February 15, p. 3; February 16, p. 3.

1909–May 25, p. 1; May 27, ed. page; November 15, p. 1; November 16, p. 1; December 31, p. 3.

1910–January 29, p. 12; January 31, p. 10.

1930–March 8, p. 1; March 9, p. 1 and p. 6.

THE VOICE OF THE NEGRO

1906–April 14, p. 2

CHATTANOOGA DAILY COMMERCIAL

1886–October 1, ed. page; October 31, ed. page; November 3, p. 1; November 4, p. 1 and ed. page.

CINCINNATI ENQUIRER

1906–March 21, p. 1.

WASHINGTON BEE
1906–March, April, October.

ATLANTA INDEPENDENT
1906–March, April.

CHATTANOOGA BLADE
1906–Spring.

VOICE OF THE PEOPLE
1906–undated issues.

WASHINGTON STAR
1906–March 21, p. 1; March 22, p. 1.

1909–May 24, p. 2; November 15, p. 1.

WASHINGTON EVENING SUN
1906–March 30.

DISSERTATIONS

Barnes, Joseph A. "The Edward Johnson Affair: Perspectives on the Motivational Bases of the Community and the Legal Profession." Ph.D. diss., University of Tennessee at Knoxville, February 24, 1977.

Cook, Stanley A. "Ties of Path to the High Bench: The Pre–Supreme Court Career of Justice Edward Terry Sanford." Ph.D. diss., University of Tennessee at Knoxville.

Legal and Behavioral Perspectives on American Vigilantism (author and publisher unknown).

"Lynchings and What They Mean: General Findings of the Southern Commission on the Study of Lynching." Tuskegee Institute, 1931.

"The Mob Still Rides." Commission on Interracial Cooperation, 1935.

SECONDARY SOURCES

MAGAZINES AND PERIODICALS

Imes, William Lloyd. "The Legal Status of Free Negroes and Slaves in Tennessee." *Journal of Negro History.* Vol. 1 (1919): 254.

Hollingsworth, Harold. "Tennessee and the Supreme Court of the United States." *East Tennessee Historical Society Publication.*

"The Supremacy of the Mob." *The Voice of the Negro.* Vol. 3, no. 5 (May 1906).

"The Supreme Court and the Negro." *The Voice of the Negro.* Vol. 1, no. 6 (June 1904).

Woodson, C. G. "Freedom and Slavery in Appalachian America," *Journal of Negro History.* Vol. 1 (1916): 132.

BOOKS

Abshire, D. M. *The South Rejects a Prophet: The Life of D. M. Key, 1824–1900*. New York: Praeger, 1967.

Alexander, Thomas B. *A Political Reconstruction in Tennessee*. Nashville: Vanderbilt University Press, 1950.

Aptheker, Herbert. *A Documentary History of the Negro People in the United States*. New York: Citadel, 1951.

Bennett, Lerone, Jr. *Before the Mayflower: A History of Black America*. New York: Penguin, 1968.

Bergman, Peter M. *The Chronological History of the Negro in America*. New York: Harper and Row, 1969.

Berry, Mary Frances. *Black Resistance, White Law*. New York: Penguin, 1994.

Beth, Loren P. *John Marshall Harlan: The Last Whig Justice*. Lexington: University Press of Kentucky, 1992.

Bickel, Alexander M. *The Least Dangerous Branch*. New Haven, Conn.: Yale University Press, 1986.

Bontemps, Arna. *One Hundred Years of Negro Freedom*. New York: Dodd, Mead, 1961.

Brown, John P. *Old Frontiers*. Kingsport, Tenn.: Southern Publishers, 1938.

Cruden, Robert. *The Negro in Reconstruction*. Englewood Cliffs, N.J.: Prentice-Hall, 1969.

Davidson, Donald. *The Tennessee: Vol 1: The Old River: Frontier to Secession*. Nashville, Tenn.: J. S. Sanders, 1991.

———. *The Tennessee; Vol 2: The New River: Civil War to TVA*. Nashville, Tenn.: J. S. Sanders, 1992.

Du Bois, W.E.B. *Black Reconstruction in America—1860 to 1880*. New York: Simon and Schuster, 1995.

Dunn, Durood. *An Abolitionist in the Appalachian South*. Knoxville: University of Tennessee Press, 1997.

Ely, James W., Jr. *The Chief Justiceship of Melville W. Fuller, 1888–1910*. Columbia: University of South Carolina Press, 1995.

Foner, Eric. *Reconstruction: America's Unfinished Revolution, 1863–1877*. New York: Harper and Row, 1989.

Franklin, John Hope. *From Slavery to Freedom*. New York: Alfred A. Knopf, 1967.

———. *Reconstruction After the Civil War*. Chicago: University of Chicago Press, 1994.

Franklin, John Hope, and August Meier, eds. *Black Leaders of the Twentieth Century*. Urbana: University of Illinois Press, 1982.

Frazier, E. Franklin. *The Negro in the United States*. New York: Macmillan, 1949.

Grant, Joanne. *Black Protest*. New York: Fawcett, 1958.

Grier, William H., and Price M. Cobbs. *Black Rage*. New York: Basic Books, 1968.

Hall, Kermit L., ed. *The Oxford Companion to the Supreme Court of the United States*. New York: Oxford University Press, 1992.

History of the Supreme Court of the United States (Oliver Wendell Holmes' Devise) Vols. 1–10 (12 vols. planned), esp. Vol. 8, by Owen Fiss. New York: Macmillan, 1993.

Jordan, Winthrop D. *White over Black: American Attitudes Toward the Negro, 1550–1812*. Chapel Hill, N.C.: University of North Carolina Press, 1968.

Kull, Andrew. *The Color-Blind Constitution*. Cambridge, Mass.: Harvard University Press, 1992.

Kolwyck, Clarence. *History of Chattanooga Bar Association—1897 to 1972*. Author: n.d.

Lamon, Lester C. *Blacks in Tennessee, 1917 to 1970*. Knoxville: University of Tennessee Press/Tennessee Historical Commission, 1981.

———. *Black Tennesseans, 1900 to 1930*. Knoxville: University of Tennessee Press, 1977.

Lazarus, Edward. *Closed Chambers: The First Eyewitness Account of the Epic Struggles Inside the Supreme Court*. New York: Times Books/Random House, 1998.

Lewis, David Levering. *W. E. B. Dubois: Biography of a Race—1868–1919*. New York: Henry Holt, 1993.

Lisandrelli, Elaine S. *Ida B. Wells-Barnett: Crusader Against Lynching*. Springfield, N.J.: Enslow Publishers, 1998.

Livingood, James W. *A History of Hamilton County*. Memphis: Memphis State University Press, 1981.

———. *The Chattanooga Country: Gateway to History*. Chattanooga, Tenn.: Chattanooga Area Historical Association, 1995.

McFeely, William. *Frederick Douglass*. New York: W. W. Norton, 1991.

McPherson, James M. *Ordeal by Fire* (Vol. 3 of *Reconstruction*). New York: Alfred A. Knopf, 1982.

———. *The Struggle for Equality*. Princeton, N.J.: Princeton University Press, 1964.

Meier, August, and Elliot M. Rudwick. *From Plantation to Ghetto*. New York: Hill and Wang, 1966.

Miller, Loren. *The Petitioners*. New York: World, 1966

Quarles, Benjamin. *The Negro in the Making of America*. New York: Simon and Schuster, 1987.

Rehnquist, William H. *The Supreme Court: How It Was, How It Is*. New York: Morrow, 1987

Shepherd, Lewis. *Personal Memoirs*. Author: n.d., 1950.

Smith, J. Clay, Jr. *Emancipation*. Philadelphia: University of Pennsylvania Press, 1993.

Stampp, Kenneth M. *The Era of Reconstruction, 1865–1877*. New York: Alfred A. Knopf, 1982.

Tribe, Laurence H. *God Save This Honorable Court*. New York: Random House, 1985

U.S. Commission on Civil Rights. *Freedom to the Free: A Century of Emancipation, A Report to the President, United States Commission on Civil Rights*. Washington, D.C.: U.S. Government Printing Office [date unknown]

Wells, Ida B. *Crusade for Justice: The Autobiography of Ida B. Wells*. Alfreda M. Duster, ed. Chicago: University of Chicago Press, 1991.

———. *Ida B. Wells on Lynching: Southern Horrors, A Red Record and Mob Rule in New Orleans*. Salem, N.H.: Ayer, 1991.

Wilkes, Donald E. *Federal Postconviction Remedies and Relief with Forms*. Tulsa, Okla.: Harrison Company, 1996.

Williamson, Joel. *The Crucible of Race*. New York: Oxford University Press, 1984.

Woodward, C. Vann. *The Strange Career of Jim Crow*. New York: Oxford University Press, 1966.

Yarbrough, Tinsley E. *Judicial Enigma: The First Justice Harlan*. New York: Oxford University Press, 1995

SOURCES FOR ILLUSTRATIONS

1. Ed Johnson's grave: Courtesy of Leroy Phillips

2. Ed Johnson's tombstone (close-up): Courtesy of Leroy Phillips

3. Styles L. Hutchins: Courtesy of the Chattanooga–Hamilton County Bicentennial Library

4. W.G.M. Thomas: Courtesy of Tennessee Circuit Court Judge Neal Thomas

5. Judge Sam McReynolds: Courtesy of the Chattanooga–Hamilton County Bicentennial Library

6. District Attorney General Matt Whitaker: Courtesy of the Chattanooga–Hamilton County Bicentennial Library

7. Noah Parden: Courtesy of the Chattanooga–Hamilton County Bicentennial Library

8. Sheriff Joseph F. Shipp: Courtesy of the Chattanooga–Hamilton County Bicentennial Library

9. The Fuller Court: Courtesy of the U.S. Supreme Court

10. Justice John Marshall Harlan: Courtesy of the U.S. Supreme Court

11. The front page of The *Chattanooga Daily Times*: Courtesy of the *Chattanooga Daily Times*

12. Cartoon from *Chattanooga News*: Courtesy of the *Chattanooga Times*

13. Order from U.S. Supreme Court: Courtesy of the U.S. Supreme Court

14. Old Senate Chamber: Courtesy of the U.S. Supreme Court

15. Courtroom in Old Senate Chamber: Courtesy of the U.S. Supreme Court

16. St. Elmo and Lookout Mountain Incline Railway: Courtesy of the Chattanooga Regional History Museum

17. Lewis Shepherd: Courtesy of the Chattanooga–Hamilton County Bicentennial Library

   Opening of the Walnut Street Bridge: Courtesy of the Chattanooga Regional History Museum

19. Reverend T. H. McCallie: Courtesy of the McCallie School

20. Representative photographs of lynchings: Courtesy of the Tuskegee University Archives.

INDEX